Watering

A g[...]t.
The extra expense [...]se
kinks less and lasts longer. Look for a hose
that has no visible veining and features a
long brass nozzle and brass screw-ends.
Even if you have a sprinkler system, you'll
need a garden hose for supplying water to
freshly planted trees and shrubs.

A **watering wand** attaches to the end of your
hose. Its long handle makes it easy to water
hard-to-reach corners of beds as well as
containers and hanging baskets. The wand's
head showers plants like raindrops instead
of blasting them with a hard stream of water.

A **watering can** always comes in handy.
Choose one with a large head to disperse
water gently. A rounded handle makes the
can easier to grip when it's full.

Timers are great for regulated watering.
Use timers to turn on garden hoses, soaker
hoses, or drip systems. Automatic
irrigation systems with underground
piping can also be controlled by specialized
timers. Because watering early in the day is
better than later, rely on timers to get the
watering done while you're still asleep.
They're also useful for keeping your
landscape healthy while you're out of town.

Soaker hoses have tiny holes that allow
water to seep into the soil and deliver
moisture directly to roots. Snake these
special hoses around the roots of plants
beneath a layer of mulch.

Drip irrigation kits are another way to
supplement Mother Nature. Like soaker
hoses, small plastic tubing lies on top of
the ground beneath a bed of mulch. Tiny
emitters release water where needed.

Automatic irrigation systems, also called
underground sprinklers, rely on a series of
pipes buried in trenches to carry water
throughout the landscape. Pop-up heads,
like this one, or heads attached to risers
spray water when turned on manually or
by a timer.

Weeding

A **weed hound** helps dig out weeds from a
standing position.

Use a **warren hoe** to chop out weeds by
their roots. The pointed blade of the
warren hoe makes it easy to cut away and
remove established root systems.

Pruning

Bypass hand pruners are essential. Buy a
good pair with blades you can sharpen.
Bypass pruners work like scissors, with
both blades moving. They make cleaner
cuts than anvil pruners, which feature one
fixed edge and one moving cutting blade.

Bypass loppers should find a home in
your toolshed. With longer handles for
leverage and bigger blades than hand
pruners, loppers are necessary for cutting
branches that are thicker than a pencil.
Using hand pruners on a large stem can
hurt both your hand and the plant. Clean
cuts are essential to good plant health.
Torn, jagged edges invite insects and
diseases. Loppers guarantee a good cut.

A **pruning saw** is needed for removing
large branches that are too big for loppers
to grasp. The small, serrated blade is
strong enough to cut into green wood but
light enough for easy handling.

Hedge trimmers have long blades and
handles. They are designed for cutting
along the surfaces of shrubs to trim,
maintain, and shape them.

A **pole pruner** easily removes overhead
branches and fronds. Wear eye protection
when you're working above your head.

Safety

Work boots are essential. You need work
boots with sturdy soles to press down on
shovels. The tough exteriors offer foot
protection and provide ankle support.

Leather gloves are necessary for
landscaping projects; cotton garden gloves
won't do. Good leather gloves protect your
hands against thorns, sharp branches, and
tools. Look for gloves with laces that
tighten at the wrist to keep out dirt.
(Rubber gloves might be required for
handling chemicals.)

Eye protection is a must. You need to wear
safety goggles whenever debris or
chemicals might become airborne, such as
when you're digging, tilling, or spraying.

Face masks prevent you from breathing
airborne particles into your mouth and
nose. If you need eye protection, you also
need a face mask. When spraying
chemicals, you might need a special
respirator that provides more protection.

A **straw hat** protects your face from the
sun. Open-weave material breathes to keep
you from overheating. Use a sun hat and
sunscreen when you're working outdoors.

Landscaping 1-2-3™ (*For Zones 5 and 6*)

Meredith Book Development Team
Project Editor: John P. Holms
Art Director: John Eric Seid
Writer and Illustrator: Jo Kellum, ASLA
Contributing Writers: Elizabeth Conner, Julie Martens, Jennie McIlwain, Lisa Wolfe Williams
Photographer: Doug Hetherington
Designer: Ann DuChaine—Ann DuChaine Creative
Contributing Designer: Tim Abramowitz
Copy Chief: Catherine Hamrick
Copy and Production Editor: Terri Fredrickson
Contributing Copy Editors: Lorraine Ferrell, Sherry Rindels, Margaret Smith
Contributing Proofreaders: Janet Anderson, Maria Duryee, Dan Degen
Indexer: Donald Glassman
Managers, Book Production: Pam Kvitne, Marjorie J. Schenkelberg
Electronic Production Coordinator: Paula Forest
Editorial Assistants: Renee McAtee, Karen Schirm

Meredith® Books
Editor in Chief: James D. Blume
Design Director: Matt Strelecki
Managing Editor: Gregory H. Kayko
Executive Editor, Home Depot Books: Benjamin W. Allen

Director, Retail Sales and Marketing: Terry Unsworth
Director, Sales, Special Markets: Rita McMullen
Director, Sales, Premiums: Michael A. Peterson
Director, Sales, Retail: Tom Wierzbicki
Director, Book Marketing: Brad Elmitt
Director, Operations: George A. Susral
Director, Production: Douglas M. Johnston

Vice President, General Manager: Jamie L. Martin

Meredith Publishing Group
President, Publishing Group: Stephen M. Lacy
Vice President, Finance and Administration: Max Runciman

Meredith Corporation
Chairman and Chief Executive Officer: William T. Kerr

Chairman of the Executive Committee: E. T. Meredith III

The Home Depot®
Senior Vice President, Marketing and Communications: Dick Hammill
Marketing Manager: Nathan Ehrlich
Wisdom of the Aisles: Countless Home Depot store associates

Copyright © 2001 by Homer TLC, Inc.
All rights reserved. Printed in the United States of America.
First Edition—00
Library of Congress Catalog Card Number: 00-135014
ISBN: 0-696-21254-4 Distributed by Meredith Corporation

Note to the Reader: Due to differing conditions, tools, and individual skills, Meredith Corporation and The Home Depot assume no responsibility for any damages, injuries suffered, or losses incurred as a result of following the information published in this book. Before beginning any project, review the instructions carefully, and if any doubts or questions remain, consult local experts or authorities. Because codes and regulations vary greatly, you always should check with authorities to ensure that your project complies with all applicable local codes and regulations. Always read and observe all of the safety precautions provided by any tool or equipment manufacturer, and follow all accepted safety procedures.

Contact us by any of these methods:

1 Leave a voice message at **(800) 678-2093**

2 Write to **Meredith Books, Home Depot Books; 1716 Locust St; Des Moines, IA 50309-3023**

3 Send e-mail to **hi123@mdp.com**. Visit The Home Depot website at **homedepot.com**

Landscaping 1-2-3

Regional Edition
Zones 5-6
(See page 5)

Selection & Design

Trees

Shrubs

Groundcovers & Vines

STEP-BY-STEP

Meredith BOOKS

Landscaping 1-2-3

for Zones 5 and 6

How to Use this Book . . . 4

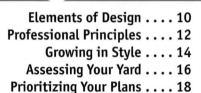

Chapter 1
design 10

Elements of Design 10
Professional Principles 12
Growing in Style 14
Assessing Your Yard 16
Prioritizing Your Plans 18

Chapter 2
selection 20

The Right Plant in the Right Place 20
Choosing Plants for Zone 5 22
Choosing Plants for Zone 6 24
Screening and Privacy 26
Sun and Shade 30
Choosing Plants for Full Sun 32
Choosing Plants for Shade 34
Soil Conditions 36
Project: Perc Test 37
Soil pH 38
Choosing Plants for Special Site Conditions 40
Windbreaks 42

Chapter 3
how to 44

Getting the Job Done 44
Project: Marking a Bedline 44
Project: Making a Bed 45
Project: Grass Removal 47
Bed Preparation 48
Keeping Plants Happy 50
Project: Drainage Solutions 51
Fertilizing 52
Project: Planting Bare-Root Roses 54
Project: Planting Containerized Roses 55
Caring for Roses 56

*Sea Thrift
(Armeria maritima)
Page 178*

Chapter 4

trees 58

The Value of Trees 58
Buying a Tree 60
Project: Planting a Container-Grown Tree 62
Project: Planting a Tree on a Slope 63
Project: Planting a B&B Tree 64
Choosing Trees for Seasonality 66
Trees for Every Need 68
Tree Encyclopedia 70
Project: Pruning Bradford Pear 100

*Red Maple
(Acer rubrum)
Page 74*

Chapter 5

shrubs 110

Depend on Shrubs 110
Foundation Planting 112
Project: Planting a Container Shrub 114
Project: Planting Shrubs on Slopes 115
Project: Pruning Evergreen Shrubs 116
Project: Pruning Flowering Shrubs 118
Choosing Shrubs by Characteristics 120
Choosing Shrubs by Needs 122
Choosing Shrubs for Seasonal Interest 124
Shrub Encyclopedia 126
Project: Rejuvenating Overgrown Lilacs 165

*Redtip Photinia
(Photinia x fraseri)
Page 149*

Chapter 6

groundcovers/vines 168

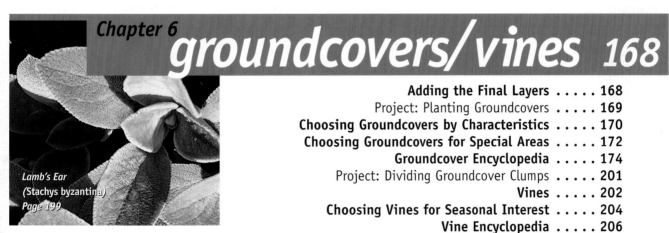

Adding the Final Layers 168
Project: Planting Groundcovers 169
Choosing Groundcovers by Characteristics 170
Choosing Groundcovers for Special Areas 172
Groundcover Encyclopedia 174
Project: Dividing Groundcover Clumps 201
Vines 202
Choosing Vines for Seasonal Interest 204
Vine Encyclopedia 206
Project: Pruning Chinese Wisteria 215

*Lamb's Ear
(Stachys byzantina)
Page 199*

Index....216

Landscaping *1-2-3*

How to Use this Book

Landscaping 1-2-3 Overview 4
Find Your Climate Zone 5
Planning and Executing Your Landscape . . 6
How to Pick the Right Plants 8
Special Features 9

Learn Landscaping from the Experts

L *andscaping 1-2-3* from the landscaping experts at The Home Depot® is specifically tailored for Climate Zones 5 and 6. Inside you'll find everything you need to help you plan, design, select, install, and care for a landscape that will make your yard a showcase.

First, you will become familiar with some basic landscaping terminology. Then you'll learn how to find your climate zone. Pages 6 and 7 explain how the book is arranged and lay out the steps to creating a great landscape. Pages 8 and 9 introduce you to features in this book that will make putting your plans to work quick and easy.

The Language of Landscaping

Knowing a few basic landscaping terms will help you understand what the pros are talking about when they're making a plan.

• **Evergreen** An evergreen keeps fresh-looking leaves all year, even in winter. Evergreens shed leaves and grow new ones but never lose their leaves completely.

• **Deciduous** A deciduous plant sheds its leaves and goes through a yearly period of dormancy. Deciduous plants are often noted for fall colors.

• **Perennial** Most perennials, with the exception of some evergreens, go into dormancy during the winter months and reappear in spring.

• **Tree** A tree is a woody plant that has one or more main trunks. It grows at least to the height of an adult person. Trees can be evergreen or deciduous. Some palms are listed

as trees, according to their use in the landscape.

• **Shrub** Shrubs are evergreen or deciduous. They vary in height and width but are generally lower and have a wider spread than trees. Some palms are listed as shrubs, according to their use in the landscape.

Trees, shrubs, groundcover, and vines as well as flowering accents are all part of this beautiful and effective backyard landscape.

• **Groundcover** This is not a true horticultural term. There are differing opinions on what is or is not a groundcover. Groundcovers here are evergreen or deciduous plants that spread to cover large areas of ground or to act as the low, front layer of a planting bed. Vines growing prostrate, spreading shrubs, low compact shrubs, ornamental grasses, clumping plants, flat spreading plants, or even perennials might be considered groundcovers.

• **Vine** Vines are climbers. Some have tendrils to grasp any nearby support. Others twist and twine over anything in their path. Still others attach themselves with tiny aerial rootlets to cover hard surfaces. Though some trailing plants are included as groundcovers, plants listed as vines are those used primarily to grow vertically on fences, posts, arbors, trellises, and walls.

Find Your Climate Zone

The first step to landscaping success is understanding climate zones and their effect on plant selection and care. Plants that are right for your climate zone, soil type, and watering needs will make themselves at home in your yard and are less likely to be troubled by insects and disease. *All the plant selection guides, projects, and landscaping information in the book are specific to Zones 5 and 6.*

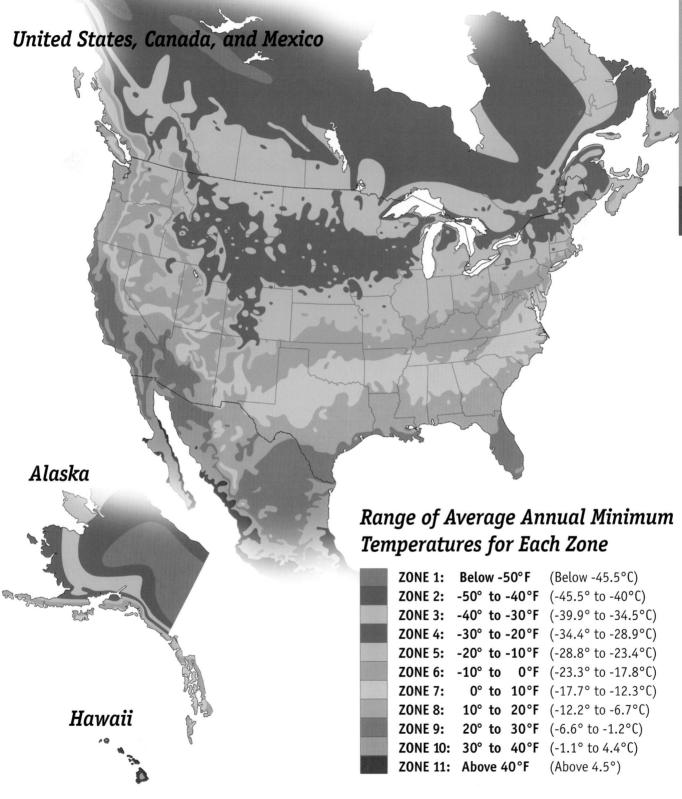

United States, Canada, and Mexico

Alaska

Hawaii

Range of Average Annual Minimum Temperatures for Each Zone

ZONE 1:	Below -50°F	(Below -45.5°C)
ZONE 2:	-50° to -40°F	(-45.5° to -40°C)
ZONE 3:	-40° to -30°F	(-39.9° to -34.5°C)
ZONE 4:	-30° to -20°F	(-34.4° to -28.9°C)
ZONE 5:	-20° to -10°F	(-28.8° to -23.4°C)
ZONE 6:	-10° to 0°F	(-23.3° to -17.8°C)
ZONE 7:	0° to 10°F	(-17.7° to -12.3°C)
ZONE 8:	10° to 20°F	(-12.2° to -6.7°C)
ZONE 9:	20° to 30°F	(-6.6° to -1.2°C)
ZONE 10:	30° to 40°F	(-1.1° to 4.4°C)
ZONE 11:	Above 40°F	(Above 4.5°)

Planning and Executing Your Landscape

 This book is organized the way you should organize your landscaping plans.

Chapter One–*Design* gives you basic design concepts.

Chapter Two–*Selection* helps you choose the right plant for your yard. All the selection guides are specific to Zones 5 and 6.

Chapter Three–*How-To* shows you how to install and care for plants.

Chapters Four, Five, and Six–*Trees, Shrubs, Groundcovers, and Vines* guide you through the specifics of selection, care, and feeding.

The path to a great landscape is easy to take if you've done your homework and have a solid plan.

Four Steps to a Great Landscape

1) Plan Before You Plant

Make landscaping decisions in an orderly manner to create an orderly landscape. Like building a house, planning comes first, then the foundation, walls, and roof.

2) Layout Bedlines

Lay out shapes for lawn areas and planting beds first. Work around existing plants you'd like to keep within new planting beds. Fill new

beds by starting with trees. Then add shrubs. Complete the design with groundcovers and vines. The goal is an attractive, balanced composition that makes the most of outdoor areas while defining and complementing your home.

Because plants mature at different rates, be patient as your landscape takes shape. Balance rapid and slow growers in the design mix so you can have plants to enjoy as you move through the growing phases.

3) Place Trees and Shrubs

Trees and shrubs are the foundation, forming the structure of the landscape. Make decisions about these big plants first. They are also the walls of outdoor rooms, shaping

the space within your yard and providing protection and privacy.

4) Add Groundcover and Vines

Groundcovers define the landscape by filling in planting beds that frame lawns. They give planting areas a lush, rich look, adding layers of greenery and flowers. Vines emphasize overhead structures, such as trellises and arbors, drawing the eye down and into the landscape.

Ideally, grass should be added when the rest of the work is done. However, you might want to incorporate some of your present lawn into a new landscape design. The key is to not let the current shape of grassy areas dictate where planting areas should go. Changing the size and shape of an old lawn can give you a refreshing new look.

Finishing Touches

Seasonal flowers are accessories, giving the finished landscape interest and accent. However, they can be in the way while you're working. Grow them in pots instead of beds while the yard is a work-in-progress. You should be focused on the basics—layout and structure—not tiptoeing around plants that have been placed out of order in the landscape.

The Bottom Line

Unless you've done your homework and your plan is well thought out, all the flowers in the world won't make your landscape a success. That's why you should go step-by-step through the entire landscaping process, starting with design in Chapter One. Before you begin, check pages 8 and 9 for special features that will help you along the way.

Placement of trees and shrubs adds privacy around a hot tub area. Seasonals add impact and color.

Wisdom of the Aisles

Call Before You Dig

Cutting through a cable or gas line is potentially dangerous and can be hazardous to your pocketbook as well. Utility and cable companies are happy to mark the locations of underground lines for you at no charge. Pick up the phone before you pick up a shovel to avoid cutting lines and cutting off your service.

If You Want to Hire a Pro

If design and planning have you stumped, consult an expert. **Associates** at home and garden centers often offer informal design advice as part of their service. If you want to consult a professional gardener, you have several options. **Landscape architects** are professionals licensed to prepare plans and guide planting, grading, and landscape construction. **Garden designers** might not be licensed, but they are often very qualified and can offer advice on planning and preparing your landscape. **Design/build contractors** will often provide free design services as long as they're hired to do the work as well.

Always ask for references, visit sites in progress, and see completed jobs before you negotiate a contract. Show the designer yardscapes you like. Don't be satisfied until you get what you want. Set a budget and stick to it. Never pay the entire fee up-front. Expect a licensed architect to charge a higher fee.

How to Pick the Right Plants

1) Selection Guides Plant selection guides that range from the general to the specific make shopping decisions easier. First you'll find comprehensive lists of plants that grow within Zones 7, 8, 9, and 10. (See Chapter Two: "Selection," page 20.) Then throughout the book there are lists designed to help you narrow your choices into groups of plants that will work in your landscape and stay healthy. These lists will also spark your imagination and offer plant choices you might not otherwise have considered.

Use these dedicated selection guides to determine the right plant for the right job. Establishing privacy or blocking poor views might be a top priority. Selection guides, such as the one shown above, list plants suitable for screening and filtering. There are lists for sun or shade, for different soil conditions, and for particular site conditions (slopes, small spaces, or salt spray). You'll find selection guides that group plants by similar characteristics or solve similar landscaping problems. Each plant listed refers you to the page where the plant is described in detail.

2) Plant Descriptions These entries, as shown below, tell you about outstanding features, growth rate, mature size, light requirements, and form. You'll see from the photos what each plant looks like. There's also a description of how to grow each plant and its purpose in the landscape. Each description contains both botanical and common names. The "More Choices" entry will refer you to specific selection guides for proper use of the featured plant.

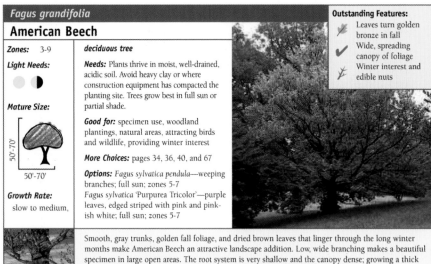

Fagus grandifolia

American Beech

Zones: 3-9

Light Needs:

Mature Size:

50'-70'

50'-70'

Growth Rate:
slow to medium,

deciduous tree

Needs: Plants thrive in moist, well-drained, acidic soil. Avoid heavy clay or where construction equipment has compacted the planting site. Trees grow best in full sun or partial shade.

Good for: specimen use, woodland plantings, natural areas, attracting birds and wildlife, providing winter interest

More Choices: pages 34, 36, 40, and 67

Options: *Fagus sylvatica pendula*—weeping branches; full sun; zones 5-7
Fagus sylvatica 'Purpurea Tricolor'—purple leaves, edged striped with pink and pinkish white; full sun; zones 5-7

Outstanding Features:
- Leaves turn golden bronze in fall
- Wide, spreading canopy of foliage
- Winter interest and edible nuts

Smooth, gray trunks, golden fall foliage, and dried brown leaves that linger through the long winter months make American Beech an attractive landscape addition. Low, wide branching makes a beautiful specimen in large open areas. The root system is very shallow and the canopy dense; growing a thick stand of grass can be a challenge. Mulch instead for improved tree health and less work for you. Nuts are edible and enjoyed by several species of birds and squirrels.

Understanding Rates of Growth

How fast a plant will grow depends on site conditions, how quickly it settles into its new home, and length of the growing season. With so many variables, it isn't possible to predict the number of inches or feet you can expect a plant to grow per year, but they can be generally classified as rapid, medium, and slow growers.

The Name Game

Common vs. Botanical

Cross-Referencing by Common and Botanical Names Makes Plants Easy to Identify.

Common names for plants vary greatly from region to region. The same plant can even have several different common names. This creates the potential for confusion. Plant experts have agreed to use botanical (Latin) names to maintain consistency and make sure everyone is talking about the same thing.

Selection Guides are **alphabetized by common names.** Because most people recognize plants by their common names, the Selection Guides reflect the most common usage.

Plant Descriptions are **alphabetized by botanical names.** Latin is the language for accurate plant identification. It's a good idea to know the botanical name even if you're not sure how to say it. Don't worry about how the words are pronounced. Knowing a little Latin will help you get the right plant.

Multiple Indexes Selection Guides and *Plant Descriptions* are cross-referenced throughout the book. Beginning on page 216 you'll find a **general index** for easy access to projects and landscaping information. There's also an **index** of **botanical** and **common names** to make plants easy to find no matter what they're called.

Note: Availability of specific plants varies by area and local conditions (see page 21). Check with your garden center for plants that will thrive in your particular area.

Special Features for Quick Reference

✔ Information about hardiness and climate will help you eliminate plants that won't live where you do and help you pick the right ones for your planting zone.

In the Zone

New plants need daily watering for the first few weeks, especially during hot weather. In cooler seasons, you can water every other day for the first week. After that, cut back to once a week for 2 to 3 months, then reduce to once a month, until shrubs have weathered a full growing season. Water faithfully unless nature supplies at least one-half inch of water during the week. Once established, properly sited plants will need supplemental water only during hot, dry spells.

✔ Every project includes a list of tools and materials you'll need to get the job done right.

STUFF YOU'LL NEED
✔ Garden hose that you don't mind getting paint on
✔ Sharp-shooter or trenching shovel
✔ Marking paint (not regular spray paint)
✔ Inexpensive gloves
✔ Old shoes

What to Expect
You'll probably try several patterns with the hose before you're satisfied with the bedline. Don't rush the process. You'll live with your choice for a long time.

Step-by-Step Projects

Planting Bare-Root Roses

Whether you're planting bare-root roses or plants grown in containers, learn how to get new roses off to the best start.

Bare-root roses are shipped without soil, making them less expensive. They look like stubby sticks. You'll find these plants for sale in late winter or early spring. Plant them soon after purchasing.

1 Carefully open the packaging. Avoid cutting roots. Gently remove packing material from roots and discard. Place the roots in a bucket of water mixed with root stimulator and allow them to soak in a dark, cool, dry location such as a garage. Soak roots no longer than eight hours.

2 Dig a hole in a spot that receives at least six hours of sun daily. The hole should be 12 to 18 inches deep. Mix bagged compost with some of the native soil in a wheelbarrow or on a tarp to create a mixture that's about two-thirds organic matter and one-third native soil. The soil mixture should appear dark and rich.

3 Shovel the good soil mixture into the hole until it's nearly full. Use your hands to form a cone of soil in the center of the hole. Make the top of the cone slightly below the level of adjacent, undisturbed soil. Position the rose on top of the cone, spreading roots evenly around it.

4 Backfill around the rose with soil. Make sure the scion (the ridge where the rose was grafted to the rootstock) is still visible above the soil. Add a thick layer of compost for mulch. Use excess native soil to form a moat around the freshly planted rose. Fill moat with a slowly trickling hose.

STUFF YOU'LL NEED
✔ Bucket
✔ Root stimulator
✔ Hand pruner
✔ Organic matter such as bagged compost
✔ Round-point shovel

What to Expect
Your newly planted bare-root rose will look like a stick poking up out of the ground until new shoots and leaves appear in a few weeks.

BUYER'S GUIDE

Pick up several bare-root roses before you buy one. If one feels heavier than the others or has more water dripping from its packaging, it's not the one you want to take home to plant in your yard. Roses that are bare should stay moist but not wet during shipping.

54   How-to

TOOL TIP

Round-point shovels are great for digging holes and scooping out soil. Shovels with fiberglass handles usually last longer than those with wooden handles.

✔ Having the right tool and knowing how to use it can make a world of difference.

Design Tip

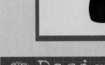

The front yard is more heavily influenced by architecture than the backyard. Your house and front yard landscape are seen together from the street. On the other hand, the backyard is usually seen when looking from the house, not at it. If the architecture makes a formal style appropriate, use a traditional approach to design in front; if you also like informally styled outdoor spaces, grow a more free-form landscape in the back.

✔ Hints from a landscape architect will make your yard look its best.

Homer's Hindsight

When I landscaped our first home, I picked out plants by purchasing whatever caught my eye at the garden center. The yard looked all right at first, but after a while, it was a mess! And it was a lot of work trying to keep that many different kinds of plants healthy and neat. Landscaping is easier with a strategy.

✔ Homer helps you avoid mistakes before you make them.

BUYER'S GUIDE

If you want a larger tree than those in stock, ask a garden associate about ordering a B&B tree for you. Some stores stock balled-and-burlapped trees only upon request. Inquire about the approximate measurements of the root ball and dig the proper-sized hole before the tree arrives. Ask if delivery is available for a fee when you order your tree. If so, find out where the tree will be left—don't be surprised if the delivery driver will take it no further than the curb. You'll probably need a sturdy wheelbarrow waiting to get the tree to the hole. You might want to hire a professional or get a friend to help with a big tree; B&B trees are heavy.

✔ Solid shopping tips from the pros.

Wisdom of the Aisles

Most trees and shrubs require no fertilizer at all during their first year in your landscape. That's because they've been heavily fertilized during nursery production to make them look their best on the shelves. If you add fertilizer at planting and then apply more fertilizer later in the growing season, you've probably given your new plants a double-dose of chemicals they don't need. Wait until the second year of growth.

✔ Great advice you can't get anywhere else—tried-and-true wisdom of the aisles from the experts at Home Depot.

✔ Good ideas go along with step-by-step instructions to make projects even easier.

Good idea! **Put the Best Face on Things.** Before backfilling, turn your shrub so that its best side is facing the direction from which it will be viewed. Once the dirt's in the hole, it's harder to adjust the shrub's direction.

Chapter 1
design

A successful landscape design defines the function of outdoor spaces. Lush foliage around the pond on the left creates a sense of privacy and tranquillity for this backyard getaway, while carefully placed combinations of color and form beckon along garden paths.

Four Elements of Design

This is where you unlock the secrets of landscape design. Start with the four building blocks that form the basis of outdoor composition.

1) Color is the first element—easy to identify, but challenging to use correctly. So many colors are appealing that it can be hard to limit your choices.

Flower beds are obvious sources of color, but trees, shrubs, groundcovers, and vines are bloomers as well. Leaf color, seasonal variations, and the hues of bark and branches also have impact. Both flowers and foliage need to work with other features—paving, outdoor furniture and fabrics, and the colors of your home.

Color evokes an emotional response. Bright colors give a garden

a cheerful, pleasing look. Just one noticeable color contrasting with green leaves gives a landscape a sophisticated appearance. Too many colors in too many places compete for attention and overwhelm the design. Carefully placed color directs your guests right to your front door.

2) Texture is a subtle but important element of good design. The more you know about texture and how it works, the more professional your landscape will be.

You might think of texture as something you touch—the roughness of sandpaper or the

smoothness of silk—but it's also something you see. Coarsely textured plants have big leaves, large flowers, or rough, peeling bark. They are characterized as bold or architectural. Finely textured plants have tiny leaves and twigs, or flowers with many small petals. Many species of plants fall somewhere between. Leaf texture matters in landscape design because flowering time is usually brief.

Textures blend or contrast. If you're using a lot of different colors in your landscape, minimize the difference in textures. Conversely, if you have a shady yard with few hues, a variety of textures adds interest. Place a large-leaf, coarsely textured plant, such as Catawba Rhododendron, behind a tiny-leaf, finely textured plant, such as Maidenhair Fern. The contrast in textures will be eye-catching.

3) *Line* impacts landscape design. The horizontal outlines of walkways, patios, driveways, and bedlines carve fluid shapes and create spaces. They separate planting areas from the lawn, creating areas for trees, shrubs, groundcovers, and vines. Bedlines should complement existing

Design Tip

A picture is still worth a thousand words. Colors that seem so attractive in the store might not work when planted near your home. Picking complementary colors from memory is tough. Even if you're sure of the color scheme, take some snapshots of the outside of your house with you when you go plant shopping. It'll help the salespeople and possibly eliminate a return trip.

landscaping—the shape of your house on the land, paved areas, trees, and fences.

Vertical lines are also important. If everything is the same height, your landscape will appear flat and dull. Trees are the most obvious example. Upright, spiky foliage, such as iris leaves, also adds a vertical accent to the landscape. Fencing and posts will contribute vertical lines to your yard. Too many vertical lines, however, will make a yard small and crowded. The goal is to frame and balance open spaces with vertical lines.

4) *Form* defines the physical presence of a plant and the space it takes up in your yard. Knowing the mature shape of a plant is critical when plant shopping. If you want a plant that will stay low and neat, don't buy one that is naturally large and arching. You won't be able to prune it into a compact shape, and the plant won't be attractive when confined to an unnatural form.

The shape of a young plant is not necessarily the same as it will be when it matures. Study the form symbols with the plant descriptions in this book or on plant tags. Ask before you buy. You will hear the

A garden bench becomes a focal point because it contrasts with its setting. The texture of ornamental grasses, the curving lawn, and arching and mounded plant forms provide visual contrast.

terms regular or irregular. Regular forms are symmetrical—neatly rounded, compact, pyramidal, or oval. Irregular forms are uneven, resist pruning, and are described as airy, natural, loose, arching, spreading, or sculptural. What you buy depends on your design. Choose regular shrubs for a neatly clipped hedge or formal garden. If you're seeking an airy backdrop for a cottage garden or a woodland scene, irregular forms are best. A single plant with uneven form can serve as a living sculpture.

Choosing Colors That Work with Your Home

Welcome the seasons by choosing plants to color your landscape with spring or summer flowers, fall foliage, or bright winter stems.

If your home is a neutral color, such as tan, buff, gray, beige, brown, or white, just about any flower or foliage color will look good beside it. Houses featuring unusual colors, such as lavender-painted siding or pink-tinted stucco, should depend heavily on dark greens and whites. But keep things fun by repeating the house color in nearby plants. Matching the color or using flower hues a little darker will emphasize the scheme.

Bold color schemes present other challenges. Hot pink flowers and yellow, golden, or bluish foliage won't work well with a red brick house. Plant lots of dark green instead, and stick to white, dark purple, or pale pink flowers. Yellow can work if separated from the brick by a layer of dark green leaves. Oranges and reds will clash; use them elsewhere in your yard, away from the house.

Design Principles   11

Professional Principles of Design

Now that you've gone through the elements of design, the next step is learning how to apply them in your landscape. The methods professionals use to manipulate design elements are known as the principles of design. Here's what they are and how they can help you create a beautiful and functional landscape. If you need help planning your landscape, work with a professional designer to give your yard style.

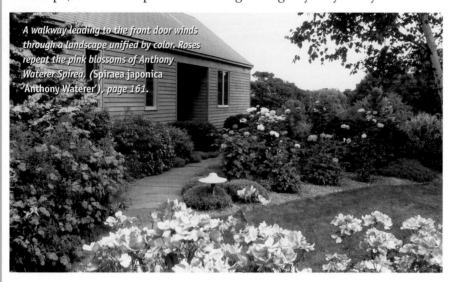

A walkway leading to the front door winds through a landscape unified by color. Roses repeat the pink blossoms of Anthony Waterer Spirea, (Spiraea japonica 'Anthony Waterer'), page 161.

Planting the same kind of plant in more than one place is a surefire way to add unity to your landscape through repetition. But you can also repeat a characteristic common to different kinds of plants. For example, wispy ornamental grasses have fine texture. So do delicate ferns, some grasslike clumping groundcovers, and shrubs with tiny leaves. Plant them together to create a mass of fine texture, which makes an excellent background for showing off a coarse-textured, large-leaved plant as an accent. Set plants with similar textures in different places throughout your yard. This makes it easier to deal with different conditions. In the example above, you can plant ferns in the shade and ornamental grasses in the sun, repeating the fine textures of both plants and unifying your landscape. Texture isn't the only element you can repeat. Using similar colors, lines, or forms will also add unity.

1) **Unity** is the glue that holds a landscape together, and repetition is the means to achieve it. Without unity a yard is a hodgepodge of plants. Trees, shrubs, groundcovers, and vines are lovely individually, but they must work together to make your design cohesive.

At first, examples of unity can be hard to spot. But look closely at yards you admire in your neighborhood or study attractive landscapes in books and magazines. You will notice that, no matter how much styles vary, well-designed landscapes all share a certain elusive quality: The plants in well-designed landscapes seem to belong where they are placed. The secret is unity, and here's how to get it.

Repetition gives your landscape a unified look. Even cottage gardens, which contain a multitude of flowers, are held together by repetition of one or more elements: color, texture, line, or form. For example, in a cottage garden the flowers might be united by a color theme of mostly pinks or shades of yellow. Perhaps there are many bright colors tied together with generous helpings of white. Landscapes that feature multitudes of flowers need a good solid background for structure. Evergreen trees and shrubs, walls, or picket fences are common choices of unifying materials.

You don't have to have a cottage garden to need unity in your landscape. Start by selecting the trees and shrubs that form the backbone of your composition. Limit yourself to a core group of plants that grow well in your area. Using 8-2-2 (8 kinds of shrubs, 2 kinds of trees, and 2 kinds of groundcovers) is a proven combination. You can vary this, but

When color schemes are simplified, other design elements become more noticeable. The textures and forms of a bed of conifers and heathers capture attention.

don't be tempted to introduce too many different plants at this early stage. Think of these core plants as wardrobe basics; you can mix and match them for different looks. Using the same kind of plant in more than one place in your yard is an example of repetition and a good way to achieve unity.

When you're ready to add more plants to your basic landscape, keep the value of repetition in mind. Set showier plants together in groups, known as masses, so they'll have an attractive impact on the composition. (Scattering plants tends to dilute their effect.) Adding masses of the same species of plant in more than one place will create a cohesive and unified look.

2) Accent is the second principle of landscape design. This is the fun stuff: eye-catching plants with brightly colored flowers, unusual forms, or noticeable leaves. A showy plant isn't necessarily an accent. Like real estate, it's all about location, location, location.

A plant must stand out from its

Delicate spring blossoms of white-flowering redbud (Cercis canadensis 'Alba'), page 81, are welcoming. In summer, the small tree is covered with heart-shaped leaves, turning yellow in fall.

surroundings to serve as an accent. Too many varieties of showy plants too close together will compete for attention. Contrast is the key. A plant becomes distinctive when its color, texture, line, or form contrasts with its setting.

Create contrast by placing an eye-catching plant in a mass of similar plants. Your accent plant will be showcased, making its special qualities noticeable. You can choose a single accent plant, known as a specimen, to stand alone, or set a few of the same kind of accent plants together for a bigger impact. Groups of three work well in many settings.

Coarse-textured leaves of hosta (Hosta spp.), page 187, contrast with the lacy leaves of Japanese maple (Acer palmatum), page 73, to create an accent in the garden.

Creating Focal Points

Evergreen trees and shrubs offer ample opportunity for dressing up an entry walk with beds and containers of seasonal flowers. The bright colors lead the way to the front door.

Position colorful plants where they'll draw attention to what you want your visitors to see.
Your landscape should focus first on the house and then on your front door. If it's hard to tell which house is yours, add an address plate near a bright, eye-catching planting so the mailbox isn't the only indication of your house number. This way, you'll focus attention on your home, not your mailbox. Use attractive plantings at property entrances and in parking areas. This makes guests feel welcome. Lead them to the door with landscaping—putting the brightest colors there denotes a destination.

Growing in Style

The exterior of your home should fit your personal style, just as the interior does. The appearance of your home—its architectural style—has a big role in setting the scene. A bungalow, a stately mansion, a rustic log home, and an adobe house: All have their own distinctive look. Though you could choose the same plants for any of these houses, the way you arrange the plants to create a setting is the essence of style. Setting a style for your landscape is the result of a combination of influences. Understanding them will make it easier for you to create a landscape in the style that's right for you.

1) *Formal style* will complement many traditional types of architecture, characterized by an even number of windows symmetrically placed, balanced wings, or formal columns. This style also works well in small city gardens. Formality is achieved by arranging plants, walkways, benches, and other outdoor features along an invisible line, known as an axis. Plants on one side of the axis match, or mirror, those on the opposite, creating symmetry. Arrange plants in groups that are evenly divisible by two. Pairs of plants establish instant symmetry as do two matching shrubs on each side of a walkway. Plants set in rows or in recognizable geometric patterns, such as squares, diamonds, rectangles, and circles, also lend a formal style to a landscape. (Repeat shapes found on your house, such as windows or trim.) The more symmetry, the more formal your design. Formal landscaping shows the designer's hand in nature. Your choice of plant material also affects formality. Plants that can be clipped into smooth hedges, round balls, or neat cones add a formal touch.

Regional Styles

Let where you live influence the style of your landscape. Including native plants will make your landscape look appropriate for its location, and the plants will be more likely to survive. Using other indigenous materials will also give your landscape a local flavor. Local plants and materials look best when paired with architectural styles that are typical of the region. Paving materials, such as brick, stone, tile, or pebbles, may be produced in your region, as well as the kind of wood and finish you choose for fences, gates, benches, rails, and arbors. If your house features a look borrowed from elsewhere, design the landscape's style to match the architecture first and the region second. Include native plants whenever their natural forms are appropriate to the landscape style that suits your house.

From the mirror-image layout of planting beds and graveled pathways to a pair of pineapple finials, the concept of symmetry is present everywhere in this formal landscape design.

2) Informal style

is the natural arrangement of elements. It complements a wide range of architectural styles. Informal landscapes are asymmetrical—their components don't match up like a mirror. Instead of dividing the landscape with an axis, arrange planting beds in broad, sweeping curves. This will soften the hard lines of any house and make it seem nestled into the landscape.

Though they don't feature mirror images, asymmetrical landscapes must be balanced. If you have a large shade tree at one end of a planting bed, balance it with three large shrubs at the far end. This approach sets a scene that looks balanced instead of lopsided.

Plants with natural and irregular forms are informal. Those that arch, spread, twist, or seem fluffy or airy give landscapes a casual style.

3) Combining styles

should be done carefully. As long as you don't have formal features competing with informal ones, you can combine styles successfully. Use one style to set the dominant tone of your landscape, then create little accent areas of the opposite style. A landscape full of curving bedlines without a central axis is informal, but you can add formal touches. For example, a pair of ornamental trees framing a view adds a touch of formality, but won't be out of place in an informal setting.

Asymmetrical composition gives this landscape an informal air. Plants were chosen to please the eye with no thought of creating matching patterns.

Combining styles can also add contrast. A formally clipped hedge surrounding a bed of plants with delicate flowers and foliage on lanky stems will create an appealing scene showing off both kinds of plants to their best advantage.

How much work do you want to do?

Maintenance considerations affect choice of style. If you enjoy pruning, try a formal landscape with lots of plants clipped into neat shapes. If you want to spend more time admiring your landscape than working in it, an informal style might suit your needs. To reduce maintenance chores, avoid mixing many different kinds of plants closely together. You'll find it difficult to meet their individual needs unless you enjoy puttering with plants. Consider growing conditions when choosing plants. The right plant in the right place is still the first rule of landscaping.

The front yard is more heavily influenced by architecture than the backyard. Your house and front yard landscape are seen together from the street. On the other hand, the backyard is usually seen when looking from the house, not at it. If the architecture makes a formal style appropriate, use a traditional approach to design in front; if you also like informally styled outdoor spaces, grow a more free-form landscape in the back.

A pair of pots adds a formal touch to an informally designed landscape, drawing attention to the bench. A pair of matching shrubs or small trees could do the same.

Assessing Your Yard

Great landscapes start at home, not at the store. The first things you need to decide are what you've got that's worth keeping, what you need to get rid of, and what problems need to be solved before you can start making improvements.

1) Create a Base and Site Map

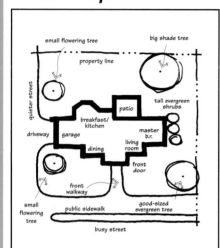

A base map doesn't have to be neat or accurate. It's just the first step in assessing your property.

To assess your yard, you'll need to take an objective look at your property. It helps to have a sketch on which you can take notes. Make a photocopy of your original survey if you have one. If you can't find your survey, make a rough sketch showing the shape of your lot with the house and any paving on it. Don't worry about making the drawing neat and pretty or getting accurate dimensions. The purpose of this sketch is to make it easier to take notes about different areas. Mark approximate locations of trees, water features, and existing bedlines to indicate the locations and shapes of planting beds and lawn areas. The result is a rough base map.

With your base map in hand, walk your property. Look at the exterior spaces from different angles, including from across the street. Note the parking areas and walkways. Go inside the house and look out windows; views from the inside are part of landscaping, too.

You're looking for assets and liabilities for the site analysis. Assets are things that you want to keep. Attractive planting areas, healthy shrubs, big shade trees, small accent trees, good stands of lawn, and pretty vines are assets. Mark good views looking into your property and looking outward. Nicely paved areas, welcoming walkways, and interesting architectural features on your home are also worth noting. Anything you like is an asset.

Now it's time to be blunt. List all the liabilities you see. Scribble notes and arrows all over your sketch. Use a different color ink to contrast with the notes you made about assets.

Liabilities include unattractive or unhealthy plants, trees or shrubs that block good views or make interior rooms dark and gloomy, plants that are messy or require constant maintenance, scraggly lawn areas, or deteriorating paving, walls,

or fences. Include poor views seen while looking at your home, out the windows, or from within your yard looking out toward adjacent properties. Note areas that don't have enough privacy, shade, or seating to be comfortable.

Other common liabilities include traffic noises, glare, inadequate parking, and noticeable utility areas.

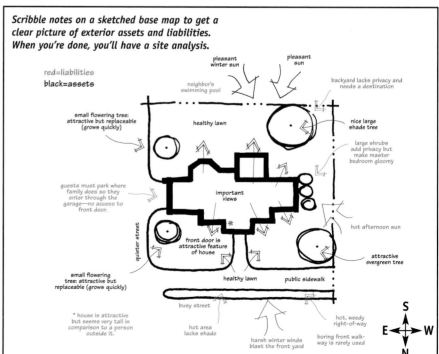

Scribble notes on a sketched base map to get a clear picture of exterior assets and liabilities. When you're done, you'll have a site analysis.

Look for unattractive aspects of your house. Blank, windowless walls; old closed-in garages with driveways leading nowhere; and tall foundations will make your list. Drainage problems should be noted, too: Spots that stay wet or are difficult to keep moist are important factors in plant selection.

Good landscaping overcomes liabilities and makes the most of the assets of your home. It could be painful to be objective now, but it's easier to fix problems if you know what they are.

2) *Inventory Your Needs*

Landscape architects and garden designers visit with their clients before beginning work. They learn about a family's likes and dislikes, their budget, and their priorities before they begin. You'll need to do the same thing. Though it seems as though all the answers would be obvious (after all, you're your own client), a little research goes a long way toward setting obtainable landscaping goals.

List your needs and your goals. Some things might be obvious, such as providing additional parking or adding more shade. Others will take more thought—making your walkway more inviting or adding privacy to make your patio more usable or more intimate.

Follow these observations with notations about the cause of the current condition. For example, if your walkway is uncomfortable, it might be too narrow. Adding borders of bricks, pavers, or stones can widen the paving to make it more inviting. Or, crumbling, uneven paving might need replacing.

3) *Set a Budget*
Decide how much you'd like to spend and then research the costs of plants, materials, delivery, and labor if you're hiring help. Most people find that landscaping costs more than they think, so budgets have to be flexible. Compared with the cost of your house, landscaping is a reasonable investment. If you're building a new home, set aside 10 percent of the cost for landscaping. If that's impossible, find a percentage you can live with and stick to it. You'll be glad you didn't spend all your money on the interior when it comes time to dress up the exterior—after all, that's the area most people will see.

Smart Design—Inside and Out
You're missing a design bet if you don't plan your landscape to work from both the inside and outside of your home. Windows are picture frames that invite you into a living world. Creating great views from favorite interior spaces such as bedrooms, family rooms, kitchens, and living rooms will give you hours of enjoyment when you can't be outside.

Landscape Assessment Quiz

How well do you know your property?

Answer these questions before you head for the garden center. Prepare a packet with all the notes you've gathered, including the snapshots of your home and yard, and bring it along. Accurate information will help you get you what you want.

1) What's your exposure?
Knowing the direction your house faces (the exposure) will help you design your landscape and select the right plant. Some plants will thrive on southern exposure but freeze on the northern side of your house. Others grow in eastern sun but wilt in hot, western sun. Use a compass to find north or track where the sun rises (east) and sets (west). If you're facing west, north is to your right.

2) How's your sun and shade?
Knowing how the amount of sun or shade affects plants is essential to their survival. (See pages 32-33.) Observe at various times of the day (10 a.m., noon, 3 p.m., and 5 p.m.) to see how the sun affects your property. Buildings, walls, evergreen trees, and shrubs also might provide shade most of the year. Trees, shrubs, and vines will allow winter sunlight to filter through during dormancy but will cast shade during the summer. Does the project area receive morning sun or afternoon sun? Refer to your notes and combine that with information about exposure: East-facing areas receive morning light unless shaded, and west-facing spots generally receive afternoon sun.

3) What's your soil like?
Dig a few sample holes in your project area and examine the soil. (See page 38 for information on soil and percolation tests.) Some basic questions are: What color is the soil a few inches beneath the surface? Is the soil moist or dry? The ideal soil will roll into a ball yet crumble easily, will be dark in color, and will hold water and nutrients. For a detailed analysis, visit your county extension service and arrange for a soil test.

If a cozy retreat is what you crave, concentrate your efforts on private areas of your landscape right away. You may need to begin by adding screening with fences and plants.

Prioritizing Your Plans

Plan your design and then break it down into manageable projects. Completing work on specific areas is more satisfying than scattering your efforts. Improving your landscape in phases stretches your budget, too. Before you choose which project area to work on first, prioritize your needs. First, look at your public and private spaces.

1) Public Spaces

The exterior area around your house can be broadly classified in two categories—public and private. Public spaces are the parts of your yard that you present to guests and the public, including passersby and workers who access your property. For many people, these public areas are a top priority. Completing this portion of a landscape makes a home look its best from the street and beautifies the neighborhood. Making public areas the first priority is a practical decision, too. A well-designed landscape welcomes people, gives them a place to park, and provides clear access to the house. Good landscaping adds value to your home by enhancing curb appeal. If you're making improvements to enhance sales value, public spaces will be your priority.

On most lots, the front yard is the public space, and many people begin their landscape efforts there. That's fine if public space is your top priority. In fact, most builders will spend the entire landscape allowance on the front yard because that's what helps sell the house. But don't automatically concentrate on the front yard if you'd really rather begin by working on more private family areas. Prioritize your efforts to meet your family's needs, or you might never get around to sprucing up the area you'd use the most.

Pay attention to the public spaces of your yard. Landscaping around the front door will make your home welcoming and attractive.

2) Private Spaces

Family entries, entertainment areas, and spots to sit, read, talk, or snooze in the fresh air are quiet private spaces. Active private areas include children's play areas and places for growing vegetables or favorite flowers. Utility areas are also

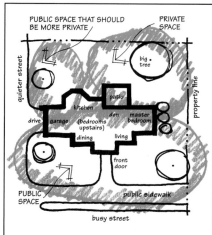

Before beginning work, you'll want to sketch the public and private areas of your landscape to help set priorities.

Brick steps, pots of flowers, and a pretty garden gate mark the entry to somewhere special. Lush plantings and walls make this backyard patio private and comfortable.

private—there's no need for neighbors to share a view of garbage cans, dog runs, and storage spots.

Most backyards and some side yards are private spaces. If you don't enjoy being in your backyard, or feel you're on display when you sit there, make some changes. A lack of destination, poor views, no privacy, drainage problems, too little or too much shade, and unattractive plants are common backyard problems. If some of these descriptions sound like your backyard, working on it might be more important than working on the public spaces. Let

family members have a say. The landscape is part of your home and should meet everyone's needs — including pets.

Focus Your Work
Dividing your landscaping goals into phases makes achieving them more likely. It's much more satisfying to complete a project area within your yard than it is to get bogged down trying to do all the work at once. Doing the job in phases is also a good way to stretch a budget. Set priorities to concentrate your efforts.

Design Tip

Multiple Priorities Planning phases for landscaping public and private spaces isn't an either/or proposition. You can devise a plan that includes major work on a private space, such as the backyard, as well as minor improvements for the front. Those changes can make it immediately more presentable and create the groundwork for a bigger overhaul later on.

Combined Spaces

Lots don't always divide neatly in half, with the front as public space and the back as private space.
You can also carve out private spaces within the front yard, increasing the area's usefulness. Low hedges, walls, or fences distinguish a private space from a public one. Waist-high barriers seem friendly and unchallenging, giving you the best of both worlds—you can have a public conversation and still offer privacy with outdoor seating behind the hedge.

You might need to separate a private area to make the public space more appealing. If everyone is entering your house through a messy garage strewn with toys and tools, rethink your landscape. Block views of doors that you don't want people to use. A vine-covered trellis or artfully arranged trees and shrubs keep family entries from becoming visible targets for guests. Make the public area welcoming by including a wide, inviting, well-lit walkway close to where people get out of their cars or approach

from public sidewalks. (Consider creating separate guest parking.) Keep the landscape fresh and tidy around the door you'd like guests to use. If it looks like no one ever goes there, no one ever will.

Design Principles   **19**

selection

White Fir
(Abies concolor)
Page 70

A thriving landscape full of healthy plants isn't an accident. It's the result of thorough research and careful planning. Good plant selection is the key.

Yellowwood
(Cladrastis lutea)
Page 82

The Right Plant in the Right Place

If there's a common equation for good results in the landscaping trade, it would be something like this: right + right + right = success. But you don't need chalk and a blackboard to figure out that the *right* plant in the *right* place with the *right* care will guarantee landscaping success.

Saxifrage
(Bergenia cordifolia)
Page 179

Proper plant selection is critical. A lovely plant in the wrong place won't thrive or serve its intended purpose, and will require constant attention. A poorly chosen plant might grow too large for the space and require excessive pruning. Choosing the wrong location for a plant means that conditions are unfavorable for growth, resulting in more work on your part. Finally, there's an artistic issue. The wrong plant in the wrong place just won't work well within your landscape design.

Follow these steps to choose the right plant for the right place:

1) Determine Your Needs

Chapter One is a road map for figuring out what you want; if you skipped it, go back and work through the exercises so you'll understand the roles each plant plays within your landscape design. You might need some plants to supply privacy, others to dress up the front of your house, and still others to add interest to a backyard patio. Before plant shopping, pick a specific project area within your yard and list the purposes new plants should serve to make that area work.

Make existing elements on your site work for you. Selecting plants that thrive in rocky soil and full sun turns this barren stone outcropping into a garden.

Wisdom of the Aisles

Reduce yard work. Proper plant selection in the beginning will help keep maintenance requirements at a manageable level later on. That's because plants that thrive in their setting are less susceptible to insects and disease problems than those that struggle to survive. Plants that are right for their location require less coaxing to grow. Plants that are correctly sited have room to mature. Their natural forms fit their chosen sites well and require little pruning.

2) Define Existing Conditions

You need to know what conditions exist within your project area and which plants will thrive there. Refer to notes you made during your site analysis (see page 16), but repeat the exercise focusing on your project area. Note whether the area is hilly or flat; wet, moist, or dry; and sunny or shady in mornings and afternoons. Learn which direction your area faces and whether it's protected from harsh winds or exposed to them. Check to see whether the soil is hard and compacted or rich and soft. Look for any special conditions, such as salt spray from ocean breezes, confined root space, or city conditions such as car exhaust.

BUYER'S GUIDE

Don't overlook a good plant just because it isn't in full bloom at the store.. You're better off buying a vigorous plant that's shaped properly according to its species than you would be if you made flowers the top shopping criteria. Your purchases are for the long run.

3) Study Your Options

Use the selection guides that follow to help you get started in the decisionmaking process. These lists of plants are a good first step toward choosing the right plants for the right places in your yard. They'll help you match your needs, your desires, and the conditions of your yard with a variety of suitable plants. To get a complete picture of your options, you'll need to look up descriptions of plants on the pages listed. It's also important to supplement your research with observations about what grows in your area. Seek the advice of local experts, too. Talented gardeners and associates at garden centers are valuable sources of information when it comes to choosing plants for your region.

Examine the selection guides and eliminate any plant that doesn't include your climate zone within its growing range (see page 5 to determine your climate zone). But keep in mind that not every plant with a zone number that matches yours will grow where you live. That's because climate zones are based on the minimal temperatures at which plants will thrive. This

Kousa Dogwood (Cornus kousa) Page 83

information is valuable, but it's not the final word in plant selection. Other climate factors, such as annual rainfall and humidity, also play a role in choosing plants. Local soil conditions and soil pH affect which plants you'll find for sale in your area, too. Availability is also dependent in part upon local growers who supply plants to stores.

Plants for Zone 5

Locate your area on the map on page 5 to determine the number of your climate zone. The plants in the following lists will thrive in Zone 5.

Availability varies by area and conditions (see page 21). These lists categorize plants by height. Follow the page number listed to the encyclopedia entries, which will give you complete information on the plants you're considering.

Trees for Zone 5

Common Name	Zones	Page
◆ **Small Trees (30 feet or under)**		
American Arborvitae	2-9	107
Thuja occidentalis		
Amur Maple	2-6	71
Acer tataricum ginnala		
Blue Holly	5-8	88
Ilex x meserveae		
Downy Serviceberry	4-9	76
Amelanchier arborea		
European Mountain Ash	3-6	104
Sorbus aucuparia		
Flowering Dogwood	5-9	82
Cornus florida		
Japanese Flowering Crabapple	4-8	92
Malus floribunda		
Japanese Maple	5-8	73
Acer palmatum		
Japanese Snowbell	5-8	105
Styrax japonicum		
Japanese Tree Lilac	3-7	106
Syringa reticulata		
Kousa Dogwood	5-8	83
Cornus kousa		
Kwanzan Cherry	5-8	98
Prunus serrulata 'Kwanzan'		
Paperbark Maple	4-8	72
Acer griseum		
Plumleaf Crabapple	4-9	92
Malus prunifolia		
Possum Haw	3-9	87
Ilex decidua		
Purple-Leaf Plum	4-8	97
Prunus cerasifera 'Atropurpurea'		
Redbud	3-9	81
Cercis canadensis		
Russian Olive	3-8	84
Elaeagnus angustifolia		
Saucer Magnolia	5-9	91
Magnolia x soulangiana		
Savannah Holly	5-9	88
Ilex opaca 'Savannah'		
Skyrocket Juniper	4-8	89
Juniperus scopulorum 'Skyrocket'		
Star Magnolia	4-9	91
Magnolia stellata		
Trident Maple	4-8	71
Acer buergerianum		
Washington Hawthorn	3-9	83
Crataegus phaenopyrum		
Weeping Cherry	4-8	99
Prunus subhirtella 'Pendula'		
◆ **Medium Trees (30 to 60 feet)**		
Amur Chokecherry	2-6	97
Prunus maackii		
Bradford Pear	4-8	100
Pyrus calleryana 'Bradford'		
Chinese Elm	5-9	109
Ulmus parvifolia		
Colorado Blue Spruce	2-7	95
Picea pungens glauca		
Eastern Red Cedar	3-9	89
Juniperus virginiana		
European Hornbeam	4-7	78
Carpinus betulus		
Frasier Fir	4-7	70
Abies fraseri		
Green Ash	3-9	86
Fraxinus pennsylvanica		
Japanese Stewartia	5-7	105
Stewartia pseudocamellia		
Japanese Zelkova	5-9	109
Zelkova serrata		
Katsura Tree	4-8	80
Cercidiphyllum japonicum		
Norway Maple	3-7	72
Acer platanoides		

Common Name	Zones	Page
Norway Spruce	2-7	93
Picea abies		
Pyramidal Japanese Yew	4-7	107
Taxus cuspidata 'Capitata'		
Quaking Aspen	2-6	96
Populus tremuloides		
Red Maple	3-9	74
Acer rubrum		
Sugarberry	5-9	80
Celtis laevigata		
Weeping Willow	4-9	104
Salix babylonica		
White Fir	3-7	70
Abies concolor		
White Spruce	2-6	94
Picea glauca		
Whitespire Birch	4-7	77
Betula mandschurica japonica 'Whitespire'		
◆ **Large Trees (60 feet or more)**		
American Beech	3-9	85
Fagus grandifolia		
Bald Cypress	4-10	106
Taxodium distichum		
California Incense Cedar	4-8	78
Calocedrus decurrens		
Canadian Hemlock	3-7	108
Tsuga canadensis		
Canoe Birch	2-5	77
Betula papyrifera		
Dawn Redwood	4-8	93
Metasequoia glyptostroboides		
Douglas Fir	4-6	99
Pseudotsuga menziesii		
Fruitless American Sweetgum	5-9	90
Liquidambar styraciflua 'Rotundiloba'		
Ginkgo	3-9	86
Ginkgo biloba		
Honeylocust	3-8	87
Gleditsia triacanthos inermis		
Japanese Black Pine	5-7	96
Pinus thunbergii		
Littleleaf Linden	3-7	108
Tilia cordata		
Northern Red Oak	4-7	103
Quercus rubra		
Pin Oak	4-8	102
Quercus palustris		
River Birch	4-9	76
Betula nigra		
Sargent Cherry	4-7	98
Prunus sargentii		
Scarlet Oak	4-9	101
Quercus coccinea		
Serbian Spruce	4-7	94
Picea omorika		
Shumard Oak	5-9	103
Quercus shumardii		
Silver Maple	3-9	75
Acer saccharinum		
Sugar Maple	4-8	75
Acer saccharum		
White Oak	4-9	101
Quercus alba		
White Pine	3-8	95
Pinus strobus		
Willow Oak	4-8	102
Quercus phellos		

Shrubs for Zone 5

Common Name	Zones	Page
◆ **Small Shrubs (3 feet or under)**		
Bird's Nest Spruce	2-7	150
Picea abies 'Nidiformis'		
Blue Star Juniper	4-8	146
Juniperus squamata 'Blue Star'		

Common Name	Zones	Page
Carol Mackie Daphne	4-8	136
Daphne x burkwoodii 'Carol Mackie'		
Dwarf Alberta Spruce	3-8	150
Picea glauca 'Conica'		
Dwarf Hinoki False Cypress	4-8	132
Chamaecyparis obtusa 'Nana Gracilis'		
Green Beauty Boxwood	5-9	130
Buxus microphylla 'Green Beauty'		
Heller Japanese Holly	5-8	142
Ilex crenata 'Helleri'		
Iceberg Rose	4-9	157
Rosa 'Iceberg'		
Korean Boxwood	5-9	131
Buxus microphylla koreana		
Margo Koster Rose	5-8	157
Rosa 'Margo Koster'		
Parson's Juniper	3-9	145
Juniperus chinensis 'Parsonii'		
Shrubby Cinquefoil	2-7	152
Potentilla fruticosa		
The Fairy Rose	4-9	159
Rosa 'The Fairy'		
◆ **Medium Shrubs (3 to 6 feet)**		
Annabelle Hydrangea	3-9	139
Hydrangea arborescens 'Annabelle'		
Anthony Waterer Spirea	3-9	161
Spiraea japonica 'Anthony Waterer'		
Baby's Breath Spirea	2-8	162
Spiraea thunbergii		
Betty Prior Rose	4-9	155
Rosa 'Betty Prior'		
Bridalwreath Spirea	5-8	162
Spiraea prunifolia		
Butterfly Bush	5-9	129
Buddleia davidii		
Carefree Beauty Rose	4-8	155
Rosa Carefree Beauty		
Carolina Azalea	4-9	127
Azalea carolinianum		
Chinese Beautyberry	5-8	132
Callicarpa dichotoma		
Compact Japanese Holly	5-8	143
Ilex crenata 'Compacta'		
Coralberry	4-7	163
Symphoricarpos orbiculatus		
Drooping Leucothoe	5-8	147
Leucothoe fontanesiana		
Dwarf Burning Bush	3-8	136
Euonymus alatus 'Compacta'		
Dwarf Flowering Almond	4-8	153
Prunus glandulosa 'Rosea'		
Exbury Azalea	4-7	127
Azalea 'Exbury Hybrids'		
Fru Dagmar Hastrup Rose	2-9	156
Rosa 'Fru Dagmar Hastrup'		
Graham Thomas Rose	5-9	156
Rosa Graham Thomas		
Inkberry	3-9	143
Ilex glabra 'Compacta'		
Japanese Barberry	4-8	129
Berberis thunbergii		
Korean Spice Viburnum	4-8	167
Viburnum carlesii		
Little Giant Arborvitae	3-7	166
Thuja occidentalis 'Little Giant'		
Manhattan Spreading Euonymus	4-8	137
Euonymus kiautschovicus 'Manhattan'		
Mountain Pieris	4-8	151
Pieris floribunda		
Mugo Pine	2-7	152
Pinus mugo		
Northern Lights Azalea	4-7	128
Azalea 'Northern Lights'		
Oakleaf Hydrangea	5-9	141
Hydrangea quercifolia		
Peace Rose	5-8	158
Rosa 'Peace'		

Common Name	Zones	Page
Pink Meidiland Rose *Rosa Pink Meidiland*	5-8	158
Rosa Rubrifolia *Rosa rubrifolia*	4-9	159
Sea Green Juniper *Juniperus chinensis 'Sea Green'*	4-8	145
Shibori Spirea *Spiraea japonica 'Shibori'*	4-8	161
Snowberry *Symphoricarpos albus*	3-7	163
Tam Juniper *Juniperus sabina 'Tamariscifolia'*	3-7	146
Yukon Belle Firethorn *Pyracantha angustifolia Yukon Belle*	4-9	154

◆ Large Shrubs (6 feet or more)

Common Name	Zones	Page
Andromeda *Pieris japonica*	5-8	151
Arnold's Red Tatarian Honeysuckle *Lonicera tatarica 'Arnold's Red'*	3-9	148
Catawba Rhododendron *Rhododendron catawbiense*	4-8	154
Common Lilac *Syringa vulgaris*	3-7	165
Common Witch Hazel *Hamamelis virginiana*	3-8	138
Coral Embers Willow *Salix alba 'Britzensis'*	2-8	160
Cornelian Cherry *Cornus mas*	4-8	134
Cornell Pink Azalea *Azalea mucronulatum 'Cornell Pink'*	4-7	128
Cutleaf Lilac *Syringa x laciniata*	4-8	164
Doublefile Viburnum *Viburnum plicatum tomentosum*	4-8	167
European Cranberrybush *Viburnum opulus 'Roseum'*	3-8	167
Golden Vicary Privet *Ligustrum x vicaryi*	5-8	148
Gray Dogwood *Cornus racemosa*	4-7	134
Green Lustre Japanese Holly *Ilex crenata 'Green Lustre'*	4-6	142
Hick's Upright Yew *Taxus x media 'Hicksii'*	4-7	166
Large Fothergilla *Fothergilla major*	4-8	138
Miss Kim Lilac *Syringa patula 'Miss Kim'*	3-7	164
Mountain Laurel *Kalmia latifolia*	4-9	147
Northern Bayberry *Myrica pensylvanica*	2-6	149
PeeGee Hydrangea *Hydrangea paniculata 'Grandiflora'*	3-8	140
Persian Lilac *Syringa x persica*	3-7	164
Redtwig Dogwood *Cornus alba*	2-8	133
Serviceberry *Amelanchier alnifolia*	4-5	126
Summersweet *Clethra alnifolia*	3-9	133
Winterberry *Ilex verticillata*	3-9	144
Yellow-Twig Dogwood *Cornus stolonifera 'Flaviramea'*	3-8	135

Groundcover for Zone 5

Common Name	Zones	Page

◆ Low Groundcovers (12" or less)

Common Name	Zones	Page
Ajuga *Ajuga reptans*	4-9	175
Allegheny Foam Flower *Tiarella cordifolia*	4-9	200
Bar Harbor Juniper *Juniperus horizontalis 'Bar Harbor'*	3-9	190
Bath's Pink *Dianthus gratianopolitanus 'Bath's Pink'*	4-9	182
Blue Chip Juniper *Juniperus horizontalis 'Blue Chip'*	3-9	190
Blue-Eyed Mary *Omphalodes verna*	5-9	194

Common Name	Zones	Page
Blue Rug Juniper *Juniperus horizontalis 'Wiltonii'*	3-9	191
Bunchberry *Cornus canadensis*	2-7	181
Corsican Mint *Mentha corsica*	5-9	193
Creeping Phlox *Phlox stolonifera*	2-8	195
Creeping Thyme *Thymus leucotrichus*	5-9	200
Cypress Spurge *Euphorbia cyparissias*	4-8	184
Dragon's Blood Sedum *Sedum spurium 'Dragon's Blood'*	3-8	198
Dwarf Blue Fescue *Festuca glauca*	4-9	184
English Ivy *Hedera helix*	5-9	186
Evergreen Candytuft *Iberis sempervirens*	4-8	189
Forget-Me-Not *Myosotis scorpioides*	3-8	193
Geum *Geum reptans*	4-7	186
Green and Gold *Chrysogonum virginianum*	5-8	181
Kinnikinick *Arctostaphylos uva-ursi*	2-7	177
Lady's Mantle *Alchemilla mollis*	4-7	175
Lily-of-the-Valley *Convallaria majalis*	2-9	181
Littleleaf Periwinkle *Vinca minor*	4-8	201
Maidenhair Fern *Adiantum pedatum*	3-8	174
Memorial Rose *Rosa wichuraiana*	4-9	197
Moneywort *Lysimachia nummularia*	3-8	193
Moss Phlox *Phlox subulata*	2-9	196
Mountain Sandwort *Arenaria montana*	3-6	177
Pachysandra *Pachysandra terminalis*	4-9	195
Pink Panda Strawberry *Fragaria 'Pink Panda'*	3-9	184
Rockcress *Arabis caucasica*	3-7	177
Rock Jasmine *Androsace lanuginosa*	5-7	176
Rock Rose *Helianthemum nummularium*	5-8	186
Royal Carpet Honeysuckle *Lonicera pileata*	5-9	192
Snow-on-the-Mountain *Aegopodium podagraria 'Variegatum'*	3-9	174
Spring Cinquefoil *Potentilla tabernaemontani*	4-8	196
Spring Heath *Erica carnea*	4-8	183
Sundrop Primrose *Oenothera missouriensis*	4-8	194
Yellow Archangel *Lamiastrum galeobdolon 'Variegatum'*	3-9	192

◆ Tall Groundcovers (12" or more)

Common Name	Zones	Page
Aaron's Beard *Hypericum calycinum*	5-9	188
Alba Meidiland Rose *Rosa Alba Meidiland*	4-8	197
Andorra Compact Juniper *Juniperus horizontalis 'Plumosa Compacta'*	3-9	191
Bearberry Cotoneaster *Cotoneaster dammeri*	5-9	182
Blanket Flower *Gaillardia x grandiflora*	2-9	185
Bloody Cranesbill *Geranium sanguineum*	3-8	185
Blue Pacific Shore Juniper *Juniperus conferta 'Blue Pacific'*	5-9	190
Blue Star *Amsonia tabernaemontana*	3-9	175
Bog Rosemary *Andromeda polifolia*	2-6	176

Common Name	Zones	Page
Catmint *Nepeta x faassenii*	4-8	194
Coral Bells *Heuchera sanguinea*	3-8	187
Dwarf Japanese Garden Juniper *Juniperus procumbens 'Nana'*	4-9	191
Flower Carpet Rose *Rosa 'Flower Carpet'*	4-10	197
Fountain Grass *Pennisetum alopecuroides*	5-9	195
Germander *Teucrium prostratum*	4-9	199
Goldmoss *Sedum acre*	4-9	198
Hosta *Hosta species*	3-8	187
Houttuynia *Houttuynia cordata*	5-9	188
Japanese Blood Grass *Imperata cylindrica 'Red Baron'*	5-9	189
Japanese Painted Fern *Athyrium nipponicum 'Pictum'*	4-9	179
Japanese Primrose *Primula japonica*	5-8	196
Lamb's Ear *Stachys byzantina*	4-8	199
Plumbago *Cerotostigma plumbaginoides*	5-9	180
Prostrate Chenault Coralberry *Symphoricarpos x chenaultii 'Hancock'*	4-7	199
Purple-Leaf Wintercreeper *Euonymus fortunei 'Coloratus'*	4-8	183
Saxifrage *Bergenia cordifolia*	3-8	179
Scotch Heather *Calluna vulgaris*	3-8	180
Sea Thrift *Armeria maritima*	3-8	178
Siberian Forget-Me-Not *Anchusa myosotidiflora*	3-7	176
Silver Brocade Artemisia *Artemisia stelleriana 'Silver Brocade'*	3-9	178
Spotted Dead Nettle *Lamium maculatum*	3-9	192
Stonecrop *Sedum spectabile*	3-10	198

Vines for Zone 5

Common Name	Zones	Page
American Bittersweet *Celastrus scandens*	3-8	208
Blaze Climbing Rose *Rosa 'Blaze'*	5-10	212
Boston Ivy *Parthenocissus tricuspidata*	4-8	211
Chinese Wisteria *Wisteria sinensis*	5-9	215
Chocolate Vine *Akebia quinata*	5-9	206
Climbing Hydrangea *Hydrangea petiolaris*	4-7	209
Climbing Iceberg Rose *Rosa 'Climbing Iceberg'*	4-10	213
Climbing Peace Rose *Rosa 'Climbing Peace'*	5-9	213
Dropmore Scarlet Honeysuckle *Lonicera x brownii 'Dropmore Scarlet'*	3-7	210
Hardy Kiwi *Actinidia arguta*	4-8	206
Hybrid Clematis *Clematis hybrid*	3-9	209
Joseph's Coat Climbing Rose *Rosa 'Joseph's Coat'*	4-10	214
Porcelain Vine *Ampelopsis brevipedunculata*	4-8	207
Silver Lace Vine *Polygonum aubertii*	4-9	212
Trumpet Honeysuckle *Lonicera sempervirens*	4-9	210
Trumpet Vine *Campsis radicans*	4-9	208
Virginia Creeper *Parthenocissus quinquefolia*	4-8	211

Plants for Zone 6

Locate your home on the map on page 5 to determine your climate zone. The plants in the following lists are good for Zone 6. Availability varies by area and conditions (see page 21). Check with your garden center. Plants on these lists are categorized by height. Turn to the pages listed for more information about growth rate and for ranges of height and spread.

Trees for Zone 6

Common Name	Zones	Page
◆ **Small Trees (30 feet or under)**		
American Arborvitae	2-9	107
Thuja occidentalis		
Amur Maple	2-6	71
Acer tataricum ginnala		
Blue Holly	5-8	88
Ilex x meserveae		
Downy Serviceberry	4-9	76
Amelanchier arborea		
Flowering Dogwood	5-9	82
Cornus florida		
Japanese Flowering Crabapple	4-8	92
Malus floribunda		
Japanese Maple	5-8	73
Acer palmatum		
Japanese Snowbell	5-8	105
Styrax japonicum		
Japanese Tree Lilac	3-7	106
Syringa reticulata		
Kousa Dogwood	5-8	83
Cornus kousa		
Kwanzan Cherry	5-8	98
Prunus serrulata 'Kwanzan'		
Paperbark Maple	4-8	72
Acer griseum		
Plumleaf Crabapple	4-9	92
Malus prunifolia		
Possum Haw	3-9	87
Ilex decidua		
Purple-Leaf Plum	4-8	97
Prunus cerasifera 'Atropurpurea'		
Redbud	3-9	81
Cercis canadensis		
Russian Olive	3-8	84
Elaeagnus angustifolia		
Saucer Magnolia	5-9	91
Magnolia x soulangiana		
Savannah Holly	5-9	88
Ilex opaca 'Savannah'		
Star Magnolia	4-9	91
Magnolia stellata		
Trident Maple	4-8	71
Acer buergerianum		
Washington Hawthorn	3-9	83
Crataegus phaenopyrum		
Weeping Cherry	4-8	99
Prunus subhirtella 'Pendula'		
◆ **Medium Trees (30 to 60 feet)**		
Amur Chokecherry	2-6	97
Prunus maackii		
Bradford Pear	4-8	100
Pyrus calleryana 'Bradford'		
Chinese Elm	5-9	109
Ulmus parvifolia		
Colorado Blue Spruce	2-7	95
Picea pungens glauca		
Eastern Red Cedar	3-9	89
Juniperus virginiana		
European Hornbeam	4-7	78
Carpinus betulus		
Frasier Fir	4-7	70
Abies fraseri		
Green Ash	3-9	86
Fraxinus pennsylvanica		
Japanese Stewartia	5-7	105
Stewartia pseudocamellia		
Japanese Zelkova	5-9	109
Zelkova serrata		
Katsura Tree	4-8	80
Cercidiphyllum japonicum		
Leyland Cypress	6-9	84
X Cupressocyparis leylandii		
Norway Maple	3-7	72
Acer platanoides		
Norway Spruce	2-7	93
Picea abies		

Common Name	Zones	Page
Pyramidal Japanese Yew	4-7	107
Taxus cuspidata 'Capitata'		
Quaking Aspen	2-6	96
Populus tremuloides		
Red Maple	3-9	74
Acer rubrum		
Sugarberry	5-9	80
Celtis laevigata		
Weeping Willow	4-9	104
Salix babylonica		
White Fir	3-7	70
Abies concolor		
White Spruce	2-6	94
Picea glauca		
Whitespire Birch	4-7	77
Betula mandschurica japonica 'Whitespire'		
Yellowwood	6-8	82
Cladrastis lutea		
◆ **Large Trees (60 feet or more)**		
American Beech	3-9	85
Fagus grandifolia		
Bald Cypress	4-10	106
Taxodium distichum		
Blue Atlas Cedar	6-8	79
Cedrus libani 'Glauca'		
California Incense Cedar	4-8	78
Calocedrus decurrens		
Canadian Hemlock	3-7	108
Tsuga canadensis		
Dawn Redwood	4-8	93
Metasequoia glyptostroboides		
Deodar Cedar	6-9	79
Cedrus deodara		
Douglas Fir	4-6	99
Pseudotsuga menziesii		
Ginkgo	3-9	86
Ginkgo biloba		
Honeylocust	3-8	87
Gleditsia triacanthos inermis		
Japanese Black Pine	5-7	96
Pinus thunbergii		
Littleleaf Linden	3-7	108
Tilia cordata		
Northern Red Oak	4-7	103
Quercus rubra		
Pin Oak	4-8	102
Quercus palustris		
River Birch	4-9	76
Betula nigra		
Sargent Cherry	4-7	98
Prunus sargentii		
Shumard Oak	5-9	103
Quercus shumardii		
Silver Maple	3-9	75
Acer saccharinum		
Southern Magnolia	6-10	90
Magnolia grandiflora		
Sugar Maple	4-8	75
Acer saccharum		
White Oak	4-9	101
Quercus alba		
White Pine	3-8	95
Pinus strobus		
Willow Oak	4-8	102
Quercus phellos		

PeeGee Hydrangea
(*Hydrangea paniculata* 'Grandiflora')
Page 140

Shrubs for Zone 6

Common Name	Zones	Page
◆ **Small Shrubs (3 feet or under)**		
Bird's Nest Spruce	2-7	150
Picea abies 'Nidiformis'		
Dwarf Alberta Spruce	3-8	150
Picea glauca 'Conica'		
Dwarf Hinoki False Cypress	4-8	132
Chamaecyparis obtusa 'Nana Gracilis'		
Edging Boxwood	6-8	131
Buxus sempervirens 'Suffruticosa'		
Green Beauty Boxwood	5-9	130
Buxus microphylla 'Green Beauty'		
Heller Japanese Holly	5-8	142
Ilex crenata 'Helleri'		
Iceberg Rose	4-9	157
Rosa 'Iceberg'		
Korean Boxwood	5-9	131
Buxus microphylla koreana		
Margo Koster Rose	5-8	157
Rosa 'Margo Koster'		
Otto Luyken Laurel	6-8	153
Prunus laurocerasus 'Otto Luyken'		
Parson's Juniper	3-9	145
Juniperus chinensis 'Parsonii'		
Rockspray Cotoneaster	6-9	135
Cotoneaster horizontalis		
Shrubby Cinquefoil	2-7	152
Potentilla fruticosa		
The Fairy Rose	4-9	159
Rosa 'The Fairy'		
◆ **Medium Shrubs (3 to 6 feet)**		
Annabelle Hydrangea	3-9	139
Hydrangea arborescens 'Annabelle'		
Anthony Waterer Spirea	3-9	161
Spiraea japonica 'Anthony Waterer'		
Baby's Breath Spirea	2-8	162
Spiraea thunbergii		
Betty Prior Rose	4-9	155
Rosa 'Betty Prior'		
Bridalwreath Spirea	5-8	162
Spiraea prunifolia		
Butterfly Bush	5-9	129
Buddleia davidii		
Carolina Azalea	4-9	127
Azalea carolinianum		
Chinese Beautyberry	5-8	132
Callicarpa dichotoma		
Compact Japanese Holly	5-8	143
Ilex crenata 'Compacta'		
Coralberry	4-7	163
Symphoricarpos orbiculatus		
Drooping Leucothoe	5-8	147
Leucothoe fontanesiana		
Dwarf Burning Bush	3-8	136
Euonymus alatus 'Compacta'		
Dwarf Flowering Almond	4-8	153
Prunus glandulosa 'Rosea'		
Exbury Azalea	4-7	127
Azalea 'Exbury Hybrids'		
Fru Dagmar Hastrup Rose	2-9	156
Rosa 'Fru Dagmar Hastrup'		
Graham Thomas Rose	5-9	156
Rosa Graham Thomas		
Inkberry	3-9	143
Ilex glabra 'Compacta'		
Japanese Barberry	4-8	129
Berberis thunbergii		
Japanese Boxwood	6-9	130
Buxus microphylla japonica		
Japanese Skimmia	6-9	160
Skimmia japonica		

Common Name	Zones	Page
Korean Spice Viburnum *Viburnum carlesii*	4-8	167
Little Giant Arborvitae *Thuja occidentalis 'Little Giant'*	3-7	166
Mugo Pine *Pinus mugo*	2-7	152
Nikko Blue Hydrangea *Hydrangea macrophylla 'Nikko Blue'*	6-9	140
Northern Lights Azalea *Azalea 'Northern Lights'*	4-7	128
Oakleaf Hydrangea *Hydrangea quercifolia*	5-9	141
Peace Rose *Rosa 'Peace'*	5-8	158
Pink Meidiland Rose *Rosa Pink Meidiland*	5-8	158
Rosa Rubrifolia *Rosa rubrifolia*	4-9	159
Sea Green Juniper *Juniperus chinensis 'Sea Green'*	4-8	145
Shibori Spirea *Spiraea japonica 'Shibori'*	4-8	161
Snowberry *Symphoricarpos albus*	3-7	163
Tam Juniper *Juniperus sabina 'Tamariscifolia'*	3-7	146
Yukon Belle Firethorn *Pyracantha angustifolia Yukon Belle*	4-9	154

◆ Large Shrubs (6 feet or more)

Common Name	Zones	Page
Andromeda *Pieris japonica*	5-8	151
Arnold's Red Tatarian Honeysuckle *Lonicera tatarica 'Arnold's Red'*	3-9	148
Border Forsythia *Forsythia x intermedia*	6-9	137
Catawba Rhododendron *Rhododendron catawbiense*	4-8	154
Common Lilac *Syringa vulgaris*	3-7	165
Common Witch Hazel *Hamamelis virginiana*	3-8	138
Cornelian Cherry *Cornus mas*	4-8	134
Cornell Pink Azalea *Azalea mucronulatum 'Cornell Pink'*	4-7	128
Cutleaf Lilac *Syringa x laciniata*	4-8	164
Doublefile Viburnum *Viburnum plicatum tomentosum*	4-8	167
Dwarf Burford Holly *Ilex cornuta 'Bufordii Nana'*	6-9	141
European Cranberrybush *Viburnum opulus 'Roseum'*	3-8	167
Golden Vicary Privet *Ligustrum x vicaryi*	5-8	148
Gray Dogwood *Cornus racemosa*	4-7	134
Hick's Upright Yew *Taxus x media 'Hicksii'*	4-7	166
Large Fothergilla *Fothergilla major*	4-8	138
Miss Kim Lilac *Syringa patula 'Miss Kim'*	3-7	164
Mountain Laurel *Kalmia latifolia*	4-9	147
Nellie R. Stevens Holly *Ilex 'Nellie R. Stevens'*	6-9	144
Northern Bayberry *Myrica pensylvanica*	2-6	149
PeeGee Hydrangea *Hydrangea paniculata 'Grandiflora'*	3-8	140
Persian Lilac *Syringa x persica*	3-7	164
Redtwig Dogwood *Cornus alba*	2-8	133
Rose of Sharon *Hibiscus syriacus*	5-9	139
Vanhoutte Spirea *Spiraea x vanhouttei*	3-8	162
Winterberry *Ilex verticillata*	3-9	144
Yellow-Twig Dogwood *Cornus stolonifera 'Flaviramea'*	3-8	135

Groundcover for Zone 6

◆ Low Groundcovers (12" or less)

Common Name	Zones	Page
Ajuga *Ajuga reptans*	4-9	175
Allegheny Foam Flower *Tiarella cordifolia*	4-9	200
Bar Harbor Juniper *Juniperus horizontalis 'Bar Harbor'*	3-9	190
Bath's Pink *Dianthus gratianopolitanus 'Bath's Pink'*	4-9	182
Blue Chip Juniper *Juniperus horizontalis 'Blue Chip'*	3-9	190
Blue Rug Juniper *Juniperus horizontalis 'Wiltonii'*	3-9	191
Bunchberry *Cornus canadensis*	2-7	181
Corsican Mint *Mentha corsica*	5-9	193
Creeping Phlox *Phlox stolonifera*	2-8	195
Creeping Thyme *Thymus leucotrichus*	5-9	200
Dragon's Blood Sedum *Sedum spurium 'Dragon's Blood'*	3-8	198
Dwarf Blue Fescue *Festuca glauca*	4-9	184
English Ivy *Hedera helix*	5-9	186
Evergreen Candytuft *Iberis sempervirens*	4-8	189
Forget-Me-Not *Myosotis scorpioides*	3-8	193
Geum *Geum reptans*	4-7	186
Green and Gold *Chrysogonum virginianum*	5-8	181
Hardy Ice Plant *Delosperma nubigenum*	6-9	182
Kinnikinick *Arctostaphylos uva-ursi*	2-7	177
Lily-of-the-Valley *Convallaria majalis*	2-9	181
Littleleaf Periwinkle *Vinca minor*	4-8	201
Maidenhair Fern *Adiantum pedatum*	3-8	174
Memorial Rose *Rosa wichuraiana*	4-9	197
Moneywort *Lysimachia nummularia*	3-8	193
Moss Phlox *Phlox subulata*	2-9	196
Mountain Sandwort *Arenaria montana*	3-6	177
Pachysandra *Pachysandra terminalis*	4-9	195
Pink Panda Strawberry *Fragaria 'Pink Panda'*	3-9	184
Rockcress *Arabis caucasica*	3-7	177
Rock Jasmine *Androsace lanuginosa*	5-7	176
Rock Rose *Helianthemum nummularium*	5-8	186
Royal Carpet Honeysuckle *Lonicera pileata*	5-9	192
Spring Cinquefoil *Potentilla tabernaemontani*	4-8	196
Spring Heath *Erica carnea*	4-8	183
Yellow Archangel *Lamiastrum galeobdolon 'Variegatum'*	3-9	192

◆ Tall Groundcovers (12" or more)

Common Name	Zones	Page
Aaron's Beard *Hypericum calycinum*	5-9	188
Alba Meidiland Rose *Rosa Alba Meidiland*	4-8	197
Andorra Compact Juniper *Juniperus horizontalis 'Plumosa Compacta'*	3-9	191
Arum *Arum italicum*	6-10	178
Bearberry Cotoneaster *Cotoneaster dammeri*	5-9	182
Blanket Flower *Gaillardia x grandiflora*	2-9	185

Common Name	Zones	Page
Blue Pacific Shore Juniper *Juniperus conferta 'Blue Pacific'*	5-9	190
Blue Star *Amsonia tabernaemontana*	3-9	175
Bog Rosemary *Andromeda polifolia*	2-6	176
Catmint *Nepeta x faassenii*	4-8	194
Coral Bells *Heuchera sanguinea*	3-8	187
Dwarf Japanese Garden Juniper *Juniperus procumbens 'Nana'*	4-9	191
Flower Carpet Rose *Rosa 'Flower Carpet'*	4-10	197
Fountain Grass *Pennisetum alopecuroides*	5-9	195
Germander *Teucrium prostratum*	4-9	199
Goldmoss *Sedum acre*	4-9	198
Hosta *Hosta species*	3-8	187
Japanese Painted Fern *Athyrium nipponicum 'Pictum'*	4-9	179
Lamb's Ear *Stachys byzantina*	4-8	199
Lenten Rose *Helleborus orientalis*	4-8	187
Plumbago *Ceratostigma plumbaginoides*	5-9	180
Prostrate Chenault Coralberry *Symphoricarpos x chenaultii 'Hancock'*	4-7	199
Purple-Leaf Wintercreeper *Euonymus fortunei 'Coloratus'*	4-8	183
Scotch Heather *Calluna vulgaris*	3-8	180
Sea Thrift *Armeria maritima*	3-8	178
Siberian Forget-Me-Not *Anchusa myosotidiflora*	3-7	176
Spotted Dead Nettle *Lamium maculatum*	3-9	192
Stonecrop *Sedum spectabile*	3-10	198
Variegated Japanese Sedge *Carex morrowii 'Variegata'*	6-9	180

Vines for Zone 6

Common Name	Zones	Page
American Bittersweet *Celastrus scandens*	3-8	208
Blaze Climbing Rose *Rosa 'Blaze'*	5-10	212
Boston Ivy *Parthenocissus tricuspidata*	4-8	211
Chinese Wisteria *Wisteria sinensis*	5-9	215
Chocolate Vine *Akebia quinata*	5-9	206
Climbing Cecil Brunner Rose *Rosa 'Climbing Cecil Brunner'*	6-10	214
Climbing Hydrangea *Hydrangea petiolaris*	4-7	209
Cross-Vine *Bignonia capreolata*	6-9	207
Dropmore Scarlet Honeysuckle *Lonicera x brownii 'Dropmore Scarlet'*	3-7	210
Hardy Kiwi *Actinidia arguta*	4-8	206
Hybrid Clematis *Clematis hybrid*	3-9	209
Joseph's Coat Climbing Rose *Rosa 'Joseph's Coat'*	4-10	214
Porcelain Vine *Ampelopsis brevipedunculata*	4-8	207
Silver Lace Vine *Polygonum aubertii*	4-9	212
Trumpet Honeysuckle *Lonicera sempervirens*	4-9	210
Trumpet Vine *Campsis radicans*	4-9	208
Virginia Creeper *Parthenocissus quinquefolia*	4-9	211

Screening and Privacy

The results of your assessment revealed some views that should be blocked, such as unappealing garbage cans or air conditioners within your own yard. Other scenes might be off your property—a neighbor's messy garage, ugly signs, or unkempt alleyways will spoil your time outdoors. The beauty of landscaping is that you don't have to look at anything you don't want to. You can make unwanted views disappear behind plants, fences, arbors, or walls.

Evergreens make dense barriers that block views to the outside and guarantee privacy.

1) Define Privacy Needs

In addition to pinpointing unpleasant views, your site analysis reveals areas that might be unusable because they lack privacy. Blocking views to add or enhance privacy is important. However, it's rarely necessary to block every view from every angle. Doing so turns your home into a fortress. Instead, look at your yard notes on public and private spaces. Are the private spaces truly private? Do you need to make changes to increase privacy and make these spaces more usable? Would some public areas be better as private spaces?

2) Concentrate Efforts

When you've answered these questions, you'll know where to add privacy. Walk those areas. Identify the directions from which people can see into private areas. (Don't forget to look up; a neighboring multistory home or building might pose a problem.) These directions are angles of view. Identifying them will help you place plants to block views and enhance privacy without walling in your entire yard.

3) Filter Views Now

that you know which views to block, it's time to add screening. This term describes plants or objects positioned to block views. There are several screening options: fences, arbors, walls, and plants.

Evergreen plants are often used as screens because they retain their foliage year-round. Some are so dense they form screens like living walls.

Adding privacy can be as simple as planting a hedge or as elaborate as creating a beautiful hillside garden.

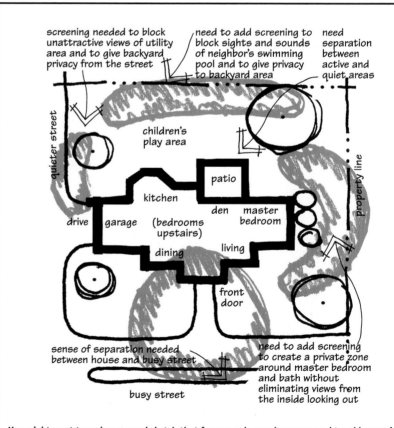

screening needed to block unattractive views of utility area and to give backyard privacy from the street

need to add screening to block sights and sounds of neighbor's swimming pool and to give privacy to backyard area

need separation between active and quiet areas

quieter street

children's play area

patio

kitchen

drive | garage | (bedrooms upstairs) | den | master bedroom

dining | living

property line

front door

sense of separation needed between house and busy street

need to add screening to create a private zone around master bedroom and bath without eliminating views from the inside looking out

busy street

You might want to make a second sketch that focuses only on where you need to add screening to provide privacy, to block views looking outward, to conceal unattractive areas on your property, or to provide a sense of separation between areas of your yard. Use your earlier sketches and notes as references.

Strong climbers such as Climbing Hydrangea (H. petiolaris), page 209, add texture to fences.

Deciduous plants can also be used for screening, though you'll rarely find such notations in their descriptions. Look for plants with a rapid growth rate or ones described as good choices for informal hedges.

Rapid-growing deciduous plants are good choices when you need to establish a sense of separation. This means that you add screening to

Design Tip

During warm months when you're out in your yard, deciduous trees, shrubs, and vines block unwanted views with their foliage. These views will become visible again in fall, winter, and early spring when plants are bare. The structure of the plant (its trunk and branches) still filters views after leaves have fallen, which may provide a sense of adequate separation. If not, combine fast-growing deciduous plants with slower-growing evergreens. Deciduous plants are good choices for screening along the southern exposure. When leaves fall, they'll let in winter sunlight.

Use plants and the terrain of your yard to carve out private spaces. Here, an intimate patio nestled against a slope is surrounded by trees and shrubs. Shrubs planted between the house and paving make the spot comfortable.

distinguish between your public and private space. Instead of blocking views completely, you enhance some spots in your yard by filtering the views that look inward or out toward another area. A filtered view is not blocked completely. There is enough screening to establish some distinction between areas. Adding a

filtered screen to your yard creates an illusion of privacy without sacrificing breezes or views you enjoy. Though you can see out through the filtered screen and others can see in through it, the presence of something between areas creates a sense of separation necessary for a feeling of privacy.

Planting trees, shrubs, or vines first to give your yard the privacy it needs will pay off for years to come.

Plant Selection   27

Properly balanced screening keeps the neighbors at a distance without making the backyard feel like a fortress.

Plants for Privacy

Evergreen trees for screening

Common Name	Zones	Page	Growth
American Arborvitae	2-9	107	M
Thuja occidentalis			
Blue Atlas Cedar	6-8	79	S
Cedrus libani 'Glauca'			
Blue Holly	5-8	88	S
Ilex x meserveae			
California Incense Cedar	4-8	78	M
Calocedrus decurrens			
Canadian Hemlock	3-7	108	M
Tsuga canadensis			
Colorado Blue Spruce	2-7	95	S
Picea pungens glauca			
Deodar Cedar	6-9	79	M
Cedrus deodara			
Douglas Fir	4-6	99	M
Pseudotsuga menziesii			
Eastern Red Cedar	3-9	89	M
Juniperus virginiana			
Frasier Fir	4-7	70	S
Abies fraseri			
Japanese Black Pine	5-7	96	M
Pinus thunbergii			
Leyland Cypress	6-9	84	R
X Cupressocyparis leylandii			
Norway Spruce	2-7	93	M
Picea abies			
Pyramidal Japanese Yew	4-7	107	S
Taxus cuspidata 'Capitata'			
Savannah Holly	5-9	88	S
Ilex opaca 'Savannah'			
Serbian Spruce	4-7	94	S
Picea omorika			
Skyrocket Juniper	4-8	89	S
Juniperus scopulorum 'Skyrocket'			
Southern Magnolia	6-10	90	S
Magnolia grandiflora			
White Fir	3-7	70	M
Abies concolor			
White Pine	3-8	95	R
Pinus strobus			
White Spruce	2-6	94	M
Picea glauca			

Evergreen shrubs for screening

Common Name	Zones	Page	Growth
Catawba Rhododendron	4-8	154	S
Rhododendron catawbiense			
Dwarf Burford Holly	6-9	141	M
Ilex cornuta 'Bufordii Nana'			
Glossy Abelia	6-9	126	M
Abelia x grandiflora			
Golden Vicary Privet	5-8	148	S
Ligustrum x vicaryi			
Green Lustre Japanese Holly	4-6	142	S
Ilex crenata 'Green Lustre'			
Hick's Upright Yew	4-7	166	R
Taxus x media 'Hicksii'			
Inkberry	3-9	143	M
Ilex glabra 'Compacta'			
Little Giant Arborvitae	3-7	166	S
Thuja occidentalis 'Little Giant'			
Manhattan Spreading Euonymus	4-8	137	R
Euonymus kiautschovicus 'Manhattan'			
Mountain Laurel	4-9	147	S
Kalmia latifolia			
Nellie R. Stevens Holly	6-9	144	M
Ilex 'Nellie R. Stevens'			
Northern Bayberry	2-6	149	R
Myrica pensylvanica			
Redtip Photinia	6-9	149	R
Photinia x fraseri			

Rate of Growth:

R: Rapid M: Medium S: Slow

Botanical name in italics

Evergreen vines for screening

Common Name	Zones	Page	Growth
Chocolate Vine	5-9	206	M
Akebia quinata			
Cross-Vine	6-9	207	R
Bignonia capreolata			
Dropmore Scarlet Honeysuckle	3-7	210	M
Lonicera x brownii 'Dropmore Scarlet'			

Wisdom of the Aisles

Though you may be eager to plant flowers, adding privacy and blocking poor views should be one of your top priorities. The sooner you get trees, shrubs, and vines in the ground, the sooner they can start growing. Even if you've picked a particular area of your yard to concentrate on, you may want to plant living screens in other areas you've identified so plants can get a head start on growth.

Deciduous shrubs for screening

Common Name	Zones	Page	Growth
Arnold's Red Tatarian Honeysuckle *Lonicera tatarica 'Arnold's Red'*	3-9	148	R
Baby's Breath Spirea *Spiraea thunbergii*	2-8	162	R
Border Forsythia *Forsythia x intermedia*	6-9	137	R
Bridalwreath Spirea *Spiraea prunifolia*	5-8	162	R
Common Lilac *Syringa vulgaris*	3-7	165	S
Coralberry *Symphoricarpos orbiculatus*	4-7	163	R
Coral Embers Willow *Salix alba 'Britzensis'*	2-8	160	R
Cornelian Cherry *Cornus mas*	4-8	134	R
Cornell Pink Azalea *Azalea mucronulatum 'Cornell Pink'*	4-7	128	S
Cutleaf Lilac *Syringa x laciniata*	4-8	164	M
Doublefile Viburnum *Viburnum plicatum tomentosum*	4-8	167	R
Dwarf Burning Bush *Euonymus alatus 'Compacta'*	3-8	136	S
European Cranberrybush *Viburnum opulus 'Roseum'*	3-8	167	R
Gray Dogwood *Cornus racemosa*	4-7	134	S
Large Fothergilla *Fothergilla major*	4-8	138	S
Miss Kim Lilac *Syringa patula 'Miss Kim'*	3-7	164	S
Northern Bayberry *Myrica pensylvanica*	2-6	149	R
PeeGee Hydrangea *Hydrangea paniculata 'Grandiflora'*	3-8	140	R
Persian Lilac *Syringa x persica*	3-7	164	M
Redtwig Dogwood *Cornus alba*	2-8	133	R
Rose of Sharon *Hibiscus syriacus*	5-9	139	R
Serviceberry *Amelanchier alnifolia*	4-5	126	M
Summersweet *Clethra alnifolia*	3-9	133	S
Vanhoutte Spirea *Spiraea x vanhouttei*	3-8	162	R
Winterberry *Ilex verticillata*	3-9	144	S
Yellow-Twig Dogwood *Cornus stolonifera 'Flaviramea'*	3-8	135	R

Rapid-growing deciduous vines for screening

Common Name	Zones	Page
American Bittersweet *Celastrus scandens*	3-8	208
Boston Ivy *Parthenocissus tricuspidata*	4-8	211
Chinese Wisteria *Wisteria sinensis*	5-9	215
Climbing Cecil Brunner Rose *Rosa 'Climbing Cecil Brunner'*	6-10	214
Hardy Kiwi *Actinidia arguta*	4-8	206
Silver Lace Vine *Polygonum aubertii*	4-9	212
Trumpet Honeysuckle *Lonicera sempervirens*	4-9	210
Trumpet Vine *Campsis radicans*	4-9	208
Virginia Creeper *Parthenocissus quinquefolia*	4-9	211

Rapid-growing deciduous trees for filtered views

Common Name	Zones	Page
Bald Cypress *Taxodium distichum*	4-10	106
Bradford Pear *Pyrus calleryana 'Bradford'*	4-8	100
Chinese Elm *Ulmus parvifolia*	5-9	109
Green Ash *Fraxinus pennsylvanica*	3-9	86
Japanese Zelkova *Zelkova serrata*	5-9	109
Pin Oak *Quercus palustris*	4-8	102
Purple-Leaf Plum *Prunus cerasifera 'Atropurpurea'*	4-8	97
Red Maple *Acer rubrum*	3-9	74
Redbud *Cercis canadensis*	3-9	81

Saucer Magnolia
(Magnolia x soulangiana)
Page 91

Common Name	Zones	Page
River Birch *Betula nigra*	4-9	76
Saucer Magnolia *Magnolia x soulangiana*	5-9	91
Scarlet Oak *Quercus coccinea*	4-9	101
Shumard Oak *Quercus shumardii*	5-9	103
Silver Maple *Acer saccharinum*	3-9	75
Willow Oak *Quercus phellos*	4-8	102

Combining Plants and Materials

Choose a variety of evergreen or deciduous plants to screen for privacy or to block unpleasant views.

Plant a combination of the two to enjoy the advantages of both. This works particularly well when rapid-growing deciduous trees are planted among slower-growing evergreen shrubs. The trees quickly establish a sense of separation, while the shrubs slowly fill in to block views completely from a lower angle. Such combinations add privacy to low decks, patios, and other outdoor seating areas. The shrubs eventually block views from eye-level while you're seated, making the area seem comfortably private. The trees filter higher views that need not be obscured completely. Open space between the top of the shrubs and the bottom of the tree canopies will be filtered by tree trunks but won't be closed in. This permits sunlight and breezes to enter without walling off the seating area.

You can also combine evergreen and deciduous plants with fences, walls, trellises, or arbors to enhance privacy and block unattractive sights. These structures have the advantage of immediate impact. Use them where you can't wait for plants to grow. (First compare the cost of construction to the expense of adding big plants.) Use vines, shrubs, and trees to give the hard surfaces of these structures a softer look. Leaves, stems, branches, and trunks will also make the screen denser and block unwanted views more completely.

Choose sun-loving plants for open areas to enjoy profuse blossoms and lush foliage. Such plants usually need midday and afternoon sun to grow well.

Sun and Shade

Understanding sun and shade requirements for your plants is **important.** The symbols for sun and shade on plant tags tell you how much sunlight a plant needs to thrive. To find the right plants for your yard, learn to interpret the tags. If you find a tag with all three symbols, the plant can grow successfully in any light condition.

Full sun A tag with a circle or sun shape that isn't blackened indicates a plant that will tolerate a full day of hot, direct sun. The hottest climates are a possible exception; protection from the sun might be necessary during the hottest part of the day. The intensity and heat of the sun diminishes as you move into northern zones. Plants that have only the full-sun symbol on their tags will not grow well in partially shaded spots.

Part shade A circle half shaded and half open indicates that partial shade is the optimum condition. Morning sunlight followed by afternoon shade is best for these plants. The term partial shade also describes areas where the sun is filtered by overhead canopies, allowing some rays to penetrate during the day. Plant tags describe this condition as dappled or filtered shade. Both terms mean the same thing and are different types of partial shade.

Full sun/part shade Though plant tags don't differentiate between morning and afternoon sun, you can still decide what a plant needs by looking for combinations of symbols. Tags with both full-sun and partial-shade symbols indicate a plant can grow in conditions ranging from sunny all day long to sunny for just part of the day. Choose plants with both of these symbols to grow in areas of your yard that are sunny all day or sunny in the afternoons. In hotter

Homer's Hindsight

I had always heard that roses need a lot of sun, but I wasn't sure how much was enough. After several seasons of skimpy blooms and puny foliage, I finally cut my rose plants back, dug them up, and moved them to a brighter location. Now I know that, unless a particular kind of rose is known for its shade tolerance, I need to find a spot in my yard that gets at least six hours of direct sun each day to grow bountiful roses.

climates, intense midday and afternoon sun can be deadly to plants requiring some shade. If the plant tag has a full-sun symbol, it should tolerate a half day of hot afternoon sun. Remember, the partial-shade symbol tells you the plant can thrive with less than a full day of sun.

If you have dappled shade areas that receive some direct sunlight during a portion of the day, look for plants that include both the full-sun circle and the partial-shade symbol on their tags.

Design Tip

Light levels in your landscape vary during the day and during the year. Areas that may be full sun early in the spring may turn to deep shade when your oak and maple trees leaf out. Make sure you consider the light levels over the entire growing season, not just for a single day.

Choosing plants that thrive in shade turns dim corners into lovely and useful areas of your landscape.

Stop, Look, and Listen

Plants can't talk, but they will tell you when something is wrong. Look for signs that plants aren't seeing the right kind of light. After allowing a few months for them to establish, the only solution is to move plants to where the light better suits them..

Too much sun: Leaves wilt (even shortly after watering) and quickly become brown and crispy.

Too much shade: Growth is tall, weak, and spindly; stems lean toward the light; foliage and flowers are sparse.

Part shade/deep shade

Plants that need some sunlight filtered through other plant canopies but should stay deeply shaded most of the day have both the deep-shade symbol and the partial-shade symbol. These plants thrive in conditions that range from almost no light to a half-day's sun. Morning sun is usually best for plants with these symbols on their tags, though weak winter rays of afternoon sun are probably okay.

Deep shade

If you need plants where there is little or no direct sunlight, look for plants with a solid dark circle on their tags. These plants thrive with low light levels, though nothing grows in the dark. Too much sun is fatal for deep shade-loving plants. But the farther north you live, the less likely the sun is to harm even those plants that prefer deep shade. However, it's best to protect these plants from afternoon sun in summer.

Plants for Full Sun

You can take the guesswork out of buying plants. This section groups plants into selection guides by light requirements. Check out the lists on the following pages for plants that thrive in full sun, partial shade, and deep shade. You'll see plants on more than one list; they grow in varying amounts of sunlight. Look for plants that include your zone within their growing range. (If you don't know what planting zone you live in, see page 5.) Then, turn to the pages listed for photos and a complete description of plants you'd like to know more about. Availability varies by area and conditions (see page 21). Check with your garden center.

Trees for full sun

Common Name	Zones	Page
American Arborvitae	2-9	107
Thuja occidentalis		
American Beech	3-9	85
Fagus grandifolia		
Amur Chokecherry	2-6	97
Prunus maackii		
Amur Maple	2-6	71
Acer tataricum ginnala		
Bald Cypress	4-10	106
Taxodium distichum		
Blue Atlas Cedar	6-8	79
Cedrus libani 'Glauca'		
Blue Holly	5-8	88
Ilex x meserveae		
Bradford Pear	4-8	100
Pyrus calleryana 'Bradford'		
California Incense Cedar	4-8	78
Calocedrus decurrens		
Canadian Hemlock	3-7	108
Tsuga canadensis		
Canoe Birch	2-5	77
Betula papyrifera		
Chinese Elm	5-9	109
Ulmus parvifolia		
Chinese Fringe Tree	6-8	81
Chionanthus retusus		
Colorado Blue Spruce	2-7	95
Picea pungens glauca		
Dawn Redwood	4-8	93
Metasequoia glyptostroboides		
Deodar Cedar	6-9	79
Cedrus deodara		
Douglas Fir	4-6	99
Pseudotsuga menziesii		
Downy Serviceberry	4-9	76
Amelanchier arborea		
Eastern Red Cedar	3-9	89
Juniperus virginiana		
European Hornbeam	4-7	78
Carpinus betulus		
European Mountain Ash	3-6	104
Sorbus aucuparia		
Frasier Fir	4-7	70
Abies fraseri		
Fruitless American Sweetgum	5-9	90
Liquidambar styraciflua 'Rotundiloba'		
Ginkgo	3-9	86
Ginkgo biloba		
Green Ash	3-9	86
Fraxinus pennsylvanica		
Honeylocust	3-8	87
Gleditsia triacanthos inermis		
Japanese Black Pine	5-7	96
Pinus thunbergii		
Japanese Flowering Crabapple	4-8	92
Malus floribunda		
Japanese Snowbell	5-8	105
Styrax japonicum		
Japanese Stewartia	5-7	105
Stewartia pseudocamellia		
Japanese Tree Lilac	3-7	106
Syringa reticulata		
Katsura Tree	4-8	80
Cercidiphyllum japonicum		
Kousa Dogwood	5-8	83
Cornus kousa		
Kwanzan Cherry	5-8	98
Prunus serrulata 'Kwanzan'		
Leyland Cypress	6-9	84
X Cupressocyparis leylandii		
Littleleaf Linden	3-7	108
Tilia cordata		
Northern Red Oak	4-7	103
Quercus rubra		

Common Name	Zones	Page
Norway Maple	3-7	72
Acer platanoides		
Norway Spruce	2-7	93
Picea abies		
Paperbark Maple	4-8	72
Acer griseum		
Pin Oak	4-8	102
Quercus palustris		
Plumleaf Crabapple	4-9	92
Malus prunifolia		
Possum Haw	3-9	87
Ilex decidua		
Purple-Leaf Plum	4-8	97
Prunus cerasifera 'Atropurpurea'		
Pyramidal Japanese Yew	4-7	107
Taxus cuspidata 'Capitata'		
Quaking Aspen	2-6	96
Populus tremuloides		
Redbud	3-9	81
Cercis canadensis		
River Birch	4-9	76
Betula nigra		
Russian Olive	3-8	84
Eleagnus angustifolia		
Sargent Cherry	4-7	98
Prunus sargentii		
Saucer Magnolia	5-9	91
Magnolia x soulangiana		
Savannah Holly	5-9	88
Ilex opaca 'Savannah'		
Scarlet Oak	4-9	101
Quercus coccinea		
Serbian Spruce	4-7	94
Picea omorika		
Shumard Oak	5-9	103
Quercus shumardii		
Silver Maple	3-9	75
Acer saccharinum		
Skyrocket Juniper	4-8	89
Juniperus scopulorum 'Skyrocket'		
Southern Magnolia	6-10	90
Magnolia grandiflora		
Sugar Maple	4-8	75
Acer saccharum		
Sugarberry	5-9	80
Celtis laevigata		
Trident Maple	4-8	71
Acer buergerianum		
Washington Hawthorn	3-9	83
Crataegus phaenopyrum		
Weeping Cherry	4-8	99
Prunus subhirtella 'Pendula'		
Weeping Willow	4-9	104
Salix babylonica		
White Fir	3-7	70
Abies concolor		
White Oak	4-9	101
Quercus alba		
White Pine	3-8	95
Pinus strobus		
White Spruce	2-6	94
Picea glauca		
Whitespire Birch	4-7	77
Betula mandschurica japonica 'Whitespire'		
Willow Oak	4-8	102
Quercus phellos		
Yellowwood	6-8	82
Cladrastis lutea		

Shrubs for full sun

Common Name	Zones	Page
Andromeda	5-8	151
Pieris japonica		
Annabelle Hydrangea	3-9	139
Hydrangea arborescens 'Annabelle'		
Anthony Waterer Spirea	3-9	161
Spiraea japonica 'Anthony Waterer'		
Arnold's Red Tatarian Honeysuckle	3-9	148
Lonicera tatarica 'Arnold's Red'		
Baby's Breath Spirea	2-8	162
Spiraea thunbergii		
Betty Prior Rose	4-9	155
Rosa 'Betty Prior'		
Bird's Nest Spruce	2-7	150
Picea abies 'Nidiformis'		
Blue Star Juniper	4-8	146
Juniperus squamata 'Blue Star'		
Border Forsythia	6-9	137
Forsythia x intermedia		
Bridalwreath Spirea	5-8	162
Spiraea prunifolia		
Butterfly Bush	5-9	129
Buddleia davidii		
Carefree Beauty Rose	4-8	155
Rosa Carefree Beauty		
Carol Mackie Daphne	4-8	136
Daphne x burkwoodii 'Carol Mackie'		
Carolina Azalea	4-9	127
Azalea carolinianum		
Catawba Rhododendron	4-8	154
Rhododendron catawbiense		
Chinese Beautyberry	5-8	132
Callicarpa dichotoma		
Common Lilac	3-7	165
Syringa vulgaris		
Common Witch Hazel	3-8	138
Hamamelis virginiana		
Compact Japanese Holly	5-8	143
Ilex crenata 'Compacta'		
Coralberry	4-7	163
Symphoricarpos orbiculatus		
Coral Embers Willow	2-8	160
Salix alba 'Britzensis'		
Cornelian Cherry	4-8	134
Cornus mas		
Cornell Pink Azalea	4-7	128
Azalea mucronulatum 'Cornell Pink'		
Cutleaf Lilac	4-8	164
Syringa x laciniata		
Doublefile Viburnum	4-8	167
Viburnum plicatum tomentosum		
Dwarf Alberta Spruce	3-8	150
Picea glauca 'Conica'		
Dwarf Burford Holly	6-9	141
Ilex cornuta 'Bufordii Nana'		
Dwarf Burning Bush	3-8	136
Euonymus alatus 'Compacta'		
Dwarf Flowering Almond	4-8	153
Prunus glandulosa 'Rosea'		
Dwarf Hinoki False Cypress	4-8	132
Chamaecyparis obtusa 'Nana Gracilis'		
Edging Boxwood	6-8	131
Buxus sempervirens 'Suffruticosa'		
European Cranberrybush	3-8	167
Viburnum opulus 'Roseum'		
Exbury Azalea	4-7	127
Azalea 'Exbury Hybrids'		
Fru Dagmar Hastrup Rose	2-9	156
Rosa 'Fru Dagmar Hastrup'		

Common Name	Zones	Page
Glossy Abelia	6-9	126
Abelia x grandiflora		
Golden Vicary Privet	5-8	148
Ligustrum x vicaryi		
Graham Thomas Rose	5-9	156
Rosa Graham Thomas		
Gray Dogwood	4-7	134
Cornus racemosa		
Green Beauty Boxwood	5-9	130
Buxus microphylla 'Green Beauty'		
Green Lustre Japanese Holly	4-6	142
Ilex crenata 'Green Lustre'		
Heller Japanese Holly	5-8	142
Ilex crenata 'Helleri'		
Hick's Upright Yew	4-7	166
Taxus x media 'Hicksii'		
Iceberg Rose	4-9	157
Rosa 'Iceberg'		
Inkberry	3-9	143
Ilex glabra 'Compacta'		
Japanese Barberry	4-8	129
Berberis thunbergii		
Japanese Boxwood	6-9	130
Buxus microphylla japonica		
Korean Spice Viburnum	4-8	167
Viburnum carlesii		
Large Fothergilla	4-8	138
Fothergilla major		
Little Giant Arborvitae	3-7	166
Thuja occidentalis 'Little Giant'		
Manhattan Spreading Euonymus	4-8	137
Euonymus kiautschovicus 'Manhattan'		
Margo Koster Rose	5-8	157
Rosa 'Margo Koster'		
Miss Kim Lilac	3-7	164
Syringa patula 'Miss Kim'		
Mountain Laurel	4-9	147
Kalmia latifolia		
Mountain Pieris	4-8	151
Pieris floribunda		
Mugo Pine	2-7	152
Pinus mugo		
Nellie R. Stevens Holly	6-9	144
Ilex 'Nellie R. Stevens'		
Nikko Blue Hydrangea	6-9	140
Hydrangea macrophylla 'Nikko Blue'		
Northern Bayberry	2-6	149
Myrica pensylvanica		
Northern Lights Azalea	4-7	128
Azalea 'Northern Lights'		
Parson's Juniper	3-9	145
Juniperus chinensis 'Parsonii'		
Peace Rose	5-8	158
Rosa 'Peace'		
PeeGee Hydrangea	3-8	140
Hydrangea paniculata 'Grandiflora'		
Persian Lilac	3-7	164
Syringa x persica		
Pink Meidiland Rose	5-8	158
Rosa Pink Meidiland		
Redtip Photinia	6-9	149
Photinia x fraseri		
Redtwig Dogwood	2-8	133
Cornus alba		
Rockspray Cotoneaster	6-9	135
Cotoneaster horizontalis		
Rosa Rubrifolia	4-9	159
Rosa rubrifolia		
Rose of Sharon	5-9	139
Hibiscus syriacus		
Sea Green Juniper	4-8	145
Juniperus chinensis 'Sea Green'		
Serviceberry	4-5	126
Amelanchier alnifolia		
Shibori Spirea	4-8	161
Spiraea japonica 'Shibori'		
Shrubby Cinquefoil	2-7	152
Potentilla fruticosa		
Snowberry	3-7	163
Symphoricarpos albus		
Tam Juniper	3-7	146
Juniperus sabina 'Tamariscifolia'		
The Fairy Rose	4-9	159
Rosa 'The Fairy'		

Common Name	Zones	Page
Vanhoutte Spirea	3-8	162
Spiraea x vanhouttei		
Winterberry	3-9	144
Ilex verticillata		
Yellow-Twig Dogwood	3-8	135
Cornus stolonifera 'Flaviramea'		
Yukon Belle Firethorn	4-9	154
Pyracantha angustifolia Yukon Belle		

Groundcover for full sun

Common Name	Zones	Page
Ajuga	4-9	175
Ajuga reptans		
Alba Meidiland Rose	4-8	197
Rosa Alba Meidiland		
Andorra Compact Juniper	3-9	191
Juniperus horizontalis 'Plumosa Compacta'		
Arum	6-10	178
Arum italicum		
Bar Harbor Juniper	3-9	190
Juniperus horizontalis 'Bar Harbor'		
Bath's Pink	4-9	182
Dianthus gratianopolitanus 'Bath's Pink'		
Bearberry Cotoneaster	5-9	182
Cotoneaster dammeri		
Blanket Flower	2-9	185
Gaillardia x grandiflora		
Bloody Cranesbill	3-8	185
Geranium sanguineum		
Blue Chip Juniper	3-9	190
Juniperus horizontalis 'Blue Chip'		
Blue Pacific Shore Juniper	5-9	190
Juniperus conferta 'Blue Pacific'		
Blue Rug Juniper	3-9	191
Juniperus horizontalis 'Wiltonii'		
Bog Rosemary	2-6	176
Andromeda polifolia		
Catmint	4-8	194
Nepeta x faassenii		
Coral Bells	3-8	187
Heuchera sanguinea		
Corsican Mint	5-9	193
Mentha corsica		
Creeping Thyme	5-9	200
Thymus leucotrichus		
Cypress Spurge	4-8	184
Euphorbia cyparissias		
Dragon's Blood Sedum	3-8	198
Sedum spurium 'Dragon's Blood'		
Dwarf Blue Fescue	4-9	184
Festuca glauca		
Dwarf Japanese Garden Juniper	4-9	191
Juniperus procumbens 'Nana'		
English Ivy	5-9	186
Hedera helix		
Evergreen Candytuft	4-8	189
Iberis sempervirens		
Fleabane	2-10	183
Erigeron hybrid		
Flower Carpet Rose	4-10	197
Rosa 'Flower Carpet'		
Forget-Me-Not	3-8	193
Myosotis scorpioides		
Fountain Grass	5-9	195
Pennisetum alopecuroides		
Germander	4-9	199
Teucrium prostratum		
Geum	4-7	186
Geum reptans		
Goldmoss	4-9	198
Sedum acre		
Hardy Ice Plant	6-9	182
Delosperma nubigenum		
Houttuynia	5-9	188
Houttuynia cordata		
Japanese Blood Grass	5-9	189
Imperata cylindrica 'Red Baron'		
Kinnikinick	2-7	177
Arctostaphylos uva-ursi		
Lamb's Ear	4-8	199
Stachys byzantina		

Common Name	Zones	Page
Littleleaf Periwinkle	4-8	201
Vinca minor		
Memorial Rose	4-9	197
Rosa wichuraiana		
Moss Phlox	2-9	196
Phlox subulata		
Mountain Sandwort	3-6	177
Arenaria montana		
Pink Panda Strawberry	3-9	184
Fragaria 'Pink Panda'		
Plumbago	5-9	180
Ceratostigma plumbaginoides		
Prostrate Chenault Coralberry	4-7	199
Symphoricarpos x chenaultii 'Hancock'		
Purple-Leaf Wintercreeper	4-8	183
Euonymus fortunei 'Coloratus'		
Rockcress	3-7	177
Arabis caucasica		
Rock Rose	5-8	186
Helianthemum nummularium		
Royal Carpet Honeysuckle	5-9	192
Lonicera pileata		
Saxifrage	3-8	179
Bergenia cordifolia		
Scotch Heather	3-8	180
Calluna vulgaris		
Silver Brocade Artemisia	3-9	178
Artemisia stelleriana 'Silver Brocade'		
Spring Cinquefoil	4-8	196
Potentilla tabernaemontani		
Spring Heath	4-8	183
Erica carnea		
Stonecrop	3-10	198
Sedum spectabile		
Sundrop Primrose	4-8	194
Oenothera missouriensis		
Sweet Woodruff	4-8	179
Asperula odorata		
Variegated Japanese Sedge	6-9	180
Carex morrowii 'Variegata'		
Warley Rose	5-8	174
Aethinoema x warleyense		

Vines for full sun

Common Name	Zones	Page
American Bittersweet	3-8	208
Celastrus scandens		
Blaze Climbing Rose	5-10	212
Rosa 'Blaze'		
Boston Ivy	4-8	211
Parthenocissus tricuspidata		
Chinese Wisteria	5-9	215
Wisteria sinensis		
Chocolate Vine	5-9	206
Akebia quinata		
Climbing Cecil Brunner Rose	6-10	214
Rosa 'Climbing Cecil Brunner'		
Climbing Hydrangea	4-7	209
Hydrangea petiolaris		
Climbing Iceberg Rose	4-10	213
Rosa 'Climbing Iceberg'		
Climbing Peace Rose	5-9	213
Rosa 'Climbing Peace'		
Cross-Vine	6-9	207
Bignonia capreolata		
Dropmore Scarlet Honeysuckle	3-7	210
Lonicera x brownii 'Dropmore Scarlet'		
Hardy Kiwi	4-8	206
Actinidia arguta		
Hybrid Clematis	3-9	209
Clematis hybrid		
Joseph's Coat Climbing Rose	4-10	214
Rosa 'Joseph's Coat'		
Porcelain Vine	4-8	207
Ampelopsis brevipedunculata		
Silver Lace Vine	4-9	212
Polygonum aubertii		
Trumpet Honeysuckle	4-9	210
Lonicera sempervirens		
Trumpet Vine	4-9	208
Campsis radicans		
Virginia Creeper	4-9	211
Parthenocissus quinquefolia		

Plants for Shade

Trees for shade

Need help finding plants to grow in shaded areas? These lists are guides to help you find trees, shrubs, groundcovers, and vines for partial or deep shade. If you see plants on more than one list, they grow in varying degrees of shade. Look for plants that include your zone within their growing range and skip plants that don't. (If you don't know what planting zone you live in, see page 5.) Then turn to the pages listed for photos and a complete description of plants you'd like to know more about. Availability varies by area and conditions (see page 21). Check with your garden center.

Common Name	Zones	Page	Shade
American Beech	3-9	85	P
Fagus grandifolia			
Amur Chokecherry	2-6	97	P
Prunus maackii			
Amur Maple	2-6	71	P
Acer tataricum ginnala			
Blue Holly	5-8	88	P
Ilex x meserveae			
California Incense Cedar	4-8	78	P
Calocedrus decurrens			
Canadian Hemlock	3-7	108	P
Tsuga canadensis			
Chinese Fringe Tree	6-8	81	P/D
Chionanthus retusus			
Downy Serviceberry	4-9	76	P
Amelanchier arborea			
European Hornbeam	4-7	78	P
Carpinus betulus			
European Mountain Ash	3-6	104	P
Sorbus aucuparia			
Flowering Dogwood	5-9	82	P/D
Cornus florida			
Frasier Fir	4-7	70	P
Abies fraseri			
Japanese Maple	5-8	73	P
Acer palmatum			
Japanese Snowbell	5-8	105	P
Styrax japonicum			
Japanese Stewartia	5-7	105	P
Stewartia pseudocamellia			
Kousa Dogwood	5-8	83	P
Cornus kousa			
Norway Maple	3-7	72	P
Acer platanoides			
Pin Oak	4-8	102	P
Quercus palustris			
Possum Haw	3-9	87	P
Ilex decidua			
Pyramidal Japanese Yew	4-7	107	P/D
Taxus cuspidata 'Capitata'			
Red Maple	3-9	74	P
Acer rubrum			
Redbud	3-9	81	P
Cercis canadensis			
River Birch	4-9	76	P
Betula nigra			
Sargent Cherry	4-7	98	P
Prunus sargentii			
Saucer Magnolia	5-9	91	P
Magnolia x soulangiana			
Savannah Holly	5-9	88	P
Ilex opaca 'Savannah'			
Serbian Spruce	4-7	94	P
Picea omorika			

Common Name	Zones	Page	Shade
Silver Maple	3-9	75	P
Acer saccharinum			
Southern Magnolia	6-10	90	P
Magnolia grandiflora			
Star Magnolia	4-9	91	P
Magnolia stellata			
Sugar Maple	4-8	75	P
Acer saccharum			
Sugarberry	5-9	80	P
Celtis laevigata			
Washington Hawthorn	3-9	83	P
Crataegus phaenopyrum			
Weeping Cherry	4-8	99	P
Prunus subhirtella 'Pendula'			
White Spruce	2-6	94	P
Picea glauca			
Yellowwood	6-8	82	P
Cladrastis lutea			

Shrubs for shade

Common Name	Zones	Page	Shade
Andromeda	5-8	151	P
Pieris japonica			
Annabelle Hydrangea	3-9	139	P
Hydrangea arborescens 'Annabelle'			
Anthony Waterer Spirea	3-9	161	P
Spiraea japonica 'Anthony Waterer'			
Baby's Breath Spirea	2-8	162	P
Spiraea thunbergii			
Bridalwreath Spirea	5-8	162	P
Spiraea prunifolia			
Carol Mackie Daphne	4-8	136	P
Daphne x burkwoodii 'Carol Mackie'			
Catawba Rhododendron	4-8	154	P/D
Rhododendron catawbiense			
Chinese Beautyberry	5-8	132	P
Callicarpa dichotoma			
Common Lilac	3-7	165	P
Syringa vulgaris			
Common Witch Hazel	3-8	138	P
Hamamelis virginiana			
Compact Japanese Holly	5-8	143	D
Ilex crenata 'Compacta'			
Coralberry	4-7	163	P/D
Symphoricarpos orbiculatus			
Cutleaf Lilac	4-8	164	P
Syringa x laciniata			
Doublefile Viburnum	4-8	167	P
Viburnum plicatum tomentosum			
Drooping Leucothoe	5-8	147	P/D
Leucothoe fontanesiana			
Dwarf Alberta Spruce	3-8	150	P
Picea glauca 'Conica'			
Dwarf Burford Holly	6-9	141	P
Ilex cornuta 'Bufordii Nana'			
Dwarf Burning Bush	3-8	136	P
Euonymus alatus 'Compacta'			
Dwarf Flowering Almond	4-8	153	P
Prunus glandulosa 'Rosea'			
Edging Boxwood	6-8	131	P
Buxus sempervirens 'Suffruticosa'			
Glossy Abelia	6-9	126	P
Abelia x grandiflora			

Common Name	Zones	Page	Shade
Green Beauty Boxwood	5-9	130	P
Buxus microphylla 'Green Beauty'			
Green Lustre Japanese Holly	4-6	142	P
Ilex crenata 'Green Lustre'			
Heller Japanese Holly	5-8	142	P/D
Ilex crenata 'Helleri'			
Hick's Upright Yew	4-7	166	P/D
Taxus x media 'Hicksii'			
Iceberg Rose	4-7	157	P
Rosa 'Iceberg'			
Inkberry	3-9	143	P
Ilex glabra 'Compacta'			
Japanese Barberry	4-8	129	P/D
Berberis thunbergii			
Japanese Boxwood	6-9	130	P
Buxus microphylla japonica			
Japanese Skimmia	6-9	160	P/D
Skimmia japonica			
Korean Spice Viburnum	4-8	167	P
Viburnum carlesii			
Manhattan Spreading Euonymus	4-8	137	P/D
Euonymus kiautschovicus 'Manhattan'			
Miss Kim Lilac	3-7	164	P
Syringa patula 'Miss Kim'			
Mountain Laurel	4-9	147	P/D
Kalmia latifolia			
Mountain Pieris	4-8	151	P
Pieris floribunda			
Mugo Pine	2-7	152	P
Pinus mugo			
Nellie R. Stevens Holly	6-9	144	P
Ilex 'Nellie R. Stevens'			
Nikko Blue Hydrangea	6-9	140	P/D
Hydrangea macrophylla 'Nikko Blue'			
Northern Bayberry	2-6	149	P
Myrica pensylvanica			
Oakleaf Hydrangea	5-9	141	P
Hydrangea quercifolia			
Otto Luyken Laurel	6-8	153	P/D
Prunus laurocerasus 'Otto Luyken'			
PeeGee Hydrangea	3-8	140	P
Hydrangea paniculata 'Grandiflora'			
Persian Lilac	3-7	164	P
Syringa x persica			
Redtip Photinia	6-9	149	P
Photinia x fraseri			
Rose of Sharon	5-9	139	P
Hibiscus syriacus			
Serviceberry	4-5	126	P
Amelanchier alnifolia			
Shibori Spirea	4-8	161	P
Spiraea japonica 'Shibori'			
Shrubby Cinquefoil	2-7	152	P
Potentilla fruticosa			
Snowberry	3-7	163	P/D
Symphoricarpos albus			
Summersweet	3-9	133	P
Clethra alnifolia			
The Fairy Rose	4-9	159	P
Rosa 'The Fairy'			
Vanhoutte Spirea	3-8	162	P
Spiraea x vanhouttei			
Winterberry	3-9	144	P
Ilex verticillata			
Yellow-Twig Dogwood	3-8	135	P
Cornus stolonifera 'Flaviramea'			
Yukon Belle Firethorn	4-9	154	P
Pyracantha angustifolia Yukon Belle			

Level of Shade:
P: Partial   D: Deep
Botanical name in italics

European Mountain Ash (Sorbus aucuparia)
Page 104

Groundcover for shade

Sweet Woodruff
(Asperula odorata)
Page 179

Common Name	Zones	Page	Shade
Aaron's Beard	5-9	188	P/D
Hypericum calycinum			
Ajuga	4-9	175	P
Ajuga reptans			
Alba Meidiland Rose	4-8	197	P
Rosa Alba Meidiland			
Allegheny Foam Flower	4-9	200	P/D
Tiarella cordifolia			
Arum	6-10	178	P/D
Arum italicum			
Bath's Pink	4-9	182	P
Dianthus gratianopolitanus 'Bath's Pink'			
Bearberry Cotoneaster	5-9	182	P
Cotoneaster dammeri			
Bloody Cranesbill	3-8	185	P
Geranium sanguineum			
Blue Star	3-9	175	P
Amsonia tabernaemontana			
Blue-Eyed Mary	5-9	194	P
Omphalodes verna			
Bog Rosemary	2-6	176	P
Andromeda polifolia			
Bunchberry	2-7	181	P/D
Cornus canadensis			
Catmint	4-8	194	P
Nepeta x faassenii			
Coral Bells	3-8	187	P
Heuchera sanguinea			
Creeping Phlox	2-8	195	P/D
Phlox stolonifera			
Cypress Spurge	4-8	184	P
Euphorbia cyparissias			
English Ivy	5-9	186	P/D
Hedera helix			
Evergreen Candytuft	4-8	189	P
Iberis sempervirens			
Fleabane	2-10	183	P
Erigeron hybrid			
Forget-Me-Not	3-8	193	P
Myosotis scorpioides			

Common Name	Zones	Page	Shade
Green and Gold	5-8	181	P
Chrysogonum virginianum			
Hosta	3-8	187	P/D
Hosta species			
Houttuynia	5-9	188	P
Houttuynia cordata			
Japanese Blood Grass	5-9	189	P
Imperata cylindrica 'Red Baron'			
Japanese Painted Fern	4-9	179	P/D
Athyrium nipponicum 'Pictum'			
Japanese Primrose	5-8	196	D
Primula japonica			
Kinnikinick	2-7	177	P
Arctostaphylos uva-ursi			
Lady's Mantle	4-7	175	P
Alchemilla mollis			
Lenten Rose	4-8	187	P/D
Helleborus orientalis			
Lily-of-the-Valley	2-9	181	P/D
Convallaria majalis			
Littleleaf Periwinkle	4-8	201	P
Vinca minor			
Maidenhair Fern	3-8	174	P/D
Adiantum pedatum			
Moneywort	3-8	193	P/D
Lysimachia nummularia			
Pachysandra	4-9	195	P/D
Pachysandra terminalis			

Common Name	Zones	Page	Shade
Pink Panda Strawberry	3-9	184	P
Fragaria 'Pink Panda'			
Prostrate Chenault Coralberry	4-7	199	P/D
Symphoricarpos x chenaultii 'Hancock'			
Rockcress	3-7	177	P
Arabis caucasica			
Rock Jasmine	5-7	176	P
Androsace lanuginosa			
Royal Carpet Honeysuckle	5-9	192	P
Lonicera pileata			
Saxifrage	3-8	179	P
Bergenia cordifolia			
Sea Thrift	3-8	178	P
Armeria maritima			
Siberian Forget-Me-Not	3-7	176	P/D
Anchusa myosotidiflora			
Snow-on-the-Mountain	3-9	174	P/D
Aegopodium podagraria 'Variegatum'			
Spotted Dead Nettle	3-9	192	P/D
Lamium maculatum			
Sweet Woodruff	4-8	179	P
Asperula odorata			
Variegated Japanese Sedge	6-9	180	P
Carex morrowii 'Variegata'			
Wintergreen	3-8	185	P
Gaultheria procumbens			
Yellow Archangel	3-9	192	P/D
Lamiastrum galeobdolon 'Variegatum'			

Bath's Pink
(Dianthus gratianopolitanus 'Bath's Pink')
Page 182

Vines for shade

Common Name	Zones	Page	Shade
American Bittersweet	3-8	208	P/D
Celastrus scandens			
Boston Ivy	4-8	211	P
Parthenocissus tricuspidata			
Chinese Wisteria	5-9	215	P
Wisteria sinensis			
Chocolate Vine	5-9	206	P
Akebia quinata			
Climbing Hydrangea	4-7	209	P/D
Hydrangea petiolaris			
Cross-Vine	6-9	207	P
Bignonia capreolata			
Hardy Kiwi	4-8	206	P
Actinidia arguta			
Hybrid Clematis	3-9	209	P
Clematis hybrid			
Silver Lace Vine	4-9	212	P/D
Polygonum aubertii			
Trumpet Vine	4-9	208	P/D
Campsis radicans			
Virginia Creeper	4-9	211	P
Parthenocissus quinquefolia			

Soil Conditions

K **nowing what kind of soil you have is the first step in choosing plants that will thrive.** Here are the basics; visit your county extension service if you want a specific soil analysis. No matter what condition you have, working the soil is beneficial to new plants, which need all the help you can offer them. Improving soil with amendments is a bonus for good growth (see pages 48-49), but don't think you can fool Mother Nature. Choose plants that thrive naturally in existing soil conditions.

River Birch
(Betula nigra)
Page 76

Get Your Hands Dirty

Begin evaluating the soil in your yard by pushing up your sleeves and digging a few inches below the surface. You're looking for three indicators—water retention, nutrient content, and drainage or "percolation" rate. (See "Wisdom of the Aisles," below.) Scoop up a handful of soil and squeeze it to check for water content. If water dribbles out, it's wet. If it can't form a lump, it's dry. If the soil forms a lump that firmly holds its shape, it's clay. If it forms a lump that easily crumbles again, the soil is moist. Next, roll it back and forth between your palms with light pressure.

Heavy Soil If it forms a snakelike form on rolling, the soil has a high clay content and is described as heavy. The pores between soil particles are very small. Nutrients do not leach out as quickly as in other soil types. However, water can be trapped in pores, resulting in sticky, wet soil. This situation creates standing water surrounding roots causing nonadapted plants to suffocate and die. When clay is dry, it is dense and hard, much like concrete. Roots can have difficulty penetrating these soils. Choose plants that can tolerate clay soil.

Porous Soil If the soil in your hand is too sandy or rocky to hold together well, it is porous. Water percolates quickly through such soil. There's no problem with water collecting around roots, but nutrients wash rapidly away. These soils are known as poor and dry. You'll need to water and fertilize plants regularly in porous soil. Select plants that tolerate poor, dry soils.

Moderate Soil Many soil types fall somewhere between these two extremes. You might be able to roll your soil into a ribbon, indicating some clay content, but it will break apart when just a few inches long. If you're able to crumble the soil easily between your fingers to its original state, your soil is moderate. Many different plants thrive in moderate soil, but they'll grow even better if you work the soil prior to planting.

Plants for Special Soil Conditions

Plants for poor, dry soil

Common Name	Zones	Page
◆ Trees		
Bald Cypress	4-10	106
Taxodium distichum		
Blue Atlas Cedar	6-8	79
Cedrus libani 'Glauca'		
Chinese Elm	5-9	109
Ulmus parvifolia		
Deodar Cedar	6-9	79
Cedrus deodara		
Eastern Red Cedar	3-9	89
Juniperus virginiana		
Ginkgo	3-9	86
Ginkgo biloba		
Green Ash	3-9	86
Fraxinus pennsylvanica		
Japanese Black Pine	5-7	96
Pinus thunbergii		
Norway Maple	3-7	72
Acer platanoides		
Pin Oak	4-8	102
Quercus palustris		
Pyramidal Japanese Yew	4-7	107
Taxus cuspidata 'Capitata'		
Red Maple	3-9	74
Acer rubrum		
Redbud	3-9	81
Cercis canadensis		
River Birch	4-9	76
Betula nigra		
Silver Maple	3-9	75
Acer saccharinum		
Skyrocket Juniper	4-8	89
Juniperus scopulorum 'Skyrocket'		
Southern Magnolia	6-10	90
Magnolia grandiflora		
Sugarberry	5-9	80
Celtis laevigata		
Washington Hawthorn	3-9	83
Crataegus phaenopyrum		

Wisdom
of the Aisles

Do a perc test. Percolation is the way water drains through soil and is one of the guides for plant selection. Determine your soil's rate of percolation by digging test holes 12 to 18 inches deep in several spots around your yard. Fill them with water and measure the water depth with a stick. After 30 minutes measure the water depth again. If the hole empties or water levels drop an inch or more within half an hour, your soil drains very quickly. Choose plants that thrive in poor, dry soil. If water remains, check levels hourly. If the hole drains about an inch an hour, it's well-drained and should support many different plant types. Less than an inch an hour indicates poor drainage. Choose plants that grow well in wet, boggy areas or will tolerate compacted soil.

Common Name	Zones	Page
Weeping Willow	4-9	104
Salix babylonica		
White Fir	3-7	70
Abies concolor		
White Oak	4-9	101
Quercus alba		
White Pine	3-8	95
Pinus strobus		
Whitespire Birch	4-7	77
Betula mandschurica japonica 'Whitespire'		
Willow Oak	4-8	102
Quercus phellos		
Yellowwood	6-8	82
Cladrastis lutea		

◆ Shrubs

Blue Star Juniper	4-8	146
Juniperus squamata 'Blue Star'		
Carol Mackie Daphne	4-8	136
Daphne x burkwoodii 'Carol Mackie'		
Coralberry	4-7	163
Symphoricarpos orbiculatus		
Dwarf Alberta Spruce	3-8	150
Picea glauca 'Conica'		
Dwarf Burford Holly	6-9	141
Ilex cornuta 'Bufordii Nana'		
Fru Dagmar Hastrup Rose	2-9	156
Rosa 'Fru Dagmar Hastrup'		
Hick's Upright Yew	4-7	166
Taxus x media 'Hicksii'		
Manhattan Spreading Euonymus	4-8	137
Euonymus kiautschovicus 'Manhattan'		
Nellie R. Stevens Holly	6-9	144
Ilex 'Nellie R. Stevens'		
Northern Bayberry	2-6	149
Myrica pensylvanica		
Parson's Juniper	3-9	145
Juniperus chinensis 'Parsonii'		
Rose of Sharon	5-9	139
Hibiscus syriacus		
Sea Green Juniper	4-8	145
Juniperus chinensis 'Sea Green'		
Tam Juniper	3-7	146
Juniperus sabina 'Tamariscifolia'		

◆ Groundcovers

Bath's Pink	4-9	182
Dianthus gratianopolitanus 'Bath's Pink'		
Bearberry Cotoneaster	5-9	182
Cotoneaster dammeri		
Blanket Flower	2-9	185
Gaillardia x grandiflora		
Blue Chip Juniper	3-9	190
Juniperus horizontalis 'Blue Chip'		
Blue Pacific Shore Juniper	5-9	190
Juniperus conferta 'Blue Pacific'		
Catmint	4-8	194
Nepeta x faassenii		
Creeping Thyme	5-9	200
Thymus leucotrichus		
Dragon's Blood Sedum	3-8	198
Sedum spurium 'Dragon's Blood'		
Dwarf Blue Fescue	4-9	184
Festuca glauca		
Fountain Grass	5-9	195
Pennisetum alopecuroides		
Goldmoss	4-9	198
Sedum acre		
Hardy Ice Plant	6-9	182
Delosperma nubigenum		
Kinnikinick	2-7	177
Arctostaphylos uva-ursi		
Lily-of-the-Valley	2-9	181
Convallaria majalis		
Moss Phlox	2-9	196
Phlox subulata		
Mountain Sandwort	3-6	177
Arenaria montana		
Prostrate Chenault Coralberry	4-7	199
Symphoricarpos x chenaultii 'Hancock'		
Rock Jasmine	5-7	176
Androsace lanuginosa		
Rock Rose	5-8	186
Helianthemum nummularium		
Sea Thrift	3-8	178
Armeria maritima		

Carol Mackie Daphne (Daphne x burkwoodii 'Carol Mackie') Page 136

Common Name	Zones	Page
Silver Brocade Artemisia	3-9	178
Artemisia stelleriana 'Silver Brocade'		
Snow-on-the-Mountain	3-9	174
Aegopodium podagraria 'Variegatum'		
Spotted Dead Nettle	3-9	192
Lamium maculatum		
Spring Cinquefoil	4-8	196
Potentilla tabernaemontani		
Stonecrop	3-10	198
Sedum spectabile		
Sundrop Primrose	4-8	194
Oenothera missouriensis		

◆ Vines

American Bittersweet	3-8	208
Celastrus scandens		
Boston Ivy	4-8	211
Parthenocissus tricuspidata		
Porcelain Vine	4-8	207
Ampelopsis brevipedunculata		
Silver Lace Vine	4-9	212
Polygonum aubertii		
Trumpet Vine	4-9	208
Campsis radicans		
Virginia Creeper	4-9	211
Parthenocissus quinquefolia		

Plants for wet, boggy soil

Common Name	Zones	Page
◆ Trees		
Bald Cypress	4-10	106
Taxodium distichum		
Eastern Red Cedar	3-9	89
Juniperus virginiana		
Green Ash	3-9	86
Fraxinus pennsylvanica		
Possum Haw	3-9	87
Ilex decidua		
River Birch	4-9	76
Betula nigra		
Southern Magnolia	6-10	90
Magnolia grandiflora		
Sugarberry	5-9	80
Celtis laevigata		
Weeping Willow	4-9	104
Salix babylonica		

◆ Shrubs

Coral Embers Willow	2-8	160
Salix alba 'Britzensis'		
European Cranberrybush	3-8	167
Viburnum opulus 'Roseum'		
Inkberry	3-9	143
Ilex glabra 'Compacta'		
Redtwig Dogwood	2-8	133
Cornus alba		
Summersweet	3-9	133
Clethra alnifolia		
Vanhoutte Spirea	3-8	162
Spiraea x vanhouttei		
Winterberry	3-9	144
Ilex verticillata		
Yellow-Twig Dogwood	3-8	135
Cornus stolonifera 'Flaviramea'		

◆ Groundcovers

Bearberry Cotoneaster	5-9	182
Cotoneaster dammeri		
Forget-Me-Not	3-8	193
Myosotis scorpioides		
Japanese Primrose	5-8	196
Primula japonica		
Snow-on-the-Mountain	3-9	174
Aegopodium podagraria 'Variegatum'		

Plants for heavy, clay soil

Common Name	Zones	Page
◆ Trees		
American Arborvitae	2-9	107
Thuja occidentalis		
Bald Cypress	4-10	106
Taxodium distichum		
Blue Atlas Cedar	6-8	79
Cedrus libani 'Glauca'		
Dawn Redwood	4-8	93
Metasequoia glyptostroboides		
Eastern Red Cedar	3-9	89
Juniperus virginiana		
European Hornbeam	4-7	78
Carpinus betulus		
European Mountain Ash	3-6	104
Sorbus aucuparia		
Ginkgo	3-9	86
Ginkgo biloba		
Green Ash	3-9	86
Fraxinus pennsylvanica		
Japanese Black Pine	5-7	96
Pinus thunbergii		
Littleleaf Linden	3-7	108
Tilia cordata		
Norway Maple	3-7	72
Acer platanoides		
Norway Spruce	2-7	93
Picea abies		
Paperbark Maple	4-8	72
Acer griseum		
Pin Oak	4-8	102
Quercus palustris		
Redbud	3-9	81
Cercis canadensis		
Saucer Magnolia	5-9	91
Magnolia x soulangiana		
Savannah Holly	5-9	88
Ilex opaca 'Savannah'		
Silver Maple	3-9	75
Acer saccharinum		
Sugarberry	5-9	80
Celtis laevigata		
White Pine	3-8	95
Pinus strobus		
White Spruce	2-6	94
Picea glauca		

◆ Shrubs

Annabelle Hydrangea	3-9	139
Hydrangea arborescens 'Annabelle'		
Anthony Waterer Spirea	3-9	161
Spiraea japonica 'Anthony Waterer'		
Bird's Nest Spruce	2-7	150
Picea abies 'Nidiformis'		
Border Forsythia	6-9	137
Forsythia x intermedia		
Common Lilac	3-7	165
Syringa vulgaris		
Dwarf Alberta Spruce	3-8	150
Picea glauca 'Conica'		
Dwarf Hinoki False Cypress	4-8	132
Chamaecyparis obtusa 'Nana Gracilis'		
Japanese Barberry	4-8	129
Berberis thunbergii		
Japanese Skimmia	6-9	160
Skimmia japonica		
Little Giant Arborvitae	3-7	166
Thuja occidentalis 'Little Giant'		
Mugo Pine	2-7	152
Pinus mugo		
Northern Bayberry	2-6	149
Myrica pensylvanica		
Vanhoutte Spirea	3-8	162
Spiraea x vanhouttei		

◆ Groundcovers

Bath's Pink	4-9	182
Dianthus gratianopolitanus 'Bath's Pink'		
Snow-on-the-Mountain	3-9	174
Aegopodium podagraria 'Variegatum'		

Availability varies by area and conditions (see page 21). Check with your garden center.

Soil pH

S oil can be categorized three ways based on its pH: neutral, acidic, or alkaline. Knowing which category your yard fits into will help you choose the right plants to grow there. Most soil in a given geographic area will be similar in pH, so your local garden center associates will know what's typical of where you live. For a pH reading, purchase a soil testing kit or visit your county extension agent. Your results will show a number between zero and 14. Neutral soils test around 7. Acidic soils are usually between 4 and 6. Alkaline soils yield readings higher than 7. Observing characteristics native to your area will also give you clues about soil pH. For example, areas where limestone is plentiful are naturally alkaline. Regions with high annual rainfall tend to have acidic soil because of nutrient washing. Areas with high amounts of decaying pine needles or oak leaves usually have acidic soil, too.

Exbury Azalea
(Azalea 'Exbury Hybrids')
Page 127

Plants for Special Soil Conditions

Plants for acidic soil

Common Name	Zones	Page
◆ Trees		
American Beech	3-9	85
Fagus grandifolia		
Blue Holly	5-8	88
Ilex x meserveae		
Canadian Hemlock	3-7	108
Tsuga canadensis		
Canoe Birch	2-5	77
Betula papyrifera		
Chinese Fringe Tree	6-8	81
Chionanthus retusus		
Deodar Cedar	6-9	79
Cedrus deodara		
Douglas Fir	4-6	99
Pseudotsuga menziesii		
Downy Serviceberry	4-9	76
Amelanchier arborea		
Eastern Red Cedar	3-9	89
Juniperus virginiana		
European Hornbeam	4-7	78
Carpinus betulus		
European Mountain Ash	3-6	104
Sorbus aucuparia		
Flowering Dogwood	5-9	82
Cornus florida		
Fruitless American Sweetgum	5-9	90
Liquidambar styraciflua 'Rotundiloba'		
Ginkgo	3-9	86
Ginkgo biloba		
Green Ash	3-9	86
Fraxinus pennsylvanica		
Japanese Snowbell	5-8	105
Styrax japonicum		
Japanese Stewartia	5-7	105
Stewartia pseudocamellia		
Japanese Tree Lilac	3-7	106
Syringa reticulata		
Japanese Zelkova	5-9	109
Zelkova serrata		
Katsura Tree	4-8	80
Cercidiphyllum japonicum		
Kousa Dogwood	5-8	83
Cornus kousa		
Littleleaf Linden	3-7	108
Tilia cordata		
Northern Red Oak	4-7	103
Quercus rubra		
Norway Spruce	2-7	93
Picea abies		
Pin Oak	4-8	102
Quercus palustris		

Common Name	Zones	Page
Plumleaf Crabapple	4-9	92
Malus prunifolia		
Possum Haw	3-9	87
Ilex decidua		
Purple-Leaf Plum	4-8	97
Prunus cerasifera 'Atropurpurea'		
Red Maple	3-9	74
Acer rubrum		
Redbud	3-9	81
Cercis canadensis		
River Birch	4-9	76
Betula nigra		
Russian Olive	3-8	84
Elaeagnus angustifolia		
Saucer Magnolia	5-9	91
Magnolia x soulangiana		
Savannah Holly	5-9	88
Ilex opaca 'Savannah'		
Serbian Spruce	4-7	94
Picea omorika		
Shumard Oak	5-9	103
Quercus shumardii		
Silver Maple	3-9	75
Acer saccharinum		
Star Magnolia	4-9	91
Magnolia stellata		
Sugar Maple	4-8	75
Acer saccharum		
Trident Maple	4-8	71
Acer buergerianum		
Washington Hawthorn	3-9	83
Crataegus phaenopyrum		
White Oak	4-9	101
Quercus alba		
White Spruce	2-6	94
Picea glauca		
Whitespire Birch	4-7	77
Betula mandschurica japonica 'Whitespire'		
Willow Oak	4-8	102
Quercus phellos		
◆ Shrubs		
Andromeda	5-8	151
Pieris japonica		
Annabelle Hydrangea	3-9	139
Hydrangea arborescens 'Annabelle'		
Border Forsythia	6-9	137
Forsythia x intermedia		
Carolina Azalea	4-9	127
Azalea carolinianum		
Catawba Rhododendron	4-8	154
Rhododendron catawbiense		

Catawba Rhododendron
(Rhododendron catawbiense)
Page 154

Common Name	Zones	Page
Cornell Pink Azalea	4-7	128
Azalea mucronulatum 'Cornell Pink'		
Drooping Leucothoe	5-8	147
Leucothoe fontanesiana		
Dwarf Alberta Spruce	3-8	150
Picea glauca 'Conica'		
Dwarf Burford Holly	6-9	141
Ilex cornuta 'Bufordii Nana'		
Dwarf Burning Bush	3-8	136
Euonymus alatus 'Compacta'		
Dwarf Hinoki False Cypress	4-8	132
Chamaecyparis obtusa 'Nana Gracilis'		
Exbury Azalea	4-7	127
Azalea 'Exbury Hybrids'		
Glossy Abelia	6-9	126
Abelia x grandiflora		
Hick's Upright Yew	4-7	166
Taxus x media 'Hicksii'		
Inkberry	3-9	143
Ilex glabra 'Compacta'		
Japanese Skimmia	6-9	160
Skimmia japonica		
Korean Boxwood	5-9	131
Buxus microphylla koreana		
Korean Spice Viburnum	4-8	167
Viburnum carlesii		
Large Fothergilla	4-8	138
Fothergilla major		
Mountain Laurel	4-9	147
Kalmia latifolia		
Mountain Pieris	4-8	151
Pieris floribunda		
Nellie R. Stevens Holly	6-9	144
Ilex 'Nellie R. Stevens'		
Northern Lights Azalea	4-7	128
Azalea 'Northern Lights'		
Oakleaf Hydrangea	5-9	141
Hydrangea quercifolia		
PeeGee Hydrangea	3-8	140
Hydrangea paniculata 'Grandiflora'		
Serviceberry	4-5	126
Amelanchier alnifolia		
Summersweet	3-9	133
Clethra alnifolia		
Winterberry	3-9	144
Ilex verticillata		

◆ Groundcovers

Common Name	Zones	Page
Allegheny Foam Flower	4-9	200
Tiarella cordifolia		
Bath's Pink	4-9	182
Dianthus gratianopolitanus 'Bath's Pink'		
Bearberry Cotoneaster	5-9	182
Cotoneaster dammeri		
Blue Pacific Shore Juniper	5-9	190
Juniperus conferta 'Blue Pacific'		
Blue-Eyed Mary	5-9	194
Omphalodes verna		
Bog Rosemary	2-6	176
Andromeda polifolia		
Bunchberry	2-7	181
Cornus canadensis		
Creeping Phlox	2-8	195
Phlox stolonifera		
Dwarf Japanese Garden Juniper	4-9	191
Juniperus procumbens 'Nana'		
Green and Gold	5-8	181
Chrysogonum virginianum		
Japanese Primrose	5-8	196
Primula japonica		
Maidenhair Fern	3-8	174
Adiantum pedatum		
Purple-Leaf Wintercreeper	4-8	183
Euonymus fortunei 'Coloratus'		
Scotch Heather	3-8	180
Calluna vulgaris		
Snow-on-the-Mountain	3-9	174
Aegopodium podagraria 'Variegatum'		
Spring Heath	4-8	183
Erica carnea		
Sweet Woodruff	4-8	179
Asperula odorata		
Wintergreen	3-8	185
Gaultheria procumbens		

◆ Vines

Common Name	Zones	Page
Blaze Climbing Rose	5-10	212
Rosa 'Blaze'		
Boston Ivy	4-8	211
Parthenocissus tricuspidata		
Climbing Cecil Brunner Rose	6-10	214
Rosa 'Climbing Cecil Brunner'		
Climbing Iceberg Rose	4-10	213
Rosa 'Climbing Iceberg'		
Climbing Peace Rose	5-9	213
Rosa 'Climbing Peace'		
Cross-Vine	6-9	207
Bignonia capreolata		
Joseph's Coat Climbing Rose	4-10	214
Rosa 'Joseph's Coat'		
Porcelain Vine	4-8	207
Ampelopsis brevipedunculata		
Virginia Creeper	4-9	211
Parthenocissus quinquefolia		

Joseph's Coat Climbing Rose
(Rosa 'Joseph's Coat')
Page 214

Plants for alkaline soil

◆ Trees

Common Name	Zones	Page
American Arborvitae	2-9	107
Thuja occidentalis		
Chinese Elm	5-9	109
Ulmus parvifolia		
Deodar Cedar	6-9	79
Cedrus deodara		
Eastern Red Cedar	3-9	89
Juniperus virginiana		
European Hornbeam	4-7	78
Carpinus betulus		
Ginkgo	3-9	86
Ginkgo biloba		
Green Ash	3-9	86
Fraxinus pennsylvanica		
Honeylocust	3-8	87
Gleditsia triacanthos inermis		
Japanese Flowering Crabapple	4-8	92
Malus floribunda		
Japanese Zelkova	5-9	109
Zelkova serrata		
Katsura Tree	4-8	80
Cercidiphyllum japonicum		
Littleleaf Linden	3-7	108
Tilia cordata		
Norway Maple	3-7	72
Acer platanoides		
Possum Haw	3-9	87
Ilex decidua		
Purple-Leaf Plum	4-8	97
Prunus cerasifera 'Atropurpurea'		
Redbud	3-9	81
Cercis canadensis		
Serbian Spruce	4-7	94
Picea omorika		
Shumard Oak	5-9	103
Quercus shumardii		
Silver Maple	3-9	75
Acer saccharinum		
Sugarberry	5-9	80
Celtis laevigata		
Washington Hawthorn	3-9	83
Crataegus phaenopyrum		
Willow Oak	4-8	102
Quercus phellos		
Yellowwood	6-8	82
Cladrastis lutea		

◆ Shrubs

Common Name	Zones	Page
Border Forsythia	6-9	137
Forsythia x intermedia		
Carol Mackie Daphne	4-8	136
Daphne x burkwoodii 'Carol Mackie'		
Dwarf Burning Bush	3-8	136
Euonymus alatus 'Compacta'		
Dwarf Hinoki False Cypress	4-8	132
Chamaecyparis obtusa 'Nana Gracilis'		
Glossy Abelia	6-9	126
Abelia x grandiflora		
Little Giant Arborvitae	3-7	166
Thuja occidentalis 'Little Giant'		

Common Name	Zones	Page
Oakleaf Hydrangea	5-9	141
Hydrangea quercifolia		
PeeGee Hydrangea	3-8	140
Hydrangea paniculata 'Grandiflora'		
Persian Lilac	3-7	164
Syringa x persica		
Rose of Sharon	5-9	139
Hibiscus syriacus		
Serviceberry	4-5	126
Amelanchier alnifolia		

◆ Groundcovers

Common Name	Zones	Page
Andorra Compact Juniper	3-9	191
Juniperus horizontalis 'Plumosa Compacta'		
Bar Harbor Juniper	3-9	190
Juniperus horizontalis 'Bar Harbor'		
Bath's Pink	4-9	182
Dianthus gratianopolitanus 'Bath's Pink'		
Bearberry Cotoneaster	5-9	182
Cotoneaster dammeri		
Blue Chip Juniper	3-9	190
Juniperus horizontalis 'Blue Chip'		
Blue Pacific Shore Juniper	5-9	190
Juniperus conferta 'Blue Pacific'		
Blue Rug Juniper	3-9	191
Juniperus horizontalis 'Wiltonii'		
Coral Bells	3-8	187
Heuchera sanguinea		
Creeping Thyme	5-9	200
Thymus leucotrichus		
Dwarf Japanese Garden Juniper	4-9	191
Juniperus procumbens 'Nana'		
Fountain Grass	5-9	195
Pennisetum alopecuroides		
Germander	4-9	199
Teucrium prostratum		
Goldmoss	4-9	198
Sedum acre		
Purple-Leaf Wintercreeper	4-8	183
Euonymus fortunei 'Coloratus'		
Rock Rose	5-8	186
Helianthemum nummularium		
Snow-on-the-Mountain	3-9	174
Aegopodium podagraria 'Variegatum'		
Warley Rose	5-8	174
Aethionema x warleyense		

◆ Vines

Common Name	Zones	Page
Boston Ivy	4-8	211
Parthenocissus tricuspidata		
Porcelain Vine	4-8	207
Ampelopsis brevipedunculata		
Virginia Creeper	4-9	211
Parthenocissus quinquefolia		

Availability varies by area and conditions (see page 21). Check with your garden center.

Plants for Special Site Conditions

S pecial site conditions require special plants. These selection guides will help you choose plants suitable for growing on slopes, on low-water sites, and in areas that receive ocean salts or salt from winter road crews. If parts of your yard suffer from car exhaust, reflected heat from paving, or confined root spaces, check out the list of plants for urban areas on page 41.

*Silver Lace Vine
(Polygonum aubertii)
Page 212*

Plants for slopes

Common Name	Zones	Page
◆ **Trees**		
Eastern Red Cedar	3-9	89
Juniperus virginiana		
Flowering Dogwood	5-9	82
Cornus florida		
Japanese Snowbell	5-8	105
Styrax japonicum		
Quaking Aspen	2-6	96
Populus tremuloides		
Weeping Willow	4-9	104
Salix babylonica		
◆ **Shrubs**		
Annabelle Hydrangea	3-9	139
Hydrangea arborescens 'Annabelle'		
Border Forsythia	6-9	137
Forsythia x intermedia		
Coralberry	4-7	163
Symphoricarpos orbiculatus		
Rockspray Cotoneaster	6-9	135
Cotoneaster horizontalis		
Sea Green Juniper	4-8	145
Juniperus chinensis 'Sea Green'		
Snowberry	3-7	163
Symphoricarpos albus		
◆ **Groundcovers**		
Alba Meidiland Rose	4-8	197
Rosa Alba Meidiland		
Andorra Compact Juniper	3-9	191
Juniperus horizontalis 'Plumosa Compacta'		
Bar Harbor Juniper	3-9	190
Juniperus horizontalis 'Bar Harbor'		
Bath's Pink	4-9	182
Dianthus gratianopolitanus 'Bath's Pink'		
Bearberry Cotoneaster	5-9	182
Cotoneaster dammeri		
Blanket Flower	2-9	185
Gaillardia x grandiflora		
Blue Chip Juniper	3-9	190
Juniperus horizontalis 'Blue Chip'		

Common Name	Zones	Page
Blue Pacific Shore Juniper	5-9	190
Juniperus conferta 'Blue Pacific'		
Blue Rug Juniper	3-9	191
Juniperus horizontalis 'Wiltonii'		
Cypress Spurge	4-8	184
Euphorbia cyparissias		
Dragon's Blood Sedum	3-8	198
Sedum spurium 'Dragon's Blood'		
English Ivy	5-9	186
Hedera helix		
Evergreen Candytuft	4-8	189
Iberis sempervirens		
Goldmoss	4-9	198
Sedum acre		
Hardy Ice Plant	6-9	182
Delosperma nubigenum		
Littleleaf Periwinkle	4-8	201
Vinca minor		
Moss Phlox	2-9	196
Phlox subulata		
Prostrate Chenault Coralberry	4-7	199
Symphoricarpos x chenaultii 'Hancock'		
Purple-Leaf Wintercreeper	4-8	183
Euonymus fortunei 'Coloratus'		
Rock Rose	5-8	186
Helianthemum nummularium		
Snow-on-the-Mountain	3-9	174
Aegopodium podagraria 'Variegatum'		
Spring Cinquefoil	4-8	196
Potentilla tabernaemontani		
Stonecrop	3-10	198
Sedum spectabile		
Variegated Japanese Sedge	6-9	180
Carex morrowii 'Variegata'		

> **Availability varies by area and conditions (see page 21). Check with your garden center.**

Salt-tolerant plants

Common Name	Zones	Page
◆ **Trees**		
Eastern Red Cedar	3-9	89
Juniperus virginiana		
European Mountain Ash	3-6	104
Sorbus aucuparia		
Honeylocust	3-8	87
Gleditsia triacanthos inermis		
Japanese Black Pine	5-7	96
Pinus thunbergii		
Littleleaf Linden	3-7	108
Tilia cordata		
Pyramidal Japanese Yew	4-7	107
Taxus cuspidata 'Capitata'		
Russian Olive	3-8	84
Elaeagnus angustifolia		
Southern Magnolia	6-10	90
Magnolia grandiflora		
◆ **Shrubs**		
Coral Embers Willow	2-8	160
Salix alba 'Britzensis'		
Fru Dagmar Hastrup Rose	2-9	156
Rosa 'Fru Dagmar Hastrup'		
Inkberry	3-9	143
Ilex glabra 'Compacta'		
Nikko Blue Hydrangea	6-9	140
Hydrangea macrophylla 'Nikko Blue'		
Northern Bayberry	2-6	149
Myrica pensylvanica		
Summersweet	3-9	133
Clethra alnifolia		
◆ **Groundcovers**		
Andorra Compact Juniper	3-9	191
Juniperus horizontalis 'Plumosa Compacta'		
Bar Harbor Juniper	3-9	190
Juniperus horizontalis 'Bar Harbor'		
Blanket Flower	2-9	185
Gaillardia x grandiflora		
Blue Chip Juniper	3-9	190
Juniperus horizontalis 'Blue Chip'		
Blue Pacific Shore Juniper	5-9	190
Juniperus conferta 'Blue Pacific'		
Blue Rug Juniper	3-9	191
Juniperus horizontalis 'Wiltonii'		
Kinnikinick	2-7	177
Arctostaphylos uva-ursi		
Sea Thrift	3-8	178
Armeria maritima		
Silver Brocade Artemisia	3-9	178
Artemisia stelleriana 'Silver Brocade'		
◆ **Vines**		
Silver Lace Vine	4-9	212
Polygonum aubertii		
Virginia Creeper	4-9	211
Parthenocissus quinquefolia		

*Dwarf Japanese Garden Juniper
(Juniperus procumbens 'Nana')
Page 191*

Plants for urban areas

Common Name	Zones	Page
◆ Trees		
Bradford Pear	4-8	100
Pyrus calleryana 'Bradford'		
Chinese Elm	5-9	109
Ulmus parvifolia		
European Hornbeam	4-7	78
Carpinus betulus		
Ginkgo	3-9	86
Ginkgo biloba		
Green Ash	3-9	86
Fraxinus pennsylvanica		
Honeylocust	3-8	87
Gleditsia triacanthos inermis		
Japanese Flowering Crabapple	4-8	92
Malus floribunda		
Japanese Zelkova	5-9	109
Zelkova serrata		
Littleleaf Linden	3-7	108
Tilia cordata		
Northern Red Oak	4-7	103
Quercus rubra		
Norway Maple	3-7	72
Acer platanoides		
Pin Oak	4-8	102
Quercus palustris		
Plumleaf Crabapple	4-9	92
Malus prunifolia		
Pyramidal Japanese Yew	4-7	107
Taxus cuspidata 'Capitata'		
Red Maple	3-9	74
Acer rubrum		
Saucer Magnolia	5-9	91
Magnolia x soulangiana		
Savannah Holly	5-9	88
Ilex opaca 'Savannah'		
Serbian Spruce	4-7	94
Picea omorika		
Shumard Oak	5-9	103
Quercus shumardii		
Skyrocket Juniper	4-8	89
Juniperus scopulorum 'Skyrocket'		
Sugarberry	5-9	80
Celtis laevigata		
Washington Hawthorn	3-9	83
Crataegus phaenopyrum		
Willow Oak	4-8	102
Quercus phellos		
◆ Shrubs		
Anthony Waterer Spirea	3-9	161
Spiraea japonica 'Anthony Waterer'		
Border Forsythia	6-9	137
Forsythia x intermedia		
Butterfly Bush	5-9	129
Buddleia davidii		
Dwarf Burning Bush	3-8	136
Euonymus alatus 'Compacta'		
Glossy Abelia	6-9	126
Abelia x grandiflora		
Nellie R. Stevens Holly	6-9	144
Ilex 'Nellie R. Stevens'		
Parson's Juniper	3-9	145
Juniperus chinensis 'Parsonii'		
Rockspray Cotoneaster	6-9	135
Cotoneaster horizontalis		
Snowberry	3-7	163
Symphoricarpos albus		
◆ Groundcovers		
Bar Harbor Juniper	3-9	190
Juniperus horizontalis 'Bar Harbor'		
Bearberry Cotoneaster	5-9	182
Cotoneaster dammeri		
Blanket Flower	2-9	185
Gaillardia x grandiflora		
Blue Chip Juniper	3-9	190
Juniperus horizontalis 'Blue Chip'		
Blue Pacific Shore Juniper	5-9	190
Juniperus conferta 'Blue Pacific'		
Blue Rug Juniper	3-9	191
Juniperus horizontalis 'Wiltonii'		
Catmint	4-8	194
Nepeta x faassenii		
Dwarf Japanese Garden Juniper	4-9	191
Juniperus procumbens 'Nana'		

Common Name	Zones	Page
Evergreen Candytuft	4-8	189
Iberis sempervirens		
Flower Carpet Rose	4-10	197
Rosa 'Flower Carpet'		
Fountain Grass	5-9	195
Pennisetum alopecuroides		
Goldmoss	4-9	198
Sedum acre		
Hardy Ice Plant	6-9	182
Delosperma nubigenum		
Littleleaf Periwinkle	4-8	201
Vinca minor		
Moss Phlox	2-9	196
Phlox subulata		
Prostrate Chenault Coralberry	4-7	199
Symphoricarpos x chenaultii 'Hancock'		
Purple-Leaf Wintercreeper	4-8	183
Euonymus fortunei 'Coloratus'		
Rock Rose	5-8	186
Helianthemum nummularium		
Spotted Dead Nettle	3-9	192
Lamium maculatum		
Stonecrop	3-10	198
Sedum spectabile		

*Flower Carpet Rose
(Rosa 'Flower Carpet')
Page 197*

Plants for small spaces

Common Name	Zones	Page
◆ Trees		
Bradford Pear	4-8	100
Pyrus calleryana 'Bradford'		
Flowering Dogwood	5-9	82
Cornus florida		
Ginkgo	3-9	86
Ginkgo biloba		
Japanese Maple	5-8	73
Acer palmatum		
Paperbark Maple	4-8	72
Acer griseum		
Possum Haw	3-9	87
Ilex decidua		
Purple-Leaf Plum	4-8	97
Prunus cerasifera 'Atropurpurea'		
Redbud	3-9	81
Cercis canadensis		
Savannah Holly	5-9	88
Ilex opaca 'Savannah'		
Star Magnolia	4-9	91
Magnolia stellata		
Washington Hawthorn	3-9	83
Crataegus phaenopyrum		
◆ Shrubs		
Annabelle Hydrangea	3-9	139
Hydrangea arborescens 'Annabelle'		
Butterfly Bush	5-9	129
Buddleia davidii		
Compact Japanese Holly	5-8	143
Ilex crenata 'Compacta'		
Dwarf Alberta Spruce	3-8	150
Picea glauca 'Conica'		
Dwarf Burford Holly	6-9	141
Ilex cornuta 'Bufordii Nana'		
Dwarf Burning Bush	3-8	136
Euonymus alatus 'Compacta'		
Green Lustre Japanese Holly	4-6	142
Ilex crenata 'Green Lustre'		
Heller Japanese Holly	5-8	142
Ilex crenata 'Helleri'		
Inkberry	3-9	143
Ilex glabra 'Compacta'		
Korean Boxwood	5-9	131
Buxus microphylla koreana		
Otto Luyken Laurel	6-8	153
Prunus laurocerasus 'Otto Luyken'		
Rose of Sharon	5-9	139
Hibiscus syriacus		
The Fairy Rose	4-9	159
Rosa 'The Fairy'		
◆ Groundcovers		
Andorra Compact Juniper	3-9	191
Juniperus horizontalis 'Plumosa Compacta'		
Arum	6-10	178
Arum italicum		

Common Name	Zones	Page
Bar Harbor Juniper	3-9	190
Juniperus horizontalis 'Bar Harbor'		
Bath's Pink	4-9	182
Dianthus gratianopolitanus 'Bath's Pink'		
Blanket Flower	2-9	185
Gaillardia x grandiflora		
Bloody Cranesbill	3-8	185
Geranium sanguineum		
Blue Chip Juniper	3-9	190
Juniperus horizontalis 'Blue Chip'		
Blue Pacific Shore Juniper	5-9	190
Juniperus conferta 'Blue Pacific'		
Blue Rug Juniper	3-9	191
Juniperus horizontalis 'Wiltonii'		
Catmint	4-8	194
Nepeta x faassenii		
Coral Bells	3-8	187
Heuchera sanguinea		
Corsican Mint	5-9	193
Mentha corsica		
Creeping Thyme	5-9	200
Thymus leucotrichus		
Dwarf Japanese Garden Juniper	4-9	191
Juniperus procumbens 'Nana'		
Evergreen Candytuft	4-8	189
Iberis sempervirens		
Fleabane	2-10	183
Erigeron hybrid		
Germander	4-9	199
Teucrium prostratum		
Goldmoss	4-9	198
Sedum acre		
Hosta	3-8	187
Hosta species		
Japanese Blood Grass	5-9	189
Imperata cylindrica 'Red Baron'		
Japanese Painted Fern	4-9	179
Athyrium nipponicum 'Pictum'		
Lamb's Ear	4-8	199
Stachys byzantina		
Lenten Rose	4-8	187
Helleborus orientalis		
Maidenhair Fern	3-8	174
Adiantum pedatum		
Moss Phlox	2-9	196
Phlox subulata		
Silver Brocade Artemisia	3-9	178
Artemisia stelleriana 'Silver Brocade'		
Stonecrop	3-10	198
Sedum spectabile		
Variegated Japanese Sedge	6-9	180
Carex morrowii 'Variegata'		
◆ Vines		
Climbing Hydrangea	4-7	209
Hydrangea petiolaris		
Hybrid Clematis	3-9	209
Clematis hybrid		

Creating an effective windbreak means more than planting a single row of trees.

Plants for Windbreaks

Strategically positioning plants to deflect harsh winds can make your home and yard more pleasant. The first step in planting a windbreak is to figure out where you need one. Winds come from different directions in different seasons. Cold winter winds frequently blow from the northwest, but the direction is often affected by local terrain. It's best to make your plans based upon personal observation. You can also filter summer winds that may be too gusty. Make sure you're not taking notes about prevailing wind direction during warm weather if winter or autumn winds are your main concern.

Get a Sense of Direction

Once you know the direction undesirable wind is coming from, you can figure out what area you want to shelter. The side of the windbreak opposite the direction wind is coming from is called the leeward side. A 20-foot-wide area on the leeward side next to the windbreak is the most sheltered spot. This means you'll want to plant trees and shrubs within 20 feet of sitting areas such as decks and patios if winds presently make these spots less than comfortable. Adding a windbreak can extend the season of use for a favorite outdoor spot and make it cozy a little longer. Strategically positioned trees and shrubs can also shield walkways from wind. Think about the routes that you walk to retrieve your newspaper, bring in firewood, or get into your car. If icy winds make even short trips miserable in winter, planting a windbreak can make a big difference.

Plants that deflect wind can keep your house snug, too. Blasting winter winds make interior rooms colder and drive heating costs up. Position windbreaks to shelter windows that face into the paths of harsh winds. You don't have to plant a dense screen close to your house; you can position the windbreak in the background. Though the first 20 feet of the leeward side will be the most sheltered, areas farther away will be affected, too. Wind speeds can be reduced for areas within 200 feet of a windbreak that's 20 feet tall.

Find an Informal Look

You'll have the most success with a planted windbreak if you give it an informal look. That's because letting plants grow to different heights—instead of flat-topping them to create a formal hedge—will have a big impact on wind speed. A group of plants that have staggered tops is less aerodynamic than an even-topped hedge or fence. The uneven heights create drag, slowing wind. If the rest of your yard is clipped formally, you can still have a

Trees that don't have branches all the way to the ground are not good choices for windbreaks because the airstream will be forced through the gaps beside the lower trunks. Choose full-skirted evergreen trees and shrubs instead.

Windbreaks affect the way snow accumulates.

Though the area that's closest to the leeward side of a windbreak is the most sheltered from wind, this area also receives the most snow build-up due to altered wind patterns. If drifts are a problem in your area, make sure your house and driveway are not within the first 25 percent of the sheltered area that's downwind of the windbreak; drifts will pile up there. To calculate the sheltered area, see Design Tip, below.

windbreak by using it as a background to set off your formal garden areas. Setting plants in a zigzag pattern creates a more effective windbreak than planting trees and shrubs in straight rows. Layers of plants do a better job than groupings that are only one plant wide.

Form a Solid Mass

Wind-breaks work by deflecting winds up and over, not by stopping them. So it's important to arrange plantings so that they form a solid mass from top to bottom. Any openings below the top of the highest plant are invitations for

winds to squeeze through. Such winds will blow faster as the airstream is funneled through to the leeward side of your windbreak. To prevent this, plant two or three kinds of shrubs so the forms and sizes of plants will vary and fill in gaps. Select trees that grow branches all the way to the ground, and don't trim lower branches. Trees that have exposed trunks and high branches can leave gaps in your windbreak that allow air to rush through. Evergreen plants that don't lose their leaves all at once usually make the best windbreaks because they have foliage during all the seasons, even winter.

Trees for windbreaks

Common Name	Zones	Page
California Incense Cedar *Calocedrus decurrens*	4-8	78
Canadian Hemlock *Tsuga canadensis*	3-7	108
Colorado Blue Spruce *Picea pungens glauca*	2-7	95
Eastern Red Cedar *Juniperus virginiana*	3-9	89
Japanese Black Pine *Pinus thunbergii*	5-7	96
Leyland Cypress *X Cupressocyparis leylandii*	6-9	84
Norway Maple *Acer platanoides*	3-7	72
Norway Spruce *Picea abies*	2-7	93
Skyrocket Juniper *Juniperus scopulorum 'Skyrocket'*	4-8	89
White Fir *Abies concolor*	3-7	70
White Pine *Pinus strobus*	3-8	95
White Spruce *Picea glauca*	2-6	94
Willow Oak *Quercus phellos*	4-8	102

White Pine (Pinus strobus) Page 95

Shrubs for windbreaks

Common Name	Zones	Page
Green Lustre Japanese Holly *Ilex crenata 'Green Lustre'*	4-6	142
Hick's Upright Yew *Taxus x media 'Hicksii'*	4-7	166
Inkberry *Ilex glabra 'Compacta'*	3-9	143
Little Giant Arborvitae *Thuja occidentalis 'Little Giant'*	3-7	166
Mugo Pine *Pinus mugo*	2-7	152
Nellie R. Stevens Holly *Ilex 'Nellie R. Stevens'*	6-9	144
Northern Bayberry *Myrica pensylvanica*	2-6	149
Sea Green Juniper *Juniperus chinensis 'Sea Green'*	4-8	145
Tam Juniper *Juniperus sabina 'Tamariscifolia'*	3-7	146

Availability varies by area and conditions (see page 21). Check with your garden center.

Green Lustre Japanese Holly (Ilex crenata 'Green Lustre') Page 142

Design Tip

How to calculate the area that will be protected by a windbreak.

Multiply the mature height of the trees you are planting by 10. The resulting number indicates how many feet on the leeward side of the windbreak will be sheltered when the trees reach their mature heights. The taller the trees, the more area you will shelter. Remember to combine trees with shrubs to keep wind from forcing through the windbreak below treetops. The denser your windbreak is, the more effective it will be.

Chapter 3
how-to

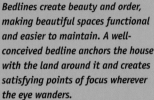

Bedlines create beauty and order, making beautiful spaces functional and easier to maintain. A well-conceived bedline anchors the house with the land around it and creates satisfying points of focus wherever the eye wanders.

Getting the Job Done

Here's where you'll learn to plant and care for your new landscape. We'll show you step-by-step how to get your carefully selected plants into the ground and keep them happy for years to come.

1) *Begin with a Bedline*

You can usually tell if a landscape was designed before planting or if trees and shrubs were put in without a great deal of thought. The first clue is the bedline. The bedline separates planting areas from lawns. How you draw the line determines the shape of the planting bed on one side and the shape of the lawn area on the other side of it.

Smooth, curving bedlines complement most homes. Such bedlines wrap around corners of houses, decks, patios, walkways, parking areas, and swimming pools.

Curving bedlines nestle man-made structures within the landscape.

2) *Keep It Simple*

It's important to keep bedlines simple. Complicated lines with little curves will make the bedline appear unnatural and the lawn more difficult to mow. Part of your goal is functionality. You should be able to easily mow a perimeter strip around the edge of the bedline before cutting the entire lawn. Plants in a bed that grow to fill in a single, smooth curve will make your landscape attractive, neat, and easy to maintain.

3) *Get It on Paper*

Lay a piece of tracing paper over your site analysis and sketch bedline schemes. The sketch will show how planting areas in your yard connect. Leave some areas open for access to doorways and utility areas. Leave access to walk around your house. Build easy routes or pathways into your design to set out trash cans, move the mower from one lawn area to another, and receive deliveries.

Once you've designed a bedline that's both artistic and functional, you're ready to get to work.

STUFF YOU'LL NEED

✔ Garden hose that you don't mind getting paint on
✔ Sharpshooter or trenching shovel
✔ Marking paint (not regular spray paint)
✔ Inexpensive gloves
✔ Old shoes

What to Expect

You'll probably try several patterns with the hose before you're satisfied with the bedline. Don't rush the process. You'll live with your choice for a long time.

Design Tip

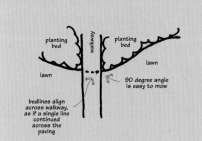

▲ **Right** Aligning bedlines across a walkway makes the entrance lead into the landscape instead of interrupting it. Always make sure bedlines meet paving or structures at 90 degrees so that lawn areas are wide enough to mow easily.

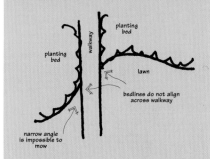

▲ **Wrong** Bedlines that don't align across a walkway make the paving look like an afterthought. Bedlines that meet paving or structures at narrow angles create slivers of lawn that are difficult to mow, inviting weed growth.

1 Use a garden hose to create an outline.
Spread a garden hose in the sun on a driveway or patio for about 15 minutes to make it flexible. Lay the garden hose on the ground in the shape of your proposed bedline. The area inside the hose will become the planting bed; the area outside the hose will remain unchanged.

2 Adjust the hose as needed.
Reposition the hose until you like the outline. Smooth the hose to eliminate any dips that give the bedline an unnatural shape. The object is to create a gently flowing curve. If that curve connects to another bedline, flow them smoothly together.

Push your mower alongside the hose to see if you can cut the grass easily. This will help you make the final decision about the shape of your bedline.

3 Spray the grass or ground with marking paint. Don't use regular spray paint and don't spray paving, stones, or plants you want to keep. Remove the hose and examine the shape of the bedline. Make sure you're happy with it before you begin to digging. You can substitute flour for marking paint, but if you do, make sure you finish the job in a day. Flour will wash away if it rains.

 Good idea! **Don't spray a thick line until you're sure.** You might change your mind. Try spraying small dashes and then standing back to look. Scuff out and correct areas you don't like, then connect the dashes into a digging line.

Making a Bed

Once you lay out your bedline, it's time to prepare the area inside it for planting. Chances are, the spot you want to convert to a lovely landscape is now full of grass and weeds. The first task is to get rid of plants you don't want.

STUFF YOU'LL NEED

✔ Rubber gloves, work boots, long pants, long-sleeved shirt
✔ Eye protection
✔ Dust mask
✔ Systemic herbicide that includes grass and weeds on the label
✔ Pump sprayer
✔ Sharpshooter or trenching shovel

1 Spray the bed. Pick a day for spraying when the weather is hot, sunny, dry, and still. (You don't want the spray to drift onto grass or plants you want to keep.) Using a pump sprayer, cover the area inside the bed with a systemic grass and weed killer. Follow sprayer directions and keep the spray head at the recommended distance above the grass and weeds. Coat all grass and weeds you want to kill. Wait three days for the product to do its work. If you notice green spots, respray as needed. If it rains, give the planting bed an extra day or two to dry out. If the grass and weeds don't appear to be dying, reapply the grass and weed killer on a sunny, still day and wait for it to do the job.

What to Expect

It's easier to keep track of where you've sprayed if you mix food coloring into the systemic herbicide before you start. Don't spray yourself into a corner; walking through fresh spray can leave footprints in your lawns.

Safety Alert!

Wear protective clothing, including eye protection and rubber gloves. Check product labels to see if a respirator is needed. Follow clean-up and disposal instructions.

 Good idea!

Don't do double duty with your garden sprayer. Herbicides and fertilizers don't mix. No matter how carefully you wash out the sprayer, residue from the weed killer will remain and damage plants you want to keep. Mark sprayers carefully, and keep them separate in your garden shed.

2 Shovel-cut the bedline when grass and weeds have turned brown. Use a narrow-bladed shovel, such as a sharpshooter, to cut a nearly vertical edge along the grassed side of your planting bed. This line separates the new planting bed from existing lawn. Scrape soil away so that the opposite side of the trench rolls upwards into the bed area. Make your V-cut about 6 inches deep so it will hold a 3-inch layer of mulch. If you're planning to install edging, do so now. (See "Edging Choices," page 47.)

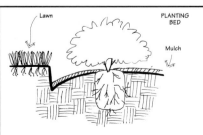

Lawn / PLANTING BED / Mulch

Homer's Hindsight

It was a little windy the Saturday morning I had planned to work in the yard. I wanted to get things going, so I went ahead and sprayed herbicide on the grass I wanted to kill within my new planting bed. Did I feel foolish the next week when my wife's prize petunias in a nearby bed began to die. Now I know to wait for a still, calm day before spraying herbicide. Sometimes I even prop up a temporary cardboard shield around flowers and plants in adjacent beds before I go to work.

3 **Using the same shovel, jab the blade under the roots of dead grass to separate them from the soil.**

Scrape and remove all roots, grass, and weeds. If you're tempted to skip these three steps and till live grass under, make sure you're not dealing with a warm-season grass such as Bermudagrass or St. Augustine grass. These deep-rooted spreading grasses will resprout if tilled into a new bed.

Get the 'Full Scoop'

Improve Your Drainage: Good drainage is essential for a thriving bed.
—See page 51

TOOL TIP

A sharpshooter is another name for trenching shovel. It features a long, narrow blade that's straight and sharp. This light shovel is easy to use and good for digging straight down.

A sod lifter has a blade attached at an angle from the handle. It's easier to slide the sharp, flat end beneath grass roots.

 **Design Tip**

Edging Choices

You can keep bedlines neat by cutting the edges with a sharp shovel every few months. Or, install edging to form a barrier.

The purposes of edging are to delineate the bedline, to make it more difficult for grass to grow into the bed or for groundcovers to spread into the lawn, and to provide a solid edge for mowing or trimming against. Brick, stone, or steel can do the job. Plastic edging is another choice. Install it carefully so the edging is inserted into the ground all the way to the rounded plastic lip. Pack soil firmly on both sides of the edging to keep it from popping out.

Edging creates neatly shaped bedlines to resist encroaching grass and weeds.

'Organic Grass Removal'

If you want to save the grass you're removing, and it's dense, thick, and free of weeds, or you don't like the idea of using herbicides, rent a sod cutter. This machine uses sharp, scissors-action blades to cut sod so you can lift and remove sections of grass. Have the associate at the rental house teach you how to use the cutter before you go to work. Lawn pieces removed with a sod cutter are suitable for planting elsewhere. Keep cut sod moist. Replant as soon as possible and water thoroughly. Keep watering regularly until the sod has reestablished itself in its new location.

A well-prepared planting bed adds more than beauty and order to your landscape. The proper balance of nutrients and good drainage helps new plants succeed.

Bed Preparation

Think of the soil in your yard as an aquarium and the plants you're adding as fish. They both have requirements for survival. Fish need the right kind of water, and plants need the right kind of soil. Prepare your bed correctly, and you'll give your landscape the right start.

The more you prep the soil prior to planting, the more hospitable it becomes for plants. Tilling, digging, and turning the ground loosens soil and makes it easier for water to percolate. Loose soil allows air to reach roots and makes it easier for them to spread.

Ideally, you should till your entire planting bed area before setting out the first plant. Prepping the entire bed is especially important when planting groundcover. Usually, these plants are set out at a smaller size than shrubs and are planted closer together. Tilling the whole bed is more efficient than digging lots of little holes and makes arranging the plants more efficient. Save the shovel for planting individual trees, shrubs, and vines. Though working the entire bed is preferable, you can improve the soil you use to fill planting holes—known as backfill—to give new trees and shrubs a good start. Whether you till or dig, mix in amendments prior to planting. Organic matter—such as well-composted manure, composted plant

debris, or leaf mold—is an excellent amendment for any soil type. When mixed into sandy or rocky soil, organic matter slows the flow of water, giving roots a chance to absorb moisture. Organic matter mixed into heavy clay soil does the opposite. It creates air spaces between the densely packed soil particles, improving drainage. Organic matter also supplies nutrients to roots.

Mix soil amendments with native soil at a ratio of 1:1. This helps plants adapt to native soil as roots spread. When you dig holes, pile the

Tilling the entire planting bed guarantees a consistent mixture of amendments in the soil. Tillers are available at most rental outlets. Get a lesson and safety tips from a qualified salesperson.

soil on a tarp or in a wheelbarrow. Mix in amendments, chopping and sifting lumps with your shovel before backfilling the hole around the roots of new plants. If the soil in the hole contains no native soil, roots are discouraged from spreading beyond the backfill. In areas with high rainfall and heavy clay soil, mix native soil with organic matter at a ratio of 4:1.

Keeping Weeds Down

Weeds will like your freshly prepared bed as much as your new plants do. Here's how to keep weeds down while your landscape gets started.

• **Apply pre-emergent herbicide.** Use on bare soil before you set out container-grown or balled-and-burlapped plants. (Follow product label instructions and don't use this kind of herbicide if you plan to sow your new bed with seeds.) Pre-emergents prevent seeds from germinating and will stop weed growth during the first growing season. Reapply each spring as needed by

scratching into the soil around plants. Pre-emergents won't hurt plants that are already growing.

• **Mulch, mulch, mulch.** The thicker the layer, the harder it is for weeds to penetrate and grow. Organic mulches, such as shredded wood, bark, or compost, are ideal because they also break down to supply nutrients to plants. Replenish mulch annually to keep layers about 3 inches thick. Tuck mulch carefully around stems of plants you want to keep; never pile mulch at the base of plants. Rock mulches also cover the ground, retarding weed growth. No matter what you do, tough weeds will eventually push their way upward. Plastic weed mats discourage weeds, but trap heat beneath them, raising soil temperatures higher than many plant roots prefer.

• **The best defense against plants you don't want is plenty of plants that you do want.** Bare soil is an invitation to weed growth. Crowd weeds out with groundcovers and shrubs. Though it's necessary to leave some soil surface bare to allow new plants room to grow, fill in bare spots with groundcover as quickly as possible.

Raised Beds

Building the soil up is an alternative to digging down. Raised beds offer the advantage of filling the entire planting area with good soil. Raised beds are good choices for spots with compacted or clay soils that don't drain well and for areas where the soil is full of tree roots. Make sure raised beds are open to the soil beneath. Sealing them with paving traps water.

In the Zone

Sweet and Sour Soils

Alkaline soil (sweet) and acidic soil (sour) occupy different ends of the pH scale and present different growing issues.

The easiest way to deal with sweet or sour soils is to grow plants that love them. You can also balance the pH to suit your needs. A pH reading of 7 (the pH of water) is considered neutral. Alkaline soils have pH numbers greater than 7. Acidic soils have pH numbers lower than 7. Average garden soil has a pH between 5 and 7. The ideal level for the largest range of plants is a pH reading between 6 and 7.

Peat moss is extremely acidic. Add it to reduce the pH of alkaline soil.

Add **ground dolomitic limestone** to raise the pH of acidic soils. See pages 38-39 for plants that prefer alkaline or acidic soil.

Wisdom of the Aisles

Dealing with heavy clay:
• Gypsum is a valuable soil amendment for improving the structure of clay soils. (It also adds calcium; don't introduce it to soil with high calcium content.) Instead of adding gypsum to backfill, mix it into native soil first, tilling or digging it in deeply to separate sticky soil particles. This works little pockets of air into the soil, allowing water to flow through more freely instead of trapping it around roots and causing plants to drown. A couple of pounds of gypsum will amend about 100 square feet of bed area.
• When planting trees and shrubs in hard clay soil, use your shovel to scrape and roughen the sides of the hole. Slick-sided holes function much like clay pots, keeping the roots confined to the hole and trapping water.
• Some plants—such as azaleas—are particularly sensitive to standing water collecting around their roots. When landscaping in clay soil, plant such shrubs high so root balls protrude an inch or two above the surface of the ground, ensuring that water will drain away from the roots.
• Gypsum does not affect soil pH.

A watering wand attached on a hose produces a spray similar to rainfall and gets in hard-to-reach places.

Keeping Plants Happy

Making sure plants get the proper amount of water is critical. Rainfall is the best source of water for plants, but it isn't always plentiful. Here's the scoop on watering.

Deep Watering makes plants tougher. You can't actually droughtproof your plants, but you can prepare them for dry spells to give your landscape a fighting chance. To deep water, apply water slowly for long periods of time at infrequent intervals. Roots learn to follow water that seeps down into soil, making them less prone to suffering during dry spells. If you water often and quickly instead, you'll only dampen the top layer of soil. As a result, roots tend to stay within this area instead of digging deeper to seek moisture. Roots near the surface are more likely to wither during dry periods than roots that grow downward.

An automatic sprinkler system makes watering easy. Valves control water flow through pipes buried underground to sprinkler heads placed at ground level. Sprinklers are turned on and off by timers. Install automatic watering systems before you plant; trenching to lay pipes can damage existing plants.

Drip irrigation systems deliver water directly to the roots instead of through the air. Watering roots conserves water and prevents many fungal problems caused by wet foliage. Most drip systems are installed by burying flexible tubing beneath mulch. They can also be controlled by timers.

Hand watering works if you're diligent and patient. Many people enjoy the time spent watering their yards—it's therapeutic. The key to hand watering is consistency. If you get off schedule, your plants suffer, especially if you go away for an extended period of time. Trees and large shrubs need water, too. A good soaking beneath the entire dripline is best, not just a quick spray while you're watering the flowers.

Winter watering will help your plants survive. Winter weather is stressful on trees and shrubs planted in late fall and for spring flowering plants. Both should be deep watered during dry winter months.

Troubleshooting is always a part of landscaping. Here are some common conditions and solutions to watering problems:

• **Too Much or Too Little** Those plants that prefer poor, dry soil will struggle with too much water. Plants requiring rich, moist soil will not thrive in dry locations.

Solution: Research plant needs thoroughly before you install.

• **Underwatering** Broad-leaved plants wilt in order to expose less leaf surface to sunshine. Foliage becomes crispy around the edges as though burned. Evergreens maintain their form but foliage becomes dry and discolored.

Solution: Check in-ground plants weekly and containerized plants daily for water needs. Poke a finger or dig a small hole a few inches below the soil surface near the plant. If the soil feels dry, the plant needs water. Apply a slow, gentle stream of water to the base, allowing the water to soak down to the roots.

• **Overwatering** Too much water produces the same symptoms as underwatering. Check the soil as above. If the soil is moist but still crumbly, lack of water is probably not the problem.

Solution: If the soil has any of the four "s" symptoms—soupy, sticky, soggy, or smelly—cut back on your watering schedule. Let the soil dry out between waterings.

Wisdom of the Aisles

When you water is as important as how you water.

The earlier in the day the better. (That's when timers come in handy.) If you wait until plants are struggling, watering becomes a form of first-aid instead of a regular part of their care. Watering in the late afternoon or evening means your plants will have suffered during the longest hours of the day. Foliage might not have a chance to dry before nightfall, making conditions ripe for fungal problems. Soil and mulch that stay damp overnight invite soft-bodied pests, such as slugs and snails.

Timers can attach directly to the hose and be programmed to provide regular watering cycles.

Drainage Solutions

Too much water can harm plants by filling air pockets in the soil and drowning roots or by washing plants away. Here are some methods for making soggy soil drier, keeping storm water from blasting plants from their beds, and preventing puddles from forming. Keep in mind that it usually isn't legal to increase the amount of water that drains across property lines, so don't dump your excess water on your neighbor's property.

French Drains

French drains disperse water that becomes trapped in soil. They're used where pounding rain spills from roof edges, confined planting beds meet paving, or retaining walls cause ground water to accumulate. To install:

• **Dig a trench that's 8 to 12 inches wide and deep.** Slope the trench downhill about one-eighth inch per foot. Extend as far from the problem area as possible.

• **Fill the trench with a layer of coarse gravel an inch or two thick.** Rinse the gravel first to keep debris from clogging pipes later. Maintain the downward slope of the trench when adding gravel.

• **Place a 3- to 4-inch-wide perforated plastic pipe on top of the gravel bed.**

• **Wrap the pipe in a filter sleeve.** This will prevent holes from clogging. You can also buy perforated plastic pipe that's already wrapped in a filter sleeve. If the pipe has holes on just one side, lay this side face down.

• **Fill the rest of the trench with washed gravel, surrounding the pipe completely.** The top of the gravel in the trench should be level with the adjacent soil.

Downspouts

Downspouts are often the culprits when plants, topsoil, and mulch are washed away by a blast of water.

Solve the problem by connecting a flexible pipe to the end of the downspout. Bury the pipe in a trench. If you can, run the pipe to a lower spot in the yard where water can flow from the far end. Wedge a flat stone beneath the end of a drain pipe where it empties onto the ground. This helps prevent erosion. If it isn't possible to "daylight" the pipe— letting the low end open onto the soil's surface—build a long French drain to disperse the water, instead (see above).

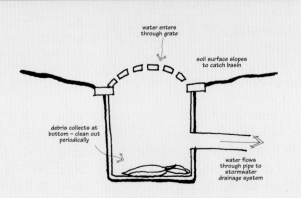

Catch Basins

Catch basins collect excess surface water so it can be moved elsewhere through underground pipes.

Set a catch basin at a low point where water puddles. Dig a hole just big enough to house the catch basin. This drainage device is topped with a grate to admit water. (Hint: domed grates help prevent mulch from washing into catch basins.) You'll need to dig a trench leading from your catch basin to an area where you want to release the water, such as a natural area or storm drainage system. Lay plastic drain pipe in the trench and connect it to the catch basin.

water enters through grate

soil surface slopes to catch basin

debris collects at bottom – clean out periodically

water flows through pipe to stormwater drainage system

Plants have varying nutritional needs. Choosing the right fertilizer and applying the right amount at the right time will keep your landscape a showplace.

Fertilizing

F ertilizing provides plants a good, balanced diet. Adding plenty of organic amendments at planting gives plants a healthy start. Properly applied fertilizers keeps them flourishing.

The Key is N-P-K

Fertilizers are combinations of major elements nitrogen (N), phosphorus (P), and potassium (K) along with other minor elements such as calcium (Ca), magnesium (Mn), and iron (Fe). N, P, and K are listed on the label in order. Bags labeled as complete fertilizers contain various percentages of N, P, and K and may contain minor elements as well. Balanced fertilizers contain equal amounts of N, P, and K. A label that reads 6-6-6 means there is 6 percent of each element; the remainder is inert matter. The larger the numbers, the higher the percentage of fertilizer. Use fertilizers with lower matching numbers in hot, dry weather to avoid chemical burns on plants. Higher matching numbers are good for cool, wet conditions when plants absorb elements easily. Different numbers indicate that the product contains N, P, and K in unequal amounts. Select fertilizers with higher percentages of specific elements to solve problems and match growing requirements. (See "It's Elemental—Know Your N-P-K," right.) A fertilizer labeled 8-12-4 contains 8 percent nitrogen, 12 percent phosphorus, and 4 percent potassium. Always read labels on fertilizers before applying. If you're confused, look for plant lists on the label or a general description that fits the plant you want to feed.

Synthetic Fertilizers

are man-made. They may be dry—in granular, powder, or pellet form—or liquid. All come with instructions for proper use. Keep dry fertilizer away from foliage and avoid mounding it at the base of plants. Instead, scratch it into the soil around plants and water well. Slow-release fertilizers have coated pellets that disintegrate, releasing fertilizer over a longer period of time and are unlikely to

Liquid or slow-release fertilizers are the best choice for tightly clustered plants to avoid burning foliage.

burn plants. Mix them into the soil at planting or around established plants. Apply liquid fertilizers directly to plant leaves or spray onto moistened soil. Liquid fertilizers allow quick plant uptake.

Natural Fertilizers also

come in dry or liquid forms. Many provide only one nutrient and are not complete fertilizers. For example, bloodmeal supplies nitrogen that will quickly green up failing plants. Bonemeal provides phosphorus for root growth and flower formation. You might need to use more than one product to provide complete fertilization. Fish emulsion is a liquid fertilizer that can be applied to damp soil or directly to leaves. Benefits of natural fertilizers are listed on each product label. Natural fertilizers are more difficult to balance than synthetics. Natural products can also be used to amend the soil pH. Cottonseed meal makes soil more acidic, while limestone makes it more alkaline. Natural fertilizers work best on warm days.

Troubleshooting

• **Overfertilizing** Plants that are overfertilized compensate by shutting down and slowing growth. Foliage turns yellow or brown but remains on branches. Plants take on a burned appearance. Flowering plants produce more leaves than blossoms.

Solution: Check the soil; you could have a watering problem. If the soil moisture is normal and you've been fertilizing frequently, stop immediately. Supply the plant with plenty of water to leach excess chemicals from the soil.

• **Underfertilizing** Foliage becomes discolored, turning a more yellowish hue. Growth becomes distorted or stunted.

Solution: Give the soil a finger-test first to find if it is too wet or too dry before fertilizing. Find a fertilizer that describes or lists your plant on the label. Follow directions carefully.

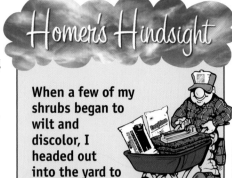
how-to 3

It's Elemental—Know Your N-P-K

Understanding package labels is necessary for using fertilizers correctly.

You'll see the letters N-P-K on lots of fertilizer labels. Here's what they mean:
N is for Nitrogen. This element promotes green growth and lush foliage. But if you use too much of it, you could end up with more leaves than flowers. That's why a balanced fertilizer is a good idea.
P is for Phosphorus. Your plants need phosphorus for good root growth and strong production of flowers and fruit.
K is for Potassium. This element is vital for the general well-being of plants. Potassium helps neutralize ground salts, which can make soil less than hospitable for growth.

You can feed at different speeds. The kind of granular fertilizer you choose affects the rate at which plants will absorb nutrients.
Slow-release. Fertilizers that are coated break down slowly so plants don't get all the good stuff at one time. This is valuable because plants have access to a longer-lasting supply of nutrients. Because slow-release fertilizers are coated, there's no need to worry about burning plants when fertilizer is freshly applied.
Fast-release. These fertilizers are good for a quick fix. But they don't last long and must be "watered in" when applied to avoid burning plants. Keep away from foliage.

Planting Bare-Root Roses

Whether you're planting bare-root roses or plants grown in containers, learn how to get new roses off to the best start.

Bare-root roses are shipped without soil, making them less expensive. They look like stubby sticks. You'll find these plants for sale in late winter or early spring. Plant them soon after purchasing.

1 **Carefully open the packaging.** Avoid cutting roots. Gently remove packing material from roots and discard. Place the roots in a bucket of water mixed with root stimulator. Allow them to soak in a dark, cool, dry location such as a garage. Soak roots no longer than eight hours.

2 **Dig a hole in a spot that receives at least six hours of sun daily.** The hole should be 12 to 18 inches deep. Mix bagged compost with some of the native soil in a wheelbarrow or on a tarp to create a mixture that's about two-thirds organic matter and one-third native soil. The soil mixture should appear dark and rich.

3 **Shovel the good soil mixture into the hole until it's nearly full.** Use your hands to form a cone of soil in the center of the hole. Make the top of the cone slightly below the level of adjacent, undisturbed soil. Position the rose on top of the cone, spreading roots evenly around it.

4 **Backfill around the rose with soil.** Make sure the scion (the ridge where the rose was grafted to the rootstock) is still visible above the soil. Add a thick layer of compost for mulch. Use excess native soil to form a moat around the freshly planted rose. Fill moat with a slowly trickling hose.

STUFF YOU'LL NEED

✔ Bucket
✔ Root stimulator
✔ Hand pruners
✔ Organic matter such as bagged compost
✔ Round-point shovel

What to Expect

Your newly planted bare-root rose will look like a stick poking up out of the ground until new shoots and leaves appear in a few weeks.

BUYER'$ GUIDE

Pick up several bare-root roses before you buy one. If one feels heavier than the others or has water dripping from its packaging, it's not the one you want to take home to plant in your yard. Roots that are bare should stay moist but not wet during shipping.

Good idea!

Before planting, use a pair of good quality hand pruners to trim away any roots that have jagged ends. This replaces rough edges with a good clean cut. Without overdoing it, remove any excessively long, dead, or broken roots.

Planting Containerized Roses

Roses grown in containers cost more than bare-root plants, but you get leaves and often buds right away.

1 **Dig a hole to the proper depth.** Check the depth by setting the rose, still in its container, into the hole. The soil in the container should be level with undisturbed soil around the hole. If the hole is too deep, remove the rose and add some soil to the bottom of the hole. If it's too shallow, you'll need to dig a little more

Nongrafted and Grafted Roses

Bury the crowns of nongrafted roses, which are also known as "own root roses." Some nongrafted roses are less likely to succumb to cold than most grafted roses. The crown of the plant is the point where branches emerge from the main stem just above the roots. Make sure it's low enough to be covered with an inch or two of soil at planting.

Keep the scion of grafted roses above ground. The scion is the ridge where the preferred variety was grafted onto sturdier rootstock. If buried, shoots may grow from the rootstock instead of the rose you want. When planting, keep the scion above the soil line. Cover the scion with mulch in winter, but be aware that plants may still freeze.

2 **Gently slide the rose from its container and place it in the hole.** Remember, it's better to destroy the pot than the plant; cut the container with a utility knife if necessary. Don't pull on the plant and don't disturb the root ball.

3 **Fill the hole to the proper depth.** Mix bagged compost with native soil to create a mixture that's about two-thirds organic matter and one-third native soil and fill around the plant. Do not add any soil to the top of root ball. Use excess soil to form a moat around the plant as wide as the depth of the hole. Mulch this area with compost before filling it slowly with a small, gentle stream from a hose. Mist newly planted roses frequently during the first week or so if the weather is hot and wilting occurs. Keep the soil around roots moist but not soggy while the plant adjusts to its new home.

Climbing Rose Care

• **When planting climbing roses, tilt the plant** in the hole so that canes lean toward supports. You'll get more blooms if you train climbers to grow horizontally, creating layers of greenery. Bend young flexible stems around supports or tie them with plant ties or rose clips.

• **Cut away dead canes in late winter,** before new greenery appears. This will encourage fresh growth in spring. Do not cut into main stems; always make cuts along the outer edges of the plant, leaving small stubs.

• **Protect climbers from freezing.** Untangle plants from their supports (or lay supports down flat) so you can cover canes completely for winter. A thick layer of mulch may do the job, but in colder areas, burying plants in a trench filled with soft soil is your best bet for survival.

Caring for Roses

Pruning roses is important to keep plants vigorous.

Prune roses at any time except before a freeze; trimming in early spring while plants are still dormant makes it easier to see the structure of the plant and what you are doing.

Right:

1 **Make the right cut.** The first order of business is making a proper cut. Cuts should be made on live canes about one-fourth inch above an outward facing bud. Angle your pruners so the tip is cut at a 45-degree slant away from the bud. Apply pruning sealer to fresh cuts to prevent damage from insects and diseases.

Cut angles away from bud and about one-fourth inch above.

Wrong:

Cut angles toward bud; rain washes to the bud.

Wrong:

Cut is too far above the bud and it's flat, not angled.

Wrong:

Cut is too close to the bud.

In the Zone

Why Prune?

Proper pruning keeps plants healthy. You'll need to trim roses each year to remove dead wood, improve air circulation, eliminate rubbing canes, reduce height, and encourage new, vigorous growth with plenty of blossoms..

2 **Cut away darkened, dead wood.** Live canes will be green, and buds will be visible.

Wisdom of the Aisles

Preventive medicine. A few simple steps now will avoid problems later on. Dip cutting tools in rubbing alcohol or bleach after each cut. This helps prevent the spread of disease. Always collect rose clippings instead of letting them fall into garden beds. Clippings may harbor pests or diseases, so you'll need to destroy them. Do not compost rose clippings.

3 **Locate any canes that rub together.** Remove the one that is angling into the center of the plant near the base. Do not cut into the main stem; instead, prune the offending cane where it emerges from the main stem, leaving a little knob of growth known as a collar. If the cane is thicker than a pencil, use bypass loppers instead of hand pruners.

4 **Thin the center of thick shrub roses to improve air circulation.** Leave strong main stems uncut and prune away selected thin, twiggy canes. Remove canes from the center of the plant only, not the outside. Choose canes randomly from the plant's center, leaving nubs of growth so cuts don't go completely back to main stems. Reduce the overall size of a shrub rose if needed. Select your desired height and cut individual canes to that level.

5 **Remove individual fading blooms.** This encourages new buds for more flowers. A good rule of thumb is to remove spent flowers by cutting the stem below the first set of five healthy leaves.

6 **Before protecting roses for winter, apply a dormant spray.** This preventive step makes sure that insects and diseases don't overwinter in your rose plants. Follow product directions.

Rose Care – Symptoms & Solutions

Roses might require spraying to control problems.

If you know what to look for and what product to use, you've already won half the battle. Here are some common culprits. When seeking advice from a garden staffer, take a sample with you. Begin your spray program as soon as first leaves appear for preventive care.

Symptom: Holes in rose blossoms; small green or tan beetles noticeable.
Solution: Hand-pick if possible. Spray large infestations with an insecticide containing carbaryl or rotenone that's labeled for roses. Erect a cheesecloth cage around plants to keep new beetles from flying in. Barrier should be taller than the plant but can be open at the top. Remove when beetles cease feeding.

Symptom: A grayish-white coating covers foliage, distorting young shoots.
Solution: Spray powdery mildew with a fungicide containing triforine, folpet, or thiophanate-methyl. Prevent by watering early in the day so leaves can dry.

Symptom: Black spots appear on foliage; leaves fall off.
Solution: Spray with a fungicide containing thiophanate-methyl, chlorothalonil, mancozeb, or triforine. Allow foliage to dry by watering early in the day to prevent this problem. Rake up and destroy fallen leaves.

Symptom: Brown buds develop and flowers are few and oddly shaped, probably caused by tiny bugs such as thrips or mites.
Solution: Spray with a systemic insecticide containing acephate. Remove buds and blooms by hand and destroy.

Symptom: New leaves are curled and stunted; foliage is shiny and sticky. Little green bugs called aphids are visible.
Solution: Knock them off with a stiff spray of water. Control with insecticidal soap or a contact-killer spray. For long-term control, apply a systemic insecticide containing acephate.

Feeding Roses

Most roses are heavy feeders—they require more fertilizer than many other landscape plants.
A fertilizer that contains higher amounts of phosphorus and potassium than nitrogen will encourage the growth of flowers instead of just leaves. Look for a fertilizer that lists a smaller first number (N) on its label than the next two numbers (P and K). Fertilizers identified as rose foods make it easy. They contain elements balanced to give roses just what they need. Slow-release fertilizers are coated to prevent all the nutrients from entering the soil at once. They supply benefits over a longer period of time than noncoated fertilizers. Some granular fertilizers also supply systemic insecticides for preventive care.

Feed roses each year when new growth is about 3 inches long. Rake away mulch and scratch dry fertilizers into the soil around plants, watering well before covering with mulch again. Feed roses again in autumn, at least a month before the first frost.
Foliar feeding. Liquid fertilizer (foliar feed) can be applied directly to leaves. Temperatures should be below 90 degrees when applying. You can use liquid fertilizer as often as every week to correct nutrient deficiencies. Always apply liquid fertilizers in the early morning to allow leaves to dry thoroughly as quickly as possible. Damp leaves can lead to fungal problems, especially if foliage is left wet overnight.

Pink Meidiland Rose (Rosa Pink Meidiland) Page 158

Chapter 4
trees

Trees are the backbone of good design, providing color, texture, line, and form. They also offer shade, protection from wind and rain, and shelter for other plants in your yard. Because most trees take longer than other plants to mature, the sooner you get new trees started in your landscape, the better.

The Value of Trees

Start your landscape with trees. A single, well-placed tree impacts your yard more than any other landscaping item. Most trees are long-lasting and embody the elements of good design—color, texture, line, and form. Planting trees first shapes planting beds and gives them a head start on growth while you work on other parts of your landscape.

Trees Solve Problems Look over the notes taken when you prepared your site analysis. Trees might solve the problem areas identified on your site analysis. Carefully chosen trees put privacy where you need it, add shade, dress up patios and entries, deflect wind, and establish a background for your landscape. Good selection is more important than quantity. Picking the right trees to fill the right needs is more effective than planting whatever you happen to find on sale. Look at the selection guides on the following pages; then go to the tree encyclopedia later in this book to help make your final decisions.

Consider These Factors
Defining the jobs you want new trees to do helps identify desirable characteristics. Think about whether you need a tree that keeps its foliage year round (evergreen) or sheds its leaves once a year (deciduous). Evergreen trees offer more privacy but usually grow more slowly than deciduous trees. Deciduous trees make good choices for producing summer shade.

Keep in mind that the right plant in the right place is critical to success. Before adding a tree to your yard, you need to know its ultimate size and how long it will take to reach maturity. After all, it's a shame to severely prune a tall, stately tree because you didn't take phone or power lines into account at planting. Knowing how big a tree will get also helps you avoid the common problem of planting a tree that will grow large too close to your house. You'll also want to know if the tree has any characteristics that make it undesirable for the purpose you have in mind. For example, trees

Rapid Growers

Rapidly growing trees can improve your landscape in a hurry. Position new trees properly in the landscape, dig large-sized planting holes, provide good soil, water adequately water (see page 50), and watch your trees take off. Find out all you can about the trees you are considering for your landscape. Growth rate is just one bit of information provided in the tree encyclopedia pages. Look on plant tags and ask garden associates for additional information if needed. Knowing the growth rate will help you decide the size of tree to purchase. If you've decided on a slow grower, consider planting one that's larger in size so you won't have to wait several years before enjoying it. A Star Magnolia used as a focal point in an entry area or courtyard is a tree worth buying big. Other trees, such as river birches, grow so quickly that you needn't go to the expense of purchasing large ones. Remember that faster-growing trees usually have weaker wood and shorter lifespans than their slower-growing counterparts.

Irregularly shaped trunks and limbs become unusual framing devices, creating points of interest in a landscape.

Common Name	Zones	Page	Common Name	Zones	Page
Amur Chokecherry *Prunus maackii*	2-6	97	Purple-Leaf Plum *Prunus cerasifera 'Atropurpurea'*	4-8	97
Bald Cypress *Taxodium distichum*	4-10	106	Quaking Aspen *Populus tremuloides*	2-6	96
Bradford Pear *Pyrus calleryana 'Bradford'*	4-8	100	Red Maple *Acer rubrum*	3-9	74
Canoe Birch *Betula papyrifera*	2-5	77	Redbud *Cercis canadensis*	3-9	81
Chinese Elm *Ulmus parvifolia*	5-9	109	River Birch *Betula nigra*	4-9	76
Dawn Redwood *Metasequoia glyptostroboides*	4-8	93	Russian Olive *Elaeagnus angustifolia*	3-8	84
Green Ash *Fraxinus pennsylvanica*	3-9	86	Saucer Magnolia *Magnolia x soulangiana*	5-9	91
Honeylocust *Gleditsia triacanthos inermis*	3-8	87	Scarlet Oak *Quercus coccinea*	4-9	101
Japanese Zelkova *Zelkova serrata*	5-9	109	Shumard Oak *Quercus shumardii*	5-9	103
Katsura Tree *Cercidiphyllum japonicum*	4-8	80	Silver Maple *Acer saccharinum*	3-9	75
Northern Red Oak *Quercus rubra*	4-7	103	Weeping Willow *Salix babylonica*	4-9	104
Pin Oak *Quercus palustris*	4-8	102	Whitespire Birch *Betula mandschurica japonica 'Whitespire'*	4-7	77
Possum Haw *Ilex decidua*	3-9	87	Willow Oak *Quercus phellos*	4-8	102

Availability varies by area and conditions (see page 21). Check with your garden center.

with large root systems that buckle paving are poor choices for planting next to patios, sidewalks, parking areas, or streets. These areas need trees that have well-behaved roots. They should also thrive next to the reflected heat of paving. (Always check easements and right-of-way restrictions before planting.) Find out if trees have invasive roots so you can avoid planting them around septic and drainage systems. Finally, know what it takes to care for your new trees before you plant them. Don't make high-maintenance choices if you desire a low-maintenance landscape. Throughout the following pages, you'll find the details to help you choose the right trees for your landscape.

see page 21

Design Tip

Legacy Trees

Celebrating a major family event by planting a tree is a time-honored tradition. Trees that are known for slow growth and large size are also good choices for longevity. Ginkgos, White Oaks, and Sugar Maples are trees that will commemorate great moments for many generations to come.

Planting a legacy tree such as this White Oak (Quercus alba), page 101, connects generations, establishing a family home.

Wisdom of the Aisles

Trees can actually affect the climate around your home. Trees suitable for use as windbreaks make a big difference when positioned to deflect harsh northwestern winter winds. Deciduous trees planted along the southern and southeastern sides of your home offer cooling shade during the warm seasons. Then they shed their leaves, allowing winter rays to light and warm your home. Choosing trees known for providing leafy shade can make a big difference when positioned to block hot afternoon summer sun coming from the west.

trees 4

Well-placed trees can frame the front door of your home, making it an enticing destination for visitors.

Buying a Tree

Choosing a good tree and getting it home from the store safely are the first steps in creating a landscape.

Trees are sold as container-grown, balled-and-burlapped, and bare-root. Container-grown trees have lived their lives in nursery pots. Balled-and-burlapped trees, also known as B&B, start their lives in tree farm fields. After they're dug up with tree spades, their root balls are wrapped with fabric for shipping. Bare-root types (such as fruit trees) come with roots carefully surrounded with packing inside a plastic bag or set in sawdust.

Trees with big broad leaves provide shade and protection from the elements.

Container vs. B&B Trees grown in containers are often smaller than ones wrapped in burlap. Root growth is limited by the size of the container. Because they don't have to be removed from the ground, container-grown trees are less likely to go into shock and lose their leaves when planted. Garden shops, home centers, and nurseries carry wide selections of container-grown trees. They are often easier for most consumers to handle and are available for a longer period of time during the growing season. The best times to buy B&B trees are early spring or late fall.

Shopping Tips

• **Choose a tree with bigger caliper.** A thick trunk is sturdier than a tall, skinny-trunked tree.

• **Check the firmness of the root ball.** If the tree and root ball move as one, it has developed a good, firm root ball. If the tree is loose within the soil in the container, it has only recently been "stepped up" from a smaller pot into the larger container. Roots are the most important thing you buy when you purchase any plant. Bypass a tree that hasn't been in its container long enough to develop roots to fill the container. If the root ball of a B&B tree is cracked or crumbling, find another tree.

• **Look at the tree roots.** A tree that has long white roots protruding from the bottom drainage hole has been in its container too long and is root-bound. Though you can grow such a tree successfully, it shouldn't be your first choice. A root-bound tree takes longer to put out fresh feeder roots in its new home.

- **Avoid trees that have nicks or wounds to their trunks.** These trees are damaged and may attract insects or develop disease problems.
- **Know the form of the mature tree.** If a tree is supposed to have multiple trunks, that's one thing. But if a particular kind of tree normally has a single, straight trunk, don't purchase one that divides into a double trunk. Water collecting in the crotch can cause splitting because of rot or the formation of ice. High winds may damage an improperly formed tree, too. It pays to know what form is correct before you buy.
- **Check the tree container.** Trees with burlap-wrapped root balls are sometimes set in containers for easier handling. A layer of bark is then added to cover the burlap and keep the root ball moist. These are good trees, just not container grown. Check beneath the mulch to see what you're getting. If you see

Evergreens have their place, but don't forget to choose some trees to help you celebrate the changing of the seasons.

burlap, the tree was dug from a nursery field and is balled-and-burlapped, not container grown.

Fall is for Planting

Autumn is an excellent time to plant woody trees and shrubs. Cold weather slows growth above ground, so a plant's energy is put into expanding roots beneath the ground. Cool weather puts less stress on new trees than hot weather does. Regular watering is not as critical. Insect and disease problems are fewer in fall and winter than in spring and summer. Planting in the fall gives you a jump on next spring.

Tree Mortality

Plants that have been transported from one location to another and then replanted are under a great deal of stress. Some will die through no fault of yours. If the plant is mishandled at any point during the shipping process, the damage has been done before you buy it.

Newly planted trees and shrubs that turn completely brown and hold their leaves instead of dropping them are not going into transplant shock (see page 64). This symptom usually indicates that the plant has died. To test whether your tree is dead or alive, use your fingernail to scratch the thin bark of a branch. If you see green, your tree is alive. If you see brown or gray beneath the bark, try again on other branches or even on the trunk. If none are green, your tree is dead.

Trunk damage is one of the leading reasons that healthy trees die. Trunk wounds destroy the tissues that transport water and nutrients from the roots to the upper portions of the tree. Wounds also invite insects and disease. In the landscape, string trimmers and mowers often cause this damage. Avoid planting grass near tree trunks to eliminate potential problems.

Don't ignore mature trees. They can suffer during the stress of drought. Shallow-rooted trees such as dogwoods are particularly vulnerable during prolonged periods of extremely hot, dry weather. Curling leaves that turn crispy brown along the edges are a sign that a tree needs water. Foliage may also drop prematurely. Water trees by turning a hose on to a slow trickle and placing it around the base of the tree and at various places under the dripline for several hours at a time to give the tree a good soaking. If water flows across the surface of the ground, your hose is turned on too hard.

Homer's Hindsight

I bought a new tree and was eager to get it home. My first mistake was putting it in the trunk with the top sticking out. The tree was destroyed by the time I got home. Even though I'd driven slowly, the wind shredded the leaves and dried them out. Next time, I'll get a tarp and bungee cords to bundle up the tree or at least lay it down in the bed of a pickup truck to give it some wind protection during the ride home.

Planting a Container-Grown Tree

It's easy to add trees to your landscape. Follow these guidelines for planting those that are container-grown.

1 Dig a hole that's one-and-a-half to two times as wide as the tree's container. The hole should be as deep as the container is tall. Use a shovel handle to take a rough measurement; if your hole is too deep, add soil to the bottom and tamp it in place to keep the tree from settling. If you're planting in an area with heavy clay soil, scrape the sides of the hole with a shovel to roughen them. A slick-sided hole acts like a big clay pot and restricts root growth. Add gypsum to clay soil, too (see page 49).

What to Expect

Your newly planted tree will look shorter than it did at the garden center because the container itself seems to add height. When the tree is planted, the roots are buried beneath the soil surface.

Good idea! **Have a tarp or wheelbarrow handy.** As you shovel, place soil onto a tarp or in a wheelbarrow instead of on your lawn. This will make it easier to mix amendments into the soil before putting it back into the hole around the root ball. This trick also makes cleaning up easier.

2 **Mix amendments into the removed soil.** Amendments vary according to existing soil conditions and plant requirements. Compost and bagged, composted manure are good organic amendments to use. The amended mixture should contain half native soil and half organic matter. The use of native soil helps the tree adapt to its new home and spread roots out into the soil beyond the planting hole.

Wisdom of the Aisles

Moving a tree correctly

▲ **Right** Support the heavy root ball from below to prevent damaging tree roots.

3 **Gently slide the tree from its container.** Cut the container with a utility knife if you can't get it off without tugging. (Pulling on the trunk can damage roots.) When the container is off, lay the tree on its side. Gently score the root ball with a sharp shovel or utility knife to encourage the growth of new roots outside the pot-shaped mass of roots. It's important to keep the root ball intact; limit the scores on the root ball.

▲ **Wrong** Transport trees to the planting site by the container, not the tree trunk.

4 Position the tree in its hole.

The top of the root ball should be level with adjacent, undisturbed soil. In areas with heavy clay soil, trees should be planted higher so the root ball protrudes an inch or two above the soil surface. This prevents water from puddling around roots. Before filling the hole, gently swivel the tree so it looks best at the angle from which you'll see it the most. Check to make sure the tree is straight from all directions.

Round-point shovels are great for digging holes and scooping out soil. Shovels with fiberglass handles usually last longer than those with wooden handles.

5 Fill the hole with amended soil mixture.

Add soil around the root ball pressing it firmly with your hands as you go. If planting during hot weather, water the soil as you fill the hole. Watering may settle the soil; add a little more soil the next day, if needed. Avoid stomping on the soil to tamp it down. This destroys soil porosity making it difficult for water and air to reach

plant roots. Because you have dug the hole only as deep as the container is tall, the tree should be sitting on a firm base that won't settle.

Use the excess soil to form a moat around the tree. Make the moat as wide as the hole. Pat the soil firmly in place with your hands. The moat walls should be 3 inches wide and tall. Mulch the area inside the moat and fill with water from a slowly

trickling hose. Place the hose at the base of the tree's trunk to soak the root ball; otherwise, the water will run past the root ball into the looser soil in the hole. The moat allows the water to seep down to the roots instead of running off the soil's surface. Weather will eventually melt your moat; but by then, your tree will no longer need it.

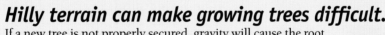

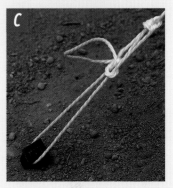

Planting a Tree on a Slope

Hilly terrain can make growing trees difficult.

If a new tree is not properly secured, gravity will cause the root ball to pivot in its hole before roots grow into the adjacent soil. When this happens, the tree leans downhill and grows at an angle instead of straight up and down. Use a tree-staking kit to secure the tree on the uphill side. (To secure a newly planted tree on level soil in areas prone to high winds, use three cables to anchor the tree from all sides.) Watering is also a major concern. Here's how to solve both potential problems.

1) Form a moat on the downhill side of the tree. Now the soil is level, preventing water run off (see A). Deep watering (see page 50) is particularly important for trees planted on slopes. Roots growing downward to seek water give the tree stability.

2) Pass the roping through plastic tubes. Loop tubes around the trunk above a limb and position the hose to prevent wire from cutting into the tree (see B).

3) Secure each rope to a stake driven into the soil on the uphill side. (The two stakes should form the points of a triangle, with the tree at the apex.) Wrap the roping around the hook in each stake, pulling until roping is taut. Make sure the tree is straight from all angles. Tie a brightly colored flag to each rope to make it visible (see C).

Remove the roping and stakes after the tree has been in place for one complete growing season. If your area is prone to high winds, leave trees–even those not planted on slopes–roped for one year (but no longer than a year). Check the lines periodically and tighten as needed. As the root system develops, the tree becomes securely anchored in the ground.

Planting a B&B Tree

Trees that come from the store with balled-and-burlapped root balls are known as B&B trees. Planting them is slightly different than planting container-grown trees.

1 **Dig a hole that's twice as wide as the tree's root ball.** The hole should be as deep as the root ball is tall. Use a shovel handle to take a rough measurement. If your hole is too deep, add soil to the bottom and tamp it in place to keep the tree from settling. If you're planting in an area with heavy clay soil, scrape the sides of the hole with a shovel to roughen them. A slick-sided hole acts like a big clay pot and restricts root growth.

2 **Mix amendments into the removed soil.** The resulting mixture is usually half native soil and half organic matter. Amendments vary according to existing soil conditions and plant requirements. In areas with high rainfall and heavy clay soil, mix native soil with organic matter at a reduced ratio of 4:1. Organic materials such as bagged compost make excellent soil additions.

3 **Cut back all metal or plastic fasteners from the root ball and peel back the top third of the burlap after the tree is set in the hole.** It's important to remove metal or plastic fasteners wrapped around the burlap at the base of the trunk. Leaving these will eventually girdle the tree, killing it. However, if the B&B root ball is sitting in a wire basket, do not remove it. This helps keep the root ball intact. The roots will grow through the wire and the wire will eventually rust away.

Wisdom of the Aisles

Topping trees **Don't flat-top your trees.** Cutting branches so they're all the same level encourages the development of many fast-growing sprouts from the tips of remaining stubs. Though the tree's canopy will appear dense and bushy for a while, the sprouts will shoot upward, requiring more pruning. Thick, gnarled scars can appear after cuts are made in the same place year after year. Cutting branches off to make the tree resemble a lollipop prohibits the development of the tree's natural form. Instead, shoots angle upward, close to the trunk. Narrow crotches result, which may accumulate water and rot wood or form ice that will split the branches from the tree. Topping trees also severely limits the size of a tree's canopy; eventually, the trunk grows thicker, making it appear out of proportion to the limited canopy. Topping is also known as pollarding or dehorning.

STUFF YOU'LL NEED

✔ Round-point shovel
✔ Water supply and hose within reach of work site
✔ Organic matter such as bagged compost
✔ Tarp (optional)
✔ Gypsum for clay soil

What to Expect

It may be difficult to pry fasteners from root balls with your fingers; try using a flat-head screwdriver, instead.

TOOL TIP

A digging bar is essential when you're digging holes in rocky, compacted, or hard clay soil. Use a sledgehammer to drive it into the soil to pry chunks loose and get your hole started.

In the Zone

Transplant Shock

If your new tree drops all its leaves shortly after planting, don't give it up for dead. A balled-and-burlapped tree has many roots severed when it is dug from the ground. It is more likely to experience transplant shock than a container-grown tree. Trees in shock shed their foliage and go into a survival mode. Given enough time and water, such trees will most likely recover. Keep the soil lightly moist. Though it appears a little silly to be watering something that looks dead, keep doing it!

Design Tip

Plan your bedlines around existing or future trees.

Though you shouldn't plant right up to the trunks of trees, you can surround them with a bed of shrubs and groundcovers. Keep lawns away from the base of trees to avoid trunk damage from mowers and string trimmers. You'll also avoid the problems caused by the different watering needs of trees and grass.

4 **Position the tree in its hole.**
Peel back the fabric to reveal the top third of the root ball. Leave the fabric in place unless it is nonbiodegradable plastic, which will need to be removed before the ball goes in the hole. The top of the root ball should be level with adjacent, undisturbed soil. This is easily checked with the handle of a shovel. In clay soil, trees need to be planted so the root ball is an inch or two above the soil surface so water won't puddle around roots. Make sure the tree is straight from all sides.

5 **Fill the hole with the amended soil mixture.** Add soil around the root ball, pressing it firmly with your hands as you go. If planting during hot weather, water the soil as you fill in the hole. Avoid stomping on the soil to tamp it down. This destroys soil porosity, making it difficult for water and air to reach plant roots. Because you have dug the hole only as deep as the root ball is tall, the tree is sitting on a firm base and shouldn't settle.

Good idea! **Capture a wonderful family occasion by taking pictures as you plant your new tree.** Everyone will treasure the memories, and the moment will become part of your family history.

6 **Use the excess soil to form a moat around the tree.** The moat should be as wide as the hole and 3 inches wide and tall. Pat it in place with your hands to make it sturdy. Mulch the inside and fill the area with water from a trickling hose placed at the base of the trunk. The moat allows the water to seep down to the roots instead of running off the surface of the soil. Fill the moat slowly several times, letting the water soak in each time. Weather will eventually wear away your moat, but after establishment, your tree will no longer need it.

Trees 65

trees

4

Lush summer foliage provides a rich backdrop for the spray from a fountain in a backyard pond.

Choosing Trees for Seasonality

Decorate the seasons. Choose trees for beauty throughout the year. You'll find plenty of different kinds with attractive flowers, foliage, berries, or bark. The selection guides on these pages offer a range of choices. Eliminate any trees that don't include your planting zone within their range. Turn to the pages listed for photographs and more information.

Japanese Flowering Crabapple (Malus floribunda) Page 92

Autumn has arrived when the fan-shaped leaves of a Ginkgo turn golden.

Japanese Tree Lilac (Syringa reticulata) Page 106

Trees with autumn interest

Common Name	Zones	Page
American Beech	3-9	85
Fagus grandifolia		
Amur Chokecherry	2-6	97
Prunus maackii		
Amur Maple	2-6	71
Acer tataricum ginnala		
Bradford Pear	4-8	100
Pyrus calleryana 'Bradford'		
Canoe Birch	2-5	77
Betula papyrifera		
Chinese Elm	5-9	109
Ulmus parvifolia		
Downy Serviceberry	4-9	76
Amelanchier arborea		
European Hornbeam	4-7	78
Carpinus betulus		
European Mountain Ash	3-6	104
Sorbus aucuparia		
Flowering Dogwood	5-9	82
Cornus florida		
Fruitless American Sweetgum	5-9	90
Liquidambar styraciflua 'Rotundiloba'		
Ginkgo	3-9	86
Ginkgo biloba		
Green Ash	3-9	86
Fraxinus pennsylvanica		
Honeylocust	3-8	87
Gleditsia triacanthos inermis		
Japanese Flowering Crabapple	4-8	92
Malus floribunda		
Japanese Maple	5-8	73
Acer palmatum		
Japanese Snowbell	5-8	105
Styrax japonicum		
Japanese Stewartia	5-7	105
Stewartia pseudocamellia		
Japanese Zelkova	5-9	109
Zelkova serrata		
Katsura Tree	4-8	80
Cercidiphyllum japonicum		
Kousa Dogwood	5-8	83
Cornus kousa		
Kwanzan Cherry	5-8	98
Prunus serrulata 'Kwanzan'		
Littleleaf Linden	3-7	108
Tilia cordata		
Northern Red Oak	4-7	103
Quercus rubra		
Norway Maple	3-7	72
Acer platanoides		
Paperbark Maple	4-8	72
Acer griseum		
Pin Oak	4-8	102
Quercus palustris		
Possum Haw	3-9	87
Ilex decidua		
Quaking Aspen	2-6	96
Populus tremuloides		
Red Maple	3-9	74
Acer rubrum		
Redbud	3-9	81
Cercis canadensis		
Sargent Cherry	4-7	98
Prunus sargentii		
Scarlet Oak	4-9	101
Quercus coccinea		
Shumard Oak	5-9	103
Quercus shumardii		
Silver Maple	3-9	75
Acer saccharinum		
Southern Magnolia	6-10	90
Magnolia grandiflora		
Star Magnolia	4-9	91
Magnolia stellata		
Sugar Maple	4-8	75
Acer saccharum		
Trident Maple	4-8	71
Acer buergerianum		
Washington Hawthorn	3-9	83
Crataegus phaenopyrum		
Weeping Cherry	4-8	99
Prunus subhirtella 'Pendula'		
White Oak	4-9	101
Quercus alba		
Whitespire Birch	4-7	77
Betula mandschurica japonica 'Whitespire'		
Yellowwood	6-8	82
Cladrastis lutea		

Spring-flowering trees

Common Name	Zones	Page
Amur Chokecherry	2-6	97
Prunus maackii		
Bradford Pear	4-8	100
Pyrus calleryana 'Bradford'		
Chinese Fringe Tree	6-8	81
Chionanthus retusus		
Downy Serviceberry	4-9	76
Amelanchier arborea		
European Mountain Ash	3-6	104
Sorbus aucuparia		
Flowering Dogwood	5-9	82
Cornus florida		
Japanese Flowering Crabapple	4-8	92
Malus floribunda		
Japanese Snowbell	5-8	105
Styrax japonicum		
Kousa Dogwood	5-8	83
Cornus kousa		
Kwanzan Cherry	5-8	98
Prunus serrulata 'Kwanzan'		
Plumleaf Crabapple	4-9	92
Malus prunifolia		
Red Maple	3-9	74
Acer rubrum		
Redbud	3-9	81
Cercis canadensis		
Russian Olive	3-8	84
Elaeagnus angustifolia		
Sargent Cherry	4-7	98
Prunus sargentii		
Saucer Magnolia	5-9	91
Magnolia x soulangiana		
Star Magnolia	4-9	91
Magnolia stellata		
Washington Hawthorn	3-9	83
Crataegus phaenopyrum		
Weeping Cherry	4-8	99
Prunus subhirtella 'Pendula'		
Yellowwood	6-8	82
Cladrastis lutea		

Summer-flowering trees

Common Name	Zones	Page
Japanese Snowbell	5-8	105
Styrax japonicum		
Japanese Stewartia	5-7	105
Stewartia pseudocamellia		
Japanese Tree Lilac	3-7	106
Syringa reticulata		
Littleleaf Linden	3-7	108
Tilia cordata		
Russian Olive	3-8	84
Elaeagnus angustifolia		
Southern Magnolia	6-10	90
Magnolia grandiflora		
Yellowwood	6-8	82
Cladrastis lutea		

Trees with winter interest

Common Name	Zones	Page
American Beech (bark)	3-9	85
Fagus grandifolia		
Amur Chokecherry (bark)	2-6	97
Prunus maackii		
Amur Maple (shape)	2-6	71
Acer tataricum ginnala		
Blue Holly (berries)	5-8	88
Ilex x meserveae		

Common Name	Zones	Page
Canadian Hemlock (bark)	3-7	108
Tsuga canadensis		
Canoe Birch (bark)	2-5	77
Betula papyrifera		
Chinese Elm (bark)	5-9	109
Ulmus parvifolia		
Eastern Red Cedar (bark)	3-9	89
Juniperus virginiana		
Japanese Black Pine (shape)	5-7	96
Pinus thunbergii		
Japanese Maple (shape)	5-8	73
Acer palmatum		
Japanese Snowbell (shape)	5-8	105
Styrax japonicum		
Japanese Stewartia (bark)	5-7	105
Stewartia pseudocamellia		
Kwanzan Cherry (bark)	5-8	98
Prunus serrulata 'Kwanzan'		
Paperbark Maple (bark)	4-8	72
Acer griseum		
Plumleaf Crabapple (berries)	4-9	92
Malus prunifolia		
Possum Haw (berries)	3-9	87
Ilex decidua		
River Birch (bark)	4-9	76
Betula nigra		
Sargent Cherry (bark)	4-7	98
Prunus sargentii		
Saucer Magnolia (shape)	5-9	91
Magnolia x soulangiana		
Savannah Holly (berries)	5-9	88
Ilex opaca 'Savannah'		
Sugarberry (bark)	5-9	80
Celtis laevigata		
Washington Hawthorn (berries)	3-9	83
Crataegus phaenopyrum		
Whitespire Birch (bark)	4-7	77
Betula mandschurica japonica 'Whitespire'		

Peeling bark on a River Birch trunk becomes more noticeable in winter when leaves are down.

Availability varies by area and conditions (see page 21). Check with your garden center.

Honeylocust (Gleditsia triacanthos inermis), page 87, is known for its bright-green foliage. The leaf color is especially noticeable in spring.

Trees for Every Need

Some trees are better suited for special jobs than others. Use these selection guides as a starting point for choosing the right tree for the right place. You may find other choices for sale, too.

Weeping Willow
(Salix babylonica)
Page 104

Patio trees

Common Name	Zones	Page
Amur Maple	2-6	71
Acer tataricum ginnala		
Bradford Pear	4-8	100
Pyrus calleryana 'Bradford'		
Chinese Elm	5-9	109
Ulmus parvifolia		
European Hornbeam	4-7	78
Carpinus betulus		
European Mountain Ash	3-6	104
Sorbus aucuparia		
Flowering Dogwood	5-9	82
Cornus florida		
Fruitless American Sweetgum	5-9	90
Liquidambar styraciflua 'Rotundiloba'		
Ginkgo	3-9	86
Ginkgo biloba		
Japanese Flowering Crabapple	4-8	92
Malus floribunda		
Japanese Maple	5-8	73
Acer palmatum		
Japanese Snowbell	5-8	105
Styrax japonicum		
Japanese Stewartia	5-7	105
Stewartia pseudocamellia		
Japanese Tree Lilac	3-7	106
Syringa reticulata		
Japanese Zelkova	5-9	109
Zelkova serrata		
Kousa Dogwood	5-8	83
Cornus kousa		
Kwanzan Cherry	5-8	98
Prunus serrulata 'Kwanzan'		
Littleleaf Linden	3-7	108
Tilia cordata		
Paperbark Maple	4-8	72
Acer griseum		
Possum Haw	3-9	87
Ilex decidua		
Purple-Leaf Plum	4-8	97
Prunus cerasifera 'Atropurpurea'		
Red Maple	3-9	74
Acer rubrum		
Redbud	3-9	81
Cercis canadensis		
River Birch	4-9	76
Betula nigra		
Russian Olive	3-8	84
Elaeagnus angustifolia		
Savannah Holly	5-9	88
Ilex opaca 'Savannah'		
Shumard Oak	5-9	103
Quercus shumardii		
Star Magnolia	4-9	91
Magnolia stellata		
Trident Maple	4-8	71
Acer buergerianum		
Washington Hawthorn	3-9	83
Crataegus phaenopyrum		
Weeping Cherry	4-8	99
Prunus subhirtella 'Pendula'		
Whitespire Birch	4-7	77
Betula mandschurica japonica 'Whitespire'		
Willow Oak	4-8	102
Quercus phellos		
Yellowwood	6-8	82
Cladrastis lutea		

Availability varies by area and conditions (see page 21). Check with your garden center.

Composting Fallen Leaves

Natural Recycling is Nature's Bonus

Turn the leaves on your lawn into carbon-rich compost. Collect fallen leaves by raking or mowing and deposit them in a compost bin that's no larger than 6 feet and no smaller than 4 feet. (Larger bins won't have adequate oxygen levels while smaller bins can't maintain internal temperatures necessary for decomposition throughout cold winters.) Shredding leaves is fine, but don't pack them down. Have a hose handy to water layers of leaves as you add them to the bin. For each four bushels of leaves in the pile, add a cup or two of nitrogen-rich fertilizer (such as 21-0-0). Fertilizer should not contain weed killers. That's all you need to do until next spring, when it'll be time to turn your compost with a shovel or pitchfork. This will speed the decomposition process. Don't turn your compost pile in fall; doing so will allow heat to escape and keep internal temperatures too low for leaves to begin decomposing.

Trees for open areas

Common Name	Zones	Page
Deodar Cedar	6-9	79
Cedrus deodara		
Eastern Red Cedar	3-9	89
Juniperus virginiana		
Ginkgo	3-9	86
Ginkgo biloba		
Northern Red Oak	4-7	103
Quercus rubra		
River Birch	4-9	76
Betula nigra		
Saucer Magnolia	5-9	91
Magnolia x soulangiana		
Silver Maple	3-9	75
Acer saccharinum		
Southern Magnolia	6-10	90
Magnolia grandiflora		
Sugar Maple	4-8	75
Acer saccharum		
Sugarberry	5-9	80
Celtis laevigata		
Weeping Willow	4-9	104
Salix babylonica		

Shade trees

Common Name	Zones	Page
Fruitless American Sweetgum	5-9	90
Liquidambar styraciflua 'Rotundiloba'		
Green Ash	3-9	86
Fraxinus pennsylvanica		
Honeylocust	3-8	87
Gleditsia triacanthos inermis		
Japanese Zelkova	5-9	109
Zelkova serrata		
Littleleaf Linden	3-7	108
Tilia cordata		
Northern Red Oak	4-7	103
Quercus rubra		
Norway Maple	3-7	72
Acer platanoides		
Pin Oak	4-8	102
Quercus palustris		
Red Maple	3-9	74
Acer rubrum		
Redbud	3-9	81
Cercis canadensis		
Sargent Cherry	4-7	98
Prunus sargentii		
Saucer Magnolia	5-9	91
Magnolia x soulangiana		
Scarlet Oak	4-9	101
Quercus coccinea		
Shumard Oak	5-9	103
Quercus shumardii		
Silver Maple	3-9	75
Acer saccharinum		
Sugar Maple	4-8	75
Acer saccharum		
Trident Maple	4-8	71
Acer buergerianum		
White Oak	4-9	101
Quercus alba		
Willow Oak	4-8	102
Quercus phellos		
Yellowwood	6-8	82
Cladrastis lutea		

Accent trees

Common Name	Zones	Page
Amur Chokecherry	2-6	97
Prunus maackii		
Bradford Pear	4-8	100
Pyrus calleryana 'Bradford'		
Chinese Fringe Tree	6-8	81
Chionanthus retusus		
Downy Serviceberry	4-9	76
Amelanchier arborea		
European Mountain Ash	3-6	104
Sorbus aucuparia		
Flowering Dogwood	5-9	82
Cornus florida		
Ginkgo	3-9	86
Ginkgo biloba		
Japanese Flowering Crabapple	4-8	92
Malus floribunda		
Japanese Maple	5-8	73
Acer palmatum		
Japanese Snowbell	5-8	105
Styrax japonicum		
Japanese Stewartia	5-7	105
Stewartia pseudocamellia		
Japanese Tree Lilac	3-7	106
Syringa reticulata		
Kousa Dogwood	5-8	83
Cornus kousa		
Kwanzan Cherry	5-8	98
Prunus serrulata 'Kwanzan'		
Plumleaf Crabapple	4-9	92
Malus prunifolia		
Purple-Leaf Plum	4-8	97
Prunus cerasifera 'Atropurpurea'		
Quaking Aspen	2-6	96
Populus tremuloides		
Redbud	3-9	81
Cercis canadensis		
Sargent Cherry	4-7	98
Prunus sargentii		
Saucer Magnolia	5-9	91
Magnolia x soulangiana		
Savannah Holly	5-9	88
Ilex opaca 'Savannah'		
Skyrocket Juniper	4-8	89
Juniperus scopulorum 'Skyrocket'		
Star Magnolia	4-9	91
Magnolia stellata		
Sugar Maple	4-8	75
Acer saccharum		
Washington Hawthorn	3-9	83
Crataegus phaenopyrum		
Weeping Cherry	4-8	99
Prunus subhirtella 'Pendula'		

Streetside trees

Common Name	Zones	Page
Bradford Pear	4-8	100
Pyrus calleryana 'Bradford'		
Chinese Elm	5-9	109
Ulmus parvifolia		
Chinese Fringe Tree	6-8	81
Chionanthus retusus		
Dawn Redwood	4-8	93
Metasequoia glyptostroboides		
European Hornbeam	4-7	78
Carpinus betulus		
Fruitless American Sweetgum	5-9	90
Liquidambar styraciflua 'Rotundiloba'		
Ginkgo	3-9	86
Ginkgo biloba		
Green Ash	3-9	86
Fraxinus pennsylvanica		
Honeylocust	3-8	87
Gleditsia triacanthos inermis		
Japanese Flowering Crabapple	4-8	92
Malus floribunda		
Japanese Zelkova	5-9	109
Zelkova serrata		
Katsura Tree	4-8	80
Cercidiphyllum japonicum		
Kwanzan Cherry	5-8	98
Prunus serrulata 'Kwanzan'		
Littleleaf Linden	3-7	108
Tilia cordata		
Northern Red Oak	4-7	103
Quercus rubra		
Norway Maple	3-7	72
Acer platanoides		
Pin Oak	4-8	102
Quercus palustris		
Plumleaf Crabapple	4-9	92
Malus prunifolia		
Pyramidal Japanese Yew	4-7	107
Taxus cuspidata 'Capitata'		
Red Maple	3-9	74
Acer rubrum		
River Birch	4-9	76
Betula nigra		
Russian Olive	3-8	84
Elaeagnus angustifolia		
Saucer Magnolia	5-9	91
Magnolia x soulangiana		
Savannah Holly	5-9	88
Ilex opaca 'Savannah'		
Serbian Spruce	4-7	94
Picea omorika		
Shumard Oak	5-9	103
Quercus shumardii		
Sugarberry	5-9	80
Celtis laevigata		
Trident Maple	4-8	71
Acer buergerianum		
Washington Hawthorn	3-9	83
Crataegus phaenopyrum		
Willow Oak	4-8	102
Quercus phellos		

Kousa Dogwood (Cornus kousa) Page 83

Abies concolor

White Fir

Zones: 3-7

Light Needs:

Mature Size:

30'-50'

15'-30'

Growth Rate:
slow to medium

evergreen tree

Needs: Plant in rich, moist, well-drained, sandy loam soil. Trees will tolerate rocky or dry soil, but growth is slower. Tolerates heat and cold equally well. Grow in full sun. Plant in a location where you won't need to prune.

Good for: specimen tree use, windbreaks, screening, background, adding fine texture, winter interest, and blue color to landscape compositions

More Choices: pages 28, 32, 37, and 43

Grow White Fir where its bright, blue-tinted needles can show off against the sky or dark green plants. This easy-care tree keeps fresh foliage year-round and a conical shape throughout its life. This is the best fir for the Midwest and Eastern Seaboard. More tolerant of city conditions than other firs. Also known as Concolor Fir. Foliage is fragrant.

Abies fraseri

Frasier Fir

Zones: 4-7

Light Needs:

Mature Size:

30'-40'

20'-25'

Growth Rate:
slow

evergreen tree

Needs: Grow in full sun or partial shade. Plant in moist, well-drained soil. Trees tolerate drier soil, but young trees will require watering during the first few years until well established. Not tolerant of heat or excessive drought.

Good for: specimen use, winter interest, screening to add privacy or to block poor views, providing background for shrubs and other trees

More Choices: pages 28, 32, and 34

These easy-care evergreens offer a sweet evergreen fragrance in a classic Christmas-tree-shaped package. Frasier Firs are not picky about where they sink their roots; they will thrive in most ordinary, well-drained soils. Their only demand is that they are not planted in hot, dry locations. For a family activity that will bring joy for years to come, plant Frasier Firs in your yard and decorate them for the holiday season. The dark green foliage will also provide a backdrop to more colorful plants throughout the year. May be sold as Southern Balsam Fir.

Acer buergerianum

Trident Maple

Zones: 4-8

Light Needs:

Mature Size:

20'-30'
20'-30'

Growth Rate:
slow

deciduous tree

Needs: Plant in spring in well-drained, acidic soil. Provide full sun for best growth. Can grow in partial shade. Trees are drought tolerant. Position where low branches can spread naturally or remove limbs to allow room for walking or parking beneath trees. Make cuts in summer or autumn when sap flow is reduced.

Good for: shade tree use, lawns, planting along streets, near patios and decks, in small yards, containers, bonsai

More Choices: pages 32, 38, 67, 68, and 69

Plant this small, graceful tree to add summer shade and head-turning fall color to your yard or outdoor sitting area. Three-lobed foliage is glossy green during the summer months and turns on the color show later in the fall than other maples. Old trunks exfoliate to reveal shades of gray, brown, and orange. Known as a hard maple.

Acer tataricum ginnala

Amur Maple

Zones: 2-6

Light Needs:

Mature Size:

15'-18'
18'-20'

Growth Rate:
slow

deciduous tree

Needs: Grow in moist, well-drained soil, but will thrive in drier soils as well. Plant in full sun or partial shade. Prune in summer or fall to minimize bleeding sap. Can withstand heavy pruning. Easy to transplant.

Good for: planting beside patios or decks, entries, in front of blank walls, multi-stemmed specimen tree, containers

More Choices: pages 32, 34, 67, and 68

Options: 'Red Fruit' boasts large quantities of bright red-winged seeds
'Flame' has outstanding fall color

You can grow this hardy little maple as a traditional single-stemmed tree or in a multitrunk form. Trees grown in full sun develop the best fall color. Ornamental seed turns from green to red to brown in late summer and fall. Trees are pest-free and adaptable. They adapt well to life in above-ground containers. Known as a hard maple.

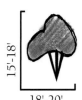

trees

4

Acer griseum

Paperbark Maple

Zones: 4-8

Light Needs:

Mature Size:

20'-30'

15'-30'

Growth Rate:
slow

deciduous tree

Needs: Plant in full sun in moist soil. Clay or well-drained soil is fine as long as moisture is available; these maples are not drought tolerant. Adapts to a wide range of soil pH. Transplant balled-and-burlapped or container-grown trees in spring. Exfoliating bark characteristic develops with age.

Good for: planting near patios and decks, lawn and speciman use, near flower beds, adding interest to winter scenes

More Choices: pages 32, 37, 41, 67, and 68

The cinnamon-colored bark on this maple peels away as the tree ages—the trunk looks as though it's covered with curly wood shavings. Snow cover provides an excellent foil for the winter interest this plant provides. Because it is slow-growing, plant this tree as soon as you begin your landscaping project. Three-lobed leaves possess a bluish-green color during the summer and develop a bronze or red color in the fall. Very ornamental. Known as a hard maple.

Acer platanoides

Norway Maple

Zones: 3-7

Light Needs:

Mature Size:

40'-50'

30'-40'

Growth Rate:
medium

deciduous tree

Needs: Plant in well-drained soil ranging from sandy to clay, acidic to alkaline. Hot, dry conditions and polluted air are no problem either.

Good for: lawn, street, and shade tree use in large areas

More Choices: pages 32, 34, 36, 37, 39, 41, 43, 67, and 69

Options: 'Crimson King'—slow growing, rich maroon-colored foliage
'Deborah'—new foliage emerges red and matures dark green; golden yellow in fall
'Royal Red'— maroon leaves turn bronze-red in autumn

'Crimson King'

Plant this tough tree for its large leaves that cast cooling shade in summer. Varieties are available with varying foliage colors and mature tree size. Roots can buckle nearby concrete. Grass doesn't grow well under its dense shade or shallow roots. Try this cultivar as well: 'Schwedleri'—new leaves are purple, turning dark green in summer and changing to gold in fall. Known as a hard maple.

Acer palmatum

Japanese Maple

Zones: 5-8

Light Needs:

Mature Size:

15'-20'

10'-15'

Growth Rate:
slow

deciduous tree

Needs: Plant in fertile soil that's moist but well-drained. Add compost at planting; mulch roots well to keep them cool. Grow in full sun or partial shade; protect selections with fine-textured leaves from afternoon sun in hotter climates. Grow green-leaved varieties in sun for brilliant fall color. Trees tolerate confined spaces if watered regularly.

Good for: specimen planting, accents and focal points, winter interest, patios, decks, entries, courtyards, understory trees, adding human scale, small gardens

More Choices: pages 34, 41, 67, 68, and 69

Options: 'Atropupurea'—red-purple summer foliage turns brighter red in autumn; medium-textured leaves
Upright—tree size:
'Bloodgood'—red-purple summer foliage turns brighter red in autumn; fine-textured leaves
'Linearilobum'—bright green, fine-textured leaves turn yellow in fall
'Burgundy Lace'—red-purple leaves, deeply cut for a lacy look
'Shishio'—new leaves and autumn foliage are red; summer leaves are green
var. heptalobum—broader leaves have coarser texture; green foliage turns bright orange to red in fall
'Sango Kaku'—green leaves with coral bark; good winter interest
'Oshio Beni'—bright red foliage during the growing season
Weeping—smaller size:
'Dissectum' (threadleaf)—very fine-textured foliage; mounding form
'Crimson Queen'—reddish purple leaves; fine-textured foliage
'Ever Red'—very fine-textured foliage, dark red-purple in color; mounding form
'Inaba Shidare'—red leaves
'Viridis'—green leaves

'Bloodgood'

Outstanding Features:

- Lacy leaves provide color and texture
- Sculptural form is graceful and elegant
- Small and neat with well-behaved roots

This tree is so graceful that it's an accent even in winter when it's as bare as a bone. Delicate leaves vary among named selections in shape, color, size, and texture; all are shaped somewhat like a hand. Green-leaved selections tend to have the best fall color, turning brilliant shades of orange, gold, or crimson. Trees are often multitrunked. Picturesque form shows best against solid backgrounds, such as walls or tall evergreen shrubs.

trees

4

Acer rubrum

Red Maple

Zones: 3-9

Light Needs:

Mature Size:

40'-50'

30'-40'

Growth Rate:
rapid

deciduous tree

Needs: Grow in any kind of soil, from alkaline to acidic, rich to poor, or wet to dry. Grow in full sun or partial shade. Water new trees regularly for the first growing season; after that, trees rarely need water. Tolerates heat and car exhaust.

Good for: shade trees, parking areas, street trees, lining long driveways, woodlands, patios, decks, fast-growing deciduous screens, beside ponds or creeks, boggy areas, hot, dry spots, natural areas

More Choices: pages 29, 34, 36, 38, 41, 59, 67, 68, and 69

Options: 'Autumn Flame'—leaves turn vivid red in early fall
'October Glory'—brilliant orange or red fall foliage
'Red Sunset'—foliage turns red in early fall
'Bowhall'—symmetrical, narrow canopy, yellow to red fall leaves
'Columnare'—narrow canopy about 10 feet wide, red fall foliage
'Indian Summer'—vigorous, very cold-hardy; leaves turn red-orange in fall

In the Zone

Pruning Red Maples

Most Red Maples never require pruning, but it's OK to remove low branches that are in the way. The best time to make cuts is in late fall or early winter when temperatures are cool. At this time of year, sap is not rising and trees won't "bleed" as heavily as they do if pruned in the spring or summer. Sap may ooze from pruning cuts for a year before the wounds heal. This is a normal response for many maples and will not kill the tree. However, it can be messy and attractive to insects.

Grow this tough native tree for a delicate blush of red in spring, leafy shade in summer, and brightly colored foliage in fall. Red Maples adapt to a variety of growing conditions. These trees grow naturally in swamps but are equally at home in a hot, dry parking area. Known as a hard maple.

Acer saccharinum

Silver Maple

Zones: 3-9

Light Needs:

Mature Size:

50'-70'
35'-50'

Growth Rate:
rapid

deciduous tree

Needs: Plant in full sun or partial shade. This tree tolerates a variety of soils, from acidic to alkaline and sandy loam to clay. Plant away from buildings, paving, and pipes.

Good for: shading, screening, adding quick shade and height to new yards while longer-lived trees mature; large open spaces

More Choices: pages 29, 32, 34, 36, 37, 38, 39, 59, 67, and 69

Options: 'Silver Queen'—oval form, bears fewer seeds; 'Skinneri'—stronger wood, deeply cut leaves

Outstanding Features:
- Grows quickly; transplants easily
- Large leaves cast abundant shade
- Grows in a variety of soil conditions

Plant a Silver Maple to provide quick shade in broad, open areas. Silvery-back leaves turn lemon yellow in autumn. Because of its rapid growth, wood is weak and trees will break apart during storms; keep trees away from powerlines or houses for this reason. Plant where roots can't invade septic or drainage systems. Keep roots away from paving. Short-lived compared to other maples. Known as a soft maple.

Acer saccharum

Sugar Maple

Zones: 4-8

Light Needs:

Mature Size:

60'-75'
40'-50'

Growth Rate:
slow

deciduous tree

Needs: Plant in acidic soil that's moist but well-drained; avoid compacted clay, wet soil, or city conditions. Grow in full sun or partial shade. Fall color is best in sun.

Good for: shade trees, lawn trees, lining driveways and streets, large open spaces, seasonal accent, natural areas, large estates, formal landscapes, mountainsides

More Choices: pages 32, 34, 38, 67, and 69

Options: 'Green Mountain'—thick, deep green foliage
'Bonfire'—grows slightly faster
'Green Column'—leaves turn yellow-orange

Outstanding Features:
- Leaves turn brilliant colors in autumn
- Oval canopy provides deep shade
- Long-lived, enduring, provides stability

trees

4

Leafy summer shade followed by traffic-stopping fall color makes Sugar Maple an excellent choice for growing in large lawns or in rows along streets or driveways. Roots require large open spaces rather than restricted growing areas. Plants will grow well in the cooler areas of Zone 8. Known as a hard maple. Try these cultivars: 'Legacy'—drought-resistant; 'Flax Mill Majesty'—faster growing, red-orange leaves.

Amelanchier arborea

Downy Serviceberry

Zones: 4-9

Light Needs:

Mature Size:

15'-25'

20'-30'

Growth Rate:
medium

deciduous tree

Needs: Plant in fertile, acidic soil that's moist but well-drained. Tolerates a variety of soil conditions. Grow in full sun or partial shade. Little or no pruning is required.

Good for: planting along edges of woods, natural areas, small yards, sideyards, perennial beds or near evergreens, accent, specimen use, use as a single or multi-stemmed small tree, attracting birds

More Choices: pages 32, 34, 38, 67, and 69

Outstanding Features:
- White, saucer-shaped flowers in spring
- Fruit ripens in early summer, attracts birds
- Fall leaves turn golden yellow to dusky red

This easy-care tree goes on display three out of four seasons. Spring brings white flowers, summer brings purple-black berries, and fall brings brightly colored foliage. Berries can stain paving but the birds usually take care of the fruit before that becomes a problem. Best used at the edges of woodlands or in naturalized settings. May be sold as Juneberry.

Betula nigra

River Birch

Zones: 4-9

Light Needs:

Mature Size:

40'-70'

40'-60'

Growth Rate:
rapid

deciduous tree

Needs: Plant in almost any soil from dry to soggy, poor or fertile. Acidic pH suits it best. Grow in full sun or partial shade. Prune only to remove obstructing low-hanging branches.

Good for: boggy areas, watersides, natural areas, beside patios and decks, along walkways, groves, open areas, deciduous screens, winter interest

More Choices: pages 29, 32, 34, 36, 37, 38, 59, 67, 68, and 69

Options: 'Heritage'—outstanding peely bark

Outstanding Features:
- Coarse-textured, peeling bark
- Fast-growing and adaptable
- Multiple trunks have instant presence

The best way to make a brand-new or flat landscape look better is to add a fast-growing tree. River Birch adds height, shade, and texture quickly. Peeling bark adds to its ornamental value throughout the year. River Birch is tolerant of a variety of growing conditions; it will even tolerate standing in water. Heat-tolerant too, this is the best birch tree for the South. Other birches become stressed when temperatures rise, making them more susceptible to damaging and potentially deadly pests. River Birch is NOT susceptible to borers; definitely an added landscaping bonus.

Betula papyrifera

Canoe Birch

Zones: 2-5

Light Needs:

Mature Size:

50'-70'

25'-40'

Growth Rate:
medium to rapid

deciduous tree

Needs: Plant in full sun in acidic soil that's moist but well-drained. This birch thrives in cool, northern climates and transplants easily. Plant where low branches are not a problem. Or, remove obstructing branches in summer or fall when sap flow is less and bleeding from cuts is reduced.

Good for: specimen tree use, planting in groves, natural areas, adding interest to winter landscapes, large yards

More Choices: pages 32, 38, 59, and 67

Outstanding Features:

- Peeling bark; reddish orange inner bark
- Adaptable to cool, moist locations
- Leaves turn yellow to orange in fall

When you plant a Canoe Birch, you're planting a piece of history. Native American Indians used the bark for making utensils, wigwam covers, and—hence the name—canoes. You'll want nothing more than to enjoy the beauty of its chalky white bark which peels away in papery layers. Canoe Birch is especially striking when planted against a backdrop of evergreens. The trees tower over 70 feet tall and add to fall's color show with leaves that turn shades of yellow and orange. Will not thrive in polluted areas. Also sold as Paper Birch.

Betula mandschurica japonica 'Whitespire'

Whitespire Birch

Zones: 4-7

Light Needs:

Mature Size:

30'-50'

20'-25'

Growth Rate:
medium to rapid

deciduous tree

Needs: Plant in acidic soil that's either moist or dry. Grow in full sun. Prune in summer or fall to prevent bleeding of sap. Plants are resistant to potentially deadly bronze birch borer infestations.

Good for: specimen tree, planting in groves, natural areas, adding winter interest, planting beside patios

More Choices: pages 32, 37, 38, 59, 67, and 68

Outstanding Features:

- Showy, chalk-white bark on trunks
- Yellow fall foliage adds seasonal interest
- Very resistant to bronze birch borer problems

The glossy, green leaves of this tree shimmer in summer breezes, turn yellow in autumn, and fall to reveal showy white branches in winter. Bark doesn't turn white until branches are about three to four years old. Bark does not peel like other species of Birch.

trees

4

Calocedrus decurrens

California Incense Cedar

Zones: 4-8

Light Needs:

Mature Size:
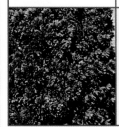
30'-60'
8'-10'

Growth Rate:
slow

evergreen tree

Needs: Plant in fertile soil that's moist or wet. Grow in full sun or partial shade. Trees don't like wind-swept or smoggy conditions, but they will survive the heat and humidity of the Southeast.

Good for: specimen use, windbreaks, planting in groves beside large lawns and formal estates

More Choices: pages 28, 32, 34, and 43

These trees stand like soldiers at attention, lending an air of formality to the large landscape. Their height complements the larger landscapes but may prove too large for small lots or single-story homes. Though it prefers moist sites, California Incense Cedar is adaptable to the heat and drought found in Southern growing areas. Makes a beautiful large specimen tree.

Carpinus betulus

European Hornbeam

Zones: 4-7

Light Needs:

Mature Size:
40'-60'
30'-40'

Growth Rate:
slow to medium

deciduous tree

Needs: Grow in full sun or partial shade and provide well-drained soil. Roots won't tolerate standing water. Plants are tolerant of acidic or alkaline soil pH.

Good for: parking areas, entries, street trees, including in small yards, lawns, near patios, in paving cut-outs, lining driveways, a high hedge

More Choices: pages 32, 34, 37, 38, 39, 41, 67, 68, and 69

Options: C. caroliniana (American Hornbeam)—multi-stemmed or single-stemmed tree; 20' to 30' tall by 40' to 50' wide; Zones 2-9

This small, adaptable tree is easy to grow. Branches are arranged around trunks like a spiral staircase to form dense, tidy canopies. Trees are pest- and disease-free. Foliage turns yellow in fall. Also look at 'Asplenifolia'—leaves are deeply lobed; 'Columnaris'—slow-growing columnar form, 30' tall by 20' wide; 'Fastigiata' (also sold as 'Pyramidalis')—vase-shaped tree, 30' to 50' tall by 20' to 40' wide.

Cedrus libani 'Glauca'

Blue Atlas Cedar

Zones: 6-9

Light Needs:

Mature Size:

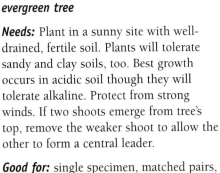

40'-60'

30'-40'

Growth Rate:
slow

evergreen tree

Needs: Plant in a sunny site with well-drained, fertile soil. Plants will tolerate sandy and clay soils, too. Best growth occurs in acidic soil though they will tolerate alkaline. Protect from strong winds. If two shoots emerge from tree's top, remove the weaker shoot to allow the other to form a central leader.

Good for: single specimen, matched pairs, large estates, background, screening, winter interest

More Choices: pages 28, 32, 36, and 37

Outstanding Features:
- Silvery blue needles provide color contrast
- Elegant branches sweep the ground
- Plants develop a picturesque form

Known for its sweeping branches and silvery blue needles, Blue Atlas Cedar grows to a majestic size and requires plenty of room to develop fully. Pruning to control size ruins the form of this tree. Allow a minimum of 30 feet of open space per tree. May grow 120' tall by 100' wide. Also try: 'Pendula'—weeping form.

Cedrus deodara

Deodar Cedar

Zones: 6-9

Light Needs:

Mature Size:

40'-70'

25'-30'

Growth Rate:
medium

evergreen tree

Needs: Plant in any well-drained or dry soil, from acidic to alkaline. Grow in full sun and provide protection from sweeping winds that can deform the tree.

Good for: specimen use, screening to block poor views and add year-round privacy, provide background for deciduous trees and shrubs, winter interest; large, open areas

More Choices: pages 28, 32, 36, 38, 39, and 69

Outstanding Features:
- Green foliage is silvery with hints of blue
- Pyramidal form; branches pendulous
- Tolerates dry soil that's alkaline or acidic

Even if you live where it's too hot to grow most wintery-looking evergreen trees, you can grow this one. Graceful Deodar Cedar tolerates heat and poor, dry soils. Trees make excellent specimen plantings with graceful, pendulous branching. As trees mature, they widen out and become flat-topped. Older trees also produce green cones that turn reddish brown at maturity. Cones take two years to mature. Also try: 'Aurea'—golden foliage.

trees

4

Celtis laevigata

Sugarberry

Zones: 5-9

Light Needs:

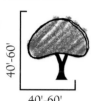

Mature Size:

40'-60'

40'-60'

Growth Rate: medium to rapid

deciduous tree

Needs: Plant in full sun to partial shade. Thrives in soils that are wet, dry, sandy, or heavy clay. Tolerates compacted and alkaline soils, as well as urban conditions. Easily transplanted and grown.

Good for: street and shade tree use, urban landscapes, floodplains, compacted soils, large, open areas, damp or boggy locations

More Choices: pages 32, 34, 36, 37, 39, 41, 67, and 69

Options: *C. occidentalis*—70' tall by 50' wide; Zones 2-9

Here's a tree that's tolerant of adverse conditions, forms a broad canopy, and features smooth gray bark on massive limbs. It grows quickly even in compacted, urban landscapes. Proper pruning when trees are young prevents problems in old age. Sometimes sold as Hackberry or Sugar Hackberry. Avoid planting trees near sidewalks and drives as roots may buckle paving.

Cercidiphyllum japonicum

Katsura Tree

Zones: 4-8

Light Needs:

Mature Size:

40'-60'

20'-30'

Growth Rate: medium to rapid

deciduous tree

Needs: Plant in full sun in soil that's well-drained and fertile. Grow in alkaline or acidic soils. Water young trees during periods of heat and drought. If several main stems emerge, prune the tree to a single trunk in late winter or early spring.

Good for: specimen use, patio areas, small yards, street trees, entries, courtyards, and parking areas

More Choices: pages 32, 38, 39, 59, 67, and 69

Outstanding Features:
- Leaves provide multi-season interest
- Roots will not disturb paving or sidewalks
- No special care; maintenance-free

Here's a tree anyone can grow. Its size fits well with small home landscapes. Foliage emerges a reddish color in the spring, matures to a blue-green hue, and turns red and gold in the fall, providing three-season interest. Fall color is best when grown in acidic soil. Fallen leaves smell of cinnamon or burnt sugar. Avoid planting in areas with northwestern exposure in the winter or where winds are extremely harsh.

Redbud

Zones: 3-9

Light Needs:

Mature Size:

20'-30'
25'-35'

Growth Rate:
medium

Outstanding Features:
- Purplish pink flowers appear before leaves
- Heart-shaped leaves turn yellow in fall
- Native tree proves tough and adaptable

deciduous flowering tree

Needs: Plant in any soil type from sandy to clay and soil pH from acidic to alkaline. Prefers dry over soggy soil. Grow in full sun to partial shade. Prune to remove dead wood and open the canopy for light penetration.

Good for: specimen, patio, understory, small lawn tree use, seasonal accent, in groundcover, shrub beds, woodland areas

More Choices: pages 29, 32, 34, 36, 37, 38, 39, 41, 59, 67, 68, and 69

Options: 'Alba'—white flowers 'Forest Pansy'—purple leaves in spring and fall

'Alba'

Spring arrives early if you have a Redbud in your yard. April blooms appear on trees just a few years old. Older trees actually form flower buds on tree trunks and provide a conversation topic through the entire neighborhood. Attractive, heart-shaped leaves turn yellow in fall; color quality varies with genetics and light. Tree trunks divide close to the ground and then develop graceful, ascending branches.

Chinese Fringe Tree

Zones: 6-8

Light Needs:

Mature Size:
10'-25'
8'-10'

Growth Rate:
slow to medium

Outstanding Features:
- Fragrant white flowers in late spring
- Adaptable to various growing conditions
- Small size and rounded form for accent use

deciduous flowering tree

Needs: Plant in full sun or deep shade in fertile soil that's wet or dry. Acidic soils are ideal, but alkaline conditions are tolerable. It can be grown as a small tree or large shrub. To grow as a small tree, prune away undesired stems in late winter or early spring. Trees are male or female.

Good for: specimen use, small yards, seasonal accent, empty corners, attracting birds, natural areas, planting beds

More Choices: pages 32, 34, 38, 67, and 69

Here's a pretty little tree that's covered with unusual-looking blooms in late spring. Fleecy-looking panicles are snow white in color. Male trees produce larger, showier blooms and no fruit. Females produce attractive flowers as well as ornamental fruit. Older plants produce ornamental bark that is gray to brown in color and peeling. Trees are not picky about growing conditions; they will tolerate almost anything. May be sold as Grancy Graybeard.

trees

4

Cladrastis lutea

Yellowwood

Zones: 6-8

Light Needs:

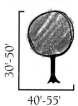

Mature Size:

30'-50'

40'-55'

Growth Rate:
medium

deciduous flowering tree

Needs: Plant in fertile, well-drained soil. Alkaline soils are ideal but not required. Shelter the tree from hot sun by planting in partial shade. This tree is not drought-tolerant and requires adequate moisture throughout the growing season. Protect from strong winds. Prune in the summer to reduce bleeding sap.

Good for: single specimen use or as a shade tree for small yards. Group several together for a grove of bloom. Plant near outdoor seating areas to enjoy the fragrance of flowers.

More Choices: pages 32, 34, 37, 67, 68, and 69

Outstanding Features:

- Dangling white flowers in late spring
- Coarse-textured leaves turn yellow in fall
- Upright form with spreading lower limbs

Fragrant blossoms appear to drip like white rain when this tree blooms in late spring and early summer. Foliage emerges a bright yellow-green in the spring and provides a nice contrast with the dark green leaves of maples and oaks. Fall color is yellow though not as outstanding as maple. Gray-colored bark is smooth and resembles beech bark. Try the cultivar 'Rosea' if you prefer pink flowers.

Cornus florida

Flowering Dogwood

Zones: 5-9

Light Needs:

Mature Size:

20'-25'

20'-25'

Growth Rate:
slow to medium

deciduous flowering tree

Needs: Plant in rich, acidic soil that's moist but well-drained. Grow in partial to dense shade. Trees bloom best in sun, but require afternoon shade in hotter climates unless watered regularly. Supply all dogwoods with extra water during droughts.

Good for: specimen trees, seasonal accents, understory plantings, natural areas, edges of woodlands, filling empty corners of yards, near patios, decks, or benches, corners of houses, attracting birds in fall and winter

More Choices: pages 34, 38, 39, 40, 41, 67, 68, and 69

Outstanding Features:

- Showy white flowers in early spring
- Scarlet fall leaf color followed by red fruit
- Graceful tiered branch habit; irregular form

Plant a single dogwood or several together to welcome spring with drifts of white. Flowers appear before the foliage. The leaves of these graceful trees turn varying shades of red to purple in autumn. Bare trees form interesting silhouettes in winter. Pink-flowering selections are not as heat-tolerant as white flowering cultivars. Try these cultivars: 'Cherokee Chief'—dark pink flowers and reddish-colored new foliage; 'Plena'—white, double flowers.

Cornus kousa

Kousa Dogwood

Outstanding Features:

- Pointy, white flowers in late spring
- Leaves turn bright scarlet in autumn
- Horizontal layers of foliage and flowers

Zones: 5-8

Light Needs:

Mature Size:

20'-30'

20'-30'

Growth Rate:
slow to medium

deciduous flowering tree

Needs: Plant in well-drained, acidic soil with some organic matter. Grow in partial shade or full sun with regular watering. Roots are shallow; all dogwoods will need extra water during droughts.

Good for: specimen trees, seasonal accents, courtyard and patios, edges of woodlands, natural areas, shrub and groundcover beds

More Choices: pages 32, 34, 38, 67, 68, and 69

Options: *C. alternifolia*—small white flowers, blue-black fruit, horizontal branching

Kousa Dogwood extends spring by blooming later than the flowering dogwoods. Horizontal layers of leaves are in place before the flowers appear. White in color, they remain attractive for more than six weeks. Edible, pinkish-colored fruit develops in late summer through fall. Fall foliage is eye-catching in shades of red and purple. Plant form and attractive peeling bark provide winter interest for the landscape. Named selections are more pest-resistant than many cultivars of *C. florida*.

Crataegus phaenopyrum

Washington Hawthorn

Outstanding Features:

- Clusters of white flowers in spring
- Leaves turn orange or red in autumn
- Red berries provide winter interest

Zones: 3-9

Light Needs:

Mature Size:

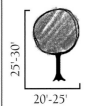

25'-30'

20'-25'

Growth Rate:
medium

deciduous flowering tree

Needs: Plant in any soil, from acidic to alkaline, dry to moist, or poor to fertile. Grow in full sun or partial shade. Tolerates urban pollution and paving. Remove low-hanging branches for clearance if desired. Avoid planting in high-traffic areas because of the thorns.

Good for: specimen trees, seasonal accents, natural areas, growing in clusters, attracting birds, winter interest, narrow spaces, and hedges

More Choices: pages 32, 34, 36, 38, 39, 41, 67, 68, and 69

Here's a small tree that isn't picky about its growing conditions. Plant a few anywhere you want to add year-round color in the yard. White flowers tinged with pink start off the spring season followed by glossy green summer foliage. Colorful fall foliage raises the curtain for red fruit that persists throughout the winter. Thorny twigs add fine texture during the winter as well.

trees

4

Trees 83

X Cupressocyparis leylandii

Leyland Cypress

Zones: 6-9

Light Needs:

Mature Size:

60'-70'

10'-15'

Growth Rate:
fast

evergreen tree

Needs: Grow in any soil that's well-drained. Plant in full sun and water regularly for fastest growth. Supply extra water during dry spells.

Good for: quick screening of unwanted views, provide privacy, evergreen background for deciduous trees and shrubs, tolerant of salt spray

More Choices: pages 28, 32, and 43

Options: If you can't water regularly, substitute Eastern Red Cedar, *Juniperus virginiana*, in areas with long, hot summers and sandy soils.

Outstanding Features:
- Dense, fluffy foliage stays green year-round
- Fast-growing; more than 3 feet a year
- Low maintenance; tolerant of soil extremes

Feathery foliage and columnar form make a graceful, airy addition to the landscape. Bluish green color provides interesting contrast. Leyland Cypress will block poor views or add privacy in a hurry. Perfect for use as a living fence. Trees may decline in hot climates without regular watering. Design tip: When planting a screen, stagger trees so they form a zigzag pattern. This will provide a thicker planting and add depth to the area.

Elaeagnus angustifolia

Russian Olive

Zones: 3-8

Light Needs:

Mature Size:

12'-20'

12'-20'

Growth Rate:
medium to rapid

deciduous tree

Needs: Plant in area with coastal winds, salty, poor soil and drought. This tough tree can actually be planted in any kind of soil except soggy. Grow in full sun. Prune after flowering for a rounded shape. Or, let trees grow naturally into irregular forms. Roots will not disturb paving.

Good for: coastal areas, Xeriscaping, patio trees, street trees (withstands road salt), specimen use, natural areas, entries

More Choices: pages 32, 38, 40, 59, 67, 68, and 69

Outstanding Features:
- Tolerates salt, drought, and wind
- Fragrant flowers in late spring, summer
- Silvery, gray-green foliage adds contrast

This tough tree takes cold, salt, wind, and dry soil. Foliage has silvery undersides and can't be beat for providing foliage contrast in the landscape. Trees add interest to areas enjoyed in the evening and tolerate troublesome areas. Tiny, yellowish flowers are fragrant. Keep plants growing vigorously for best performance.

American Beech

Zones: 3-9

Light Needs:

Mature Size:

50'-70'

50'-70'

Growth Rate:

slow to medium

deciduous tree

Needs: Plant in moist, well-drained, acidic soil. Avoid heavy clay or where construction equipment has compacted the planting site. Trees grow best in full sun or partial shade.

Good for: specimen use, woodland plantings, natural areas, attracting birds and wildlife, providing winter interest

More Choices: pages 32, 34, 38, and 67

Fagus sylvatica pendula

deciduous tree

True to its name, the branches of this tree grow downward, reaching nearly to the ground. Be sure to plant it where there's plenty of room for the spreading canopy to grow so you won't need to trim the gracefully weeping branches. Plant a single tree for an accent.

Zones: 5-7

Light Needs:

Mature Size:
60' tall, 40'-50' wide

Growth Rate:
medium

Fagus sylvatica 'Tricolor'

deciduous tree

Add an unusual touch of color to your landscape with a Tricolor Beech. The form of this tree resembles American Beech, but the foliage is distinctive. Leaves are dark purple with pinkish-white stripes and borders. For a weeping tree with solid purple leaves, choose *F. sylvatica* 'Purpurea Pendula'.

Also sold as *F. sylvatica* 'Purpurea Tricolor' or 'Roseomarginata'

Zones: 5-7

Light Needs:

Mature Size:
50'-60' tall, 35'-45' wide

Growth Rate:
medium

trees

4

Smooth gray trunks, golden fall foliage, and dried brown leaves that linger through the long winter months make American Beech an attractive landscape addition. Low, wide branching makes a beautiful specimen in large open areas. The root system is very shallow and the canopy dense; growing a thick stand of grass can be a challenge. Mulch instead for improved tree health and less work for you. Nuts are edible and enjoyed by several species of birds and squirrels.

Fraxinus pennsylvanica

Green Ash

Zones: 3-9

Light Needs:

Mature Size:

50'-60'

25'-30'

Growth Rate:
rapid

deciduous tree

Needs: Plant in soils ranging from acidic to alkaline, wet to dry, compacted or loose. Green Ash tolerates drought, reflected heat from paving, and car exhaust. Roots won't buckle paving.

Good for: providing shade; lining walkways, driveways, or roadsides; planting in open lawns and parking areas

More Choices: pages 29, 32, 36, 37, 38, 39, 41, 59, 67, and 69

Options: 'Marshall's Seedless'—rapid growth, seedless, insect-resistant *F. americana* Autumn Purple—purple to chocolate brown fall color

Outstanding Features:

- Transplants easily; fast-growing shade
- Leafy, spreading canopy turns yellow in fall
- Tolerates a range of growing conditions

Need shade? Grow Green Ash. This tree grows fast, lives a long life, and tolerates whatever growing conditions are thrown its way. Roots are well-behaved and will not buckle paving, though they will clog drains if given the opportunity. Trees are widely planted because of their ease of growth. Choose seedless varieties for less mess in the landscape. For a tree with a narrow, egg-shaped crown, choose 'Summit'.

Ginkgo biloba

Ginkgo

Zones: 3-9

Light Needs:

Mature Size:

50'-80'

30'-50'

Growth Rate:
slow

deciduous tree

Needs: Plant in a range of soils including acidic, alkaline, sandy, or clay. Ginkgo grows best in full sun. Trees are drought-resistant but grow faster with regular watering and a spring feeding of balanced fertilizer. No pruning is necessary except to remove lower limbs for clearance beneath the tree. Tolerates urban conditions, confined root spaces, heat, and cold.

Good for: specimen use, seasonal accents, street trees, lining walkways or drives, parking areas, open lawns, large estates

More Choices: pages 32, 36, 37, 38, 39, 41, 67, 68, and 69

Outstanding Features:

- Striking golden fall foliage color
- Adaptable, easy to grow, and pest-free
- Angular limbs, pyramidal to spreading form

Hold that rake; let the fallen leaves stay on the ground awhile. When Ginkgo's fan-shaped leaves turn golden in autumn, they hold their color even after dropping to the ground. This tree is considered one of the most attractive deciduous trees grown. Female trees produce messy fruit with an objectionable odor. There are several male clones available that do not produce fruit, including 'Autumn Gold' and the narrow-formed 'Fastigiata'.

Gleditsia triacanthos inermis

Honeylocust

Zones: 3-8

Light Needs:

Mature Size:

70'-100'

50'-70'

Growth Rate: rapid

deciduous tree

Needs: Plant in fertile, well-drained soil in full sun. Trees tolerate salt, drought, polluted air, and alkaline soils. Prune as needed to shape or remove dead wood.

Good for: shade, lawn, street, or specimen use; coastal areas, city conditions, areas prone to salting by winter road crews

More Choices: pages 32, 39, 40, 41, 59, 67, and 69

Options: 'Shademaster'—seedless, 30' to 45' tall and wide
'Skyline'—pyramidal shape, to 50' tall
'Sunburst'—conical shape, new leaves yellow, 40' tall by 30' wide

You can grow grass beneath this broad shade tree. Fine-textured leaves are yellow-green in spring, bright green in summer, and golden yellow in fall. The true Honeylocust tree has dangerous thorns present on the trunk. Named selections are all thornless and most are seedless as well. Select one with the growth habit you desire for your yard.

Ilex decidua

Possum Haw

Zones: 3-9

Light Needs:

Mature Size:

15'-25'

8'-20'

Growth Rate: rapid

deciduous tree

Needs: Plant in soil that's well-drained or swampy, acidic or alkaline. Provide a location with full sun or partial shade. Trees require little if any pruning; they look best when maintained in their naturally irregular form.

Good for: small specimen use, winter interest, natural areas, understory use, parking areas, soggy locations, courtyards and entries

More Choices: pages 32, 34, 37, 38, 39, 41, 59, 67, and 68

Options: 'Warren's Red'—upright form, profuse berries

This tough holly is different from most; it loses its leaves in the winter and grows well in swampy, alkaline soils. Irregular in form, the branches are horizontal and ascending. Yellow fall foliage color provides beautiful color contrast to the red fruit before dropping. Berries show off against bare branches providing winter interest for the landscape. Plant female trees in showy locations, but be sure to include a male tree nearby for pollination purposes.

trees

4

Ilex opaca 'Savannah'

Savannah Holly

Zones: 5-9

Light Needs:

Mature Size:

20'-25'
10'-15'

Growth Rate:
slow

evergreen tree

Needs: Plant in full sun or partial shade. Soil conditions should be fertile, acidic, moist, yet well-drained. Prune trees in the winter if they need shaping. Female plants produce showy red berries. Males are necessary for pollination. Plant one male for every two to three females.

Good for: specimen use, low-growing street tree, providing winter interest, patio plantings, parking areas, screening, background plantings in shrub beds

More Choices: pages 28, 32, 34, 37, 38, 41, 67, 68, and 69

Outstanding Features:

 Pyramidal form, yellow-green foliage
Prolific red fruit in winter
Tolerates air pollution and paving

This versatile holly produces bumper crops of berries that last from late fall through the winter. Trees have naturally pyramidal forms. Leave lower branches all the way to the ground or prune them to expose a portion of the trunk. Foliage is normally a yellow-green color; if leaves turn noticeably yellow, fertilize with acid-loving plant food.

Ilex x meserveae

Blue Holly

Zones: 5-8

Light Needs:

Mature Size:

10'-15'
8'-10'

Growth Rate:
slow

evergreen tree

Needs: Grow in fertile, moist soil with an acidic pH. Use a fertilizer formulated for acid-loving plants in the spring. Grows well in full sun and partial shade. Prune to shape in late winter or early spring. Both male and female plants are necessary for fruit production.

Good for: specimen use, screening poor views, privacy, winter interest, hedging, attracting birds

More Choices: pages 28, 32, 34, 38, and 67

Options: 'Blue Girl'—female, glossy blue-green foliage, abundant, bright red berries 'Blue Boy'—male pollinator, glossy leaves

Outstanding Features:

Lustrous blue-green foliage all year-round
Bright red winter berries on female plants
Neat, small size fits in with many landscapes

Glossy blue-green leaves earn this holly its name. Plant one male for every dozen female plants if you want the attractive, red berries. Protect plants from desiccating winter winds especially in colder climates. This is one of the most cold hardy of the hollies.

Juniperus virginiana

Eastern Red Cedar

Zones: 3-9

Light Needs:

Mature Size:

40-50'

8'-20'

Growth Rate: medium

evergreen tree

Needs: Grow in any soil from acidic to alkaline, sandy to clay, wet to dry. Plant in full sun for densest growth. Trees grown in partial shade will be more open. Tolerates wind, salt, and drought. Water new trees regularly the first year to help them establish.

Good for: screening, privacy, windbreaks, shelter belts, seaside landscapes, hillsides, natural areas, providing background for deciduous trees and shrubs, attracting birds, hedges, topiaries

More Choices: pages 28, 32, 36, 37, 38, 39, 40, 43, 67, and 69

Outstanding Features:
- Dense foliage stays green year-round
- Withstands wind, salt, and dry conditions
- Conical form becomes pendulous with age

Grow this durable native to block winds and screen poor views, provide a background for your garden, or to add needed privacy in the landscape. Trees are tough enough to plant at the beach and anywhere else you need their wide adaptability. Numerous cultivars are available with varying sizes, forms, and foliage color.

Juniperus scopulorum 'Skyrocket'

Skyrocket Juniper

Zones: 4-8

Light Needs:

Mature Size:

15'-20'

1'-2'

Growth Rate: slow

evergreen tree

Needs: Plant in full sun. This tree thrives in moist, well-drained soil but will grow in poor, dry soil, too. Tolerant of city conditions. Do not plant in soggy soil.

Good for: vertical accent, arid landscapes, hedges, screens, growing in groups as windbreaks, urban landscapes, Xeriscaping

More Choices: pages 28, 32, 36, 41, 43, and 69

Outstanding Features:
- Tolerant of wind and poor, dry, or rocky soil
- Narrow, pencil-shaped form for accent
- Silvery-blue color provides contrast

Don't despair if your soil is dry and rocky and your region is windy. None of these conditions will faze 'Skyrocket Juniper'. Sometimes sold as Rocky Mountain Juniper, 'Skyrocket' is a preferred selection chosen especially for its narrow upright form and silvery-blue coloration. Plants tolerate the harsh growing conditions of the Midwest. Growth may be limited in clay soils.

trees

4

Liquidambar styraciflua 'Rotundiloba'

Fruitless American Sweetgum

Zones: 5-9

Light Needs:

Mature Size:

60'-75'

40'-50'

Growth Rate:
medium

deciduous tree

Needs: Plant in full sun. Moist, slightly acidic soil is required for growth. Trees do not tolerate pollution, city life, or areas where their fleshy roots are limited. Remove lower branches in late winter if needed to walk or park beneath trees.

Good for: shading lawns, parking areas, or decks; street tree use

More Choices: pages 32, 38, 67, 68, and 69

Large lobed leaves turn various hues in fall, from yellow to red to dark purple. Young trees have a distinctly pyramidal outline that becomes more rounded as they mature. Neat in appearance, and because this variety is fruitless, it is neat all the way around. Give roots room to spread—avoid planting areas surrounded by paving. In milder climates, fall color may not be as showy as those that bear fruit. Also try *L. styraciflua*—produces spiny gumballs, bright fall foliage; *L. formosana*—leaves are five-lobed, tree shape is conical, bright fall foliage.

Magnolia grandiflora

Southern Magnolia

Zones: 6-10

Light Needs:

Mature Size:

50'-80'

30'-50'

Growth Rate:
slow to medium

evergreen flowering tree

Needs: Grows best in well-drained rich soil, but trees tolerate poor soils and wet locations. Soil should be acidic. Plant in full sun or partial shade. Protect from winter winds in northern areas.

Good for: specimen tree, open lawn areas, large estates, screening, soggy soil, espalier blank walls

More Choices: pages 28, 32, 34, 36, 37, 40, 67, and 69

Options: 'Bracken's Brown Beauty'— cold-tolerant, brown-backed leaves
'Little Gem'—shrubby form, small sizes
'D.D. Blancher'—tree with upright form

Everything about this magnolia is big—its size, its foliage, its flowers, and its fruit. Blooms up to 12 inches across appear in late spring emitting a scent better than almost any perfume. Rose red fruit ripens in late fall. Trees need plenty of room to grow and develop their stately form. Avoid planting this tree in small areas. Look for trees that are named; they are generally superior in strength and quality to unnamed varieties.

Magnolia stellata

Star Magnolia

Zones: 4-9

Light Needs:

Mature Size:

15'-20'
10'-15'

Growth Rate:
slow

deciduous flowering tree

Needs: Plant in moist, well-drained soil that's rich in organic matter and acidic. Mulch trees well and water regularly to keep soil moist during summer months. Grows best in partial shade. Plant in warmer parts of Zone 4.

Good for: small specimen trees, seasonal accent, foundation planting, narrow spaces, beside walkways or steps, natural areas, understory trees, woodlands, shaded courtyards

More Choices: pages 34, 38, 41, 67, 68, and 69

Outstanding Features:

- Fragrant, white starry blooms in early spring
- Neat, small size for foundation planting
- Green summer foliage turns yellow in fall

Starry white blooms brighten shady spots during the gray days between winter and spring. This tree stays small and tidy. This is the earliest-blooming magnolia. Planting on a northern exposure may delay flowering and reduce flower loss due to freezing temperatures. Trees look great planted against red brick walls and buildings.

Magnolia x soulangiana

Saucer Magnolia

Zones: 5-9

Light Needs:

Mature Size:

20'-30'
20'-30'

Growth Rate:
medium

deciduous flowering tree

Needs: Plant in rich soil high in organic matter. Slightly acidic soil is best, but trees tolerate some alkalinity. Mulch well and water regularly in summer to keep soil moist. Prune after flowering and only as needed because cuts heal slowly.

Good for: specimen use, seasonal accents, open lawn areas, large planting beds, groupings, near buildings

More Choices: pages 29, 32, 34, 37, 38, 41, 59, 67, and 69

Options: Northern Japanese Magnolia, *M. kobus*—blooms in midspring

Outstanding Features:

- Big, 5- to 10-inch flowers in early spring
- Coarse-textured leaves provide dense shade
- Sculptural form for specimen use

Big, beautiful blooms in shades of white to pink and purple accent this ornamental tree. Often jumping the gun on spring, it blooms during the slightest warm spell, often resulting in flower loss due to frost. Flowering occurs before leaves emerge. Planting on a northern exposure may help to delay flowering and reduce flower loss. Hybrids with girls' names bloom a bit later as well. Branches emerge low on the trunk and spread widely to form a crown with an attractive rounded outline.

Malus floribunda

Japanese Flowering Crabapple

Zones: 3-8

Light Needs:

Mature Size:

15'-25'

15'-25'

Growth Rate: medium

deciduous flowering tree

Needs: Plant in moist, well-drained, slightly acidic soil. Grow in full sun. Prune shoots to shape trees by late spring.

Good for: specimen use, small yards, seasonal accent, lining driveways, framing patios, low decks, or shrub beds

More Choices: pages 32, 39, 41, 67, 68, and 69

Options: Selections known for disease-resistance and persistent fruit include:
M. 'Pink Spires'—lavender-pink blooms
M. x *robusta* 'Red Siberian'—white blooms
M. 'Prairie Fire'—pinkish-red blooms
M. 'Red Splendor'—pink blooms, dark foliage turns reddish purple in fall

Outstanding Features:
- Scented flowers open before leaves
- Ornamental red fruit in fall
- Broad, rounded form; multitrunked

Crabapples are known for their spring beauty, especially when they burst into bloom. Japanese Flowering Crabapple has deep pink to red buds that open into fading white flowers. Developing fruits are yellow to red in color and add another season of show. They do not persist on the tree during the winter. This selection may be sold as Showy Crabapple. Numerous species, cultivars, and varieties of crabapples are available. Additional cultivars include M. 'Royalty'—crimson-purple blooms; M. 'Profusion'—purple-pink blooms; M. 'Spring Snow'—white blooms with no fruit.

Malus prunifolia

Plumleaf Crabapple

Zones: 3-8

Light Needs:

Mature Size:

10'-12'

10'-12'

Growth Rate: medium

deciduous flowering tree

Needs: Grow in full sun. A heavy loam soil that's well-drained, moist, and acidic is ideal, but trees will grow in sites less than ideal. Remove water sprouts—non-blooming, thin twigs growing straight up from main branches.

Good for: specimen use, lawn tree, seasonal accent, lining driveways, planting along fences, adding winter interest, attracting birds

More Choices: pages 32, 38, 41, 67, and 69

Outstanding Features:
- Pinkish buds open into white flowers
- Edible red fruit adds winter interest
- Small size and overall rounded shape

Spring brings clouds of fragrant, white flowers before leaves emerge on this tree. Red fruit dangles like holiday ornaments through winter snows. One-inch fruit can be messy. Avoid planting near patios and walkways. Rake away fallen leaves and fruit to help control apple scab disease.

Metasequoia glyptostroboides

Dawn Redwood

Zones: 4-8

Light Needs:

Mature Size:

70'-100'

20'-25'

Growth Rate:
rapid

deciduous conifer tree

Needs: Plant in moist—but not soggy—soil. Acidic soils are preferred over alkaline. Grow in full sun. Seldom requires any pruning.

Good for: large, open lawns or natural areas; groves, lining streets or long driveways, large estates

More Choices: pages 32, 37, 59, and 69

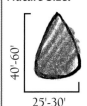

If you have room for a big tree, look no further. Dawn Redwoods can top 100 feet. Feathery foliage turns bronze in autumn before dropping. The large size of this tree will dwarf most single-story houses. Plant away from smaller buildings to avoid comparison or place near larger structures. Trunks of older trees develop buttressed, fluted bases and possess exfoliating bark.

Picea abies

Norway Spruce

Zones: 2-7

Light Needs:

Mature Size:

40'-60'

25'-30'

Growth Rate:
medium to rapid

evergreen tree

Needs: Plant in acidic soil that's moist but well-drained. Water diligently during the early years of growth. After establishment, spruces can tolerate drier conditions. Clean air is necessary. Plants require little pruning. Grows best in cool climates.

Good for: windbreaks, background planting, large specimen use, defining property lines, screening, large estates, sheltering wild birds

More Choices: pages 28, 32, 37, 38, and 43

Options: 'Aurea'—yellow-green needles

Spruce have the toughness and durability necessary to survive in colder climates. Wind and below zero temperatures are no problem for Norway Spruce. Trees grow to be quite large, so give them plenty of room from the start. Big cones, 4 to 6 inches long, persist on branches through winter. Also try: 'Pendula'—weeping shrub.

Picea glauca

White Spruce

Zones: 2-6

Light Needs:

Mature Size:

40'-60'

10'-20'

Growth Rate:
medium

evergreen tree

Needs: Plant in acidic soil that's moist but well-drained. Water diligently during the early years of growth. After establishment, spruces can tolerate drier conditions. Clean air is necessary. Little pruning is needed. Grow in full sun or shade.

Good for: windbreaks, large specimen trees, screening to add privacy or block poor views, tall hedges

More Choices: pages 28, 32, 34, 37, 38, and 43

Outstanding Features:

- Tolerates a wide range of harsh conditions
- Conical form adds formality in the yard
- Dense foliage stays green year-round

This tree withstands wind, heat, cold, shade, and drought—all the growing conditions found in the Plains States. No wonder it thrives there. Trees can tolerate overcrowding and transplant easily. Dense foliage stays green year-round. Cones are less than two inches long, green at first, then turning brown upon maturity.

Picea omorika

Serbian Spruce

Zones: 4-7

Light Needs:

Mature Size:

50'-70'

10'-20'

Growth Rate:
slow

evergreen tree

Needs: Grow in full sun or partial-shade. Plant in soil that is deep, rich, and moist but well-drained. Acidic or alkaline soil conditions are fine. Protect from strong winds, especially in cold winter climates. Very adaptable and tolerates city air.

Good for: tall, narrow specimen tree, mass plantings in large yards, winter interest

More Choices: pages 28, 32, 34, 38, 39, 41, and 69

Options: 'Nana'—8' to 10' high, conical to irregular in outline

Outstanding Features:

- Narrow, pyramidal shape; graceful outline
- Tolerates alkaline soils and city air pollution
- Evergreen foliage adds winter interest

Growing much taller than it does wide, this graceful spruce stands like a spire in the landscape. It withstands a variety of soil types, pH levels, and air pollution. Branches droop down near the trunk and turn up slightly at the ends. Cones are about 2 inches long, bluish-black when young, and ripen to a cinnamon brown color. Trees can reach heights of 100' or more with time.

Picea pungens glauca

Colorado Blue Spruce

Zones: 2-7

Light Needs:

Mature Size:

30'-60'
10'-20'

Growth Rate:
slow

evergreen tree

Needs: Grow in full sun. Trees grow best in rich, moist soil. They will tolerate dry soil conditions.

Good for: large specimen use, winter interest, windbreaks, grouping beside long driveways or in the corners of large yards, screening, sheltering wild birds

More Choices: pages 28, 32, and 43

Options: 'Koster'—silvery foliage 'Hoopsii'—blue-white needles; dense, pyramidal form

Outstanding Features:

- Blue to blue-green needles year-round
- Dense branches extend to the ground
- Adaptability to a range of soil conditions

The blue foliage color of a Colorado Blue Spruce is attractive year-round. The degree of blueness can vary from tree to tree. Compare the colors and select the trees that fit your needs. Blue tree color can conflict with house colors. Select the color appropriately or plant trees away from the house. Cones grow two to four inches long.

Pinus strobus

White Pine

Zones: 3-8

Light Needs:

Mature Size:

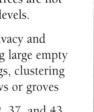

50'-80'
20'-40'

Growth Rate:
rapid

evergreen tree

Needs: Plant in any well-drained soil; trees thrive in many extremes except heavy clay soil. Grow in full sun. Trees transplant easily into the landscape. Trees are not tolerant of high pollution levels.

Good for: screening for privacy and blocking poor views, filling large empty areas, background plantings, clustering together or planting in rows or groves

More Choices: pages 28, 32, 37, and 43

Outstanding Features:

- Fluffy, soft needles have a bluish hue
- Grows quickly for screen and hedge use
- Full-skirted, graceful pyramidal form

It's hard to find a screening tree that grows as quickly or is as pretty as White Pine. Bluish green needles are three to five inches long, soft, and touchable. Given room to grow, trees may reach 150 feet in height. They can also be sheared for hedging use. Allow fallen needles to accumulate as water-conserving, weed-controlling mulch. Water during dry spells. In colder areas, protect from sweeping winds and road salt. Also try: 'Nana'—dwarf globe white pine, a rounded shrub.

trees

4

Pinus thunbergii (also listed as Pinus thunbergiana)

Japanese Black Pine

Zones: 5-7

Light Needs:

Mature Size:

20'-80'

20'-25'

Growth Rate:
medium

evergreen tree

Needs: Plant in fertile soil that's moist but well-drained. Will grow on sandy soils. Grow in full sun. Plants are salt tolerant.

Good for: seaside landscapes, specimen use, windbreaks, screening, Japanese gardens, bonsai, stabilizing sand dunes

More Choices: pages 28, 32, 36, 37, 40, 43, and 67

Options: 'Oculus-draconis'—needles striped with yellow bands

Outstanding Features:
- Irregular, sculptural form
- Needles stay dark green year-round
- Tolerates salt spray and sandy soil

The sculptural, irregular form of Japanese Black Pine suggests a dainty garden, but this tree is tough enough for growing at the beach. This pine will tolerate salt and sand. Prune to emphasize bonsailike form, if desired in the landscape. Knock heavy snow off branches to prevent them from breaking.

Populus tremuloides

Quaking Aspen

Zones: 2-6

Light Needs:

Mature Size:

40'-50'

20'-30'

Growth Rate:
rapid

deciduous tree

Needs: Grow in full sun or part shade. Trees grow best in well-drained, fertile soil but will grow in any soil that isn't waterlogged.

Good for: accent use, groves, natural areas, hillsides, new construction areas

More Choices: pages 32, 40, 59, 67, and 69

Outstanding Features:
- Leaves shake and shimmer in the breeze
- Leaves turn a brilliant golden yellow in fall
- Transplants easily and grows quickly

When breezes blow, the leaves of Quaking Aspen shake, shimmer, and whisper in the wind. Yellow autumn leaves are showy against silvery trunks. Trees are very adaptable to a range of growing conditions and fast-growing. Unfortunately they are short-lived. The usual life span is under 35 years.

Prunus cerasifera 'Atropurpurea'

Purple-Leaf Plum

Zones: 4-8

Light Needs:

Mature Size:

15'-30'

15'-25'

Growth Rate:
rapid

deciduous flowering tree

Needs: Plant in any soil that is well-drained. They will not tolerate wet feet. Trees aren't particular about soil pH. Grow in full sun for best color development. Prune after flowering. Keep plants growing vigorously for best pest resistance.

Good for: specimen trees, seasonal accent, lining driveways, patio trees, planting in clusters at entries to property, groves

More Choices: pages 29, 32, 38, 39, 41, 59, 68, and 69

Options: 'Thundercloud'—dark pink, fragrant flowers; deep purple foliage; 20' high and wide; Zones 5-8.

Outstanding Features:
- Light pink flowers in early spring
- Dark purple foliage in summer
- Grows quickly to provide seasonal color

Fast growth and colorful foliage makes Purple-Leaf Plum a popular plant for landscapes. Pink flowers appear in early spring before the foliage; spring foliage emerges ruby-red, changing to the summer color of dark purple. Trees are usually short-lived, surviving about 20 years under good growing conditions. Trees spread by suckering. Plant them where you can easily control sucker growth through mowing or pruning. Purple foliage may clash with some house colors Also try: 'Versuvias'—double light pink flowers, purple foliage; *P.* x *blireana*—ruffled pink flowers, greenish-red foliage.

Prunus maackii

Amur Chokecherry

Zones: 2-6

Light Needs:

Mature Size:

35'-45'

20'-25'

Growth Rate:
medium to rapid

deciduous flowering tree

Needs: Plant in well-drained soil in full sun or partial shade. Naturally rounded canopy needs little or no pruning.

Good for: specimen use, seasonal accent, adding winter interest, attracting birds, fall color

More Choices: pages 32, 34, 59, 67, and 69

Outstanding Features:
- Shiny, cinnamon-colored, peeling bark
- Dense racemes of white spring flowers
- Thrives in cold regions of the country

It seems the colder the better for this spring flowering tree. White flowers are followed by small fruits ripening to black in August. Birds love them. Fruit can stain paving; avoid planting near walkways or patios. Yellow fall color completes the growing season display. The ornamental features of this tree don't end with leaf drop; shiny, cinnamon-colored bark brightens drab winter scenes. As trees mature, the bark exfoliates, providing additional winter interest.

trees

4

Prunus sargentii

Sargent Cherry

Zones: 4-7

Light Needs:

Mature Size:

40'-70'

40'-50'

Growth Rate:
medium to rapid

deciduous flowering tree

Needs: Plant in well-drained soil in full sun or partial shade. Prune to shape trees only as needed in late winter or early spring.

Good for: specimen tree, seasonal accent, shade or lawn tree use, planting near corners of large houses, attracting birds

More Choices: pages 32, 34, 67, and 69

Options: 'Columnaris'—narrow, columnar form; 40' high by 10' wide
P. x yedoensis—Yoshino Cherry features fragrant flowers

These trees combine beauty with usefullness for a tree suitable for almost any landscape. Pink flowers appear in mid- to late-spring followed by glossy, crimson-colored fruit. The foliage emerges with a red tinge and turns a dark, glossy green during the summer. Orange-red fall foliage completes the fall wardrobe. Trees possess shiny, reddish-brown bark that's pretty during winter months. Avoid planting near areas where fruit may stain paving.

Prunus serrulata 'Kwanzan'

Kwanzan Cherry

Zones: 5-8

Light Needs:

Mature Size:

30'-40'

30'-40'

Growth Rate:
medium to rapid

deciduous flowering tree

Needs: Plant in moist, well-drained soil. Grow in full sun. Protect from harsh wind. Trees are naturally vase-shaped (spreading upward like a "V") and require little or no pruning to keep them that way.

Good for: specimen use, lawn trees, street trees, patio trees, seasonal accents, courtyards, groves

More Choices: pages 32, 67, 68, and 69

Options: 'Mt. Fuji'—pink buds, white flowers; 20' high by 25' wide; spreading 'Shirofugen'—pink buds, white flowers that fade back to pink, leaves deep bronze at emergence; 25' high by 30' wide

Welcome spring to your yard with the pink, double blooms of Kwanzan Cherry. This tree boasts glossy, coppery-colored bark and bright fall foliage, too. This tree may also be sold as Japanese Flowering Cherry. Kwanzan is a particular selection. Selected varieties are often grafted onto *P. avium* rootstock. Trees grow quickly and are often short-lived in the landscape.

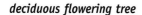

Prunus subhirtella 'Pendula'

Weeping Cherry

Zones: 4-8

Light Needs:

Mature Size:

20'-40'

15'-30'

Growth Rate:
medium to rapid

deciduous flowering tree

Needs: Plant in well-drained soil. Grow in full sun or partial shade. Prune to shape trees as needed after bloom.

Good for: specimen tree use, accent, courtyards, entries, near patios and decks, Japanese gardens

More Choices: pages 32, 34, 67, 68, and 69

Options: 'Yae-shidare-higan'—pink, double flowers are long-lasting 'Autumnalis'—semi-double pink blooms appear in fall as well as in early spring

Outstanding Features:
- Rounded, weeping form for speciman use
- Pink flowers in early spring before foliage
- Green leaves turn golden yellow in fall

Each cascading branch of this tree is covered with pink flowers in spring and golden leaves in fall. Cherrylike red fruit ripens to nearly black. Bare weeping stems are attractive in winter. Plants make excellent specimen plantings in the landscape. Avoid planting near areas where fruits might drop and stain paving. Varieties are usually grafted about four to six feet high on *P. avium* rootstock.

Pseudotsuga menziesii

Douglas Fir

Zones: 4-6

Light Needs:

Mature Size:

40'-80'

12'-20'

Growth Rate:
medium

evergreen tree

Needs: Plant in well-drained, moist soil with an acidic pH. Trees will not tolerate dry, poor soils or windy conditions. Grow in full sun.

Good for: specimen use, large groves, corners of yards, large estates, screening views, mass plantings

More Choices: pages 28, 32, and 38

Options: 'Fastigiata'—very upright, conical shape; 40' to 80' high, spread to 20' var. *glauca*—needles are blue-green; 40' to 80' high, spread 12' to 20' 'Oudemansii'—15' to 30' high, spread 12' to 20'

Outstanding Features:
- Classic, pyramidal shape; impressive size
- Evergreen needles stay fresh year-round
- Pendulous cones are light brown in color

Plant this stately tree where it will have room to grow up to its fullest potential. Slightly curving branches grow in pyramidal fashion. A traditional forest tree that makes the transition to the landscape beautifully. Trees are not suitable for use in windbreaks. May be sold as *P. douglasii*.

trees

4

Pyrus calleryana 'Bradford'

Bradford Pear

Zones: 4-8	***deciduous tree***

Light Needs:

Mature Size:

30'-50'

20'-35'

Growth Rate:
rapid

Needs: Plant in any soil that's well-drained and receives full sun. Trees tolerate city conditions including polluted air and reflected heat from paving. Roots are well-behaved and won't buckle paving. Prune in late winter or early spring.

Good for: parking, lawns, and street trees, specimens, patios, courtyards, entries, lining driveways, growing in large planting beds, providing seasonal accent

More Choices: pages 29, 32, 41, 59, 67, 68, and 69

Outstanding Features:
- ✔ Uniform shape like big lollipops
- ✱ White spring flowers before leaves
- 🍂 Foliage turns shiny scarlet to purple in fall

Bradford Pear combines all the features desired in an ornamental tree—rapid growth, spring bloom, summer shade, no fruit, and autumn color. See below for pruning information that will help minimize winter damage. Tends to be weak-wooded. Flowers have an unpleasant odor. Look at these cultivars as well for use in the landscape. 'Aristocrat'—less prone to splitting, 30' to 35' high, 20' to 25' wide; 'Capital'—fall leaves coppery, 40' high, 15' wide; 'Chanticleer'—less susceptible to freeze damage than 'Bradford', 30' high, 20' wide; 'Cleveland Select'—blooms very young, 30' to 35' high, 20' wide.

Pruning Bradford Pear

These ornamental pear trees are known for their uniformly shaped canopies. Pruning is essential to keep trees from splitting apart during icy weather.

STUFF YOU'LL NEED

✔ Pruning saw
✔ Work gloves

What to Expect
You may be advised by tree companies to flat-top your Bradford Pears, but that's not the best pruning method for these trees.

1 **To remove branches,** make the first cut with a pruning saw from the underside of the branch, about a foot from the trunk. Saw about a third of the way through. This cut stops the branch from ripping and splitting the bark.

2 **Make the second cut** about an inch farther along the branch than the first one. Cut from the top of the branch until it comes off cleanly.

3 **Place the saw against the joint** where the branch attaches to the trunk, known as the branch bark ridge. Don't cut into this ridge. Instead, remove the remaining foot-long branch stub by cutting upward from the bottom.

4 **Watersprouts are shoots that grow** straight up from branches. They cross other branches, rubbing against them and catching high winds. Remove them with loppers or hand pruners.

Quercus alba

White Oak

Zones: 4-9

Light Needs:

Mature Size:

80'-100'+
50'-80'

Growth Rate:
slow to medium

deciduous tree

Needs: Plant in acidic soil that's moist and well-drained. Grow in full sun. Avoid planting in areas where construction has compacted soils. Make any pruning cuts in late winter or early spring.

Good for: shade trees, large specimen trees, natural areas, woodlands

More Choices: pages 32, 37, 38, 67, and 69

Outstanding Features:
- Purple fall color, leaves remain on tree
- Spreading canopies provide dense shade
- Long-lived, durable tree in the landscape

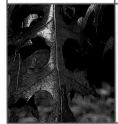

Large landscapes deserve at least one White Oak to provide generations of leafy shade. Dark green summer foliage turns in the fall to a reddish wine and finally to brown. Leaves are large, coarse, and may remain on the tree throughout the winter. Wood is sturdy.

Quercus coccinea

Scarlet Oak

Zones: 4-9

Light Needs:

Mature Size:

70'-75'
40'-50'

Growth Rate:
medium to rapid

deciduous tree

Needs: Plant in acidic soil that's moist and well-drained. It will tolerate dry, sandy soils. Grow in full sun. Prune in late winter or early spring to prevent spread of disease.

Good for: shade tree, large specimen tree, lawn tree, natural areas, woodland landscapes

More Choices: pages 29, 32, 59, 67, and 69

Outstanding Features:
- Rounded, spreading canopies with age
- Leaves turn bright red in fall
- Impressive size is best suited for large areas

For dense summer shade and bright fall color, add Scarlet Oak to your yard. Trees grow to an impressive size that works well with multistory homes and buildings. Young trees have a pyramidal form with a strong central leader and pendulous lower branches that drop off as the tree matures.

Quercus palustris

Pin Oak

Zones: 4-8

Light Needs:

Mature Size:

60'-70'

25'-40'

Growth Rate:
rapid

deciduous tree

Needs: Plant in moist, acidic soil—dry soil is OK, but not alkaline. Grow in full sun or partial shade. Endures confined roots, reflected heat from paving, and air pollution.

Good for: shade and street tree use, lining driveways, parking areas, urban conditions, parks, and golf courses

More Choices: pages 29, 32, 34, 36, 37, 38, 41, 59, 67, and 69

Outstanding Features:

✔ One of the fastest-growing oaks

Tolerates a range of difficult conditions

Pyramidal form; pendulous branches

In acidic soils there is nothing better than Pin Oak for a big, fast-growing shade tree. Roots won't buckle paving. Foliage turns scarlet in fall; brown leaves remain until spring. Surround with shade-tolerant groundcover, mulch, or paving; shade is too dense for a nice lawn. Remove lower branches for parking or walking beneath trees. Iron chlorosis is a common ailment of trees grown in alkaline soils. It is difficult to nearly impossible to remedy on a long-term basis. Select another tree species more suited to alkaline locations.

Quercus phellos

Willow Oak

Zones: 4-8

Light Needs:

Mature Size:

40'-60'+

30'-40'

Growth Rate:
rapid

deciduous tree

Needs: Grow in fertile, moist acidic soil. Wet clays and loams are not a problem. Trees will tolerate dry, slightly alkaline soil though not the ideal. City conditions don't pose a problem. Transplants easily.

Good for: large specimen, shade, and street tree use; lining long driveways; large patio trees

More Choices: pages 29, 32, 37, 38, 39, 41, 43, 59, 68, and 69

Outstanding Features:

Fine-textured foliage; unusual in large trees

Wide, shady canopy; oval form with age

✔ Behaved roots won't buckle paving

Majestic in size, this oak is big enough to shade your house and your landscape. Long narrow leaves provide fine-textured appearance different from most oaks. Leaves turn varying shades of yellow in the fall. Remove lower limbs to park or walk beneath your tree safely. Iron chlorosis may develop in alkaline soils. Check your pH before planting. Acorns produce numerous seedlings for transplanting.

Quercus rubra

Northern Red Oak

Zones: 4-7

Light Needs:

Mature Size:

60'-80'

50'-70'

Growth Rate:
rapid

deciduous tree

Needs: Plant in acidic soil that's moist but well-drained. Easy to transplant because it doesn't produce a taproot. Tolerates polluted city air. Plant in full sun.

Good for: shade and street tree use (in sites not confined by paving), specimen trees, large estates, open areas

More Choices: pages 32, 38, 41, 59, 67, and 69

More Choices: pages 32, 38, 41, 59, 67, and 69

Outstanding Features:

Glossy leaves turn dark red in fall

Tolerates Midwest growing conditions

Dense, rounded canopy provides shade

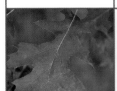

Though it's native to many parts of the United States, Northern Red Oak grows particularly well in the Midwest. Trees produce large, rounded canopies upon maturity. New foliage has a pinkish or reddish color when unfolding, turning dark green in summer. Foliage is coarse-textured and lobed. Fall color varies from dark to bright red depending on environmental conditions. Trees produce dense shade; it may be difficult to grow grass beneath the leafy canopies.

Quercus shumardii

Shumard Oak

Zones: 5-9

Light Needs:

Mature Size:

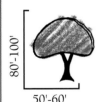

80'-100'

50'-60'

Growth Rate:
rapid

deciduous tree

Needs: Plant in soil that's acidic or alkaline, well-drained or damp. Grow in full sun. Roots won't buckle paving. Tolerates reflected heat and air pollution. Easy to grow.

Good for: shade, lawn, or street tree use, lining long driveways, parking areas, large patios, natural areas, damp locations

More Choices: pages 29, 32, 38, 39, 41, 59, 67, 68, and 69

More Choices: pages 29, 32, 38, 39, 41, 59, 67, 68, and 69

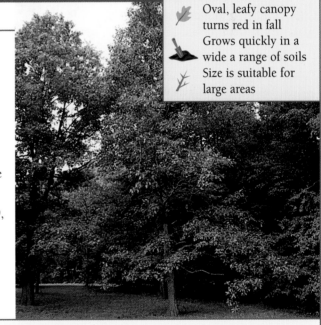

Outstanding Features:

Oval, leafy canopy turns red in fall

Grows quickly in a wide a range of soils

Size is suitable for large areas

If you need a shade tree that's tough, try this one; it'll grow just about anywhere. Shumard Oaks feature big canopies and red fall color.

trees

4

Salix babylonica

Weeping Willow

Zones: 4-9

Light Needs:

Mature Size:

30'-40'

30'-40'

Growth Rate:
rapid

deciduous tree

Needs: Plant in soil that's wet or dry, fertile, or poor. Lush, fast growth occurs when grown in moist locations. Grow in full sun. Leaves will shed prematurely during droughts.

Good for: specimen trees, beside ponds or streams, damp, boggy areas, hillsides, large spaces

More Choices: pages 32, 37, 40, 59, and 69

Options: 'Niobe'—golden bark

Outstanding Features:

- Pendulous branches sweep the ground
- Grows quickly to provide screening
- Large, dramatic form in the landscape

If you have a large pond, you need a weeping willow to reflect on the water's surface. Streamerlike stems dangle to the water; roots love the soggy soil. Roots are invasive; don't plant this tree near waterlines, swimming pools, drain lines, or septic fields. Though they grow quickly, trees may be short-lived. Leaves, twigs, and branches drop frequently resulting in the need for constant cleanup.

Sorbus aucuparia

European Mountain Ash

Zones: 3-6

Light Needs:

Mature Size:

30'-50'

15'-25'

Growth Rate:
medium

deciduous flowering tree

Needs: Plant in fertile soil that's moist but well-drained. Neutral to acidic soil is best. Grow in full sun or partial shade. This tree thrives where summers are cool. Plants are not tolerant of summer heat or drought.

Good for: specimen use, seasonal accent, patio trees, courtyards, entries, attracting birds to the landscape

More Choices: pages 32, 34, 37, 38, 40, 67, 68, and 69

Options: *S. decora* (Showy Mountain Ash)—white flowers, red berries, orange-red fall foliage; Zones 3-8

Outstanding Features:

- Clusters of white flowers in spring
- Orange-red berries in summer
- Fine-textured leaves; attractive in fall

Three seasons of color make this tree a good choice for cooler climates. White spring flowers are followed by orange-red summer fruit and finally by yellow-red fall foliage. The scent of the flowers is unpleasant to some. Birds love the fruit and consume it as quickly as it ripens. Available as single or multitrunked trees.

Stewartia pseudocamellia

Japanese Stewartia

Zones: 5-7

Light Needs:

Mature Size:

30'-40'

20'-25'

Growth Rate:
slow

deciduous flowering tree

Needs: Plant in acidic soil that's moist but well-drained. Add composted leaves or peat to the soil at planting time; fertilize with acid-loving plant food in spring. Grow in full sun or partial shade. Provide shade during the hottest part of the day in warm climates.

Good for: specimen use, seasonal accents, patio trees, entries, courtyards, small areas, planting in shrub or perennial beds, providing winter interest

More Choices: pages 32, 34, 38, 67, 68, and 69

Outstanding Features:
White, camellialike blossoms in summer
Fall foliage color; yellow, red, to purple
Smooth, peeling bark adds winter interest

This slow-growing tree provides year-round interest in the landscape. Green spring and summer foliage, summer blooms, excellent fall color, and peeling bark make its slow growth worth the wait. Trees form an oval to pyramidal crown. Grows in the milder areas of Zone 5.

Styrax japonicum

Japanese Snowbell

Zones: 5-8

Light Needs:

Mature Size:

20'-30'

15'-25'

Growth Rate:
medium

deciduous flowering tree

Needs: Plant in fertile, acidic, well-drained soil; water regularly to keep soil moist. Add organic matter to the soil before planting. These will not tolerate extreme heat or drought. Grow in full sun or partial shade. Position plants in protected areas in cold climates. Prune to shape into small trees by removing shrubby branches from the base of plants.

Good for: specimen tree use, seasonal accents, hillsides, entries, beside patios or outdoor seating areas, planting beds, and mixed borders

More Choices: pages 32, 34, 38, 40, 67, 68, and 69

Outstanding Features:
Slender, smooth trunks have sculptural form
Clusters of bell-like flowers in late spring
Dark green leaves turn red or yellow in fall

If you can find it, buy it. This sculptural tree features bells of white flowers in May and June followed by red or yellow fall leaves. Leaves perch on the stems like butterflies and do not hide the pendulous blooms. These trees should be planted more frequently, especially when soil conditions are appropriate. Also sold as Japanese Snowdrop Tree.

Syringa reticulata

Japanese Tree Lilac

Zones: 3-7

Light Needs:

Mature Size:

20'-30'

15'-25'

Growth Rate:
medium

deciduous tree

Needs: Plant in well-drained, slightly acidic soil. Grow in full sun for best bloom. Remove spent flowers to keep plants looking neat. Prune unwanted branches in late winter or early spring. This tree thrives where summers are cool.

Good for: small specimen trees, seasonal accents, entries, patios, planting beside the corners of houses, planted in groups for screening and as backgrounds to deciduous shrubs and perennials

More Choices: pages 32, 38, 67, 68, and 69

Options: 'Summer Snow'—compact, rounded crown; profuse flowers

A Japanese Tree Lilac in bloom is a sight to see. Covered with snowy white flowers, the dark leaves provide the ideal backdrop. Trees thrive in areas with cold winters and cool summers. The flower show may be stronger on alternate years. Bark is a glossy, reddish-brown color. Additional varieties to consider include 'Ivory Silk'—flowers appear on younger plants and 'Regent'—abundant flower production, uniform shape.

Outstanding Features:
- Creamy white flowers early to midsummer
- Dark green, heart-shaped leaves
- Resistant to borers, scale, and mildew

Taxodium distichum

Bald Cypress

Zones: 4-10

Light Needs:

Mature Size:

50'-70'

20'-30'

Growth Rate:
rapid

deciduous conifer tree

Needs: Grow in soil that's poor and dry, rich and moist, or just plain wet. Acidic soils are preferred; chlorosis develops on alkaline sites. Grow in full sun. Plants are very wind tolerant.

Good for: wet areas, compacted soils of newly constructed homes, streetside use, natural areas, beside ponds or streams, swampy sites, specimen use

More Choices: pages 29, 32, 36, 37, and 59

This swamp native can tolerate the extremes: from soggy soils to hot areas surrounded with paving. Trees form towering cones of feathery foliage. Bright green spring foliage matures to a soft, sage green in summer; fall color is a rusty brown before dropping. Trunks become buttressed with age. When grown in water or in damp, marshy spots, trees develop knobby, protruding roots known as knees. Cones are green to purple in color and mature to brown in a single growing season.

Outstanding Features:
- Fine-textured, feathery foliage; rusty fall color
- Tolerates adverse growing conditions
- Conical form and massive trunk

Taxus cuspidata 'Capitata'
Pyramidal Japanese Yew

Zones: 4-7

Light Needs:

Mature Size:

30'-40'

20'-25'

Growth Rate:
slow

evergreen tree

Needs: Plant in any type of soil that's well-drained. This yew will grow in either sun or shade. Tolerates the dust and smoke of the city. Prune as much or as little as you like, whenever you like, to shape plants into dense green canopies.

Good for: coastal areas, dry shade, city conditions, high hedges, screening to provide privacy or to block poor views, creating an evergreen background

More Choices: pages 28, 32, 34, 36, 40, 41, and 69

Outstanding Features:
- Dense evergreen foliage for screening
- Tolerates a range of harsh conditions
- Naturally pyramidal form tolerates pruning

This evergreen tree can survive nearly any type of growing condition—except standing water. Dense, needlelike leaves remain dark green throughout the year. They make dense, year-round screens for privacy or to block unwanted views.

Thuja occidentalis
American Arborvitae

Zones: 2-8

Light Needs:

Mature Size:

40'-60'

10'-15'

Growth Rate:
slow to medium

evergreen tree

Needs: Plant in full sun in moist, well-drained soil; tolerates alkaline soils well. Protect from winter winds, snow, and ice. Prune to shape shrubs during the warm season.

Good for: specimen shrub, screen, foundation planting, anchoring the corner of planting beds

More Choices: pages 30, 34, 39, 41, and 45

Options: 'Emerald'—narrow, pyramidal shrub or small tree; leaves stay bright green through winter; 10' to 15' high, 3' to 4' wide; Zones 3-8

'Emerald'

Outstanding Features:
- Easy to prune into desired shape
- Tolerates a variety of soil conditions
- Excellent used for screening and privacy

These low-care evergreens come in an assortment of shapes and sizes. There's easily one to fit every landscape setting. Many varieties have good foliage color throughout the winter months. Heavy snow or ice can break shrubs; knock snow away with a broom when it occurs. Also try: 'Pyramidalis'—narrow pyramidal shape; new leaves bright green; 12' to 15' high, 3' to 4' wide; Zones 3-8; 'Techny'—slow-growing, pyramidal form, 15' high, green all year.

trees

4

Tilia cordata

Littleleaf Linden

Zones: 3-7

Light Needs:

Mature Size:

60'-70'

30'-50'

Growth Rate:
medium

deciduous tree

Needs: Plant in any soil that's moist, including acidic or alkaline, fertile or poor. Trees can withstand the compacted soils of new construction as well as pollution and paving. Grow in full sun.

Good for: lawn, specimen, shade, and streetside use; parking areas, lining driveways, formal landscapes, patio trees

More Choices: pages 32, 37, 38, 39, 40, 41, 67, 68, and 69

Outstanding Features:
- Shiny, heart-shaped leaves; yellow in fall
- Pyramidal canopies are uniformly shaped
- Tolerates urban growing conditions

This tree's uniform shape makes it a good choice for planting in neat rows or squares and to add symmetry to the landscape. Glossy green foliage turns yellow-green in fall. Small summer flowers aren't showy but they're fragrant. Several cultivars are available that differ in form and growth rate. Trees can be grown in the warmer parts of Zone 3.

Tsuga canadensis

Canadian Hemlock

Zones: 3-7

Light Needs:

Mature Size:

40'-70'

25'-35'

Growth Rate:
medium

evergreen tree

Needs: Plant in acidic soil that's moist but well-drained. Grow in sun or partial shade in areas protected from the wind. Water new trees for two growing seasons to ensure good establishment. Afterwards, water during severe droughts. Trees are not tolerant of pollution.

Good for: screening, background, hedging along property lines, natural areas, woodlands, mountainsides, large estates

More Choices: pages 28, 32, 34, 38, 43, and 67

Options: 'Pendula'—slow-growing; gracefully drooping branches

Outstanding Features:
- Pyramidal form in youth and old age
- Fine-textured foliage lasts year-round
- Low maintenance once established

Give your garden a look reminiscent of a cool, green mountainside by planting Canadian Hemlock. They will form a screen concealing undesirable views or a backdrop for other shrubs in the planting bed. Plants can tolerate heavy pruning and are often planted in hedges. Trees look best when lower branches can remain in place all the way to the ground.

Ulmus parvifolia

Chinese Elm

- Disease-resistant and fast growing
- Suitable for shading in small areas
- Mottled bark provides seasonal interest

Zones: 5-9

Light Needs:

Mature Size:

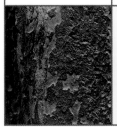

35'-45'
20'-25'

Growth Rate: rapid

deciduous tree; evergreen in frost-free areas

Needs: Plant in moist, loamy soil for best results, though trees will also grow in dry, sandy, or alkaline soils. Grow in full sun. Roots will not buckle paving. Trees endure heat, drought, and pollution.

Good for: shading small areas such as decks, patios, courtyards, and entries; streetside use, parking areas, sideyards, narrow spaces, urban landscapes

More Choices: pages 29, 32, 36, 39, 41, 59, 67, 68, and 69

Options: 'Sempervirens'—pendulous canopy 'Drake'—good heat tolerance

This just may be the ultimate patio tree. Its small size, neat habit, fast growth, and leafy shade make it ideal for sitting areas. Dark green summer foliage changes to yellow and finally to reddish purple in the fall. Ample root system makes growing grass beneath this tree difficult. Bark is a mottled combination of gray, green, orange, and brown. Very ornamental.

Zelkova serrata

Japanese Zelkova

- Upright branches and form similar to elms
- Thick, shady canopy; coarse-textured leaves
- Yellow, orange, or reddish fall foliage

Zones: 5-9

Light Needs:

Mature Size:

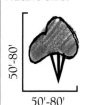

50'-80'
50'-80'

Growth Rate: medium to rapid

deciduous tree

Needs: Plant in fertile soil that's moist but well-drained. Soil pH isn't a problem. Trees grow in acidic or alkaline soils. They tolerate wind and drought once established. Reflected heat from paving and pollution don't pose a problem. Prune as needed to keep limbs overhead.

Good for: street, shade, and lawn tree use, lining walkways or drives, beside decks, entries, or patios

More Choices: pages 29, 38, 39, 41, 59, 67, 68, and 69

Consider this tree as a replacement for the disease-prone American Elm. Leafy shade, upright branches, and sturdy trunks make it perfect for patios, yards, or lining streets. Tree trunks exfoliate in old age, revealing colorful inner bark. Plants are resistant to many of the insects and diseases that plague elms.

trees

4

Chapter 5
shrubs

*Graham Thomas Rose
(Rosa Graham Thomas)
Page 156*

Shrubs add beauty to your landscape throughout the seasons. Plant groupings of the same shrubs together to show them at their best. For year-round interest, choose shrubs with various seasonal characteristics for grouping in different areas of your yard.

*Burning Bush
(Euonymus alatus)
Page 136*

Depend on Shrubs

Whether you're new to landscaping or have been working in your yard for years, this chapter helps you select, plant, and care for shrubs. The following pages offer tips and techniques. Landscaping decisions are a challenge because of the variety of available shrubs. But this chapter—complete with selection guides listing shrubs for specific purposes and growing conditions—makes it easier to buy the right shrub, plant it in the right place, and keep it thriving.

Provide the Framework

Rely on shrubs to supply the framework your landscape needs. Shrubs define spaces and hold the composition together. Use them to establish unity (see pages 12-13), provide background, screen unwanted views, complement your house, enhance privacy, and provide attractive accents. The selection guides help you select a palette of shrubs to beautify your landscape. They also provide ideas about solving problems identified when you made your site analysis. The guides match plants to the growing conditions of your yard and orchestrate a changing seasonal show of form and color.

Prepare to Purchase

After you've chosen your shrubs for planting, you'll need to determine their arrangement in your planting beds. Start by finding out the growth rate and mature plant size. Shrub descriptions begin on page 126. Knowing these facts helps you space your shrubs correctly. As a general rule, set plants so that the distance between them—measuring from the center of one plant to the center of the next plant—is equal to or slightly less than the plant's mature spread. This gives shrubs room to grow and provides the desired massed effect without large gaps at maturity. Space slow-growing species a little closer together.

On paper, draw your planting beds to scale. Fill in with circles also drawn to scale and touching slightly that represent your plants at maturity. Remember, they won't touch at planting time. Count the circles to determine how many shrubs of each type you will need before going to the store.

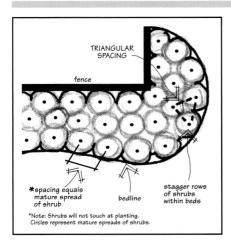

TRIANGULAR SPACING

fence

*spacing equals mature spread of shrub

bedline

stagger rows of shrubs within beds

*Note: Shrubs will not touch at planting. Circles represent mature spreads of shrubs.

Prepare to Plant

Arrange shrubs in the actual planting bed while still in their containers. You can finalize their spacing without worrying about shrubs drying out. (Always remove pots just before planting. Take only one plant out of its pot at a time.) First, position shrubs to follow the bedlines. This reinforces the shape of the bedline you spent so much time designing. Next, place shrubs in the back of the bed to follow elements that define this area, such as a fence or the wall of your home. Finally, fill the center

Wisdom of the Aisles

Plan before you plant.

Placing plants correctly in the landscape is just as impor-tant as choosing the right ones. If this step has got you stumped, consider hiring a designer to help. Always ask to be taken to view completed landscapes before agreeing to design fees. Show the designer yards that you like, too. Landscape architects are professionals licensed to prepare plans to guide planting, grading, and construction. Garden designers aren't licensed but usually have a love of plants. (Expect to pay more for a plan produced by a landscape architect than for one drawn by a garden designer.) Design/build contractors will usually provide free designs as long as you hire them to do the work.

by setting a second row behind the shrubs following the bedline. Stagger their placement in a triangular pattern (see diagram) so that no two shrubs line up. Work front to back, making adjustments and rearranging rows to avoid gaps. Before digging holes, move containers around until you're completely satisfied. Turn each shrub so that its best side faces the most important angle of view. Professionals take time with this phase. You should, too. You'll live with your decisions for a long time.

Combining potted and planted shrubs will make easy changes of pattern and color.

Shrubs for Hedges

Hedges are as functional as they are great-looking.
Will yours be formal or informal, tall growing for screening and privacy or low growing for outlining a planting bed? Use this list to help guide your selections. On the pages referenced, look for photos and information about shrubs that include your growing zone.

Common Name	Zones	Page	Common Name	Zones	Page
Andromeda	5-8	151	Iceberg Rose	4-9	157
Pieris japonica			*Rosa 'Iceberg'*		
Arnold's Red Tatarian Honeysuckle	3-9	148	Japanese Barberry	4-8	129
Lonicera tatarica 'Arnold's Red'			*Berberis thunbergii*		
Baby's Breath Spirea	2-8	162	Japanese Boxwood	6-9	130
Spiraea thunbergii			*Buxus microphylla japonica*		
Betty Prior Rose	4-9	155	Korean Boxwood	5-9	131
Rosa 'Betty Prior'			*Buxus microphylla koreana*		
Border Forsythia	6-9	137	Manhattan Spreading Euonymus	4-8	137
Forsythia x intermedia			*Euonymus kiautschovicus 'Manhattan'*		
Bridalwreath Spirea	5-8	162	Margo Koster Rose	5-8	157
Spiraea prunifolia			*Rosa 'Margo Koster'*		
Carefree Beauty Rose	4-8	155	Miss Kim Lilac	3-7	164
Rosa Carefree Beauty			*Syringa patula 'Miss Kim'*		
Common Lilac	3-7	165	Mountain Pieris	4-8	151
Syringa vulgaris			*Pieris floribunda*		
Coralberry	4-7	163	Northern Bayberry	2-6	149
Symphoricarpos orbiculatus			*Myrica pensylvanica*		
Cornelian Cherry	4-8	134	Northern Lights Azalea	4-7	128
Cornus mas			*Azalea 'Northern Lights'*		
Cutleaf Lilac	4-8	164	Parson's Juniper	3-9	145
Syringa x laciniata			*Juniperus chinensis 'Parsonii'*		
Dwarf Burford Holly	6-9	141	Peace Rose	5-8	158
Ilex cornuta 'Bufordii Nana'			*Rosa 'Peace'*		
Edging Boxwood	6-8	131	Persian Lilac	3-7	164
Buxus sempervirens 'Suffruticosa'			*Syringa x persica*		
Exbury Azalea	4-7	127	Pink Meidiland Rose	5-8	158
Azalea 'Exbury Hybrids'			*Rosa Pink Meidiland*		
Fru Dagmar Hastrup Rose	2-9	156	Redtip Photinia	6-9	149
Rosa 'Fru Dagmar Hastrup'			*Photinia x fraseri*		
Glossy Abelia	6-9	126	Rosa Rubrifolia	4-9	159
Abelia x grandiflora			*Rosa rubrifolia*		
Golden Vicary Privet	5-8	148	Serviceberry	4-5	126
Ligustrum x vicaryi			*Amelanchier alnifolia*		
Graham Thomas Rose	5-9	156	Shrubby Cinquefoil	2-7	152
Rosa Graham Thomas			*Potentilla fruticosa*		
Gray Dogwood	4-7	134	Tam Juniper	3-7	146
Cornus racemosa			*Juniperus sabina 'Tamariscifolia'*		
Green Beauty Boxwood	5-9	130	Vanhoutte Spirea	3-8	162
Buxus microphylla 'Green Beauty'			*Spiraea x vanhouttei*		
Green Lustre Japanese Holly	4-6	142	Winterberry	3-9	144
Ilex crenata 'Green Lustre'			*Ilex verticillata*		
Hick's Upright Yew	4-7	166	Yukon Belle Firethorn	4-9	154
Taxus x media 'Hicksii'			*Pyracantha angustifolia Yukon Belle*		

Availability varies by area and conditions (see page 21). Check with your garden center.

Shrubs 5

Well-chosen shrubs marry the house to the yard, making the architecture a natural fit with the land.

Foundation Planting

Plants growing close to your house are known as foundation plantings. Their primary functions are hiding the base of the house and connecting your home to the rest of the landscape. Shrubs provide numerous options for dressing up your home. Break out of the old mold— think about ways other than planting a straight hedge across the front of your home.

Include publicly visible sideyards in your foundation planting plans.

Bedlines First
Your house should seem nestled into the landscape. For all but the most contemporary styles of architecture, which might call for angular lines, smoothly curving bedlines soften the straight lines of houses. This complements architecture, making houses become part of their settings.

Start planning your foundation planting by designing the bedline (see pages 44-45). A design plan results in a much more attractive project than if you limit yourself to following the shape of the house or keeping an old landscape. After drawing a rough sketch for the bedlines around your home, take a

step back and look at your house. You'll want to enhance attractive features such as windows, stone chimneys, and the front-door area. Things you wish you didn't see— exposed foundations, meters, blank walls, and dingy siding—are candidates for screening.

Next, go inside your home and look out the windows. Do you keep the blinds shut to block glare or provide privacy? Use landscaping to solve such problems. Windows that you frequently look through should offer an attractive view. It's important that everyday living spaces such as the kitchen, breakfast room, and den have views. Make notes about what you see from them. If there's nothing to look at, it's time to add fresh landscaping for an attractive view. Remember this as you fine tune your sketches of bedlines, making the necessary adjustments.

Filling Beds Shrubs are the primary ingredient of most foundation plantings. If properly selected, they fit well beneath windows and grow together to form neat groups. Groups of shrubbery, known as masses, grow to form a single unit where individual plants are not noticed. Massing shrubs complements house size better than separate plants do. Resist the urge to prune each shrub into an individual plant; instead, let the shrubs grow together and trim only as needed to shape the mass.

Position shrubs in foundation plantings to follow bedlines, not the house. Fill curved beds with a curving arrangement of plants. If you already have a straight-line foundation planting, add more of the same shrubs in front of the hedge to stagger its shape. Then, add front layers of shorter plants arranged to follow the bedlines. Let the architecture of your house influence where you put accent plants. Fill in niches, frame attractive windows and doors, or add charming touches to porch posts and walls with trees, shrubs, groundcovers, and vines. (See page 203 to select appropriate vines that will grow on your home without damaging it.)

Foundation Shrubs

Select shrubs that include your range within their zones. Then, find more information on the pages specified. You'll need to know the mature size, rate of growth, and natural form of any plant you select to grow near your house. Don't choose naturally arching plants if what you want is a tightly clipped look.

Shrubs for foundation planting

Common Name	Zones	Page	Common Name	Zones	Page
Carefree Beauty Rose *Rosa Carefree Beauty*	4-8	155	Inkberry *Ilex glabra 'Compacta'*	3-9	143
Carolina Azalea *Azalea carolinianum*	4-9	127	Japanese Barberry *Berberis thunbergii*	4-8	129
Catawba Rhododendron *Rhododendron catawbiense*	4-8	154	Korean Boxwood *Buxus microphylla koreana*	5-9	131
Common Witch Hazel *Hamamelis virginiana*	3-8	138	Korean Spice Viburnum *Viburnum carlesii*	4-8	167
Compact Japanese Holly *Ilex crenata 'Compacta'*	5-8	143	Large Fothergilla *Fothergilla major*	4-8	138
Cornelian Cherry *Cornus mas*	4-8	134	Little Giant Arborvitae *Thuja occidentalis 'Little Giant'*	3-7	166
Cornell Pink Azalea *Azalea mucronulatum 'Cornell Pink'*	4-7	128	Mountain Laurel *Kalmia latifolia*	4-9	147
Dwarf Burford Holly *Ilex cornuta 'Burfordii Nana'*	6-9	141	Northern Bayberry *Myrica pensylvanica*	2-6	149
Exbury Azalea *Azalea 'Exbury Hybrids'*	4-7	127	Northern Lights Azalea *Azalea 'Northern Lights'*	4-7	128
Glossy Abelia *Abelia x grandiflora*	6-9	126	Otto Luyken Laurel *Prunus laurocerasus 'Otto Luyken'*	6-8	153
Golden Vicary Privet *Ligustrum x vicaryi*	5-8	148	Sea Green Juniper *Juniperus chinensis 'Sea Green'*	4-8	145
Gray Dogwood *Cornus racemosa*	4-7	134	Shrubby Cinquefoil *Potentilla fruticosa*	2-7	152

Availability varies by area and conditions (see page 21). Check with your garden center.

Some trees are not good near your home. Trees that grow large or have weak wood or invasive roots are poor choices for foundation planting. However, many small ornamental trees are just right for creating attractive focal points seen from main windows. They also offer a sense of shelter to people nearing your house along a walkway. The need to establish a transition between indoor and outdoor spaces is important, too; the sheltering effect of small trees helps do just that. Lastly, well-placed small trees help bring tall, multistory homes into human scale, making people feel more comfortable coming to your door.

Underplant such trees with shrubs and groundcovers to give your foundation planting a layered look that's sure to be an improvement over the single-row hedge style. Layers of shorter plants help to define your bedline plan and wrap your home with broad sweeps of plantings. Build a framework of evergreen plants for a solid background that enhances your home year-round to provide an anchor for landscape composition. Deciduous shrubs and small trees as well as annuals and perennials can be added in the foreground.

The foundation planting complements the casual, shingled style of this home.

Planting a Container Shrub

Planting shrubs correctly isn't difficult. Follow these steps to give your new plant the best possible start. Don't worry if you have an entire bed to fill. The more shrubs you plant, the more efficient and quicker you'll become at planting them.

STUFF YOU'LL NEED

✔ Sharpshooter or round-point shovel
✔ Topsoil or decomposed organic matter, such as compost
✔ Bagged gypsum for heavy clay soil

Optional:
✔ Tarp for collecting soil
✔ Wheelbarrow for mixing backfill soil
✔ Garden gloves

What to Expect

Workers hired to dig these holes might try to talk you out of making the holes wide. Remain firm and your shrubs will thrive as a result.

1 **Pick a spot to plant your new shrub.** Make sure growing conditions match the needs of your plant. There should be enough space around the area for the shrub to grow undisturbed for many years to come.

Dig a hole twice as wide as the plant's container. This will give roots room to grow into the good, loosened soil before venturing through into native soil. Dig the hole only as deep as the container is tall to prevent planting too deep.

2 **Carefully remove the shrub from its plastic pot and lay it on the ground.** (Don't tug on the plant to pull it out.) If the roots are pot-bound, use the shovel blade to score the root ball. The root ball should retain the container's shape. Scoring encourages feeder roots to grow beyond the root ball, establishing the plant faster. If your plant seems loose, cut away the bottom and set the plant in the hole. Slice the sides and gently remove the pot. This will help prevent damage to young roots.

In the Zone

New plants need daily watering for the first few weeks, especially during hot weather.

In cooler seasons, you can water every other day for the first week. After that, cut back to once a week for 2 to 3 months, then reduce to once a month, until shrubs have weathered a full growing season. Water faithfully unless nature supplies at least one-half inch of water during the week. Once established, properly sited plants will need supplemental water only during hot, dry spells.

3 **Set the shrub in the hole to check the depth.** The top of the root ball—where stems emerge from the soil— should be level with the surface of the undisturbed ground around the hole. If your shrub sits too low, the hole is too deep. Planting your shrub at this level causes stems to rot. Remove the plant and shovel additional soil into the bottom of the hole. Press loose soil firmly to prevent settling later. Put the plant into the hole to check the depth again. If the top of the root ball sits too high, remove the plant and dig the hole deeper. An exception to this step occurs when planting in heavy clay soils. In these locations, plant shrubs an inch or two higher than the level of the undisturbed soil to prevent water from collecting around roots.

Wisdom of the Aisles

Handling Your Shrub

▲ **Good** Always carry new plants by their nursery containers.

▲ **Not Good** Holding shrubs by their branches can stress and break roots and stems.

4 **Mix topsoil or composted organic matter** with the soil you dug from the hole, usually at a ratio of 1:1. In areas with high rainfall and heavy clay soil, reduce the amount of organic matter in the mix to 4:1.

Shovel the mixed soil around the plant, filling the hole completely. Don't tamp the soil in place because that can destroy porosity. Water to settle the soil. Add additional soil mixture as needed after settling .

Use excess soil to form a moat 3 to 4 inches high around the perimeter of the hole. Pat it firmly in place to keep water from running off the inside surface.

Good idea! → **Put the Best Face on Things.** Before backfilling, turn your shrub so that its best side is facing the direction from which it will be viewed. Once the dirt's in the hole, it's harder to adjust the shrub's direction.

5 **Mulch the area inside the moat with a 2- to 3-inch layer of organic mulch.** Mulching retains moisture, cools the soil, and prevents weeds around the plant. Hay, pine straw, ground bark, compost, or shredded leaves are ideal. (Avoid bark nuggets, which float and wash away.) Use less mulch around stems. Mulch that fills the crotches of low stems can cause fungal problems

Water your new shrub thoroughly. Lay a garden hose at the base of the plant and turn the water on to a gentle stream. Fill the moat slowly several times, letting water soak in.

Planting Shrubs on Slopes

Shrubs should always be planted upright, even if they're on sloping ground. Most upright stems will naturally reach for the vertical position as they grow, even if they have to bend to do so. Dig holes for shrubs on sloping sites much the way you would on a level site. Make sure plants are positioned straight up and down once they are placed in the hole. Build the soil moat only on the downhill side of the plant. The top of the moat should be level with the uphill soil. This prevents water from rushing down past the shrub before getting a chance to soak in. If your soil is heavy clay, omit the moat, but build up the soil to form a level planting area before setting your new shrub in place.

Shrubs 5

Pruning Evergreen Shrubs

Hold those clippers! There are things you need to know before pruning your evergreen shrubs.

First, determine what types of evergreens you have planted. Needled evergreens have needles surrounding plant stems. They may be short or long, soft or stiff depending on the plant. Broad leaf evergreens have leaves ranging from the large leaves of rhododendrons to the small leaves of boxwood.

Pruning Style

Next, decide if the plant is going to or should have an informal or formal look. Plants informally pruned are not sheared into shapes the way shrubbery in formal gardens often are. Both needled and broad leaf evergreens can be pruned to maintain a naturalistic, informal style. Shrubs with small leaves and naturally compact forms are good choices for shearing into a formal style, as are many needled shrubs.

STUFF YOU'LL NEED

✔ Hand pruners for pencil-thick branches
✔ Loppers for bigger branches
✔ Hedge trimmers for shearing
✔ Sharpening stone
✔ Garden gloves

What to Expect

If you find it necessary to trim your shrubs late in the growing season, don't be surprised if fresh growth appears and then turns brown during a cold snap. While unsightly, the plant is unharmed.

Selective Pruning

When you're finished pruning selectively, all cuts will be concealed by foliage.

Shearing

Shearing cuts the surface of a plant instead of individual branches.

Pinching

Pinching soft, new growth controls the size of evergreen shrubs.

Selective pruning removes wayward branches while retaining a plant's natural form.

Why: To keep shrubs neat and control their size while maintaining natural, informal forms.

When: Prune needled evergreen shrubs in late winter or early spring. Prune flowering, broad leaf evergreens right after bloom.

How: Reach inside shrubs and look to find where each long shoot emerges from stiff, older wood. Make pruning cuts here, inside the shrub, removing only the flexible shoot. (Cuts on stiff, older wood will not sprout again.) Do not leave any stubs. Make cuts toward the tops of plants where sunlight prompts the most new growth. Avoid pruning evergreens severely at the bottom where there's less sunlight.

To give shrubs a tightly clipped, formal look, shear them on the surface, shaping them into the desired form. Plants suitable for shearing grow new twigs and leaves from each cut, making foliage thick and dense.

Why: To create a formal, sculpted look in the landscape.

When: Shear in warm weather, promoting fresh growth. Clip frequently to keep shrubs neatly trimmed and to control the size of evergreen shrubs.

How: Angle the blades of sharpened hedge trimmers as needed to cut the surface and to shape it. Stand back frequently to assess your work. Electric hedge trimmers make shearing large hedges easy. Use care to avoid overdoing it and whittling your shrubs away to bare branches.

Bright green sprouts on pines, spruce, and fir are called candles. Pinching by hand is the best way to control plant size and keep these evergreens neat without browning the tips.

Why: To control size and shape quickly and neatly during the early part of the growing season.

When: Pinch soft, new growth on nonflowering evergreens in late spring or early summer before the shoots "harden off," becoming stiff and woody.

How: Clasp the stem of the plant where the new growth is attached to the older wood. Pinch off the portion of new growth you want removed, even the entire shoot. Buds for next year's growth will form at this point.

Know the mature form of a young plant before you prune. Check the shrub encyclopedia or ask a garden staffer to describe its natural mature form. Many beautiful plants have been ruined by improper pruning.

The larger the leaf, the less pruning an evergreen shrub requires. Broad leaf evergreens with big leaves aren't well suited for shearing. Ragged, brown-edged foliage and blunted stems producing few leaves will result. If you want shrubs that can be clipped neatly into smooth forms, choose evergreens with naturally compact shapes. These shrubs have either needled foliage or small leaves.

Trim flowering evergreen shrubs when flowers fade. Use hand pruners to cut off the dead blooms and tips of small branches. This keeps plants from becoming shaggy and overgrown. Trimming prompts fresh growth and flower bud development for next year.

Homer's Hindsight

I pruned my azaleas in autumn one year, long after they had finished blooming. The next spring, my shrubs had no flowers! Without realizing it, I had cut off all the new flower buds. Now I've learned that azaleas and lilacs bloom on "old wood." They form buds on this year's stems for next year. Pruning my azaleas and lilacs immediately after flowering ensures a beautiful display of flowers every spring.

Combining styles means that shrubs near this house are pruned formally to complement the architecture, while plants further away from the house are left in their natural form.

Pruning Hedges

▲ **Wrong** Pruning hedges wider at the top than at the bottom results in lower branches with thin, spindly foliage over time. This is caused by the top of the plant shading the bottom of the plant too much.

▲ **Right** A hedge pruned narrower at the top than the bottom will stay lush and full from the ground up. Sunlight can reach plants from all angles.

Pruning Flowering Shrubs

Flowering shrubs need occasional shaping. Keep them under control without sacrificing flowers or form.

Selective Pruning

Prune spring-flowering shrubs when blossoms fade to avoid cutting off next year's flowers.

Prune spring flowering shrubs as soon as flowers fade. Many spring-flowering shrubs, such as azaleas, bloom on "old wood." They develop next year's flower buds on this year's growth. If you wait too late in the season to prune, you will remove next spring's show of blossoms. Summer blooming shrubs can be pruned in the spring before new growth begins.

Unless a shrub is severely over-grown and warrants hard pruning, make selective pruning your goal. Selective pruning reduces size and refines shape. No cuts are evident.

Reaching into shrubs to make cuts will hide unsightly stubs and preserve natural forms.

To prune selectively, locate an overgrown branch. Reach into the center of the plant so the cut is made deep within the shrub. Make your cut just above a leaf or where the stem emerges from a main branch. New growth will begin at this point. Pruning this way achieves three things. First, foliage hides ugly stubs

from view. Second, removal of individual branches preserves the plant's natural form. Finally, selective pruning encourages prolific flowering. Sunlight reaches the center of the plant, promoting growth of new buds and leaves.

Give flowering shrubs a light pruning whenever you notice stray stems that have gone awry, giving your plant a hairy look. Use selective pruning methods to remove such branches so the natural form of the plant is preserved. (But don't get carried away and cut too much if flowering is long finished.)

Shearing a flowering shrub—cutting the outer edge of a branch to change a shrub's size and shape—eventually damages the plant. Dense, twiggy growth emerges from the multiple cuts, shading the center of the shrub. In time, leaves and flowers grow only along the outside edges of the plant, giving it a thin, scalped look. Some flowering shrubs send up long, stray shoots in protest, making trimming necessary all over again to eliminate the odd appearance of the plant.

Pruning Hydrangeas

Hydrangeas can be trimmed in fall. Hydrangeas hold their big, beautiful blooms well into autumn. Flowers fade from white, pink, or blue to various shades of cream, pinkish brown, or tan. Leave them on shrubs to enjoy them in your yard. If you need to give your shrub a trim, wait until flowers have completely dried on their stems before pruning. Then you can use the cut, dried flowers in arrangements inside your home. However, you should plan to do major pruning on most hydrangeas in spring to avoid cutting off next year's flowers.

Wisdom of the **A**isles

Rubbing alcohol is a bargain shopper's dream for plant disease prevention. Fill a spray bottle with the alcohol and make it a habit to spritz pruning tools to sterilize them between cuts, even when you're working on just a single plant. Non-sterilized tools can transfer diseases from one branch to another and spread infections throughout your entire landscape.

Annabelle Hydrangea (Hydrangea arborescens 'Annabelle') Page 139

Some plants are naturally arching, loose, and airy. Resist the urge to cut them into tight shapes.

Hard Pruning

Overgrown shrubs have big, healthy root systems, making them worth renovating.

There are times when drastic measures are justified. Neglected shrubs become large and develop poor shape. You could just start over with a new plant, but don't let your eyes convince you that the old shrub is hopeless. What you can't see is the most valuable part of the plant.

Overgrown shrubs have had time to establish big, healthy root systems. It will take years for a replacement plant to do as well.

You can start over and still save the most valuable part of the shrub. But in doing so, you have to be ruthless. Prune individual branches nearly to the ground. Stagger cutting heights some so that all branches won't be at the same level. This will make the new growth appear to fill out faster.

Late winter or early spring, before new growth emerges, is the ideal time for hard pruning. (You can do it any time of year except just before a freeze.) Pruning this severely might result in no flowers for a season or two. In the meantime, you'll be amazed and pleased at how quickly your shrub can recover and how much better it looks despite your apparent abuse.

Hard pruning is not for the soft-hearted. Cut overgrown shrubs drastically to start over.

TOOL TIP

Good pruning tools make the job easier and are better for your shrubs.

Bypass hand pruners:

This tool operates with a scissors action to make a clean cut. Hand pruners are operated with one hand, so they should be used only for cutting minor branches. You can buy them in various sizes to match your needs. For example, one-inch pruners are suitable for cutting one-inch-thick branches. Trying to force pruners to cut through too-big stems can cause wood and stems to rip, leaving a jagged edge that becomes an entry point for insects or disease.

Anvil hand pruners:

Unlike bypass pruners, which operate with both blades moving, anvil pruners have one fixed side. This is the anvil against which the sharp, movable blade presses to make the cut. Although anvil hand pruners cost less than bypass pruners, they aren't desirable pruning tools. Pressing branches against the anvil to cut them results in mashed, torn stems and jagged cuts. This pruner also requires greater hand strength than bypass pruners.

Bypass loppers:

Operated with both hands, the long handles on loppers give you greater leverage to cut larger branches. Sharp bypass blades work like scissors for smooth, clean cuts. Use loppers whenever stems are too thick for hand pruners. Use a pruning saw if you can't easily position the lopper blades around large branches.

Dwarf Burning Bush
(Euonymus alatus 'Compacta')
Page 136

Northern Lights Azalea
(Azalea 'Northern Lights')
Page 128

Low shrubs suitable for clipping, such as this Boxwood (pages 130-131), lend structure and a tidy touch to gardens containing lots of color.

Choosing Shrubs by Characteristics

I dentify particular plant characteristics that meet your needs. A plant's growth rate, its mature form, and foliage texture are other traits to consider when selecting shrubs. Availability varies by area and site conditions (see page 21). Check with your garden center.

Fragrant flowering shrubs

Common Name	Zones	Page
Arnold's Red Tatarian Honeysuckle	3-9	148
Lonicera tatarica 'Arnold's Red'		
Betty Prior Rose	4-9	155
Rosa 'Betty Prior'		
Carefree Beauty Rose	4-8	155
Rosa Carefree Beauty		
Carol Mackie Daphne	4-8	136
Daphne x burkwoodii 'Carol Mackie'		
Common Lilac	3-7	165
Syringa vulgaris		
Cutleaf Lilac	4-8	164
Syringa x laciniata		
Drooping Leucothoe	5-8	147
Leucothoe fontanesiana		
Fru Dagmar Hastrup Rose	2-9	156
Rosa 'Fru Dagmar Hastrup'		
Graham Thomas Rose	5-9	156
Rosa Graham Thomas		
Iceberg Rose	4-9	157
Rosa 'Iceberg'		

Common Name	Zones	Page
Korean Spice Viburnum	4-8	167
Viburnum carlesii		
Large Fothergilla	4-8	138
Fothergilla major		
Margo Koster Rose	5-8	157
Rosa 'Margo Koster'		
Miss Kim Lilac	3-7	164
Syringa patula 'Miss Kim'		
Mountain Pieris	4-8	151
Pieris floribunda		
Northern Lights Azalea	4-7	128
Azalea 'Northern Lights'		
Peace Rose	5-8	158
Rosa 'Peace'		
Rosa Rubrifolia	4-9	159
Rosa rubrifolia		
Summersweet	3-9	133
Clethra alnifolia		

Dwarf Hinoki False Cypress
(Chamaecyparis obtusa 'Nana Gracilis')
Page 132

Slow-growing shrubs

Common Name	Zones	Page
Bird's Nest Spruce *Picea abies 'Nidiformis'*	2-7	150
Blue Star Juniper *Juniperus squamata 'Blue Star'*	4-8	146
Carol Mackie Daphne *Daphne x burkwoodii 'Carol Mackie'*	4-8	136
Catawba Rhododendron *Rhododendron catawbiense*	4-8	154
Common Lilac *Syringa vulgaris*	3-7	165
Cornell Pink Azalea *Azalea mucronulatum 'Cornell Pink'*	4-7	128
Dwarf Alberta Spruce *Picea glauca 'Conica'*	3-8	150
Dwarf Burning Bush *Euonymus alatus 'Compacta'*	3-8	136
Dwarf Hinoki False Cypress *Chamaecyparis obtusa 'Nana Gracilis'*	4-8	132
Exbury Azalea *Azalea 'Exbury Hybrids'*	4-7	127
Gray Dogwood *Cornus racemosa*	4-7	134
Green Lustre Japanese Holly *Ilex crenata 'Green Lustre'*	4-6	142
Little Giant Arborvitae *Thuja occidentalis 'Little Giant'*	3-7	166
Miss Kim Lilac *Syringa patula 'Miss Kim'*	3-7	164
Mugo Pine *Pinus mugo*	2-7	152
Northern Lights Azalea *Azalea 'Northern Lights'*	4-7	128
Shrubby Cinquefoil *Potentilla fruticosa*	2-7	152
Summersweet *Clethra alnifolia*	3-9	133
Winterberry *Ilex verticillata*	3-9	144

Rapid-growing shrubs

Common Name	Zones	Page
Arnold's Red Tatarian Honeysuckle *Lonicera tatarica 'Arnold's Red'*	3-9	148
Baby's Breath Spirea *Spiraea thunbergii*	2-8	162
Border Forsythia *Forsythia x intermedia*	6-9	137
Bridalwreath Spirea *Spiraea prunifolia*	5-8	162
Coralberry *Symphoricarpos orbiculatus*	4-7	163
Coral Embers Willow *Salix alba 'Britzensis'*	2-8	160
Cornelian Cherry *Cornus mas*	4-8	134
Hick's Upright Yew *Taxus x media 'Hicksii'*	4-7	166
Northern Bayberry *Myrica pensylvanica*	2-6	149
PeeGee Hydrangea *Hydrangea paniculata 'Grandiflora'*	3-8	140
Redtip Photinia *Photinia x fraseri*	6-9	149
Redtwig Dogwood *Cornus alba*	2-8	133
Rose of Sharon *Hibiscus syriacus*	5-9	139
Snowberry *Symphoricarpos albus*	3-7	163
Vanhoutte Spirea *Spiraea x vanhouttei*	3-8	162
Yellow-Twig Dogwood *Cornus stolonifera 'Flaviramea'*	3-8	135
Yukon Belle Firethorn *Pyracantha angustifolia Yukon Belle*	4-9	154

Annabelle Hydrangea
(Hydrangea arborescens 'Annabelle')
Page 139

Fine-textured shrubs

Common Name	Zones	Page
Bird's Nest Spruce *Picea abies 'Nidiformis'*	2-7	150
Blue Star Juniper *Juniperus squamata 'Blue Star'*	4-8	146
Compact Japanese Holly *Ilex crenata 'Compacta'*	5-8	143
Cutleaf Lilac *Syringa x laciniata*	4-8	164
Dwarf Alberta Spruce *Picea glauca 'Conica'*	3-8	150
Dwarf Hinoki False Cypress *Chamaecyparis obtusa 'Nana Gracilis'*	4-8	132
Edging Boxwood *Buxus sempervirens 'Suffruticosa'*	6-8	131
Glossy Abelia *Abelia x grandiflora*	6-9	126
Green Beauty Boxwood *Buxus microphylla 'Green Beauty'*	5-9	130
Green Lustre Japanese Holly *Ilex crenata 'Green Lustre'*	4-6	142
Heller Japanese Holly *Ilex crenata 'Helleri'*	5-8	142
Hick's Upright Yew *Taxus x media 'Hicksii'*	4-7	166
Japanese Barberry *Berberis thunbergii*	4-8	129
Japanese Boxwood *Buxus microphylla japonica*	6-9	130
Korean Boxwood *Buxus microphylla koreana*	5-9	131
Little Giant Arborvitae *Thuja occidentalis 'Little Giant'*	3-7	166
Mugo Pine *Pinus mugo*	2-7	152
Parson's Juniper *Juniperus chinensis 'Parsonii'*	3-9	145
Rockspray Cotoneaster *Cotoneaster horizontalis*	6-9	135

Common Name	Zones	Page
Sea Green Juniper *Juniperus chinensis 'Sea Green'*	4-8	145
Tam Juniper *Juniperus sabina 'Tamariscifolia'*	3-7	146
The Fairy Rose *Rosa 'The Fairy'*	4-9	159
Yukon Belle Firethorn *Pyracantha angustifolia Yukon Belle*	4-9	154

Coarse-textured shrubs

Common Name	Zones	Page
Annabelle Hydrangea *Hydrangea arborescens 'Annabelle'*	3-9	139
Catawba Rhododendron *Rhododendron catawbiense*	4-8	154
Chinese Beautyberry *Callicarpa dichotoma*	5-8	132
Common Lilac *Syringa vulgaris*	3-7	165
Doublefile Viburnum *Viburnum plicatum tomentosum*	4-8	167
European Cranberrybush *Viburnum opulus 'Roseum'*	3-8	167
Korean Spice Viburnum *Viburnum carlesii*	4-8	167
Miss Kim Lilac *Syringa patula 'Miss Kim'*	3-7	164
Mountain Laurel *Kalmia latifolia*	4-9	147
Nikko Blue Hydrangea *Hydrangea macrophylla 'Nikko Blue'*	6-9	140
Oakleaf Hydrangea *Hydrangea quercifolia*	5-9	141
PeeGee Hydrangea *Hydrangea paniculata 'Grandiflora'*	3-8	140
Persian Lilac *Syringa x persica*	3-7	164
Rose of Sharon *Hibiscus syriacus*	5-9	139

Dwarf Burning Bush
(Euonymus alatus 'Compacta')
Page 136

shrubs

5

Arborvitae (page 166) adds a distinctive shape to the landscape year-round.

Choose shrubs to add color, texture, line, and form to your landscape.

Choosing Shrubs by Needs

Put shrubs to work in your landscape. The guides on these pages are organized by different landscaping needs. (See pages 28-29 to find lists of shrubs for privacy.) Go to the shrub encyclopedia for detailed information about individual shrubs.

Shrubs for mass planting

Common Name	Zones	Page
Annabelle Hydrangea	3-9	139
Hydrangea arborescens 'Annabelle'		
Anthony Waterer Spirea	3-9	161
Spiraea japonica 'Anthony Waterer'		
Arnold's Red Tatarian Honeysuckle	3-9	148
Lonicera tatarica 'Arnold's Red'		
Baby's Breath Spirea	2-8	162
Spiraea thunbergii		
Betty Prior Rose	4-9	155
Rosa 'Betty Prior'		
Blue Star Juniper	4-8	146
Juniperus squamata 'Blue Star'		
Border Forsythia	6-9	137
Forsythia x intermedia		
Bridalwreath Spirea	5-8	162
Spiraea prunifolia		
Carefree Beauty Rose	4-8	155
Rosa Carefree Beauty		
Carolina Azalea	4-9	127
Azalea carolinianum		
Catawba Rhododendron	4-8	154
Rhododendron catawbiense		

Common Name	Zones	Page
Coralberry	4-7	163
Symphoricarpos orbiculatus		
Cornell Pink Azalea	4-7	128
Azalea mucronulatum 'Cornell Pink'		
Doublefile Viburnum	4-8	167
Viburnum plicatum tomentosum		
Drooping Leucothoe	5-8	147
Leucothoe fontanesiana		
Dwarf Burning Bush	3-8	136
Euonymus alatus 'Compacta'		
Exbury Azalea	4-7	127
Azalea 'Exbury Hybrids'		
Fru Dagmar Hastrup Rose	2-9	156
Rosa 'Fru Dagmar Hastrup'		
Glossy Abelia	6-9	126
Abelia x grandiflora		
Graham Thomas Rose	5-9	156
Rosa Graham Thomas		
Iceberg Rose	4-9	157
Rosa 'Iceberg'		
Inkberry	3-9	143
Ilex glabra 'Compacta'		

Common Name	Zones	Page
Japanese Barberry	4-8	129
Berberis thunbergii		
Japanese Skimmia	6-9	160
Skimmia japonica		
Korean Boxwood	5-9	131
Buxus microphylla koreana		
Large Fothergilla	4-8	138
Fothergilla major		
Margo Koster Rose	5-8	157
Rosa 'Margo Koster'		
Mountain Laurel	4-9	147
Kalmia latifolia		
Mountain Pieris	4-8	151
Pieris floribunda		
Nikko Blue Hydrangea	6-9	140
Hydrangea macrophylla 'Nikko Blue'		
Northern Bayberry	2-6	149
Myrica pensylvanica		
Northern Lights Azalea	4-7	128
Azalea 'Northern Lights'		
Oakleaf Hydrangea	5-9	141
Hydrangea quercifolia		
Otto Luyken Laurel	6-8	153
Prunus laurocerasus 'Otto Luyken'		
Parson's Juniper	3-9	145
Juniperus chinensis 'Parsonii'		
Peace Rose	5-8	158
Rosa 'Peace'		
PeeGee Hydrangea	3-8	140
Hydrangea paniculata 'Grandiflora'		
Pink Meidiland Rose	5-8	158
Rosa Pink Meidiland		
Rockspray Cotoneaster	6-9	135
Cotoneaster horizontalis		
Rosa Rubrifolia	4-9	159
Rosa rubrifolia		
Sea Green Juniper	4-8	145
Juniperus chinensis 'Sea Green'		
Shibori Spirea	4-8	161
Spiraea japonica 'Shibori'		
Shrubby Cinquefoil	2-7	152
Potentilla fruticosa		
Snowberry	3-7	163
Symphoricarpos albus		
Summersweet	3-9	133
Clethra alnifolia		
Vanhoutte Spirea	3-8	162
Spiraea x vanhouttei		
Winterberry	3-9	144
Ilex verticillata		
Yukon Belle Firethorn	4-9	154
Pyracantha angustifolia Yukon Belle		

Bridalwreath Spirea (Spiraea prunifolia) Page 162

Shrubs for entries, courtyards, and patios

Common Name	Zones	Page
Annabelle Hydrangea	3-9	139
Hydrangea arborescens 'Annabelle'		
Anthony Waterer Spirea	3-9	161
Spiraea japonica 'Anthony Waterer'		
Arnold's Red Tatarian Honeysuckle	3-9	148
Lonicera tatarica 'Arnold's Red'		
Baby's Breath Spirea	2-8	162
Spiraea thunbergii		
Bridalwreath Spirea	5-8	162
Spiraea prunifolia		
Carol Mackie Daphne	4-8	136
Daphne x burkwoodii 'Carol Mackie'		
Carolina Azalea	4-9	127
Azalea carolinianum		
Common Lilac	3-7	165
Syringa vulgaris		
Compact Japanese Holly	5-8	143
Ilex crenata 'Compacta'		
Cutleaf Lilac	4-8	164
Syringa x laciniata		
Doublefile Viburnum	4-8	167
Viburnum plicatum tomentosum		
Dwarf Alberta Spruce	3-8	150
Picea glauca 'Conica'		
Dwarf Burning Bush	3-8	136
Euonymus alatus 'Compacta'		
European Cranberrybush	3-8	167
Viburnum opulus 'Roseum'		
Graham Thomas Rose	5-9	156
Rosa Graham Thomas		
Inkberry	3-9	143
Ilex glabra 'Compacta'		
Korean Boxwood	5-9	131
Buxus microphylla koreana		
Korean Spice Viburnum	4-8	167
Viburnum carlesii		
Miss Kim Lilac	3-7	164
Syringa patula 'Miss Kim'		
Mountain Pieris	4-8	151
Pieris floribunda		
Nikko Blue Hydrangea	6-9	140
Hydrangea macrophylla 'Nikko Blue'		
Otto Luyken Laurel	6-8	153
Prunus laurocerasus 'Otto Luyken'		
Parson's Juniper	3-9	145
Juniperus chinensis 'Parsonii'		
Peace Rose	5-8	158
Rosa 'Peace'		
Sea Green Juniper	4-8	145
Juniperus chinensis 'Sea Green'		
Shibori Spirea	4-8	161
Spiraea japonica 'Shibori'		
Tam Juniper	3-7	146
Juniperus sabina 'Tamariscifolia'		
Vanhoutte Spirea	3-8	162
Spiraea x vanhouttei		

Mountain Pieris
(*Pieris floribunda*)
Page 151

Shrubs for woodland gardens

Common Name	Zones	Page
Andromeda	5-8	151
Pieris japonica		
Annabelle Hydrangea	3-9	139
Hydrangea arborescens 'Annabelle'		
Border Forsythia	6-9	137
Forsythia x intermedia		
Bridalwreath Spirea	5-8	162
Spiraea prunifolia		
Carol Mackie Daphne	4-8	136
Daphne x burkwoodii 'Carol Mackie'		
Catawba Rhododendron	4-8	154
Rhododendron catawbiense		
Chinese Beautyberry	5-8	132
Callicarpa dichotoma		
Common Witch Hazel	3-8	138
Hamamelis virginiana		
Coralberry	4-7	163
Symphoricarpos orbiculatus		
Cornell Pink Azalea	4-7	128
Azalea mucronulatum 'Cornell Pink'		
Doublefile Viburnum	4-8	167
Viburnum plicatum tomentosum		
Drooping Leucothoe	5-8	147
Leucothoe fontanesiana		
European Cranberrybush	3-8	167
Viburnum opulus 'Roseum'		
Korean Spice Viburnum	4-8	167
Viburnum carlesii		
Mountain Laurel	4-9	147
Kalmia latifolia		
Mountain Pieris	4-8	151
Pieris floribunda		
Northern Lights Azalea	4-7	128
Azalea 'Northern Lights'		
Oakleaf Hydrangea	5-9	141
Hydrangea quercifolia		
PeeGee Hydrangea	3-8	140
Hydrangea paniculata 'Grandiflora'		
Serviceberry	4-5	126
Amelanchier alnifolia		
Snowberry	3-7	163
Symphoricarpos albus		
Summersweet	3-9	133
Clethra alnifolia		
Vanhoutte Spirea	3-8	162
Spiraea x vanhouttei		
Winterberry	3-9	144
Ilex verticillata		
Yellow-Twig Dogwood	3-8	135
Cornus stolonifera 'Flaviramea'		

Nikko Blue Hydrangea
(*Hydrangea macrophylla 'Nikko Blue'*)
Page 140

Shrubs for formal gardens

Common Name	Zones	Page
Annabelle Hydrangea	3-9	139
Hydrangea arborescens 'Annabelle'		
Compact Japanese Holly	5-8	143
Ilex crenata 'Compacta'		
Cornelian Cherry	4-8	134
Cornus mas		
Dwarf Alberta Spruce	3-8	150
Picea glauca 'Conica'		
Dwarf Burford Holly	6-9	141
Ilex cornuta 'Bufordii Nana'		
Dwarf Burning Bush	3-8	136
Euonymus alatus 'Compacta'		
Dwarf Hinoki False Cypress	4-8	132
Chamaecyparis obtusa 'Nana Gracilis'		
Edging Boxwood	6-8	131
Buxus sempervirens 'Suffruticosa'		
European Cranberrybush	3-8	167
Viburnum opulus 'Roseum'		
Graham Thomas Rose	5-9	156
Rosa Graham Thomas		
Green Beauty Boxwood	5-9	130
Buxus microphylla 'Green Beauty'		
Green Lustre Japanese Holly	4-6	142
Ilex crenata 'Green Lustre'		
Heller Japanese Holly	5-8	142
Ilex crenata 'Helleri'		
Hick's Upright Yew	4-7	166
Taxus x media 'Hicksii'		
Inkberry	3-9	143
Ilex glabra 'Compacta'		
Japanese Boxwood	6-9	130
Buxus microphylla japonica		
Korean Boxwood	5-9	131
Buxus microphylla koreana		
Little Giant Arborvitae	3-7	166
Thuja occidentalis 'Little Giant'		
Miss Kim Lilac	3-7	164
Syringa patula 'Miss Kim'		
Mugo Pine	2-7	152
Pinus mugo		
Nellie R. Stevens Holly	6-9	144
Ilex x 'Nellie R. Stevens'		
Nikko Blue Hydrangea	6-9	140
Hydrangea macrophylla 'Nikko Blue'		
Northern Bayberry	2-6	149
Myrica pensylvanica		
The Fairy Rose	4-9	159
Rosa 'The Fairy'		

Availability varies by area and conditions (see page 21). Check with your garden center.

Shrubs

5

Spring flowers are pretty, but don't overlook fall color when choosing shrubs for your yard.

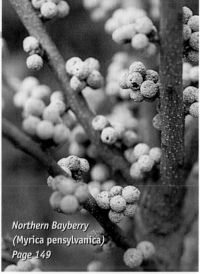

Northern Bayberry
(*Myrica pensylvanica*)
Page 149

Summersweet
(*Clethra alnifolia*)
Page 133

Choosing Shrubs for Seasonal Interest

D **ecorate your yard throughout the seasons with shrubs.** Fragrant flowers, colorful foliage, and desirable fruit add interest to the landscape throughout spring, summer, fall, and winter.

Spring-flowering shrubs

Common Name	Zones	Page
Andromeda	5-8	151
Pieris japonica		
Annabelle Hydrangea	3-9	139
Hydrangea arborescens 'Annabelle'		
Anthony Waterer Spirea	3-9	161
Spiraea japonica 'Anthony Waterer'		
Arnold's Red Tatarian Honeysuckle	3-9	148
Lonicera tatarica 'Arnold's Red'		
Baby's Breath Spirea	2-8	162
Spiraea thunbergii		
Border Forsythia	6-9	137
Forsythia x intermedia		
Bridalwreath Spirea	5-8	162
Spiraea prunifolia		
Butterfly Bush	5-9	129
Buddleia davidii		
Carol Mackie Daphne	4-8	136
Daphne x burkwoodii 'Carol Mackie'		
Carolina Azalea	4-9	127
Azalea carolinianum		
Catawba Rhododendron	4-8	154
Rhododendron catawbiense		
Common Lilac	3-7	165
Syringa vulgaris		
Cornelian Cherry	4-8	134
Cornus mas		

Common Name	Zones	Page
Cornell Pink Azalea	4-7	128
Azalea mucronulatum 'Cornell Pink'		
Cutleaf Lilac	4-8	164
Syringa x laciniata		
Doublefile Viburnum	4-8	167
Viburnum plicatum tomentosum		
Drooping Leucothoe	5-8	147
Leucothoe fontanesiana		
Dwarf Flowering Almond	4-8	153
Prunus glandulosa 'Rosea'		
European Cranberrybush	3-8	167
Viburnum opulus 'Roseum'		
Exbury Azalea	4-7	127
Azalea 'Exbury Hybrids'		
Gray Dogwood	4-7	134
Cornus racemosa		
Iceberg Rose	4-9	157
Rosa 'Iceberg'		
Japanese Skimmia	6-9	160
Skimmia japonica		
Korean Spice Viburnum	4-8	167
Viburnum carlesii		
Large Fothergilla	4-8	138
Fothergilla major		
Miss Kim Lilac	3-7	164
Syringa patula 'Miss Kim'		

Common Name	Zones	Page
Mountain Laurel	4-9	147
Kalmia latifolia		
Mountain Pieris	4-8	151
Pieris floribunda		
Northern Lights Azalea	4-7	128
Azalea 'Northern Lights'		
Otto Luyken Laurel	6-8	153
Prunus laurocerasus 'Otto Luyken'		
Persian Lilac	3-7	164
Syringa x persica		
Redtip Photinia	6-9	149
Photinia x fraseri		
Rockspray Cotoneaster	6-9	135
Cotoneaster horizontalis		
Serviceberry	4-5	126
Amelanchier alnifolia		
Vanhoutte Spirea	3-8	162
Spiraea x vanhouttei		

Availability varies by area and conditions (see page 21). Check with your garden center.

Summer-flowering shrubs

Common Name	Zones	Page
Annabelle Hydrangea	3-9	139
Hydrangea arborescens 'Annabelle'		
Anthony Waterer Spirea	3-9	161
Spiraea japonica 'Anthony Waterer'		
Betty Prior Rose	4-9	155
Rosa 'Betty Prior'		
Carefree Beauty Rose	4-8	155
Rosa Carefree Beauty		
Carolina Azalea	4-9	127
Azalea carolinianum		
Chinese Beautyberry	5-8	132
Callicarpa dichotoma		
Coralberry	4-7	163
Symphoricarpos orbiculatus		
Fru Dagmar Hastrup Rose	2-9	156
Rosa 'Fru Dagmar Hastrup'		
Glossy Abelia	6-9	126
Abelia x grandiflora		
Graham Thomas Rose	5-9	156
Rosa Graham Thomas		
Iceberg Rose	4-9	157
Rosa 'Iceberg'		
Margo Koster Rose	5-8	157
Rosa 'Margo Koster'		
Miss Kim Lilac	3-7	164
Syringa patula 'Miss Kim'		
Nikko Blue Hydrangea	6-9	140
Hydrangea macrophylla 'Nikko Blue'		
Oakleaf Hydrangea	5-9	141
Hydrangea quercifolia		
Peace Rose	5-8	158
Rosa 'Peace'		
PeeGee Hydrangea	3-8	140
Hydrangea paniculata 'Grandiflora'		
Pink Meidiland Rose	5-8	158
Rosa Pink Meidiland		
Rosa Rubrifolia	4-9	159
Rosa rubrifolia		
Rose of Sharon	5-9	139
Hibiscus syriacus		
Shrubby Cinquefoil	2-7	152
Potentilla fruticosa		
Summersweet	3-9	133
Clethra alnifolia		
The Fairy Rose	4-9	159
Rosa 'The Fairy'		
Vanhoutte Spirea	3-8	162
Spiraea x vanhouttei		
Yukon Belle Firethorn	4-9	154
Pyracantha angustifolia Yukon Belle		

Shrubs with autumn color

Common Name	Zones	Page
Annabelle Hydrangea	3-9	139
Hydrangea arborescens 'Annabelle'		
Baby's Breath Spirea	2-8	162
Spiraea thunbergii		
Bridalwreath Spirea	5-8	162
Spiraea prunifolia		
Butterfly Bush	5-9	129
Buddleia davidii		
Carefree Beauty Rose	4-8	155
Rosa Carefree Beauty		
Chinese Beautyberry	5-8	132
Callicarpa dichotoma		
Common Witch Hazel	3-8	138
Hamamelis virginiana		
Cornell Pink Azalea	4-7	128
Azalea mucronulatum 'Cornell Pink'		
Doublefile Viburnum	4-8	167
Viburnum plicatum tomentosum		
Dwarf Burning Bush	3-8	136
Euonymus alatus 'Compacta'		
European Cranberrybush	3-8	167
Viburnum opulus 'Roseum'		
Exbury Azalea	4-7	127
Azalea 'Exbury Hybrids'		
Glossy Abelia	6-9	126
Abelia x grandiflora		
Golden Vicary Privet	5-8	148
Ligustrum x vicaryi		
Graham Thomas Rose	5-9	156
Rosa Graham Thomas		
Gray Dogwood	4-7	134
Cornus racemosa		
Iceberg Rose	4-9	157
Rosa 'Iceberg'		
Japanese Barberry	4-8	129
Berberis thunbergii		
Japanese Skimmia	6-9	160
Skimmia japonica		
Large Fothergilla	4-8	138
Fothergilla major		
Little Giant Arborvitae	3-7	166
Thuja occidentalis 'Little Giant'		
Manhattan Spreading Euonymus	4-8	137
Euonymus kiautschovicus 'Manhattan'		
Northern Bayberry	2-6	149
Myrica pensylvanica		
Northern Lights Azalea	4-7	128
Azalea 'Northern Lights'		
Oakleaf Hydrangea	5-9	141
Hydrangea quercifolia		

Winterberry
(Ilex verticillata)
Page 144

Common Name	Zones	Page
Peace Rose	5-8	158
Rosa 'Peace'		
PeeGee Hydrangea	3-8	140
Hydrangea paniculata 'Grandiflora'		
Pink Meidiland Rose	5-8	158
Rosa Pink Meidiland		
Rockspray Cotoneaster	6-9	135
Cotoneaster horizontalis		
Rosa Rubrifolia	4-9	159
Rosa rubrifolia		
Serviceberry	4-5	126
Amelanchier alnifolia		
Shrubby Cinquefoil	2-7	152
Potentilla fruticosa		
Snowberry	3-7	163
Symphoricarpos albus		
Summersweet	3-9	133
Clethra alnifolia		
The Fairy Rose	4-9	159
Rosa 'The Fairy'		
Yellow-Twig Dogwood	3-8	135
Cornus stolonifera 'Flaviramea'		
Yukon Belle Firethorn	4-9	154
Pyracantha angustifolia Yukon Belle		

Shrubs with winter fruit

Common Name	Zones	Page
Carefree Beauty Rose	4-8	155
Rosa Carefree Beauty		
Dwarf Burford Holly	6-9	141
Ilex cornuta 'Burfordii Nana'		
Japanese Skimmia	6-9	160
Skimmia japonica		
Pink Meidiland Rose	5-8	158
Rosa Pink Meidiland		
Rosa Rubrifolia	4-9	159
Rosa rubrifolia		
Winterberry	3-9	144
Ilex verticillata		

Shrubby Cinquefoil
(Potentilla fruticosa)
Page 152

Abelia x grandiflora

Glossy Abelia

Zones: 6-9

Light Needs:

Mature Size:

4'-6'

3'-5'

Growth Rate: medium

semievergreen shrub

Needs: Plant in sun or part shade in well-drained soil ranging from acid to alkaline. Pinch new growth to maintain compact plants. Informal settings suit it best.

Good for: informal hedge, mass planting, or bank cover

More Choices: pages 28, 33, 34, 39, 41, 111, 113, 121, 122, and 125

Options: 'Edward Goucher'—4' high, lavender flowers
'Francis Mason'—pinkish-white flowers
'Prostrata'—2' high, white flowers
'Sherwood'—2'-3' high cascading form, white flowers

Outstanding Features:

- Glossy Abelia is heat-tolerant
- Shrubs bloom summer through fall
- Low-maintenance plants are easy to grow

Here's a low maintenance shrub that blooms in sun or part shade. Hot weather promotes flowering; pink, white, or lavender blossoms occur summer through fall. Put it with broad leaf evergreens for a textural contrast.

Amelanchier alnifolia

Serviceberry

Zones: 4-5

Light Needs:

Mature Size:

8'-12'

8'-12'

Growth Rate: medium

deciduous flowering shrub

Needs: Plant in full sun or partial shade in moist, well-drained, fertile soil. Will tolerate drier locations as well. Shrubs will grow in either acid or alkaline soil. This shrub rarely requires pruning.

Good for: specimen use, hedges, woodland areas, planting near ponds and streams, shrub borders, attracting birds

More Choices: pages 29, 33, 34, 39, 111, 123, 124, and 125

Options: 'Regent'—compact shrub with sweet fruit and attractive foliage. Grows 4' to 6' high, spreads 12' wide.

Outstanding Features:

- Star-shaped flowers in early spring
- Edible fruit ripens in July, attracting birds
- Red and yellow foliage color in the fall

Choose Serviceberry for beautiful spring flowers, which blanket the bush with white stars in early spring. Plants in flower are especially showy when planted against an evergreen hedge. Bluish purple fruit ripens in July and is attractive to birds as well as humans. Rounded, green leaves turn brilliant red and yellow in autumn. Once Serviceberry is planted, it's basically carefree. Fallen fruit can stain paving surfaces, so it is best to keep this shrub away from patios, driveways, and walkways.

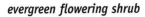

Carolina Azalea

Zones: 4-9

Light Needs:

Mature Size:

3'-6' / 3'-6'

Growth Rate:
slow

evergreen flowering shrub

Needs: Grow in full sun. Plant in fertile, acidic, moist, and well-drained soil. Set new shrubs slightly higher to prevent water from collecting around roots. Mulch to keep roots moist. Provide extra water in autumn. Prune as soon as flowering finishes by reaching into plants to remove woody stems; do not shear.

Good for: seasonal accents, background planting, foundation planting, along fences, entries, along walkways, beside patios, massing in planting beds

More Choices: pages 32, 38, 113, 122, 123, 124, and 125

Outstanding Features:
- Wide selection of flower colors
- Foliage stays green year-round
- Provides seasonal accent in spring

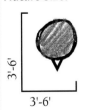

Welcome spring to your yard with Carolina Azaleas. These shrubs feature flowers in springtime shades. Leaves stay shiny green throughout the year. Can grow in Zone 4 with winter protection. Avoid planting azaleas where they'll be exposed to harsh winds or strong winter sun. Also try var. *album*—white flowers; var. *luteum*—yellow flowers. *Azalea kurume*, a smaller azalea, will grow in areas where costal influences raise minimum temperatures higher than typical conditions. *A. kurume* 'Hino Crimson' has bright red flowers.

Azalea 'Exbury Hybrids'

Exbury Azalea

Zones: 4-7

Light Needs:

Mature Size:

3'-6' / 3'-6'

Growth Rate:
slow

deciduous flowering shrub

Needs: Plant in fertile, acidic soil that's moist but well-drained. Set new shrubs slightly higher than existing ground to prevent water from collecting around roots. Mulch to keep roots moist. Supply extra water during dry periods and in autumn. Grow in full sun. Remove selected woody stems after flowering; do not shear.

Good for: seasonal accents, hedges, foundation planting, massing, planting along fences, driveways, and beneath trees

More Choices: pages 32, 39, 111, 113, 121, 122, 124, and 125

Outstanding Features:
- Midspring flowers in a range of colors
- Leaves turn yellow, orange, or red in fall
- Colorful accent in front of evergreens

These azaleas will add color to your yard in the spring when blossoms open and again in autumn when the leaves put on their fall show. Choose rose pink, red, orange, white, or yellow flower colors. Plants are also known as Knap Hill or Rothschild Hybrids. Look for these cultivars: 'Berry Rose'—rose pink blossoms; 'Firefly'—red flowers; 'Gibraltar'—bright orange flowers; and 'White Swan'—white blooms.

Shrubs 5

Azalea mucronulatum 'Cornell Pink'

Cornell Pink Azalea

Zones: 4-7

Light Needs:

Mature Size:

4'-8'

4'-8'

Growth Rate: slow

deciduous flowering shrub

Needs: Plant in fertile, acidic soil that's moist but well-drained. Set new shrubs slightly higher than existing ground to prevent water from collecting around roots. Mulch well to keep roots moist. Supply extra water during dry periods and in autumn. Grow in full sun. Remove woody stems after flowering; do not shear.

Good for: specimen use, seasonal accents, foundation plantings (with evergreen shrubs), massing, filling in planting beds, natural areas

More Choices: pages 29, 32, 39, 113, 121, 122, 123, 124, and 125

Outstanding Features:

- Lush pink flowers in early spring
- Leaves turn yellow to crimson in fall
- Tolerant of cold climates

Include these shrubs for early spring color. Flowers open before leaves unfurl, blanketing the plant in bright pink. One of the earliest azaleas to bloom. Plant these shrubs in a protected location away from winter sun. This is especially important in colder climates where warming rays may coax buds into opening too early. Freezing temperatures will damage or kill the blooms before you can enjoy them.

Azalea 'Northern Lights'

Northern Lights Azalea

Zones: 4-7

Light Needs:

Mature Size:

4'-6'

4'-6'

Growth Rate: slow

deciduous flowering shrub

Needs: Grow in full sun. Plant in fertile, moist, well-drained, acidic soil. Set new shrubs slightly higher than existing ground to prevent water from collecting around roots. Mulch. Supply extra water during dry weather and again in autumn. Prune when flowers have finished to remove woody stems; do not shear.

Good for: seasonal accents, informal deciduous hedges, foundation plantings (with evergreen shrubs), massing, natural areas, filling in planting beds

More Choices: pages 33, 39, 111, 113, 120, 121, 122, 123, 124, and 125

Outstanding Features:

- Spring flowers available in a range of colors
- Bronze, burgundy, or purple foliage in fall
- Cold-tolerant accent for the spring garden

Developed at the University of Minnesota, these azaleas can take the cold. Buds will withstand temperatures down to 45 below zero and still produce abundant blooms when spring arrives. Flowers possess a clovelike fragrance. Additional selections include 'Golden Lights'—golden flowers in late spring, bronzy-red fall foliage; 'Northern Hi-Lights'—creamy white and yellow flowers in late spring, burgundy to purple fall foliage; 'Orchid Lights'—lilac flowers in early spring, insignificant fall color; 'Rosy Lights'—rosy flowers in late spring, insignificant fall color; and 'White Lights'—pink buds open to white blossoms in late spring, bronzy-purple fall foliage.

Berberis thunbergii

Japanese Barberry

Zones: 4-8

Light Needs:

Mature Size:

3'-6'

4'-7'

Growth Rate: medium

deciduous shrub

Needs: Plant anywhere except in standing water. Japanese Barberry performs best in full sun in well-drained, fertile soil. Prune to shape after flowering. Plants tolerate urban conditions very well.

Good for: hedges, barriers, foundation planting, or border shrub

More Choices: pages 33, 34, 37, 111, 113, 121, 122, and 125

Options: var. *atropurpurea*—reddish or purple leaves, turning red in fall
'Crimson Pygmy'—deep red leaves turn orange-scarlet in fall, 2' to 3' tall and wide
'Rose Glow'—rose-red leaves in fall

Outstanding Features:
- Leaves appear early in the spring
- Fantastic foliage color in summer and fall
- Thorny plants create dense barriers

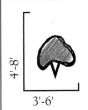

This spiny shrub will grow anywhere. It can tolerate tight root quarters, urban pollution, and neglect. Green summer foliage turns shades of orange, scarlet, or reddish purple in the fall. Spines are sharp and make effective barrier plantings, but avoid planting them where children play. The variety 'Thornless' is a better selection for these areas. Turning orange-red in the fall, it grows 3' to 5' high by 4' to 6' wide; stems are thornless. Plants tend to collect blowing debris and require cleaning out in the spring. Growth in Zone 8 is limited.

Buddleia davidii

Butterfly Bush

Zones: 5-9

Light Needs:

Mature Size:

4'-8'

3'-6'

Growth Rate: rapid

perennial or semievergreen shrub

Needs: Give plants a good start by mixing organic matter such as compost into the planting hole. Full sun yields the most flowers. Prune in either spring or fall to encourage blooming.

Good for: sunny flowerbeds or natural areas, beside patios or decks to enjoy butterflies and blossoms, enjoy cut flowers indoors

More Choices: pages 32, 41, 124, and 125

Outstanding Features:
- Flowers attract butterflies to the area
- Excellent vase life for cut flower use
- Easily grown in hot, sunny locations

Butterfly Bush is easy to grow; hot sun and limited water do little to discourage abundant flowers in shades of pink, white, purple, or red. Blooms attract butterflies. Cultivars of interest include 'Empire Blue'—large dark blue flowers; 'Fascination'—salmon-pink blossoms; 'Harlequin'—variegated leaves, maroon flowers; 'Royal Red'—dark purple-red flowers; 'Black Knight'—deep purple flowers; 'White Bouquet'—white blossoms; 'Wilsonii'—drooping, light pink-purple flower spikes.

Shrubs 5

Buxus microphylla 'Green Beauty'

Green Beauty Boxwood

Zones: 5-9

Light Needs:

Mature Size:

3'-4' (height)
3'-4' (width)

Growth Rate:
slow

evergreen shrub

Needs: Plant in full sun or light shade in well-drained, fertile soil. Boxwoods prefer cool conditions. Mulch the root area with peat or compost. Protect shrubs from strong, drying winds, especially in winter. Prune boxwood after flowering.

Good for: hedge, specimen use, topiaries. accenting entrances, formal gardens, planting beds

More Choices: pages 33, 34, 111, 121, and 123

Options: 'Winter Gem'—compact form
'Compacta'—12" high and wide
'Green Pillow'—18" tall by 3' wide

Boxwood is a shrub that is equally at home tucked into formal planters flanking a front porch or in a perennial border. It can also be used to create a lovely hedge. The evergreen leaves of boxwood make it a shrub that establishes the "bones" of a landscape. Its bright green hue remains through the march of the seasons.

Buxus microphylla japonica

Japanese Boxwood

Zones: 6-9

Light Needs:

Mature Size:

3'-6' (height)
3'-6' (width)

Growth Rate:
slow

evergreen shrub

Needs: Plant in full sun or light shade in well-drained, fertile soil. Shallow roots prefer cool growing conditions. Mulch the root area with peat or compost. Protect shrubs from strong, drying winds. Prune boxwood after flowering.

Good for: specimen shrub or hedge, foundations, edging, formal gardens

More Choices: pages 33, 34, 111, 121, and 123

Japanese Boxwood is a dense, upright shrub with lustrous evergreen leaves. Feel free to shape it to meet your yard's needs—or just let it grow. Protect plants from drying winds, especially in colder areas.

Buxus microphylla koreana

Korean Boxwood

Zones: 5-9

Light Needs:

Mature Size:

1'-2'
2'-3'

Growth Rate:
slow

evergreen shrub

Needs: Plant in fertile soil that's moist but well-drained. Slightly acidic soil is best. Mulch well to keep shallow roots cool; peat or compost is good for mulching. Protect shrubs from strong, drying winds. Prune to shape in early or midsummer.

Good for: low hedges, massing, surrounding vegetable, rose, or herb gardens; formal landscapes, courtyards, entries, winter interest, edging planting beds

More Choices: pages 39, 41, 111, 113, 121, 122, and 123

Outstanding Features:
Fine-textured foliage is bright green all year
Tolerates cold, heat, and humidity
Grows slowly and stays low

The toughest of all boxwoods, this one withstands hot or cold climates. Shrubs grow slowly, stay low, and take pruning well. Plants are easily trimmed into a variety of shapes for formal landscapes. Also sold as Korean Littleleaf Boxwood. Cultivar options: 'Wintergreen'—4' to 5' high, 3' to 4' wide, Zones 4-9; 'Suffructicosa' (edging boxwood)—3' high, 12" wide, Zones 6-8; 'Tide Hill'—15" high, 5' wide, Zones 4-9.

Buxus sempervirens 'Suffruticosa'

Edging Boxwood

Zones: 6-8

Light Needs:

Mature Size:

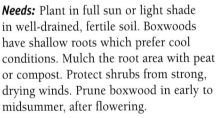
4'-6'
6'-9'

Growth Rate:
slow

evergreen shrub

Needs: Plant in full sun or light shade in well-drained, fertile soil. Boxwoods have shallow roots which prefer cool conditions. Mulch the root area with peat or compost. Protect shrubs from strong, drying winds. Prune boxwood in early to midsummer, after flowering.

Good for: low, formal hedges, specimens, mass plantings, topiaries, edging gardens

More Choices: pages 32, 34, 111, 121, and 123

Outstanding Features:
Adapts well to pruning and shearing
Leaves stay glossy green year-round
Excellent low-growing edging hedge

Shrubs 5

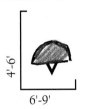

This tiny Boxwood grows slowly and, with regular pruning, will form a neat and tidy hedge around other plantings, seating areas, or walkways. Plants can be maintained at any height from just a few inches to several feet. Glossy green foliage is fragrant. Plants are resistant to leaf miner infestations.

Callicarpa dichotoma

Chinese Beautyberry

Zones: 5-8

Light Needs:

Mature Size:

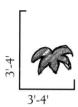

3'-4'

3'-4'

Growth Rate:
rapid

deciduous shrub

Needs: Plant in full sun or light shade in well-drained, fertile soil. Cut plants back in spring, leaving only 4" to 6" of stem. Let them resprout each year for vigorous growth, abundant flowering, and fruiting.

Good for: specimen use, mass planting, shrub borders, use along driveways, walkways, areas of high visibility

More Choices: pages 32, 34, 121, 123, and 125j

Options: var. *albifructus*—white-berries; 3' to 4' high and wide; Zones 5-8
Callicarpa japonica (Japanese Beauty berry)—purple berries; 4' to 6'; Zones 5-8

Outstanding Features:

- Lavender-pink flowers on arching branches
- Berries ripen to a bright purple color in fall
- Easily transplanted and grown

This easy-to-grow shrub has lovely flowers in summer, but autumn is when it puts on its best show. Bright clusters of purple berries combine with yellow foliage to provide a colorful contrast. Berries linger after the leaves fall, covering stems.

Chamaecyparis obtusa 'Nana Gracilis'

Dwarf Hinoki False Cypress

Zones: 4-8

Light Needs:

Mature Size:

2'-3'

3'-4'

Growth Rate:
slow

evergreen shrub

Needs: Plant in full sun in moist, well-drained, acidic soil. Plants will tolerate alkaline soils. Protect from wind.

Good for: specimen use, rock gardens, planters, adding upright, evergreen shape

More Choices: pages 32, 37, 39, 121, and 123

Options: 'Nana Lutea'—golden-yellow leaves; 12" high, 10" wide

Outstanding Features:

- Dark green needles and diminutive size
- Pyramidal form makes a beautiful specimen
- Tolerates moist, acidic soil locations

This slow-growing evergreen adds unchanging beauty to any yard. Foliage and form remain the same through the seasons and through the years. It looks like a tiny Christmas tree. This shrub is easy to grow; aside from occasional watering during times of drought, no care is needed.

Clethra alnifolia

Summersweet

Zones: 3-9

Light Needs:

Mature Size:

3'-8'

4'-8'

Growth Rate:
slow

deciduous flowering shrub

Needs: Plant in moist, acidic soil. Mix organic matter in at planting time; mulch with a 3-inch-thick layer of compost each spring. Water regularly during the growing season. Grow in partial shade. Prune in late summer after flowering to keep plants dense and oval-shaped.

Good for: massing in shady beds, woodlands, swampy spots, natural areas, beside ponds, streams, shrub borders

More Choices: pages 29, 34, 37, 39, 40, 120, 121, 122, 123, and 125

Options: 'Ruby Spice'—dark pink flowers

Don't let soggy soils or shady sites deter you. Summersweet will thrive in these locations. Fragrant flowers occur at a time when few other shrubs are blooming, usually from July to August. Shrubs get quite large and form an oval outline. They sucker to form colonies of clean, healthy plants. Plants may be sold as Sweet Pepperbush.

Cornus alba

Redtwig Dogwood

Zones: 2-8

Light Needs:

Mature Size:

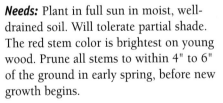

8'-10'

5'-10'

Growth Rate:
rapid

deciduous shrub

Needs: Plant in full sun in moist, well-drained soil. Will tolerate partial shade. The red stem color is brightest on young wood. Prune all stems to within 4" to 6" of the ground in early spring, before new growth begins.

Good for: shrub borders, along fences or driveways, around ponds, large displays

More Choices: pages 29, 33, 37, and 121

Options: *Cornus stolonifera* 'Cardinal'— showy red twigs, 6' tall, 12' wide
'Elegantissima'—gray-green leaves with irregular, twisted white margins
'Aurea'—leaves are soft yellow

Brighten your yard's winter appeal with Redtwig Dogwood. The new stems have a greenish color with just a hint of red. With the onset of cool weather, stems turn bright red, the perfect color to linger and glow against winter snows after the leaves blow away in the fall. The more sun plants receive, the brighter the twig color will be.

Shrubs 5

Cornus mas

Cornelian Cherry

Zones: 4-8

Light Needs:

Mature Size:

10'-20'

10'-15'

Growth Rate:
medium to rapid

deciduous flowering shrub

Needs: Plant in full sun in moist, well-drained soil. Prune any dead or damaged stems in late winter or early spring; prune to shape after flowering. Pest-free.

Good for: specimen use, shrub borders, hedges, screens, foundation plantings, small ornamental trees

More Choices: pages 29, 32, 111, 113, 121, 123, and 124

Options: 'Aureo-elegantissima'—leaves are yellow or brushed with pink
'Variegata'—leaf margins are creamy white

Outstanding Features:

Bright yellow flowers open early in spring
Edible berries attract birds to the landscape
Adaptable to various soil and pH types

Cornelian Cherry steals the show in early spring with golden blooms that burst open even before Forsythia. Edible, cherry red fruit ripens in midsummer and can be made into flavorful preserves. Or, let the birds enjoy the fruit. These shrubs require little or no care after plants become established. Plants are attractive placed against a dark green or red background.

Cornus racemosa

Gray Dogwood

Zones: 4-7

Light Needs:

Mature Size:

10'-15'

10'-15'

Growth Rate:
slow to rapid

deciduous flowering shrub

Needs: Plant in full sun in moist, well-drained soil. Prune any dead or damaged stems in late winter or early spring; prune to shape after flowering. It suckers and can be difficult to maintain in small settings.

Good for: shrub borders, hedges, poor soils, naturalized areas, winter interest, massed plantings

More Choices: pages 29, 33, 111, 113, 121, 124, and 125

Options: 'Slavinii'—dwarf with twisted leaves, 2' to 3' high, suckering spread

Outstanding Features:

Winter interest from bark and flower stems
White flowers open in late May
White berries ripen in fall and attract birds

Spring flowers turn into white, berrylike fruits that are savored by numerous species of birds. After the fruits are gone and leaves have fallen, the stems that held the fruits become visible. The pinkish stems contrast with the gray stems of the shrub, and the result is picture perfect—all winter long. Three-year-old and older stems develop the gray bark color; younger wood is reddish brown. In colder climates, shield from northwest winds by planting in a protected area, not out in the open.

Cornus stolonifera 'Flaviramea'

Yellow-Twig Dogwood

Zones: 3-8

Light Needs:

Mature Size:

6'-8'

8'-10'

Growth Rate:
rapid

deciduous shrub

Needs: Plant in full sun or part shade in moist or wet soil. The yellow stem color is brightest on young wood. Prune all stems to within 4" to 6" of the ground in early spring, before new growth begins.

Good for: shrub borders, mass plantings, use along drives or fences

More Choices: pages 29, 33, 34, 37, 121, 123, and 125

Options: 'Isanti'—bright red stems, 5' to 6' high, 8' to 10' wide; Zones 3-8

Plant Yellow-Twig Dogwood to brighten winter scenes around your home. This plant requires nothing more than well-drained soil and well-timed pruning in early spring to encourage growth of new, yellow stems. Use with caution in the landscape. The color effect can be overwhelming.

Cotoneaster horizontalis

Rockspray Cotoneaster

Zones: 6-9

Light Needs:

Mature Size:

2'-3'

5'-8'

Growth Rate:
slow to medium

evergreen shrub

Needs: Plant in full sun and well-drained soil. Susceptible to fireblight. Remove and destroy affected branches. Use spray containing streptomycin.

Good for: slopes, planters, behind retaining walls, in sunny, dry beds and as groundcover

More Choices: pages 33, 40, 41, 121, 122, 124, and 125

Options: 'Little Gem'—12" high
'Robusta'—vigorous, upright growth, heavy fruiting
'Saxatilis'—compact, few berries
'Tom Thumb'—broad spreading, dense

Shrubs 5

Rockspray Cotoneaster offers effortless seasonal interest. Showy spring flowers are followed by red berries in fall; leaves stay green year-round. Branches have interesting fish-bone pattern and create a layered effect. The level of "evergreen" depends upon the location in which it is grown. Plants are deciduous in cooler regions. *C. dammeri* 'Coral Beauty' has bigger pink flowers and a spreading form.

Daphne x burkwoodii 'Carol Mackie'

Carol Mackie Daphne

Zones: 4-8

Light Needs:

Mature Size:

2'-3'

3'-4'

Growth Rate:
slow

semievergreen shrub

Needs: Plant in full sun or part shade in cool, moist soil. Neutral to slightly alkaline soil yields best growth. Mulch to keep roots cool. Prune to remove dead wood or to shape immediately after flowering.

Good for: specimen shrubs, small yards, rock gardens, raised planting beds, entries, outdoor living areas

More Choices: pages 32, 34, 37, 39, 120, 121, 123, and 124

Outstanding Features:
- Clusters of light pink flowers in spring
- Leaves are delicately edged in cream
- Maintains foliage well into winter

Waxy, perfumed pink blooms cover this shrub in spring, scenting an entire yard with their sweet fragrance. The leaves are deep green edged in cream. Roots require cool soil that is well-drained. Once that need is met, get set for years of springtime scents and summertime beauty.

Euonymus alatus 'Compacta'

Dwarf Burning Bush

Zones: 3-8

Light Needs:

Mature Size:

5'-10'

5'-10'

Growth Rate:
slow

deciduous shrub

Needs: Plant in any well-drained soil, acidic or alkaline. Grow in full sun or partial shade. Pruning is seldom needed or desired. Maintain plants in their natural rounded form.

Good for: specimen shrubs, seasonal accents, deciduous screens, massing, parking areas, beside patios, along walkways or paths, hedges

More Choices: pages 29, 32, 34, 39, 41, 121, 122, 123, and 125

Options: Burning Bush (not dwarf; no 'Compacta' in botanical name)—12' to 15' high, 10' to 12' wide

Outstanding Features:
- Flame red fall foliage color
- Leaves grow in horizontal layers
- Naturally dense, rounded outline

If you enjoy fall color, you ought to plant Burning Bush. Leaves on these shrubs turn brilliant red in autumn. Also sold as Dwarf Winged Euonymus, so named for corky ridges present on stems.

Euonymus kiautschovicus 'Manhattan'

Manhattan Spreading Euonymus

Zones: 4-8

Light Needs:

Mature Size:

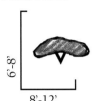

6'-8'

8'-12'

Growth Rate:
fast

evergreen shrub

Needs: Plant in full sun, part shade, or shade. Soil can be fertile or poor, but should be well-drained. Plants may die back during hard winters. Prune to remove dead branches when buds swell in spring. Shrubs will quickly regrow.

Good for: informal hedges, screens, or mass plantings

More Choices: pages 28, 33, 34, 37, 111, and 125

Outstanding Features:
- Leaves have a deep green color in summer
- Pink capsules surround orange-red fruits in fall
- Fast growth for quick hedges and screens

The dark green leaves of this shrub appear on spreading branches, making it a natural choice to create a screen or to form a loose, informal hedge. Manhattan Spreading Euonymus is easy to grow. Late summer flowers can attract flies. Locate plants away from patios and outdoor seating areas. Leaves can winter-burn in colder climates; plant where you won't view daily from inside your home.

Forsythia x intermedia

Border Forsythia

Zones: 6-9

Light Needs:

Mature Size:

8'-10'

7'-10'

Growth Rate:
rapid

deciduous shrub

Needs: Plant in a well-drained, sunny spot in a wide range of soils. Tolerant to variable levels of soil pH. Give this plant room to grow. Large, arching form is not appropriate for formal gardens or shaping.

Good for: informal hedge or screen, massed plantings, and banks

More Choices: pages 29, 32, 37, 38, 39, 40, 41, 111, 121, 122, 123, and 124

Outstanding Features:
- Arching branches provide informal form
- Yellow blooms in early spring
- Adaptable to any type of soil

This big, arching shrub welcomes spring with sunshine-yellow blooms. It's easy to grow, but give it plenty of room. Prune after flowering by removing oldest wood to the ground. Tolerant of city conditions.

Shrubs 5

Fothergilla major

Large Fothergilla

Zones: 4-8

Light Needs:

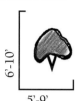

Mature Size:

6'-10'

5'-9'

Growth Rate:
slow

deciduous shrub

Needs: Plant in well-drained, fertile, acid soil. Not tolerate of alkaline soil. In northern yards, plant in full sun; in southern locales, some shade is required.

Good for: shrub borders, foundations, mass plantings, use near patios and outdoor seating areas, planting near other acid loving shrubs and perennials

More Choices: pages 29, 33, 39, 113, 120, 122, 124, and 125

Options: 'Mt. Airy'—larger flowers, more reliable fall color
F. gardenii (Dwarf Fothergilla)— 2' to 3' high and wide

Outstanding Features:
- Bottlebrush flowers are fragrant
- Showy, multicolored fall foliage
- Deep, dark green leaves are pest-free.

Large Fothergilla deserves top billing in your yard. Position it prominently where you can enjoy the show. The curtain rises in spring with the appearance of white, bottlebrushlike blooms that smell sweetly of honey. Summer leaves are dark, leathery, and free of holes and disease. In fall, the foliage explodes into a display of red-orange-scarlet-yellow fireworks. All colors are possible on the same plant and at the same time.

Hamamelis virginiana

Common Witch Hazel

Zones: 3-8

Light Needs:

Mature Size:

20'-30'

15'-20'

Growth Rate:
medium

deciduous flowering shrub

Needs: Plant in full sun or partial shade in well-drained, fertile soil. It will not thrive in dry soils. Tolerant of city conditions. This shrub will get big; give it room to grow. Prune in late winter or early spring to remove dead or damaged wood.

Good for: shrub borders, large foundation plantings or massing, naturalized areas, fragrance, shaded areas

More Choices: pages 32, 34, 113, 123, and 125

Outstanding Features:
- Golden-yellow fall foliage color
- Fragrant yellow flowers in the fall
- Disease and pest-free; low maintenance

Add flower fragrance to the scents experienced in autumn by planting Common Witch Hazel. The flowers open in fall from October to November. Green summer foliage turns a spectacular yellow in fall. Plants grown in full sun have a rounded shape while those grown in shade are more open and irregular. It can be used as a small tree or large shrub in the landscape.

Rose of Sharon

Zones: 5-9

Light Needs:

Mature Size:

8'-12'

6'-8'

Growth Rate:
medium to rapid

deciduous shrub

Needs: Plant in full sun to partial shade in any soil that's well-drained, from acidic to alkaline. Trim only as needed to shape plants; make cuts in winter to avoid removing flower buds. Underplant with shorter shrubs.

Good for: informal shrub bed or screen, narrow areas or beside paving and swimming pools, single specimen in beds and containers

More Choices: pages 29, 33, 34, 37, 39, 41, 121, and 125

Outstanding Features:
- Single or double blooms in summer
- Fast-growing, large ornamental shrub
- Tolerates wide range of growing conditions

Large flowers in pinks, reds, whites, and blues dress up this old-fashioned shrub. Rose of Sharon is a fast-growing plant that withstands poor soil, heat, and drought. May also be sold as Althea. Cultivar options: 'Aphrodite'—dark pink petals with dark red centers; 'Blue Bird'—large lavender flowers with red centers; 'Diana'—large, pure white flower; 'Oiseau Bleu'—azure blue flower with purple veining; 'Paeoniflora'—flowers double, light pink from June to September.

Annabelle Hydrangea

Zones: 3-9

Light Needs:

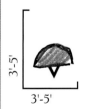

Mature Size:

3'-5'

3'-5'

Growth Rate:
rapid

deciduous shrub

Needs: Plant in fertile, slightly acidic soil that's well-drained but moist. Water regularly. Grow in full sun or partial shade—blooms best in sun but may require afternoon shade in hotter regions. Prune in late winter or early spring, cutting stems just above a bud to remove one-quarter of stem length.

Good for: specimen shrubs, seasonal accent, massing, entries, courtyards, beside patios, include in flower or shrub beds, fill in narrow spaces between walkways and walls

More Choices: pages 32, 34, 37, 38, 40, 41, 121, 122, 123, 124, and 125

Outstanding Features:
- Big, showy flowers last from spring into fall
- Grows quickly to fill in planting beds
- Tolerates both cold and hot temperatures

Shrubs 5

Get the soil right, and this shrub is easy to grow. Big blossoms are showy from spring into fall and change colors with the seasons. They start off apple green in late spring, then become white, then back to green, and finally fade to pink-blushed beige in cool weather. Position these shrubs where you can enjoy them throughout the growing season. Flowers can reach nearly a foot in diameter. Cut blossoms dry well.

Nikko Blue Hydrangea

Zones: 6-9

Light Needs:

Mature Size:

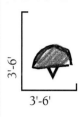

3'-6'

3'-6'

Growth Rate:
rapid

deciduous flowering shrub

Needs: Plant in fertile soil that's moist but well-drained. Grow in full sun in cooler regions, afternoon shade in hotter areas. Water regularly; plants wilt when roots are dry. Tolerates salt. Remove flower heads after color fades. Grow in sheltered spots in colder parts of Zone 6.

Good for: specimen shrubs, massing, brightening shady beds, entries, courtyards, coastal landscapes, planting in shrub beds, including in perennial beds

More Choices: pages 33, 34, 40, 121, 122, 123, and 125

Options: 'Pia'—pink flowers

Bigleaf hydrangeas will make you look like a gardening genius. Big, showy blue or pink flowers appear in warm weather set against rich green leaves. Acidic soil yields blue flowers, while plants grown in alkaline soil bloom pink. Add aluminum sulfate to soil for blue, lime for pink. Treat plants individually within a bed for a medley of blue and pink flowers.

PeeGee Hydrangea

Zones: 3-8

Light Needs:

Mature Size:

10'-20'

10'-20'

Growth Rate:
rapid

deciduous flowering shrub

Needs: Plant in rich soil that's moist but well-drained. Slightly acidic soils are best. Shrubs will adapt to any soil condition except soggy. Grow in full sun or partial shade. Avoid pruning by giving plants plenty of room; shrubs grow vigorously and get large enough to be trained into small trees.

Good for: specimen shrub, seasonal accent, informal deciduous screen, coarse-textured background, beside blank walls or fences

More Choices: pages 29, 33, 34, 39, 121, 122, 123, and 125

H. paniculata 'Tardiva'

Plant this tough, fast-growing shrub where it has room to get big. Plants fade into the background until midsummer flowers put them in the spotlight. Flowers are produced on new wood. Flower heads can reach 12 to 18 inches in length. Plants should be pruned to 5 or 10 main shoots to produce the largest heads. Ultimate plant size is quite variable. Also try 'Tardiva'—flowers in fall.

Hydrangea quercifolia

Oakleaf Hydrangea

Zones: 5-9

Light Needs:

Mature Size:

4'-8'

3'-10'

Growth Rate:
slow to medium

Outstanding Features:
- Big, drooping cones of creamy flowers
- Large, coarse leaves turn scarlet in autumn
- Mounded, irregular plant form

deciduous flowering shrub

Needs: Plant in moist, acidic or alkaline soil that's rich in organic matter. Grow in full sun in cooler regions, partial shade in hotter areas. Shrubs grow best with regular watering but will tolerate drought.

Good for: specimen shrubs, planting beneath trees, massing, coarse-textured backgrounds, shrub borders, edges of woodlands, natural areas

More Choices: pages 34, 39, 121, 122, 123, and 125

Brighten empty spots in dappled shade with Oakleaf Hydrangea. These shrubs are big, their flowers are big, and so are their leaves. Prune after flowering if necessary. Plants look best when grown into their naturally irregular form. Not a good choice for formal landscapes.

Design Tip Oakleaf Hydrangea is a good companion plant to Mountain Laurels and Rhododendrons. It also grows well in beds of Hostas.

Ilex cornuta 'Burfordii Nana'

Dwarf Burford Holly

Zones: 6-9

Light Needs:

Mature Size:

12'-18'

10'-15'

Growth Rate:
medium to rapid

Outstanding Features:
- Glossy green leaves remain year-round
- Attractive red berries in winter
- Adaptable to a range of soil conditions

evergreen shrub

Needs: Plant in full sun to partial shade in acidic soil that's either rich or poor but not too wet. Prune as needed to control size. Allow plants to form dense mass instead of individual shapes.

Good for: foundation planting, parking areas, hedges, barriers, or as a background plant

More Choices: pages 28, 32, 34, 37, 39, 41, 111, 113, 123, and 125

This tough shrub gets much larger than its name implies. You can keep hedges trimmed between 4 to 6 feet tall. Or, let single specimen plants grow tall enough to form small trees (remove lower branches to reveal trunks), as shown here. Foliage stays a glossy dark green year-round. Heavy crops of red berries appear in winter.

Shrubs 5

shrubs

Ilex crenata 'Green Lustre'

Green Lustre Japanese Holly

Outstanding Features:
- Shiny green leaves throughout the year
- Dense, solid growth makes a solid screen
- Adaptability to urban growing conditions

Zones: 4-6

Light Needs:

Mature Size:

3'-6'
5'-10'

Growth Rate: slow

evergreen shrub

Needs: Plant in either full sun or partial shade in fertile, moist soil that's high in organic matter. Prefers acidic soils. Alkaline soil (high pH) will cause leaves to turn yellow; add peat at planting if it's necessary to lower pH. Prune to shape shrubs in summer, after the new growth is mature. Tolerates city conditions and confined growing spaces.

Good for: specimen use, hedging, screening, massing in planting beds

More Choices: pages 28, 33, 34, 41, 43, 111, 121, and 123

This holly is hardy and sturdy. Its dense branching habit and thick leaf cover make it an excellent choice for creating a privacy screen or barrier hedge. Japanese Holly adapts well to urban growing conditions and to small yards. Though it prefers acidic soil, it will tolerate neutral soil pH. This holly isn't difficult to grow or to maintain. Grow this shrub in the warmer areas of Zone 4 by planting in a location shielded from harsh winter winds.

Ilex crenata 'Helleri'

Heller Japanese Holly

Outstanding Features:
- Low maintenance; no pruning required
- Fine-textured foliage stays green all year
- Dwarf, naturally mounded form

Zones: 5-8

Light Needs:

Mature Size:

2'-3'
3'-5'

Growth Rate: slow

evergreen shrub

Needs: Plant in sun or shade in soil of medium fertility and moisture. Requires acidic soil and will not thrive in alkaline or sandy soil. Pick a shadier spot if your soil is poor. Water regularly during hot, dry spells. Space new plants 2 feet apart and let them grow together to form a dense mass.

Good for: use in front of low windows or taller plants, filling large shrub beds, edging around patios and decks

More Choices: pages 33, 34, 41, 121, and 123

If you hate pruning, here's the plant for you. Heller Japanese Holly stays low and tidy all by itself. This evergreen shrub grows slowly. Start with larger plants if you want instant impact. Transplants easily into the landscape. Tolerant of city conditions.

142   Shrubs

Compact Japanese Holly

Zones: 5-8

Light Needs:

Mature Size:

3'-5'

3'-4'

Growth Rate:
rapid

evergreen shrub

Needs: Plant in sun or shade in well-drained soil. Prune if desired to maintain compact form. This disease-resistant shrub is easy to transplant.

Good for: entries, specimen use, formal gardens, foundation or background planting in shrub beds

More Choices: pages 32, 34, 41, 113, 121, and 123

Outstanding Features:

Round, dense form, dark green leaves

Resembles boxwood but grows more rapidly

Tolerates frequent repeated pruning

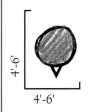

Consider this shrub a substitute for Boxwood. Though inexpensive and fast-growing in comparison, the dense form of this disease-resistant shrub has similar classic appeal. Plants are easily trimmed into formal shapes.

Inkberry

Zones: 3-9

Light Needs:

Mature Size:

4'-6'

4'-6'

Growth Rate:
slow to medium

evergreen shrub

Needs: Plant in acidic soil that's moist but well-drained. Grow in full sun or partial shade. Pest and disease-resistant. Shear or prune heavily as needed to maintain compact size.

Good for: foundation planting, screening, massing, winter interest, providing background, seaside landscapes, formal or informal gardens, parking areas, poolside, planting beside patios and walkways

More Choices: pages 28, 33, 34, 37, 39, 40, 41, 43, 113, 122, and 123

Outstanding Features:

Glossy leaves stay dark green year-round

Tolerates heat, snow, salt, and pruning

Dense, compact form; tight branching

Shrubs 5

Few shrubs are as adaptable as glossy-leaved Inkberry. You can grow it at the beach, in snow, in alkaline or acidic soils, in sunny or shady spots. Also sold as Gallberry. Compact varieties are more desired for home landscape use. Choose these selections unless you want a 10' tall shrub. Also try: 'Nigra'—3' to 4' tall; 'Shamrock'—5' to 6' tall. Thrives in the Eastern United States.

Ilex x 'Nellie R. Stevens'

Nellie R. Stevens Holly

Zones: 6-9

Light Needs:

Mature Size:

15'-20'

10'-15'

Growth Rate:
medium

large evergreen shrub

Needs: Plant in full sun or partial shade in well-drained, acidic soil. Give new plants plenty of room to grow. Mature plants can withstand drought.

Good for: corners of tall houses, screening poor views, privacy, windbreaks, specimen plants

More Choices: pages 28, 33, 34, 37, 39, 41, 43, and 123

Outstanding Features:

✔ Broad, pyramidal form in the landscape
🍃 Glossy dark green leaves year-round
🫐 Clusters of red berries in winter

With its naturally broad, pyramidal form and dark, glossy green leaves, Nellie R. Stevens Holly is a long-time favorite in the landscape. Plants get big, so give them plenty of room. They resemble a fat Christmas tree growing in the yard. Female plants fruit heavily.

Ilex verticillata

Winterberry

Zones: 3-9

Light Needs:

Mature Size:

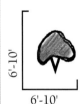

6'-10'

6'-10'

Growth Rate:
slow

deciduous flowering shrub

Needs: Plant in full sun or partial shade in fertile, moist soil that's high in organic matter. Plants prefer an acidic soil pH. They will adapt to wet soils.

Good for: wet, boggy areas, winter interest, screens or hedges, attracting birds, training as a small tree, massing

More Choices: pages 29, 33, 34, 37, 39, 111, 121, 122, 123, and 125

Options: 'Sparkleberry'—quarter-inch berries; 15' high by 12' wide; Zones 5-9 'Winter Red'—dark green leaves turn bronze in fall; berries last until spring; 8' high by 10' wide; Zones 3-9

Outstanding Features:

🫐 Big, bright red berries persist through winter
✔ Fruit attracts birds to the landscape
🪴 Grows in wet, swampy soil conditions

Grow this holly to add color to the winter landscape. Twigs covered with bright red berries attract hungry birds in cold weather. Plants require acid soils; alkaline soil will cause leaves to turn yellow and plants will not thrive. You must plant both male and female plants to get berries. Plant one male for every 10 to 12 females.

Juniperus chinensis 'Parsonii'

Parson's Juniper

Zones: 3-9

evergreen shrub

Light Needs:

Needs: Plant in full sun in moist, well-drained soil. Junipers will also grow in chalky, sandy soils that are dry. Little pruning is needed.

Mature Size:

2'-3'

3'-4'

Good for: low-growing hedge, low plantings along a walkway, or surrounding a patio or deck

More Choices: pages 33, 37, 41, 111, 121, 122, and 123

Growth Rate:
slow to medium

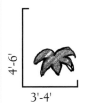

Junipers earn their keep in the landscape. Once established, they are care-free. Occasional pruning to remove any dead or damaged growth is all that is needed. Don't overwater.

Juniperus chinensis 'Sea Green'

Sea Green Juniper

Zones: 4-8

evergreen shrub

Light Needs:

Needs: Plant in full sun in moist to dry, well-drained soil. Junipers will also grow in chalky, sandy soils that are dry. Little pruning is needed.

Mature Size:

4'-6'

3'-4'

Good for: foundation plantings around homes or decks or porches

More Choices: pages 33, 37, 40, 43, 113, 121, 122, and 123

Growth Rate:
slow to medium

Easy and evergreen—that pretty much sums up Sea Green Juniper. Grow it for year-round frothy foliage in moist or poor soils in full sun.

Shrubs **5**

Juniperus sabina 'Tamariscifolia'

Tam Juniper

Zones: 3-7

Light Needs:

Mature Size:

3'-6'

5'-6'

Growth Rate:
slow to medium

evergreen shrub

Needs: Plant in full sun in well-drained soil. Grows well in chalky, sandy soils that are dry. It also can take urban growing conditions. Little pruning is needed. Remove dead or damaged branches or shape anytime from early summer to fall.

Good for: low-growing hedges, planting along walkways, surrounding patios or decks, mass plantings

More Choices: pages 33, 37, 43, 111, 121, and 123

Options: 'Arcadia'—leaves are grass green; 1' high by 4' wide; Zones 3-7

Outstanding Features:

- Rounded mound of blue-green branches
- Maintains leaf color through the seasons
- Tolerates poor, dry soil conditions with ease

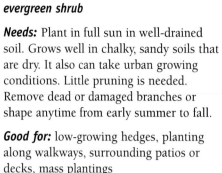

This easy-to-grow evergreen requires no effort to grow or to maintain. Simply plant it, water it in, and let it grow. Tam Juniper grows in a mounded shape, making it the perfect choice for including as part of a foundation planting or for rounding the corner of a house or deck.

Juniperus squamata 'Blue Star'

Blue Star Juniper

Zones: 4-8

Light Needs:

Mature Size:

12"-16"

2'-3'

Growth Rate:
slow

evergreen shrub

Needs: Plant in full sun in well-drained chalky, sandy, or dry soils. It grows well in urban growing conditions. Very little pruning or additional care is required.

Good for: specimen use, rock garden plantings, planting along walkways

More Choices: pages 32, 37, 121, and 122

Outstanding Features:

- Tight mound of silvery blue-green foliage
- Maintains leaf color through the seasons
- Slow growth rate; doesn't get out of hand

This blue-leafed beauty has leaves that look like little stars covering the branches of the shrub. Use it to shine by a front door or along the edge of a shrub border. Supply some night-lighting, and leaves will shine brightly at night, too.

Kalmia latifolia

Mountain Laurel

Zones: 4-9

Light Needs:

Mature Size:

7'-15'

7'-15'

Growth Rate:
slow

Outstanding Features:
- Clusters of spring flowers
- Large leaves stay green year-round
- Great for moist areas in the landscape

evergreen shrub

Needs: Plant in acidic, moist soil in sun or shade. Fewer flowers are produced in dense shade. No pruning is needed. Mulch plants well and provide water during hot, dry spells. Plants will not thrive in alkaline or very dry soil.

Good for: natural areas, large planting beds, foundation plantings, good background for summer perennials

More Choices: pages 28, 33, 34, 39, 113, 121, 122, 123, and 124

If you have the right soil condition for Mountain Laurel in your yard, don't miss the opportunity to grow this large-leaved evergreen shrub. You'll enjoy clusters of blossoms from May to June in white and shades of pink and red. Desirable cultivars include 'Alba'—white flowers; 'Myrtifolia'— stays under 6' high; 'Ostbo Red'—deep red flower buds; 'Pink Charm'—pink flower; 'Polypetala'—double feathery pink flowers; 'Sharon Rose'—deep red buds and light pink flowers, compact growth habit.

Leucothoe fontanesiana

Drooping Leucothoe

Zones: 5-8

Light Needs:

Mature Size:

3'-6'

3'-6'

Growth Rate:
slow to medium

Outstanding Features:
- Spring blooms of white fragrant flowers
- Green leaves take on a purple tinge in winter
- Arching plant form resembles a fountain

evergreen shrub

Needs: Plant in partial to full shade in acid, moist, well-drained soil. Rich, fertile soil is best. Protect plants from drying winds and drought. Rejuvenate plants by pruning to the ground after flowering.

Good for: shrub borders, planting beneath shade trees, combining with acid-loving plants, hiding fences, facing leggy plants, massing, covering shady banks

More Choices: pages 34, 39, 120, 122, 123, and 124

Options: 'Rainbow'—new leaves are mottled with rosy-pink and creamy-yellow; 5' high, 6' wide

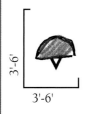

Drooping Leucothoe opens its fragrant white flowers in spring. They dangle and droop among the bright, bronzy-colored leaves. Leucothoe maintains its lustrous evergreen foliage fall through winter. Use this shrub to accompany azaleas or rhododendrons for a lovely spring show.

Shrubs 5

Ligustrum x vicaryi

Golden Vicary Privet

Zones: 5-8

Light Needs:

Mature Size:

8'-10'

8'-10'

Growth Rate:
slow to medium

evergreen shrub

Needs: Plant in full sun in well-drained soil. Full sun keeps the leaves a bright, golden color instead of yellow-green. Prune shrubs to shape after flowering.

Good for: specimen use, foundation plantings, screens, planting against dark-colored backgrounds, hedging

More Choices: pages 28, 33, 111, 113, and 125

Options: *L. sinense* 'Variegatum' (Variegated Chinese Privet)—white edged, pale green leaves; 4' to 6' tall and wide; Zones 7-9

Let the sun shine and this shrub will too. Full sun brings out the bright, golden-colored foliage. They show off best when planted against a backdrop of dark-leafed evergreens. White flowers appear in mid-summer and are followed by bluish-black fruit that birds relish.

Lonicera tatarica 'Arnold's Red'

Arnold's Red Tatarian Honeysuckle

Zones: 3-9

Light Needs:

Mature Size:

10'-12'

8'-10'

Growth Rate:
medium to rapid

deciduous flowering shrub

Needs: Plant in full sun or partial shade in well-drained, fertile soil. Prune annually after flowering to shape and maintain size. Prune anytime to tame wayward stems.

Good for: hedges, dense screens, or fence row planting; use near outdoor living areas for fragrance

More Choices: pages 29, 32, 111, 120, 121, 122, 123, and 124

Options: 'Alba' or 'Parvifolia'—fragrant white flowers
'Hack's Red'—deep purplish-red flowers
'Virginalis'—rose-pink buds and the largest flowers of any *L. tatarica* form

When 'Arnold's Red' bursts into bloom, the effect is that of a red waterfall. Blossoms give way to bright red berries that are a favorite among birds. This shrub is easy to establish and easy to care for. Fallen fruit can stain paving. Use near outside living areas but not right beside them. Dense masses of branches can catch all kinds of wind-borne trash; spring cleanup will be needed, especially if planted in open areas or near roadsides.

Myrica pensylvanica

Northern Bayberry

Zones: 2-6

Light Needs:

Mature Size:

5'-12' (height)
5'-12' (width)

Growth Rate:
medium to rapid

evergreen to deciduous shrub

Needs: Plant in full sun or partial shade. This shrub is easy to grow and adapts to a variety of soils, thriving in heavy clay, sandy, fertile, or poor soil. Prune in late winter to remove dead wood and to shape shrubs. To produce fruit, both female and male plants need to be included (check plant tags).

Good for: hedges, screens, fence rows, foundation plantings, use along streets, seaside areas, dried flower arrangements

More Choices: pages 28, 29, 33, 34, 37, 40, 43, 111, 113, 121, 122, 123, and 125

Outstanding Features:
- Aromatic, silvery berries persist through winter
- Tolerance of poor, salty soil conditions
- Attractive used with broad leaf evergreens

Northern Bayberry is one tough shrub, surviving in any kind of soil and withstanding harsh salt spray and soil salts. Its bright green leaves release a bayberry scent when rustled or crushed. Aromatic berries ripen in late summer and fall and linger on branches through winter into spring. They make a lovely addition to fall or holiday flower arrangements. Plants are evergreen in warmer areas and deciduous in colder climates.

Photinia x fraseri

Redtip Photinia

Zones: 6-9

Light Needs:

Mature Size:

10'-15' (height)
5'-7' (width)

Growth Rate:
rapid

evergreen shrub

Needs: Plant in full sun or partial shade in well-drained soil. Fertilize regularly with nitrogen to prevent deficiency. Prune heavily in late winter or early spring by cutting woody stems at their bases.

Good for: hedging or screening, single-stemmed tree

More Choices: pages 28, 33, 34, 111, 121, and 124

Outstanding Features:
- Early spring growth is bright red
- Summer leaves are a lustrous deep green
- Upright growth for hedging use

Redtip Photinia grows quickly. New growth unfolds bright red at the tops of shrubs. If left unpruned, this shrub will get very large, so give it room to grow or plan to prune. Flowers have an unpleasant smell. Die-back can kill an entire hedge quickly. Remove diseased branches as soon as they appear, rinsing loppers between cuts to avoid spreading the problem. Redtip Photinia suffers in areas with high humidity.

Shrubs 5

Picea abies 'Nidiformis'

Bird's Nest Spruce

Zones: 2-7

Light Needs:

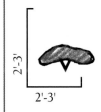

Mature Size:

2'-3' (height)

2'-3' (width)

Growth Rate:
slow

evergreen shrub

Needs: Plant in full sun in moist, well-drained soil. Spruces do not grow well in polluted, dry conditions. Prune to remove damaged wood or to shape the shrub.

Good for: specimen use, mass plantings, growing along walkways and drives, rock gardens, and perennial borders

More Choices: pages 32, 37, and 121

Outstanding Features:

✓ Slow growth, spreading more out than up

Interesting plant form creates a living "nest"

Tolerates cool climates and moist soils

Bird's Nest Spruce is an excellent plant for small gardens. Its slow growth rate and short stature make it a natural choice for planting in areas where you do not want to block views. Plant this low-growing shrub and then forget about it. It's really that easy.

Picea glauca 'Conica'

Dwarf Alberta Spruce

Zones: 3-8

Light Needs:

Mature Size:

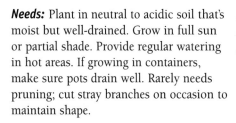

5'-8' (height)

6'-12' (width)

Growth Rate:
slow

evergreen shrub

Needs: Plant in neutral to acidic soil that's moist but well-drained. Grow in full sun or partial shade. Provide regular watering in hot areas. If growing in containers, make sure pots drain well. Rarely needs pruning; cut stray branches on occasion to maintain shape.

Good for: single specimens, matched pairs, anchoring corners of flowerbeds, formal gardens, entries, courtyards, beside walkways, gates, and patios; growing in containers or confined spaces

More Choices: pages 32, 34, 37, 39, 41, 121, and 123

Outstanding Features:

✓ Tidy, conical shape adds contrast

Small and slow-growing

Bluish green foliage stays fresh year-round

If you want a topiary but don't have time to train one, this is the plant for you. Slow-growing dwarf shrubs resemble tidy, miniature trees. These little shrubs often stay as small as 2 or 3 feet tall for many years. Easily grown.

Pieris floribunda

Mountain Pieris

Zones: 4-8

Light Needs:

Mature Size:

4'-6'
3'-10'

Growth Rate:
slow

evergreen shrub

Needs: Plant in full sun or partial shade in moist, well-drained, slightly acid soil. Boost soil acidity by mulching with composted oak leaves or by working peat moss into soil at planting time. Very little pruning is required.

Good for: specimen shrub use, informal hedges, near walkways, doors, and outdoor seating areas to enjoy the fragrance

More Choices: pages 33, 34, 39, 111, 120, 122, 123, and 124

Outstanding Features:

- Clusters of fragrant flowers in early spring
- Leaves emerge bronzy red changing to green
- Low, mounded habit forms a neat shrub

This upright shrub is smothered with sweet-smelling white flowers in early to midspring. Individual blooms dangle like tiny floral earrings from stems. Dark green leaves stay green year-round. This undemanding shrub is easy to grow if provided with proper growing conditions.

Pieris japonica

Andromeda

Zones: 5-8

Light Needs:

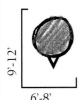

Mature Size:

9'-12'
6'-8'

Growth Rate:
slow

evergreen shrub

Needs: Plant in full sun or partial shade in moist, well-drained, acid soil. Boost acidity by mulching with composted oak leaves or by working peat moss into the soil at planting time. Prune lightly after flowering to retain form. Shelter from strong wind.

Good for: specimen use, informal hedges, shrub borders, mass plantings, plantings with evergreens, woodland areas

More Choices: pages 32, 34, 38, 111, 123, and 124

Options: 'Purity'—white flowers on upright stems; 3' high and wide

Outstanding Features:

- Clusters of fragrant flowers in early spring
- Rich bronze leaves deepen to glossy green
- Wide availability of attractive cultivars

Shrubs 5

Each spring, Andromeda is blanketed with blossoms of pure white that smell as lovely as they look. The individual blooms look like tiny bells. This is easy to grow in acidic, moist locations. In warm locations provide shade during the hottest part of the day. Plants are also sold as Japanese Pieris or Lily-of-the-Valley Bush. Additional cultivars to try include 'Valley Rose'—pastel pink flowers, to 8' high and wide; and 'Valley Valentine'—dusky red flowers, to 8' high and wide.

Pinus mugo

Mugo Pine

Zones: 2-7

Light Needs:

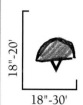

Mature Size:

18"-20'

18"-30'

Growth Rate:
slow

Outstanding Features:
- Rich, deep green needles year-round
- Slow growth makes maintenance easy
- Wide variety of heights are available

evergreen shrub

Needs: Plant in full sun or partial shade in deep, moist, well-drained soil. Pinch growing tips in late spring, removing 3" to 6" of new growth. This encourages thick, dense, bushy plants (see page 116).

Good for: specimen use, mass planting, combining with perennials and alpines in rock gardens, year-round texture

More Choices: pages 33, 34, 37, 43, 121, and 123

Options: 'Compacta'—4' tall by 5' wide; Zones 2-7
'Gnome'—15" tall by 3' wide; Zones 2-7
'Mops'—7' to 10' high, 8' wide; Zones 2-7

Mugo Pine grows slowly and makes a good filler for planting beds. There are many different varieties and forms of Mugo Pine available that range in heights from just over a foot to tree size. Be sure to read plant labels so that you can select the growth habit you desire. If you want one that stays small, select a variety that grows less than a few feet tall. If you are looking for a larger plant or even a small tree, there are selections to fill your needs as well.

Potentilla fruticosa

Shrubby Cinquefoil

Zones: 2-7

Light Needs:

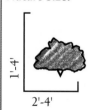

Mature Size:

1'-4'

2'-4'

Growth Rate:
slow

Outstanding Features:
- Extended flowering from summer to frost
- Bright green foliage, yellow-brown in fall
- Tolerates the extremes from cold to hot

deciduous flowering shrub

Needs: Plant in any kind of soil that is well-drained. Though full sun yields best flowering, this shrub will also grow in partial shade. Remove one-third of the stems in late winter or early spring for best flowering.

Good for: low hedges, shrub borders, foundation use, or mass planting

More Choices: pages 33, 34, 111, 113, 121, 122, and 125

Options: 'Abbottswood'—white flowers; bluish-green leaves; 30" tall, 4' wide
'Goldfinger'—bright yellow flowers; dark green leaves

This bloomer keeps going and going, from early summer until frost. The flowers of Shrubby Cinquefoil come in all shades, from white to yellow to pink and orange. The shrub stays a neat size—under 4'—and grows in all types of soil from poor to rich. Amazing cold tolerance allows this plant to grow where winter temperatures dip to a frigid 50 below zero. Additional varieties to look for include: 'Jackman's Variety'—bright yellow flowers, 3' or 4' high; 'Primrose Beauty'—primrose flowers, 3' high; 'Tangerine'—yellow-flushed-red flowers, 2' high and 4' wide.

Prunus glandulosa 'Rosea'

Dwarf Flowering Almond

Zones: 4-8

Light Needs:

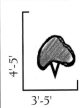

Mature Size:

4'-5'

3'-5'

Growth Rate: medium

deciduous flowering shrub

Needs: Plant in full sun in fertile, moist, well-drained soil. Full sun yields best flowering, but this shrub will grow in partial shade. Prune annually after flowering to shape the shrub. Remove any dead wood in early spring.

Good for: specimen use, shrub or perennial border, seasonal interest

More Choices: pages 32, 34, and 124

In midspring, dull twigs transform into wands of bloom, turning Dwarf Flowering Almond into a cloud of double, pink blossoms. Plants look scraggly when not in bloom; skirt them with low-growing bloomers such as Catmint, Alpine Strawberries, or Flower Carpet Roses.

Prunus laurocerasus 'Otto Luyken'

Otto Luyken Laurel

Zones: 6-8

Light Needs:

Mature Size:

5'-6'

6'-8'

Growth Rate: medium

evergreen shrub

Needs: Plant in moist, well-drained soil in partial or dense shade. Mulch roots well and water regularly. Protect from afternoon sun in hot climates. No pruning required.

Good for: foundation planting, massing beneath trees, shrub beds, background to shade gardens and perennial borders, entries, low hedges

More Choices: pages 34, 41, 113, 122, 123, and 124

Options: Schip Laurel, 'Schipkaensis'— very similar, a little hardier; 10'-15' high, good for screening; Zones 5 to 8

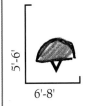

You'll love this plant for its glossy, dark green foliage. The large leaves add coarse texture to compositions as neat, spreading plants fill in shady spots. Do not prune to separate plants. Allow shrubs to grow together to form a mass of dark green. Flowers profusely even in heavy shade.

Shrubs 5

Pyracantha angustifolia Yukon Belle

Yukon Belle Firethorn

Zones: 4-9

Light Needs:

Mature Size:

5'-8'

4'-6'

Growth Rate:
medium to rapid

semievergreen to evergreen shrub

Needs: Plant in fertile, moist, well-drained soil. Full sun yields best flowering and fruiting, but this shrub will grow in partial shade. Prune as needed in any season. Plant this shrub where you want it because once this shrub is established, it doesn't take well to transplanting.

Good for: hedges, barriers, espalier on a wall or chimney as shown here

More Choices: pages 33, 34, 111, 121, 122, and 125

Options: 'Gnome'—orange berries; to 6' high and wide; Zones 4-9

Outstanding Features:

- White flowers cover the shrub in early summer
- Bright orange berries ripen in autumn
- Attractive trained on walls and chimneys

This thorny shrub spills out fountains of white flowers in early summer. Bright, orange berries follow in autumn and linger through winter, long after the leaves are gone. Birds love this shrub because of its berries and protection for nests. This shrub is very thorny. Avoid placing it in areas where children play or near walkways.

Rhododendron catawbiense

Catawba Rhododendron

Zones: 4-8

Light Needs:

Mature Size:

6'-10'

5'-8'

Growth Rate:
slow

evergreen shrub

Needs: Plant in moist, well-drained, acidic, fertile soil. Rhododendrons can take full sun in colder areas; in warmer climates, partial shade is best. Water plants in fall. Mulch beneath shrubs to help soil stay moist. Prune to remove dead branches after new growth has emerged. Snap off flowers after they fade.

Good for: specimen shrub, screen, massed, or foundation plantings

More Choices: pages 28, 32, 34, 38, 113, 121, 122, 123, and 124

Outstanding Features:

- Spring flowers in shades of lilac-purple
- Leaves stay green all year-round
- Broad, rounded outline, dense plant

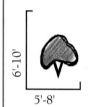

The bright lilac purple blossoms of Catawba Rhododendron are breathtaking against the dark green leaves. Catawba Rhododendron can take cold weather without sacrificing flower buds, but protect it from drying winter winds. Cultivar options: 'P.J.M.'—lavender pink flowers, shade- and drought-tolerant, 6' high to 4' wide, Zones 4-8; 'P.J.M. White'—white flowers, leaves turn burgundy in winter, 3' to 4' high and wide, Zones 4-8; 'Mollis' Hybrids—large, waxy blooms, many flower colors, deciduous, 4' to 5' high and wide, Zones 4-8.

Betty Prior Rose

Zones: 4-9

Light Needs:

Mature Size:

3'-4'

2'-3'

Growth Rate:
medium

deciduous shrub

Needs: Plant roses in full sun in moist, well-drained, fertile soil. Prune to remove dead branches and to shape shrubs after buds swell in spring. Clip faded blooms for nonstop flowers until late summer. Fertilize with rose food when blooming starts.

Good for: specimen shrub, hedge, or massed planting. Space plants 18 inches apart for a hedge of bloom. It will also grow well in a large container.

More Choices: pages 32, 111, 120, 122, and 125

Want a hedge that is as beautiful as it is functional? Plant a row of Betty Prior roses. Pink blossoms are 2 to 3 inches wide and appear from summer until frost. When planting roses, it's helpful to add super phosphate or bonemeal to the soil in the planting hole to promote root growth.

Carefree Beauty Rose

Zones: 4-8

Light Needs:

Mature Size:

3'-4'

2'-3'

Growth Rate:
medium

deciduous shrub

Needs: Plant in full sun in moist, well-drained, fertile soil. Prune to remove dead branches after buds swell in spring. Clip spent blooms to encourage ongoing flowering. Fertilize with rose food when blooming starts.

Good for: specimen shrub, hedge, or foundation planting. To grow as a hedge, space plants 18 inches apart.

More Choices: pages 32, 111, 113, 120, 122, and 125

Shrubs

5

The name says it all: Carefree Beauty. Flowers open continually from summer until frost—large, double, rose pink blooms packed with perfume. No spraying needed; they are completely disease-free. When planting roses, it's helpful to add super phosphate or bonemeal to the soil in the planting hole to promote root growth. This is probably the most famous of Griffith Buck's roses.

Fru Dagmar Hastrup Rose

Zones: 2-9

Light Needs:

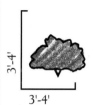

Mature Size:

3'-4'

3'-4'

Growth Rate: medium

deciduous flowering shrub

Needs: This rose prefers sandy, light soil. It will survive in warm coastal climates as well as cold. Prune in early spring each year to remove old, worn-out stems that have stopped bearing blooms. Fertilize with rose food when blooming starts and repeat monthly. Remove spent flowers to encourage additional blooms. Discontinue fertilization and deadheading four to six weeks before the first anticipated frost.

Good for: specimen shrub, hedge, back of a perennial bed

More Choices: pages 32, 37, 40, 111, 120, 122, and 125

Outstanding Features:

- One of the most disease-resistant roses
- Single flowers in shades of silvery pink
- Flowers have a rich clove scent

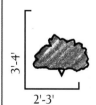

Large, single, pale pink blooms first appear in June and continue opening all summer long. At the end of the season, large scarlet hips cover the bush. Leaves are a deep green in summer, then develop shades of maroon and are golden in fall. It is a highly disease-resistant rose.

Graham Thomas Rose

Zones: 5-9

Light Needs:

Mature Size:

3'-4'

2'-3'

Growth Rate: medium

deciduous shrub

Needs: Plant roses in full sun in moist, well-drained, fertile soil. The only required pruning is removing nonflowering stems in spring. Remove faded blooms to get more flowers.

Good for: specimen shrub, hedge, massed planting, planting near sitting areas to enjoy fragrance

More Choices: pages 33, 111, 120, 122, 123, and 125

Outstanding Features:

- 3-inch-wide, golden-yellow, double blooms
- Old-fashioned rose fragrance
- Compact size and form

This David Austin rose boasts the fragrance of an old-fashioned rose in a shrub form that blooms repeatedly during the growing season. Flowers are golden yellow and double-petaled; they appear all through the growing season, including during the heat of summer. Grow where the fragrance can be enjoyed to the fullest. When grown in ideal conditions, plants may become large with age.

Iceberg Rose

Zones: 4-9

Light Needs:

Mature Size:

1'-2'

1'-2'

Growth Rate:
medium

deciduous shrub

Needs: Plant roses in full sun in moist, well-drained, fertile soil. Prune to remove dead branches and to shape plants after buds swell in spring. Clip faded blooms to keep flowers coming. Fertilize with rose food when blooming starts.

Good for: specimen shrub, hedge, massed planting, good cut flowers

More Choices: pages 33, 111, 120, 122, 124, and 125

Outstanding Features:
- Fragrant flowers in white, 3-inch clusters
- Canes are nearly thornless
- Clean, dark green foliage

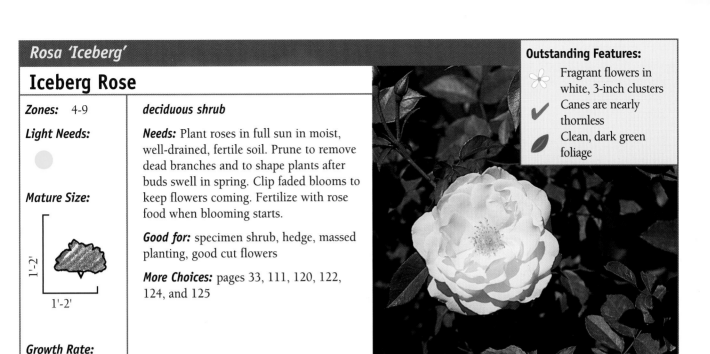

Volumes of pure white flowers open in clusters that are borne at the end of growing stems. Like all floribunda roses, Iceberg can take cold winters (to 30 degrees below zero). Iceberg is easy-care beauty at its best—you won't be disappointed with this rose. Some gardeners have had success getting this rose to bloom in partial shade.

Margo Koster Rose

Zones: 5-8

Light Needs:

Mature Size:

12"

12"-24"

Growth Rate:
medium

deciduous flowering shrub

Needs: Plant roses in full sun in moist, well-drained, fertile soil. Fertilize with rose food when blooming starts.

Good for: an edging plant, a low hedge, specimen use, edging perennial borders, near evergreen shrubs, in well-drained soil near a water garden

More Choices: pages 33, 111, 120, 122, and 125

Outstanding Features:
- Fragrant flowers are borne in small clusters
- Blooms fade in shades of salmon as they age
- Size is perfect for small landscapes

Growing a mere 12 inches high, Margo Koster is a perfect choice to edge a walkway, patio, or shrub border. The stems are nearly thornless, and flowers open in shades of salmon all summer long. This rose is a low-maintenance plant. Also try 'Nearly Wild'—nearly nonstop pink blossoms.

Shrubs 5

Rosa 'Peace'

Peace Rose

Zones: 5-8

Light Needs:

Mature Size:

3'-5'

2'-3'

Growth Rate:
medium

deciduous flowering shrub

Needs: Plant roses in full sun in moist, well-drained, fertile soil. The only required pruning is removing nonflowering stems in spring. Avoid heavy pruning on this variety. Remove spent blooms to encourage additional flowering. Fertilize with rose food when bloom begins and again in four weeks.

Good for: specimen shrub, low hedge, massed planting, near patios and entries, formal gardens surrounded by a hedge of boxwood

More Choices: pages 33, 111, 120, 122, 123, and 125

More Choices: pages 33, 111, 120, 122, 123, and 125

Outstanding Features:
- Blooms are yellow with faint pink edges
- Fragrant flowers on long stems for cutting
- Vigorous grower with dark green leaves

Yellow, high-centered blooms are tinged with pink on petal edges. Coloring is more pronounced on the large, 6-inch blooms as they mature. Vigorous plants produce blooms from early summer to fall. Long stems are great for cutting and enjoying inside. 'Peace' was developed in France in 1937 and smuggled out of the country during World War II.

Rosa Pink Meidiland

Pink Meidiland Rose

Zones: 5-8

Light Needs:

Mature Size:

3'-4'

3'-4'

Growth Rate:
medium

deciduous flowering shrub

Needs: Plant roses in full sun in moist, well-drained, fertile soil. The only required pruning is removing nonflowering stems in spring. Remove spent blooms to encourage flowering. Do not plant roses where they will be exposed to heavy winds or strong winter sun. Fertilize with rose food when blooming starts.

Good for: specimen shrub, low hedge, massed planting

More Choices: pages 33, 111, 122, and 125

More Choices: pages 33, 111, 122, and 125

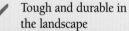

Outstanding Features:
- Pink blooms throughout summer and fall
- Small orange-red hips that attract birds
- Tough and durable in the landscape

The Meidiland roses are French-bred beauties that are tough as nails. Pink Meidiland tosses open shell pink blooms from summer until frost. The flowers are single and look like a Dogwood blossom. This rose will grow in shade and still bloom.

The Fairy Rose

Zones: 4-9

Light Needs:

Mature Size:

2'-3' (height)
2'-3' (width)

Growth Rate:
medium

deciduous flowering shrub

Needs: Plant in moist, well-drained, fertile soil in full sun or partial shade. Fertilize with rose food when blooming starts and repeat monthly. Remove spent flowers to encourage additional flowering. Discontinue fertilizing and deadheading four to six weeks before the first anticipated frost.

Good for: specimen shrub or low hedge. The Fairy is a perfect rose to grow in large container such as a whiskey barrel planter.

More Choices: pages 33, 34, 41, 121, 123, and 125

Outstanding Features:
- Clusters of pink all through the summer
- Extremely cold-hardy; tolerates below zero
- Flowering ability even in partial shade

Though dainty flowers appear delicate, this rose is hardy to 40 degrees below zero. Small, double pink blossoms open summer through fall. This rose will even bloom in partial shade.

Rosa Rubrifolia

Zones: 4-9

Light Needs:

Mature Size:

4'-6' (height)
3'-5' (width)

Growth Rate:
medium

deciduous flowering shrub

Needs: Plant roses in full sun in moist, well-drained, fertile soil. Prune stray stems as needed. Fertilize with rose food when blooming starts and repeat monthly. Remove spent flowers to encourage additional bloom. Discontinue fertilizing and deadheading four to six weeks before the first anticipated frost.

Good for: specimen shrub, hedge, anywhere you can see it from inside your home for year-round viewing

More Choices: pages 33, 111, 120, 122, and 125

Outstanding Features:
- Bright pink flowers are fragrant
- Nearly thornless purple-red stems
- Scarlet hips linger through winter

Shrubs

5

Single flowers open to a bright flamingo pink in early summer. Petal tips are pink with white bases. After they fade, the purple-tinged leaves take center stage, highlighted against bright, purple-red arching stems. In fall, hips ripen to a scarlet red color and last all winter. May be sold as *Rosa glauca*.

Salix alba 'Britzensis'

Coral Embers Willow

Zones: 2-8

Light Needs:

Mature Size:

8'-10'

5'-10'

Growth Rate:
rapid

deciduous shrub

Needs: Plant in full sun in moist, well-drained soil. Tolerates wet soil. The red stem color is most prominent on young wood; prune all stems to within a few inches of the ground in early spring before new growth begins.

Good for: shrub beds, mass planting against evergreen backgrounds, wet locations, around ponds and streams

More Choices: pages 29, 32, 37, 40, and 121

The new stems on this shrub are bright red and are most effective during winter months after the leaves fall. Stems covered in snow add winter interest. Coral Embers Willow grows in any well-drained soil as well as moist locations. The most intense color shows up on young stems. Trim plants back severely in late winter to encourage vigorous, new growth.

Skimmia japonica

Japanese Skimmia

Zones: 6-9

Light Needs:

Mature Size:

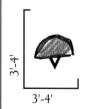

3'-4'

3'-4'

Growth Rate:
slow

evergreen shrub

Needs: Plant in fertile, acidic soil that is both moist and well-drained. Mix peat moss or composted oak leaves at planting to improve acidity. Provide a shaded or partially shaded space. Separate male and female plants are needed for fruit production. Plant one male for every six females.

Good for: fronts of planting beds, combining with shade-loving perennials, specimen use, foundations, containers

More Choices: pages 34, 37, 39, 122, 124, and 125

Skimmia is a small evergreen shrub that thrives in shaded areas. Whether in full spring flower or covered with winter fruit, plants are a picturesque addition to the landscape. Plants will withstand air pollution. Provide a protected location, and plants can be grown in Zone 6. Cultivars to try include 'Bronze Knight'—male plant with dark red flower buds; 'Fructo Albo'—green flower buds and white berries, 2' tall by 3' wide; 'Rubella'—a male plant with red flowers buds and fragrant white blooms.

Anthony Waterer Spirea

Zones: 3-9

Light Needs:

Mature Size:

3'-5' / 3'-5'

Growth Rate:
medium to rapid

deciduous flowering shrub

Needs: Plant in full sun to partial shade in any well-drained soil. Prune back in spring before new growth begins.

Good for: parking areas, entries, specimen plants, beside patios, background to summer flowerbeds, facing for taller shrubs, massed plantings, low hedges

More Choices: pages 32, 34, 37, 41, 122, 123, 124, and 125

Options: 'Little Princess'—rounded shape, about 30" high, pink flowers
'Alpina'—12" to 30" high

'Little Princess'

Outstanding Features:
- Dark pink blooms in late spring and summer
- New foliage is reddish purple in color
- Durable and adaptable in any setting

Not all spireas have white flowers in early spring. This one boasts dark pink blooms when spring is fading into summer. For durability nothing can take the place of spirea in home landscapes. May be sold as *S.* x *bumalda* 'Anthony Waterer'.

Shibori Spirea

Zones: 4-8

Light Needs:

Mature Size:

3'-4' / 3'-4'

Growth Rate:
medium

deciduous flowering shrub

Needs: Plant in full sun to partial shade in well-drained soil. Spirea will not tolerate wet sites. Prune in spring before new growth begins. Blooms best in sun.

Good for: entries, groups behind flowerbeds, specimen plants, beside patios and low decks, low hedges

More Choices: pages 33, 34, 122, and 123

Outstanding Features:
- Pink and white flowers blooming together
- Easy to grow, very adaptable
- Wide range of landscape use

Shrubs 5

Can't decide between pink or white flowers? This spirea blooms in both colors at the same time. Like all spirea, Shibori is adaptable for a variety of uses in the home landscape.

Spiraea prunifolia

Bridalwreath Spirea

Zones: 5-8

Light Needs:

Mature Size:

5'-7'

4'-6'

Growth Rate:
rapid

deciduous flowering shrub

Needs: Plant in full sun to partial shade in soil that's moderately fertile and doesn't stay wet. Prune with a light hand; over-pruning spoils the naturally arching form. Give plants room to grow.

Good for: entries, informal hedges, specimen plants, or as a background to spring flowerbeds

More Choices: pages 29, 32, 34, 111, 121, 122, 123, 124, and 125

Outstanding Features:
- Numerous buttonlike blooms in spring
- Arching branches form informal hedges
- Leaves turn orange-red in autumn

Little white flowers cover the arching branches early each spring. This is a perfect backdrop for spring flowering bulbs. Shiny dark green foliage turns orange-red in fall. Best used in informal areas.

Spiraea thunbergii

Baby's Breath Spirea

Zones: 2-8

Light Needs:

Mature Size:

3'-5'

3'-5'

Growth Rate:
rapid

deciduous flowering shrub

Needs: Plant in full sun to partial shade in soil that's moderately fertile and doesn't stay very wet. Give plants room to grow. Prune as needed, but maintain naturally arching form.

Good for: entries, accent plants, informal hedges, beside patios, as a background to beds of spring-blooming bulbs

More Choices: pages 29, 32, 34, 111, 121, 122, 123, 124, and 125

Options: 'Compacta'—grows 2' to 4' tall

Outstanding Features:
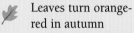
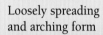

- Delicate white flowers in early spring
- Leaves turn orange-red in autumn
- Loosely spreading and arching form

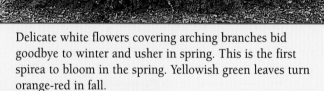

Delicate white flowers covering arching branches bid goodbye to winter and usher in spring. This is the first spirea to bloom in the spring. Yellowish green leaves turn orange-red in fall.

Spiraea x vanhouttei

Vanhoutte Spirea

Zones: 3-8

Light Needs:

Mature Size:

6'-8'

10'-12'

Growth Rate:
rapid

deciduous flowering shrub

Needs: Plant in full sun to partial shade in soil that's moderately fertile and doesn't stay wet. Blooms best in sun. Set it where you have room for a big, arching shrub. Plants are not a choice for formal areas.

Good for: entry areas, informal hedges, specimen plants, as a background to spring flowerbeds

More Choices: pages 29, 33, 34, 37, 111, 121, 122, 123, 124, and 125

Outstanding Features:

- Late spring clusters of white flowers
- Easy to grow; adaptable to various soils
- Arching form provides informality

The flowers of Vanhoutte Spirea look like tiny white bouquets in late spring and early summer. This shrub is easy to grow no matter where you put it. Not for small areas.

Symphoricarpos albus

Snowberry

Zones: 3-7

Light Needs:

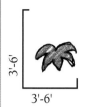

Mature Size:

3'-6' × 3'-6'

Growth Rate:
rapid

deciduous flowering shrub

Needs: Snowberry grows in sun or shade, in any type of soil, and in areas where air pollution is high. Prune in early spring to stimulate flowering on new growth. Plants will sucker and spread.

Good for: informal landscapes, woodland areas, hillsides to stabilize soil, wildlife habitat plantings

More Choices: pages 33, 34, 40, 41, 121, 122, 123, and 125

Outstanding Features:
- White berries dangle from stems in fall
- Adaptable to heavily shaded areas
- Good for stabilizing banks and slopes

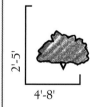

Snowberry earns its name from the abundance of white berries that cover its stems in fall. This shrub is tolerant of difficult growing conditions; use it in shady locations, on steep banks, and in areas where air pollution is high.

Symphoricarpos orbiculatus

Coralberry

Zones: 4-7

Light Needs:

Mature Size:

2'-5' × 4'-8'

Growth Rate:
rapid

deciduous flowering shrub

Needs: Plant in sun or shade in soil that is fertile or poor, moist or dry. Prune in early spring to stimulate prolific flowering.

Good for: shrub borders, informal hedges, screens, woodland plantings, stabilizing hillsides and banks, attracting birds, winter interest

More Choices: pages 29, 32, 34, 37, 40, 111, 121, 122, 123, and 125

Outstanding Features:
- Summer flowers look like tiny roses
- Purplish red berries linger through winter
- Tolerates heavy shade as well as pollution

Coralberry thrives in any growing condition. Moist or dry soil, full sun to dense shade, alkaline or acidic—it can easily fit into any yard. Winter berries attract birds. Place plants where you can view the feeding from inside. Best flowering occurs on new shoots; prune annually to encourage vigorous new growth.

Shrubs 5

Syringa x laciniata

Cutleaf Lilac

Zones: 4-8

Light Needs:

Mature Size:

6'-8'

6'-10'

Growth Rate:
medium

deciduous flowering shrub

Needs: Plant in full sun or partial shade in well-drained, fertile soil. Best flowering occurs in full sun. Add composted leaves or peat moss to soil at planting time to boost fertility. Remove faded blooms to keep plants looking neat. Prune after flowering to shape the shrub and encourage new vigorous growth.

Good for: shrub borders, hedges, screens, specimen use, entries

More Choices: pages 29, 32, 34, 111, 120, 121, 123, and 124

Outstanding Features:
- Purplish, fragrant flowers in late spring
- Leaves look like they have been cut
- Adaptable to cold and warm climates

Cutleaf Lilac is the best lilac to grow in the warmer parts of the country, even Zone 8. Use it to frame a porch or other outdoor seating area and enjoy the flowers' perfume to the fullest. Lacy foliage looks like it has been cut with scissors.

Syringa patula 'Miss Kim'

Miss Kim Lilac

Zones: 3-7

Light Needs:

Mature Size:

6'-8'

4'-5'

Growth Rate:
slow

deciduous flowering shrub

Needs: Plant in full sun to partial shade in well-drained, fertile soil. Clip off blooms after they fade. Prune only if needed, after flowering, to shape the shrub.

Good for: shrub border, informal hedge, screen, specimen shrub, near outdoor seating areas to enjoy the fragrance

More Choices: pages 29, 33, 34, 111, 120, 121, 123, 124, and 125

Outstanding Features:
- Purple flowers are very fragrant
- Leaves resist powdery mildew
- Plants are cold hardy and durable

This late-blooming lilac features single, pale lavender flowers that are rich with perfume. Leaves are glossy green in summer, then turn a burgundy red in fall. Miss Kim Lilac can survive winter temperatures of 40 degrees below zero.

Syringa x persica

Persian Lilac

Zones: 3-7

Light Needs:

Mature Size:

4'-8'

5'-10'

Growth Rate:
medium

deciduous flowering shrub

Needs: Plant in full sun to partial shade in well-drained, fertile soil. Best flowering occurs in full sun. Add composted leaves or peat moss to soil at planting time to boost fertility. Remove faded blooms to keep plants looking neat. Prune after flowering to shape plants and encourage vigorous, new growth.

Good for: shrub borders, informal hedges, specimen use, perennial beds

More Choices: pages 29, 33, 34, 39, 111, 121, and 124

Outstanding Features:
- Pale purple flowers open in midspring
- Arching branches; fountainlike form
- Compact size for use in smaller landscapes

This shrub has the same sweet, fragrant blooms as its larger lilac cousins but with more grace. Pale purple flowers grow in clusters at the tips of branches. Good for shrub borders and hedges.

Common Lilac

Zones: 3-7

Light Needs:

Mature Size:

8'-15'

6'-12'

Growth Rate:
medium

deciduous flowering shrub

Needs: Plant in full sun to partial shade in well-drained, fertile soil. Best flowering occurs in full sun. Add composted leaves or peat moss to soil at planting time to boost fertility. Remove faded blooms to keep plants looking neat. Prune after flowering to shape the shrub and encourage vigorous new growth.

Good for: shrub borders, informal hedges, screening, specimen use, planting beside entries or patios

More Choices: pages 29, 32, 34, 37, 111, 120, 121, 123, and 124

Outstanding Features:

- Spring flowers are extremely fragrant
- Numerous colors from which to choose
- Dense hedges for privacy and screening

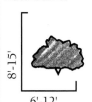

French hybrids offer big double flowers in a variety of colors including wine, pink, white, and deep purple. Powdery mildew is common on lilacs, but won't kill plants. Look for these varieties: *S. vulgaris* var. *alba*—white flowers; 'Arch McKean'—reddish-purple flowers, produces nearly no suckers; 'Charm Lilac'—pink flowers; 'Ellen Willmott'—double white flowers; 'Little Boy Blue'—single sky-blue flowers, 4' to 5' high, 5' to 6' wide; 'Primrose'—yellow flowers; 'Wedgwood Blue'—lilac pink buds open to true, blue flowers, 6' high, 6' to 8' wide.

Rejuvenating Overgrown Lilacs

An overgrown lilac is worth rescuing. Mature roots and hardy trunks make the plant valuable, even if the crown is misshapen. Combine severe pruning with patience to turn an overgrown shrub into a specimen plant.

1 **Wait until the shrub is totally bare and temperatures have dipped below freezing.** Cut away water sprouts—those stems that grow straight up and don't bloom. Remove them at ground level or flush with the branch or trunk where they emerge. Use hand pruners on small stems, loppers if it's a struggle.

2 **It's time to be ruthless.** Using loppers, cut the shrub down to about one-third or one-half its current size.

3 **Now that the shrub is at a manageable size, it's time to make final cuts.** Use a pruning saw to cut thick trunks about 2 feet above ground level, leaving these stubs.

STUFF YOU'LL NEED

- ✔ Bypass hand pruners
- ✔ Bypass loppers
- ✔ Pruning saw

What to Expect

Don't expect flowers the spring after you hard-prune your lilac. New growth will produce flower buds next year, though severe pruning may result in two bloomless years.

Get the 'Full Scoop'

Selective pruning

If your lilac requires just a little trim, make cuts in spring immediately after flowers finish blooming. This will avoid removing next year's flower buds. Don't cut your lilacs back to stubs each year. If you do, you'll never enjoy any flowers. Instead, make selective cuts on an annual basis.

—see pages 116-119

Taxus x media 'Hicksii'

Hick's Upright Yew

Zones: 4-7

Light Needs:

Mature Size:

20'-25'

6'-10'

Growth Rate:
slow

evergreen shrub

evergreen shrub

Needs: Plant in sun or shade in moist, sandy, acidic soil. Soil must be well-drained. Add composted leaves or peat moss to soil at planting time to boost soil acidity. Prune to shape the shrub during summer or early fall.

Good for: hedges, screens, specimen use; adding formal accent to entrances; forming a living fence

More Choices: pages 28, 33, 34, 37, 39, 43, 111, 121, and 123

Options: T. x *media* 'Densiformis'— dense and spreading, 4 to 6 feet wide

This is a perfect shrub to screen a fence or patio in a small yard. Its upright, narrow growth forms a dense screen without using up a lot of horizontal area. Plants add a formal touch wherever they are planted. Very low maintenance.

Thuja occidentalis 'Little Giant'

Little Giant Arborvitae

Zones: 3-7

Light Needs:

Mature Size:

4'-6'

4'-6'

Growth Rate:
slow to medium

evergreen shrub

Needs: Plant in any soil type that isn't extremely wet. Rocky, poor, dry, or alkaline conditions are fine. Grow in full sun. Prune to shape during warm months. Protect from harsh winds, ice, and snow.

Good for: specimen use, anchoring shrub and perennial planting beds, foundations

More Choices: pages 28, 33, 37, 39, 43, 113, 121, 123, and 125

Options: 'Emerald'—narrow pyramidal, green foliage; 10' to 15' high, 3' to 4' wide
'Globosa'—gray green foliage, rounded shape; 4' to 6' high and wide
'Golden Globe'—bright golden foliage

Here's a plant that looks like a big green ball in the landscape. Its evergreen foliage and rounded form make it eye-catching throughout the year. Plants are susceptible to spider mites. At first sign of fading foliage or silky webbing, spray with an insecticide labeled for spider mites. Thrives in Eastern North America.

Viburnum carlesii

Korean Spice Viburnum

Zones: 4-8

Light Needs:

Mature Size:

4'-6'
4'-6'

Growth Rate:
slow

deciduous shrub

Needs: Plant in full sun or part shade in acidic, moist, well-drained soil. Prune to shape shrubs after flowering.

Good for: specimen use, foundation plantings, shrub beds, planting beside entries, walkways, patios and outdoor seating areas for fragrance

More Choices: pages 33, 34, 39, 113, 120, 121, 123, and 124

Options: *V. davidii* (David Viburnum)— white flowers, blue-green foliage

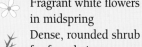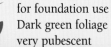
This spring bloomer features fragrant flowers in late April-May. Blooms are pink to red in bud and open pure white. It grows slowly and can be pruned to maintain desired size and shape.

Viburnum opulus 'Roseum'

European Cranberrybush

Zones: 3-8

Light Needs:

Mature Size:

8'-10'
10'-15'

Growth Rate:
medium

deciduous flowering shrub

Needs: Plant in wet or well-drained soil. This cold-hardy plant doesn't tolerate heat well; grow in afternoon shade in hotter climates, full sun elsewhere.

Good for: specimen plants, seasonal accents, focal points, large courtyards or entries, anchoring planting beds, contrasting with evergreen backgrounds, corners of houses, or yards

More Choices: pages 29, 32, 37, 121, 123, 124, and 125

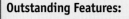

Grow, don't throw, snowballs in the spring. A blizzard of blossoms—puffy, white, and round—covers this large shrub, commanding attention in the spring. Shrubs tolerate wet soil. Sometimes sold as Snowball Viburnum or 'Sterile.'

Viburnum plicatum tomentosum

Doublefile Viburnum

Zones: 4-8

Light Needs:

Mature Size:

5'-15'
10'-18'

Growth Rate:
rapid

deciduous flowering shrub

Needs: Plant in fertile soil that's moist but well-drained. Grow in full sun to partial shade. Water regularly.

Good for: specimen plants, seasonal accents, massing, corners of houses or yards, in front of fences, balancing vertical plants, beside patios, and natural areas

More Choices: pages 29, 32, 34, 121, 122, 123, 124, and 125

For white flowers, red berries, tiered branches, all layered together in a spring display—plant a Doublefile Viburnum. You'll get all that plus scarlet fall foliage. Leaves are coarse-textured. Blooms in partial shade and full sun.

Shrubs 5

Chapter 6
groundcovers
and vines

Ever wonder why some landscapes have a gardenlike feeling while others seem to be basic and dull? Groundcovers and vines add lush layers and finishing touches to your yard. These plants also have a problem-solving practical side, too. Vines screen views and add privacy. Groundcovers anchor slopes, fill planting beds, and cover bare spots where grass won't grow.

Adding the Final Layers

This section explains how to add the final layers to your **planting beds.** Groundcovers and vines refine landscape compositions and make them appear filled out and complete. This chapter helps you choose groundcovers to control erosion, add texture and seasonal interest, and cover bare areas where grass won't grow. Selection guides indicate which groundcovers are best for growing in large beds and which are suitable for growing in confined areas, such as courtyards and entryways. For groundcovers suitable for growing in sun or shade, see pages 32 through 35.

Add pockets of groundcover for finishing touches at steps.

You'll find information about vines, too. Adding vines and climbers puts color and texture at eye level and above. They can also be used to shelter a location, enhance privacy, screen poor views, and add shade. The inclusion of vines in a landscape is an extra step professional designers take to make new landscape installations look natural and more mature.

Groundcovers

Any plant that grows close to the ground—spreading vines, prostrate plants, dwarf shrubs, and low perennials— is considered a groundcover. The selection guides and detailed information within individual plant descriptions enable you to find the plants best suited to your purpose. Local garden center staff can help, too.

Plant groundcovers after all your trees and shrubs are in place. Low-growing plants fill in empty spaces beneath taller plants, giving planting beds a finished look and preventing weeds from taking over. However, groundcovers are more than just fillers. Planting an entire bed with nothing but groundcover gives the landscape a simple, sophisticated look. To achieve this effect, make sure that bedlines are smooth and well-defined. Beds of groundcover are excellent for framing lawns with foliage that differs from grass in color, texture, or height.

Groundcovers are also handy for edging walkways, patios, and planting beds containing taller plants. Grow them in neat rows or let them spill over the edges of paving for a softer look. Some groundcovers are suitable for tucking into the crevices of rock gardens or between stepping stones. Others look best in beds all alone, set in front of a background of trees and shrubs. When you're laying out bedlines and adding trees and shrubs to your landscape, remember to save room for the last layer of the planting bed.

Slopes
When planting groundcovers on slopes, cover the soil surface with landscape fabric to keep topsoil from washing away while plants are young. (Avoid plastic that heats the soil and must be removed later.) Use any landscape fabric that will decompose over time. Lay it on the slope and cut slits through the fabric where you want the new plants to grow. For steep angles or windy areas, nail the fabric in place with spikes. Water new groundcovers thoroughly at planting and apply supplemental irrigation if necessary until plants are established.

Plant groundcover through slits in landscape fabric on steep slopes.

Planting Groundcovers

Though you don't have to dig deep holes, planting groundcover is labor-intensive.

Planting small plants means getting down on your hands and knees. If possible, till the bed area to make planting easier and establishment quicker. Spread soil amendments, such as organic matter, on the surface and work it into the soil. A loose planting bed is best for small plants sold in 4-inch pots or cell packs. Planting groundcover is labor-intensive. If you hire someone to do the planting, you might find yourself paying more for the work than for the plants.

Dig individual holes as you would for a shrub if you're planting larger groundcovers, such as those grown in 1- or 3-gallon containers. Regardless of container size, arrange the plants to fill an area before you remove them from their pots. This keeps them from drying out. Set plants in a staggered formation— like laying bricks. Avoid lining plants in perfect rows. The goal is to fill the bed with greenery, not to create a geometrical pattern that will remain recognizable for months or even years. Always set the first row of groundcover plants to follow the shape of the bedline. Set plants back from the edge of the bed a distance equal to half their mature spread. Plants then have room to grow without crossing the bedline.

Replace worn paths with stepping stones and groundcovers.

Ajuga (Ajuga reptans) Page 175

Large-leaved hostas (page 187) add coarse texture to the front of a planting bed.

Aaron's Beard
(Hypericum calycinum)
Page 188

Andorra Compact Juniper
(Juniperus horizontalis 'Plumosa Compacta')
Page 191

Choosing Groundcovers by Characteristics

The more you know about groundcovers that grow in your area, the more likely you are to pick ones with characteristics desirable for your yard. Groundcovers listed as evergreen keep their foliage year-round. Perennial groundcover disappears in late fall or early winter and comes back in spring. Coarse-textured groundcovers frame lawns, add depth to the foreground of small, confined spaces, and contrast with finer textured plants, including fine-textured groundcovers. If you want seasonal color in your yard, look at the grouped list of flowering groundcover in this chapter.

Sweet Woodruff
(Asperula odorata)
Page 179

Evergreen groundcover

Common Name	Zones	Page
Aaron's Beard	5-9	188
Hypericum calycinum		
Ajuga	4-9	175
Ajuga reptans		
Allegheny Foam Flower	4-9	200
Tiarella cordifolia		
Andorra Compact Juniper	3-9	191
Juniperus horizontalis 'Plumosa Compacta'		
Bar Harbor Juniper	3-9	190
Juniperus horizontalis 'Bar Harbor'		
Bearberry Cotoneaster	5-9	182
Cotoneaster dammeri		
Blue Chip Juniper	3-9	190
Juniperus horizontalis 'Blue Chip'		
Blue Pacific Shore Juniper	5-9	190
Juniperus conferta 'Blue Pacific'		
Blue Rug Juniper	3-9	191
Juniperus horizontalis 'Wiltonii'		
Bog Rosemary	2-6	176
Andromeda polifolia		
Coral Bells	3-8	187
Heuchera sanguinea		
Creeping Phlox	2-8	195
Phlox stolonifera		
Creeping Thyme	5-9	200
Thymus leucotrichus		
Dwarf Japanese Garden Juniper	4-9	191
Juniperus procumbens 'Nana'		

Common Name	Zones	Page
English Ivy	5-9	186
Hedera helix		
Evergreen Candytuft	4-8	189
Iberis sempervirens		
Germander	4-9	199
Teucrium prostratum		
Geum	4-7	186
Geum reptans		
Goldmoss	4-9	198
Sedum acre		
Green and Gold	5-8	181
Chrysogonum virginianum		
Kinnikinick	2-7	177
Arctostaphylos uva-ursi		
Lenten Rose	4-8	187
Helleborus orientalis		
Littleleaf Periwinkle	4-8	201
Vinca minor		
Moss Phlox	2-9	196
Phlox subulata		
Plumbago	5-9	180
Ceratostigma plumbaginoides		
Purple-Leaf Wintercreeper	4-8	183
Euonymus fortunei 'Coloratus'		
Rockcress	3-7	177
Arabis caucasica		
Rock Jasmine	5-7	176
Androsace lanuginosa		
Rock Rose	5-8	186
Helianthemum nummularium		
Royal Carpet Honeysuckle	5-9	192
Lonicera pileata		
Sandwort	3-6	177
Arenaria montana		
Scotch Heather	3-8	180
Calluna vulgaris		
Sea Thrift	3-8	178
Armeria maritima		
Silver Brocade Artemisia	3-9	178
Artemisia stelleriana 'Silver Brocade'		
Spring Heath	4-8	183
Erica carnea		
Variegated Japanese Sedge	6-9	180
Carex morrowii 'Variegata'		
Warley Rose	5-8	174
Aethinoema warleyense		

Perennial groundcover

Common Name	Zones	Page
Ajuga	4-9	175
Ajuga reptans		
Allegheny Foam Flower	4-9	200
Tiarella cordifolia		
Arum	6-10	178
Arum italicum		
Bath's Pink	4-9	182
Dianthus gratianopolitanus 'Bath's Pink'		
Blanket Flower	2-9	185
Gaillardia x grandiflora		
Bloody Cranesbill	3-8	185
Geranium sanguineum		
Blue Star	3-9	175
Amsonia tabernaemontana		
Blue-Eyed Mary	5-9	194
Omphalodes verna		
Bunchberry	2-7	181
Cornus canadensis		
Catmint	4-8	194
Nepeta x faassenii		
Coral Bells	3-8	187
Heuchera sanguinea		
Corsican Mint	5-9	193
Mentha corsica		
Creeping Phlox	2-8	195
Phlox stolonifera		
Cypress Spurge	4-8	184
Euphorbia cyparissias		
Dragon's Blood Sedum	3-8	198
Sedum spurium 'Dragon's Blood'		
Dwarf Blue Fescue	4-9	184
Festuca glauca		
Evergreen Candytuft	4-8	189
Iberis sempervirens		
Fleabane	2-10	183
Erigeron hybrid		
Forget-Me-Not	3-8	193
Myosotis scorpioides		
Fountain Grass	5-9	195
Pennisetum alopecuroides		
Geum	4-7	186
Geum reptans		

Common Name	Zones	Page
Goldmoss	4-9	198
Sedum acre		
Green and Gold	5-8	181
Chrysogonum virginianum		
Hardy Ice Plant	6-9	182
Delosperma nubigenum		
Hosta	3-8	187
Hosta species		
Houttuynia	5-9	188
Houttuynia cordata		
Japanese Blood Grass	5-9	189
Imperata cylindrica 'Red Baron'		
Japanese Painted Fern	4-9	179
Athyrium nipponicum 'Pictum'		
Japanese Primrose	5-8	196
Primula japonica		
Lady's Mantle	4-7	175
Alchemilla mollis		
Lamb's Ear	4-8	199
Stachys byzantina		
Lenten Rose	4-8	187
Helleborus orientalis		
Lily-of-the-Valley	2-9	181
Convallaria majalis		
Maidenhair Fern	3-8	174
Adiantum pedatum		
Moneywort	3-8	193
Lysimachia nummularia		
Moss Phlox	2-9	196
Phlox subulata		
Pachysandra	4-9	195
Pachysandra terminalis		
Pink Panda Strawberry	3-9	184
Fragaria 'Pink Panda'		
Plumbago	5-9	180
Ceratostigma plumbaginoides		
Rockcress	3-7	177
Arabis caucasica		
Rock Jasmine	5-7	176
Androsace lanuginosa		
Rock Rose	5-8	186
Helianthemum nummularium		
Saxifrage	3-8	179
Bergenia cordifolia		
Sandwort	3-6	177
Arenaria montana		

Rockcress
(*Arabis caucasica*)
Page 177

Common Name	Zones	Page
Sea Thrift	3-8	178
Armeria maritima		
Siberian Forget-Me-Not	3-7	176
Anchusa myosotidiflora		
Silver Brocade Artemisia	3-9	178
Artemisia stelleriana 'Silver Brocade'		
Snow-on-the-Mountain	3-9	174
Aegopodium podagraria 'Variegatum'		
Spotted Dead Nettle	3-9	192
Lamium maculatum		
Spring Cinquefoil	4-8	196
Potentilla tabernaemontani		
Stonecrop	3-10	198
Sedum spectabile		
Sundrop Primrose	4-8	194
Oenothera missouriensis		
Sweet Woodruff	4-8	179
Asperula odorata		
Variegated Japanese Sedge	6-9	180
Carex morrowii 'Variegata'		
Warley Rose	5-8	174
Aethinoema warleyense		
Wintergreen	3-8	185
Gaultheria procumbens		
Yellow Archangel	3-9	192
Lamiastrum galeobdolon 'Variegatum'		

Coarse-textured groundcover

Common Name	Zones	Page
Arum	6-10	178
Arum italicum		
Blue-Eyed Mary	5-9	194
Omphalodes verna		
Bunchberry	2-7	181
Cornus canadensis		
Coral Bells	3-8	187
Heuchera sanguinea		
English Ivy	5-9	186
Hedera helix		
Hosta	3-8	187
Hosta species		
Houttuynia	5-9	188
Houttuynia cordata		
Japanese Primrose	5-8	196
Primula japonica		
Lady's Mantle	4-7	175
Alchemilla mollis		
Lamb's Ear	4-8	199
Stachys byzantina		
Lenten Rose	4-8	187
Helleborus orientalis		
Lily-of-the-Valley	2-9	181
Convallaria majalis		
Pachysandra	4-9	195
Pachysandra terminalis		
Saxifrage	3-8	179
Bergenia cordifolia		
Stonecrop	3-10	198
Sedum spectabile		
Sweet Woodruff	4-8	179
Asperula odorata		

Availability varies by area and conditions (see page 21). Check with your garden center.

Fine-textured groundcover

Common Name	Zones	Page
Allegheny Foam Flower	4-9	200
Tiarella cordifolia		
Andorra Compact Juniper	3-9	191
Juniperus horizontalis 'Plumosa Compacta'		
Bar Harbor Juniper	3-9	190
Juniperus horizontalis 'Bar Harbor'		
Bath's Pink	4-9	182
Dianthus gratianopolitanus 'Bath's Pink'		
Bearberry Cotoneaster	5-9	182
Cotoneaster dammeri		
Bloody Cranesbill	3-8	185
Geranium sanguineum		
Blue Chip Juniper	3-9	190
Juniperus horizontalis 'Blue Chip'		
Blue Rug Juniper	3-9	191
Juniperus horizontalis 'Wiltonii'		
Catmint	4-8	194
Nepeta x faassenii		
Corsican Mint	5-9	193
Mentha corsica		
Creeping Phlox	2-8	195
Phlox stolonifera		
Creeping Thyme	5-9	200
Thymus leucotrichus		
Cypress Spurge	4-8	184
Euphorbia cyparissias		
Dwarf Blue Fescue	4-9	184
Festuca glauca		
Dwarf Japanese Garden Juniper	4-9	191
Juniperus procumbens 'Nana'		
Evergreen Candytuft	4-8	189
Iberis sempervirens		
Fountain Grass	5-9	195
Pennisetum alopecuroides		
Germander	4-9	199
Teucrium prostratum		

Common Name	Zones	Page
Geum	4-7	186
Geum reptans		
Goldmoss	4-9	198
Sedum acre		
Hardy Ice Plant	6-9	182
Delosperma nubigenum		
Japanese Blood Grass	5-9	189
Imperata cylindrica 'Red Baron'		
Kinnikinick	2-7	177
Arctostaphylos uva-ursi		
Littleleaf Periwinkle	4-8	201
Vinca minor		
Maidenhair Fern	3-8	174
Adiantum pedatum		
Moss Phlox	2-9	196
Phlox subulata		
Rockcress	3-7	177
Arabis caucasica		
Rock Jasmine	5-7	176
Androsace lanuginosa		
Sandwort	3-6	177
Arenaria montana		
Scotch Heather	3-8	180
Calluna vulgaris		
Sea Thrift	3-8	178
Armeria maritima		
Siberian Forget-Me-Not	3-7	176
Anchusa myosotidiflora		
Silver Brocade Artemisia	3-9	178
Artemisia stelleriana 'Silver Brocade'		
Spring Heath	4-8	183
Erica carnea		
Variegated Japanese Sedge	6-9	180
Carex morrowii 'Variegata'		
Warley Rose Persian Candytuft	5-8	174
Aethinoema warleyense		

groundcovers/vines

6

Groundcovers can help you turn problem places into favorite spots in your yard.

Lamb's Ear
(Stachys byzantina)
Page 199

Littleleaf Periwinkle
(Vinca minor)
Page 201

Choosing Groundcovers for Special Areas

Use these lists to find groundcovers that will fulfill your needs. Photographs of plants and detailed information can be found on the page numbers listed. Look for plants that include your growing zone within their range. To find your climate zone, turn to pages 5.

Groundcover for edging patios, entries, and garden beds

Lady's Mantle
(Alchemilla mollis)
Page 175

Common Name	Zones	Page
Alba Meidiland Rose	4-8	197
Rosa Alba Meidiland		
Andorra Compact Juniper	3-9	191
Juniperus horizontalis 'Plumosa Compacta'		
Arum	6-10	178
Arum italicum		
Bar Harbor Juniper	3-9	190
Juniperus horizontalis 'Bar Harbor'		
Bath's Pink	4-9	182
Dianthus gratianopolitanus 'Bath's Pink'		
Blanket Flower	2-9	185
Gaillardia x grandiflora		
Bloody Cranesbill	3-8	185
Geranium sanguineum		
Blue Chip Juniper	3-9	190
Juniperus horizontalis 'Blue Chip'		
Blue Rug Juniper	3-9	191
Juniperus horizontalis 'Wiltonii'		
Catmint	4-8	194
Nepeta x faassenii		
Coral Bells	3-8	187
Heuchera sanguinea		
Corsican Mint	5-9	193
Mentha corsica		
Creeping Phlox	2-8	195
Phlox stolonifera		
Creeping Thyme	5-9	200
Thymus leucotrichus		
Dragon's Blood Sedum	3-8	198
Sedum spurium 'Dragon's Blood'		
Dwarf Blue Fescue	4-9	184
Festuca glauca		
Dwarf Japanese Garden Juniper	4-9	191
Juniperus procumbens 'Nana'		
Evergreen Candytuft	4-8	189
Iberis sempervirens		

Common Name	Zones	Page
Fleabane	2-10	183
Erigeron hybrid		
Fountain Grass	5-9	195
Pennisetum alopecuroides		
Germander	4-9	199
Teucrium prostratum		
Geum	4-7	186
Geum reptans		
Hosta	3-8	187
Hosta species		
Lady's Mantle	4-7	175
Alchemilla mollis		
Lamb's Ear	4-8	199
Stachys byzantina		
Lenten Rose	4-8	187
Helleborus orientalis		
Lily-of-the-Valley	2-9	181
Convallaria majalis		
Memorial Rose	4-9	197
Rosa wichuraiana		
Moss Phlox	2-9	196
Phlox subulata		
Pink Panda Strawberry	3-9	184
Fragaria 'Pink Panda'		
Rockcress	3-7	177
Arabis caucasica		
Rock Jasmine	5-7	176
Androsace lanuginosa		
Saxifrage	3-8	179
Bergenia cordifolia		
Scotch Heather	3-8	180
Calluna vulgaris		
Sea Thrift	3-8	178
Armeria maritima		
Silver Brocade Artemisia	3-9	178
Artemisia stelleriana 'Silver Brocade'		
Spring Cinquefoil	4-8	196
Potentilla tabernaemontani		
Spring Heath	4-8	183
Erica carnea		
Sundrop Primrose	4-8	194
Oenothera missouriensis		
Variegated Japanese Sedge	6-9	180
Carex morrowii 'Variegata'		
Warley Rose	5-8	174
Aethinoema warleyense		

Flowering groundcover

Common Name	Zones	Page
Aaron's Beard	5-9	188
Hypericum calycinum		
Ajuga	4-9	175
Ajuga reptans		
Alba Meidiland Rose	4-8	197
Rosa Alba Meidiland		
Allegheny Foam Flower	4-9	200
Tiarella cordifolia		
Arum	6-10	178
Arum italicum		
Bath's Pink	4-9	182
Dianthus gratianopolitanus 'Bath's Pink'		
Bearberry Cotoneaster	5-9	182
Cotoneaster dammeri		
Blanket Flower	2-9	185
Gaillardia x grandiflora		
Bloody Cranesbill	3-8	185
Geranium sanguineum		
Blue Star	3-9	175
Amsonia tabernaemontana		
Blue-Eyed Mary	5-9	194
Omphalodes verna		
Bog Rosemary	2-6	176
Andromeda polifolia		
Bunchberry	2-7	181
Cornus canadensis		
Catmint	4-8	194
Nepeta x faassenii		
Coral Bells	3-8	187
Heuchera sanguinea		
Corsican Mint	5-9	193
Mentha corsica		
Creeping Phlox	2-8	195
Phlox stolonifera		
Creeping Thyme	5-9	200
Thymus leucotrichus		
Cypress Spurge	4-8	184
Euphorbia cyparissias		
Dragon's Blood Sedum	3-8	198
Sedum spurium 'Dragon's Blood'		
Evergreen Candytuft	4-8	189
Iberis sempervirens		
Fleabane	2-10	183
Erigeron hybrid		
Flower Carpet Rose	4-10	197
Rosa 'Flower Carpet'		
Forget-Me-Not	3-8	193
Myosotis scorpioides		
Germander	4-9	199
Teucrium prostratum		
Geum	4-7	186
Geum reptans		
Goldmoss	4-9	198
Sedum acre		
Green and Gold	5-8	181
Chrysogonum virginianum		
Hardy Ice Plant	6-9	182
Delosperma nubigenum		
Japanese Primrose	5-8	196
Primula japonica		
Kinnikinick	2-7	177
Arctostaphylos uva-ursi		
Lady's Mantle	4-7	175
Alchemilla mollis		
Lamb's Ear	4-8	199
Stachys byzantina		
Lenten Rose	4-8	187
Helleborus orientalis		
Lily-of-the-Valley	2-9	181
Convallaria majalis		
Littleleaf Periwinkle	4-8	201
Vinca minor		
Memorial Rose	4-9	197
Rosa wichuraiana		
Moneywort	3-8	193
Lysimachia nummularia		
Moss Phlox	2-9	196
Phlox subulata		
Pachysandra	4-9	195
Pachysandra terminalis		
Pink Panda Strawberry	3-9	184
Fragaria 'Pink Panda'		
Plumbago	5-9	180
Ceratostigma plumbaginoides		

Anchored with attractive groundcovers, a steep hillside becomes a backyard asset instead of a problem.

Common Name	Zones	Page
Prostrate Chenault Coralberry	4-7	199
Symphoricarpos x chenaultii 'Hancock'		
Rockcress	3-7	177
Arabis caucasica		
Rock Jasmine	5-7	176
Androsace lanuginosa		
Rock Rose	5-8	186
Helianthemum nummularium		
Royal Carpet Honeysuckle	5-9	192
Lonicera pileata		
Saxifrage	3-8	179
Bergenia cordifolia		
Sandwort	3-6	177
Arenaria montana		
Scotch Heather	3-8	180
Calluna vulgaris		
Sea Thrift	3-8	178
Armeria maritima		
Siberian Forget-Me-Not	3-7	176
Anchusa myosotidiflora		
Snow-on-the-Mountain	3-9	174
Aegopodium podagraria 'Variegatum'		
Spotted Dead Nettle	3-9	192
Lamium maculatum		
Spring Cinquefoil	4-8	196
Potentilla tabernaemontani		
Spring Heath	4-8	183
Erica carnea		
Stonecrop	3-10	198
Sedum spectabile		
Sundrop Primrose	4-8	194
Oenothera missouriensis		
Sweet Woodruff	4-8	179
Asperula odorata		
Variegated Japanese Sedge	6-9	180
Carex morrowii 'Variegata'		
Warley Rose	5-8	174
Aethinoema warleyense		
Wintergreen	3-8	185
Gaultheria procumbens		
Yellow Archangel	3-9	192
Lamiastrum galeobdolon 'Variegatum'		

Groundcover for rock gardens

Common Name	Zones	Page
Bath's Pink	4-9	182
Dianthus gratianopolitanus 'Bath's Pink'		
Bearberry Cotoneaster	5-9	182
Cotoneaster dammeri		
Bog Rosemary	2-6	176
Andromeda polifolia		
Catmint	4-8	194
Nepeta x faassenii		
Dragon's Blood Sedum	3-8	198
Sedum spurium 'Dragon's Blood'		
Dwarf Blue Fescue	4-9	184
Festuca glauca		
Evergreen Candytuft	4-8	189
Iberis sempervirens		
Germander	4-9	199
Teucrium prostratum		

Availability varies by area and conditions (see page 21). Check with your garden center.

Groundcover for woodlands

Common Name	Zones	Page
Allegheny Foam Flower	4-9	200
Tiarella cordifolia		
Arum	6-10	178
Arum italicum		
Bearberry Cotoneaster	5-9	182
Cotoneaster dammeri		
Blue-Eyed Mary	5-9	194
Omphalodes verna		
Bog Rosemary	2-6	176
Andromeda polifolia		
Bunchberry	2-7	181
Cornus canadensis		
Creeping Phlox	2-8	195
Phlox stolonifera		
English Ivy	5-9	186
Hedera helix		
Forget-Me-Not	3-8	193
Myosotis scorpioides		
Green and Gold	5-8	181
Chrysogonum virginianum		
Hosta	3-8	187
Hosta species		
Japanese Painted Fern	4-9	179
Athyrium nipponicum 'Pictum'		
Lenten Rose	4-8	187
Helleborus orientalis		
Lily-of-the-Valley	2-9	181
Convallaria majalis		
Littleleaf Periwinkle	4-8	201
Vinca minor		
Maidenhair Fern	3-8	174
Adiantum pedatum		
Prostrate Chenault Coralberry	4-7	199
Symphoricarpos x chenaultii 'Hancock'		
Snow-on-the-Mountain	3-9	174
Aegopodium podagraria 'Variegatum'		
Sweet Woodruff	4-8	179
Asperula odorata		
Wintergreen	3-8	185
Gaultheria procumbens		

Common Name	Zones	Page
Goldmoss	4-9	198
Sedum acre		
Hardy Ice Plant	6-9	182
Delosperma nubigenum		
Moss Phlox	2-9	196
Phlox subulata		
Rock Jasmine	5-7	176
Androsace lanuginosa		
Rock Rose	5-8	186
Helianthemum nummularium		
Sandwort	3-6	177
Arenaria montana		
Sea Thrift	3-8	178
Armeria maritima		
Silver Brocade Artemisia	3-9	178
Artemisia stelleriana 'Silver Brocade'		
Spring Cinquefoil	4-8	196
Potentilla tabernaemontani		
Stonecrop	3-10	198
Sedum spectabile		
Warley Rose	5-8	174
Aethinoema warleyense		

Adiantum pedatum

Maidenhair Fern

Zones: 3-8

Light Needs:

Mature Size:

8"-10"

12"-24"

Growth Rate: medium

perennial

Needs: Plant in moist soil that's rich in organic matter. Soil should be neutral or slightly acidic. Grow in partial to dense shade; protect from afternoon sun in hotter climates. Mulch for winter.

Good for: natural areas, damp sites, woodland paths, shady courtyards and entries, textural contrast among plants or stones, narrow confined spaces, shady ponds, creeks, water downspouts

More Choices: pages 35, 39, 41, 171, and 173

Outstanding Features:

- Bright green fine-textured foliage
- Thrives in damp, shady locations
- Comes back every year in the spring

If you add this plant to shady, damp spots, you'll be rewarded with bright green, delicate fronds. Leaflets seem to hover above dark, purplish stems. It may be sold as Northern Maidenhair Fern.

Aegopodium podagraria 'Variegatum'

Snow-on-the-Mountain

Zones: 3-9

Light Needs:

Mature Size:

4"-6"

indefinite

Growth Rate: rapid

perennial

Needs: Plant in any kind of soil. Grow in full sun, partial shade, or dense shade; protect from afternoon sun in hotter climates. This groundcover tolerates full sun where summers are cool.

Good for: Filling in where grass won't grow, massing, erosion control, hillsides, dry shade around tree roots, natural areas, large planting beds, brightening dim, shaded areas

More Choices: pages 35, 37, 39, 40, 171, and 173

Outstanding Features:

- Lustrous green leaves are edged with white
- Grows rapidly to cover ground completely
- Small white flowers in early summer

Here's a groundcover good in sun or shade. Green-and-white foliage spreads quickly; vigorous growth is a hallmark of this plant. It is also sold as Variegated Bishop's Weed or Goutweed. Remove any solid green foliage that appears.

Aethionema 'Warley Rose'

Warley Rose or Persian Candytuft

Zones: 5-8

Light Needs:

Mature Size:

6"-8"

6"-8"

Growth Rate: medium

evergreen or semievergreen perennial

Needs: Plant in full sun in well-drained, fertile, alkaline soil. Shear plants after the flowers fade for fresh leaves and dense growth.

Good for: edging beds or walkways, rock gardens, underplant with spring bulbs

More Choices: pages 33, 39, 170, 171, 172, and 173

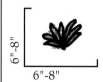

Outstanding Features:

- Pastel pink blooms in late spring
- Blue-gray leaves provide contrast
- Colorful additions to rock gardens

Here's a plant that loves limey, alkaline soil. Racemes of pink flowers are set off by blue-gray leaves. This perennial is short-lived, lasting only a few years in the garden, especially in warmer climates.

Ajuga reptans

Ajuga

Zones: 4-9

Light Needs:

Mature Size: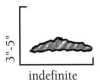

3"-5"

indefinite

Growth Rate: rapid

evergreen groundcover

Needs: Plant in any soil that's moist but well-drained. Plants won't thrive in soggy soil or in drought conditions. Grow in partial shade.

Good for: rock gardens, edging patios, stepping-stone paths, formal or informal gardens, front layer of planting beds

More Choices: pages 33, 35, 170, 171, and 173

Options: 'Alba'—white flowers 'Burgundy Lace'—dark pink flower 'Atropurpurea'—blue flowers, bronze 'Tricolor'—pink, cream, green leaves

Outstanding Features:

- Low-growing mats of flat foliage
- Blue to purple blossoms in late spring
- Grows quickly and stays low

Planted in the right conditions, Ajuga easily forms a thick carpet of rosettelike leaves. Little blue flower spikes are an added bonus. Install a solid edging to separate from lawns. Crown rot and weediness are two possible problems.

Alchemilla mollis

Lady's Mantle

Zones: 4-7

Light Needs:

Mature Size:

12"-18"

20"-24"

Growth Rate: medium

perennial

Needs: Plant in well-drained, fertile, moist soil. Partial shade is best in hotter areas; plants can take full sun in cooler regions.

Good for: edging a planting bed, planting beneath shrubs, lining a walkway

More Choices: pages 35, 171, 172, and 173

Outstanding Features:

- Gray-green, velvety leaves
- Chartreuse flowers appear in spring
- Long-lasting vase life as a cut flower

Lady's Mantle is a good low plant for in-between areas that are both shady and sunny. Chartreuse blooms are set off by silky gray-green leaves. Morning dew or rain caught by the leaves is a beautiful sight.

Amsonia tabernaemontana

Blue Star

Zones: 3-9

Light Needs:

Mature Size:

18"-24"

12"-18"

Growth Rate: medium

perennial

Needs: Plant in well-drained soil. Avoid excessively fertile soil or extra fertilization. Growth will be floppy and open if over fertilized. Trim plants back after flowering to increase density. Pick a spot that's partially shaded if your summer temperatures are warm.

Good for: wildflower gardens, perennial beds, entries, along fences, around decks, at the foot of rock walls

More Choices: pages 35, 171, and 173

Outstanding Features:

- Blue starlike blossoms begin in late spring
- Narrow green leaves turn golden in autumn
- Adapts well to poor soil conditions

Flowers cover this perennial from late spring and continue through the middle of summer. Its upright form makes a nice addition to areas where shorter groundcovers may be hidden from view.

groundcovers **6**

Anchusa myosotidiflora (also listed as Brunnera macrophylla)

Siberian Forget-Me-Not

Zones: 3-7

Light Needs:

Mature Size:
15"-18"
18"-24"

Growth Rate: medium to rapid

perennial

Needs: Plant in well-drained but moist soil. Plants thrive best in soil that's high in organic matter. Add peat moss, composted manure, or leaves to the soil at planting time. Plant in partial to dense shade. Divide when the center of plants begins to die out.

Good for: planting beneath trees, filling in shady flower beds

More Choices: pages 35, 171, and 173

Siberian Forget-Me-Not is at home in shady, organic soils beneath trees. Springtime blue flowers appear year after year. Plants self-sow and increase in number for an attractive groundcover.

Outstanding Features:

- Bright blue blooms appear in spring
- Forms a problem-free carpet of green
- Self-seeds freely to fill in an area over time

Andromeda polifolia (also listed as Andromeda rosmarinifolia)

Bog Rosemary

Zones: 2-6

Light Needs:

Mature Size:
16"-18"
18"-24"

Growth Rate: slow

evergreen shrub

Needs: Plant in well-drained, fertile, moist, acidic soil. Increase soil acidity by adding peat moss or composted oak leaves to the soil at planting time. Mulch well to conserve moisture. Plant in full sun or partial shade for best growth.

Good for: shady beds, rock gardens, woodland areas, moist locations

More Choices: pages 35, 39, 170, and 173

Options: 'Alba'—abundant white blooms, 6" high, 8" wide

As long as soil is acidic, dampness doesn't bother Bog Rosemary. White to pink flowers open in spring and continue through early summer. Leaves stay green in all seasons.

Outstanding Features:

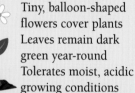

- Tiny, balloon-shaped flowers cover plants
- Leaves remain dark green year-round
- Tolerates moist, acidic growing conditions

Androsace lanuginosa

Rock Jasmine

Zones: 5-7

Light Needs:

Mature Size: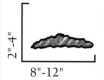
2"-4"
8"-12"

Growth Rate: slow to medium

evergreen perennial

Needs: Plant in well-drained, gritty soil. Give plants shade from hot afternoon sun in warmer climates. Water from below to keep foliage and crowns of plants dry and disease-free.

Good for: rock gardens, tucked into rock walls and vertical crevices, scree beds, containers and troughs

More Choices: pages 35, 37, 170, 171, 172, and 173

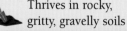

If your soil is rocky, this plant will thrive. Rock jasmine is a ground-hugging beauty that produces balls of pink blooms in mid- to late-summer. Rock Jasmine will not tolerate foot traffic.

Outstanding Features:

- Summer blooms look like small pink balls
- Silky leaves have a silvery sheen
- Thrives in rocky, gritty, gravelly soils

Arabis caucasica

Rockcress

Zones: 3-7

Light Needs:

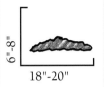

Mature Size:

6"-8"
18"-20"

Growth Rate:
medium to rapid

evergreen perennial

Needs: Plant in any soil that's well-drained in full sun or partial shade. Trim plants after flowering to promote vigorous growth. Cut stems back by two-thirds.

Good for: trailing over walls, planting beside paths, edging the front of planting beds, rock gardens

More Choices: pages 33, 35, 170, 171, 172, and 173

Options: 'Variegata'—white-edged foliage; plant in light shade

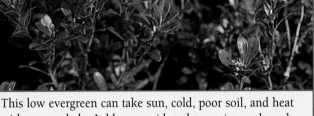

The trailing stems of Rockcress are covered with flowers each spring. Leaves remain on the plants all year, even in Zone 3. Prune plants after flowering for dense growth.

Outstanding Features:
- Flowers are white and sweetly fragrant
- Leaves on trailing stems are evergreen
- Foliage is covered with fine hairs

Arctostaphylos uva-ursi

Kinnikinick or Bearberry

Zones: 2-7

Light Needs:

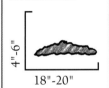

Mature Size:

4"-6"
18"-20"

Growth Rate:
slow

evergreen shrub

Needs: Plant in poor, sandy, infertile soil in full sun or partial shade. Plants rarely require pruning or fertilizer.

Good for: planting near paving, seaside gardens, foundation plantings, perennial beds, poor soils, attracting birds

More Choices: pages 33, 35, 37, 40, 170, 171, and 173

Options: 'Massachusetts'—pale pink flowers

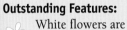

This low evergreen can take sun, cold, poor soil, and heat without any help. It blooms mid- to late-spring and produces red berries in the fall. Low maintenance plants are ideal for sites you don't have time for yet want to look good.

Outstanding Features:
- White flowers are tinged with pink
- Bright red berries attract birds to the area
- Well known for being a low maintenance plant

Arenaria montana

Mountain Sandwort

Zones: 3-6

Light Needs:

Mature Size:

2"-6"
10"-12"

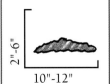

Growth Rate:
slow to medium

evergreen perennial

Needs: Plant in full sun in well-drained yet moist soil. Soils with low fertility are preferred. Plants are not drought tolerant and will need supplemental water during dry periods.

Good for: rock gardens, sunny niches, tucking into crevices of stone walls

More Choices: pages 33, 37, 170, 171, and 173

Options: *A. purpurascens* (Pink Sandwort)—pink flowers, 2" tall by 8" wide, Zones 4-7

Sandwort will grow in sunny spots and poor soil, too. Mounds of tiny, gray-green leaves last throughout the year. White flowers appear in mid- to late-spring. Provide extra water during dry spells, or plants will not survive.

Outstanding Features:
- White flowers open in late spring to summer
- Mounds of gray-green leaves last year-round
- Plants adapt to poor soils

groundcovers **6**

Armeria maritima

Sea Thrift

Zones: 3-8

Light Needs:

Mature Size:

3"-8"

10"-12"

Growth Rate:
slow to medium

evergreen perennial

Needs: Plant in full sun, well-drained soil, including sand. Afternoon shade in hot regions. Divide when centers begin to die out and flowering is reduced.

Good for: coastal areas, rock gardens, edging planting beds

More Choices: pages 35, 37, 40, 170, 171, 172, and 173

Options: 'Alba'—white flowers, 6" high
'Dusseldorf Pride'—rose-pink blooms
'Laucheana'— rose-pink blooms, 4"- 6"

Outstanding Features:

- Foliage grows in grasslike tufts
- Lollipoplike flowers in late spring
- Tolerates poor, dry, sandy soil conditions

Sea Thrift thrives by the sea as well as in any garden that has plenty of sunshine and sandy soil. This grasslike evergreen features bright pink flowers during hot months. Flowering stems rise above the foliage.

Artemisia stelleriana

Silver Brocade Artemisia

Zones: 3-9

Light Needs:

Mature Size:

18"-24"

12"-24"

Growth Rate:
medium

evergreen perennial

Needs: Plant in well-drained soil in full sun. Poor, sandy soil and coastal conditions are fine. Remove flower stalks to keep plants bushy. This is grown more for its foliage. Dig and divide plants in spring or fall when centers of crowded clumps die.

Good for: entry areas, fronts of beds, near colorful or dark-green plants, white gardens

More Choices: pages 33, 37, 40, 41, 170, 171, 172, and 173

Artemisia

Outstanding Features:

- Silvery foliage combines with white
- Tolerates dry, sandy soil conditions
- Soft texture is great for touching

Choose this low-growing plant for a sandy, sunny yard. There are several types, each boasting silvery leaves year-round.
Options: 'Powis Castle,' Zones 7-9; *Artemisia schmidtiana*, 'Silver Mound', Zones 4-10; *Artemisia ludoviciana*, Zones 4-7

Arum italicum

Arum

Zones: 6-10

Light Needs:

Mature Size:

12"-18"

6"-8"

Growth Rate:
medium

perennial

Needs: Plant in well-drained soil that's rich in organic matter. Grow in shade or sun.

Good for: planting beside patios, shady pathways, beneath covered porticoes and courtyards, woodland plantings

More Choices: pages 33, 35, 41, 171, 172, and 173

Options: 'Marmoratum'—large leaves with silvery veins
'Pictum'—leaves with gray and cream

Outstanding Features:

- Arrow-shaped leaves add interest
- Red or orange berries in fall
- Unusual growth cycle; dormant in spring

Arum is a contrary plant: Leaves emerge in fall, last through winter, and wither in spring. Summer flowers are followed by cool-season red berries.

Asperula odorata *(also listed as Galium odoratum)*

Sweet Woodruff

Zones: 4-8

Light Needs:

Mature Size:

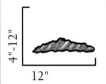

4"-12"

12"

Growth Rate:
medium to rapid

perennial

Needs: Plant in well-drained, humus-rich, acidic soil; increase soil acidity by adding peat moss, composted oak leaves, or pine straw mulch. Sweet Woodruff grows in full sun or partial shade. The hotter the climate, the more shade is required.

Good for: planting in groups beneath shade trees, along walkways, in the front of flower beds

More Choices: pages 33, 35, 39, 171, and 173

Outstanding Features:

- Bright-green leaves shaped like hands
- Starry flowers blanket plants in spring
- Plants spread quickly to cover bare areas

This groundcover grows quickly in rich soil, making it a good choice to fill in bare areas. Little white blossoms spread like snowflakes across a blanket of green in spring.

Athyrium nipponicum 'Pictum'

Japanese Painted Fern

Zones: 4-9

Light Needs:

Mature Size:

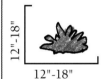

12"-18"

12"-18"

Growth Rate:
slow

perennial

Needs: Plant in moist soil that's rich in organic matter. Grow in partial or dense shade. Mulch for winter. Don't remove freeze-damaged foliage until new leaves begin to emerge

Good for: shady areas, front layer of planting beds, growing beneath trees or tall shrubs, beside shady creeks, ponds, or downspouts, at the foot of a shaded bench, woodlands

More Choices: pages 35, 41, 171, and 173

Outstanding Features:

- Dark, purplish foliage has silvery highlights
- Thrives in shady, moist locations
- Comes back every year in the spring

Grow this fern to brighten moist, shaded spots. It grows slowly, so plant ferns together in clusters for faster impact. Plants may disappear during droughts. Leaves emerge again when soil is moistened. Can grow in Zones 4 and 5 with protection.

Bergenia cordifolia

Saxifrage

Zones: 3-8

Light Needs:

Mature Size:

12"-18"

8"-12"

Growth Rate:
medium to rapid

perennial

Needs: Plant in moist but well-drained soil, in full sun or partial shade. The cooler the climate, the more sun plants can tolerate. Before new growth emerges, remove leaves burned by winter cold.

Good for: mass planting, edging perennial beds and borders, along walkways

More Choices: pages 33, 35, 171, and 173

Options: 'Bressingham Ruby'—ruby red flowers, purplish leaves in winter

Outstanding Features:

- Bright pink flowers in early to late spring
- Foliage turns bronzy fall through winter
- Plants are an attractive, year-round cover

Saxifrage offers something for every season—bell-shaped flowers in spring, bright green foliage in summer, and bronzy-red leaves in fall and winter. Add organic matter to the soil at planting time to help retain moisture.

groundcovers **6**

Calluna vulgaris

Scotch Heather

Zones: 3-8

Light Needs:

Mature Size:

4"-24"

24"-30"

Growth Rate:
medium to fast

evergreen shrub

Needs: Plant in well-drained, fertile, acidic soil in full sun. In early spring, cut branches back to within an inch of previous growth.

Good for: massing, edging walkways, flower beds, groundcover for bare areas, planting in front of shrubs

More Choices: pages 33, 39, 170, 171, 172, and 173

Options: 'Allegro'—dark red flowers 'Beoley Gold'—yellow foliage, 'County Wicklow'—pink flowers

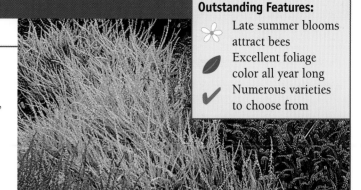

Outstanding Features:
- Late summer blooms attract bees
- Excellent foliage color all year long
- Numerous varieties to choose from

Scotch Heather's bright foliage is as eye-catching as the blooms and its leaves last year-round. Flowers occur from midsummer to fall in shades of gold, white, rose, lilac, and crimson. Scotch Heather is a low-maintenance plant.

Carex morrowii 'Variegata'

Variegated Japanese Sedge

Zones: 6-9

Light Needs:

Mature Size:

18"-20"

12"

Growth Rate:
rapid

evergreen perennial

Needs: Plant in well-drained, fertile, moist soil in full sun or partial shade. Remove dead leaves during the growing season. Plant in groups of three or more for best effect.

Good for: planting along walkways, on hillsides, in front of bigger, dark-green shrubs.

More Choices: pages 33, 35, 40, 41, 170, 171, 172, and 173

Options: 'Fisher'—cream-striped, cream-edged leaves

Outstanding Features:
- Weeping foliage adds fine texture
- Eye-catching foliage sways in the breeze
- Flower spikes emerge in late spring

Cream-and-green weeping foliage sways in the slightest breeze, adding movement in the garden. The fine texture and bright color of Variegated Japanese Sedge contrasts nicely with the larger, dark-green leaves of many shrubs.

Ceratostigma plumbaginoides

Plumbago

Zones: 5-9

Light Needs:

Mature Size:

8"-18"

12"-18"

Growth Rate:
rapid

perennial

Needs: Plant in well-drained, fertile, moist soil in full sun. Plumbago will not tolerate soggy soil conditions. Trim to the ground each spring to encourage dense growth. Plants are slow to emerge in the spring.

Good for: rock gardens, large planting beds, growing in front of shrubs, underplanting with spring bulbs, rambling over rocks

More Choices: pages 33, 170, 171, and 173

Outstanding Features:
- Late summer blooms are brilliant blue
- Bright green leaves turn reddish in fall
- Fast growing groundcover

Plumbago is a snap to grow. Full sun, well-drained soil, and light pruning each spring will keep this blue-flowered grower looking great for years to come. Plants will survive in Zone 5 with winter mulch.

Chrysogonum virginianum

Green and Gold or Goldenstar

Zones: 5-8

Light Needs:

Mature Size:

8"-10"

12"-24"

Growth Rate:
rapid

semievergreen perennial

Needs: Plant in rich, moist soil that's somewhat acidic. Choose a spot in dappled shade beneath deciduous trees. The cooler the climate, the sunnier the planting area can be.

Good for: bare shady spots, woodland gardens, planting beneath shade trees, moist areas beside downspouts, wildflower gardens, near ponds

More Choices: pages 35, 39, 170, 171, and 173

Growing less than a foot high, plants are covered with star-shaped flowers in spring, sporadically in summer, and then heavily again in fall. Plants are evergreen in mild winters and may survive in cooler locations with winter mulch.

Convallaria majalis

Lily-of-the-Valley

Zones: 2-9

Light Needs:

Mature Size:

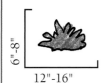

6"-8"

12"-16"

Growth Rate:
slow to rapid

perennial

Needs: Plant in any soil that's moist or receives regular watering. Grow in partial to dense shade; protect from afternoon sun in hotter climates. Tolerates full sun where summers are cool and moisture is adequate. Mulch.

Good for: shady beds, growing beneath trees or shrubs, filling in bare spots, beside shady patios, entries, or courtyards, woodland gardens, natural areas

More Choices: pages 35, 37, 171, 172, and 173

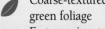
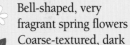

This easy-to-grow perennial spreads to cover plenty of bare ground. Delicate spring flowers show off against coarse-textured leaves. Dig and divide crowded beds in fall. Share extras with friends.

Cornus canadensis

Bunchberry

Zones: 2-7

Light Needs:

Mature Size:

3"-6"

indefinite

Growth Rate:
slow to medium

deciduous flowering shrub

Needs: Plant in well-drained, fertile, acidic soil. Choose a spot in partial to full shade where moisture is available. Improve soil acidity with peat, composted oak leaves, or pine straw mulch at planting time. Regions with cool summers are best.

Good for: shady beds, woodland gardens, planting under acid-loving shrubs and trees, cool locations

More Choices: pages 35, 39, 171, and 173

This low-growing relative of the dogwood blooms in spring. White summer flowers are followed by red berries. A little more challenging to get started than other groundcovers but worth the extra effort.

groundcovers **6**

Cotoneaster dammeri

Bearberry Cotoneaster

Zones: 5-9

Light Needs:

Mature Size:

12"–18"

3'-6'

Growth Rate:
slow to medium

semievergreen shrub

Needs: Plant in any soil, acidic or alkaline, wet or dry. Grow in full sun or partial shade.

Good for: hillsides, ditches, rock gardens, planters, filling bare planting beds, cascading over retaining walls, natural areas, parking areas, winter interest, adding fine texture

More Choices: pages 33, 35, 37, 39, 40, 41, 170, 171, and 173

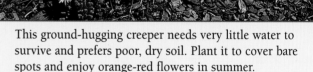

Outstanding Features:
- ✔ Prostrate form needs no pruning
- 🍃 Fine-textured foliage adds contrast
- ✳ White flowers in summer; red berries in fall

Grow this shrubby groundcover on slopes or in raised planters. Clusters of white flowers cover branches in spring and develop red berries in autumn. Extreme heat and excess fertilization make them vulnerable to fire blight.

Delosperma nubigenum

Hardy Ice Plant

Zones: 6-9

Light Needs:

Mature Size:

1"–2"

indefinite

Growth Rate:
rapid

perennial

Needs: Plant in any soil, no matter how poor, as long as it's well-drained. Grow in full sun.

Good for: rock gardens, hillsides, bare spots where there's little topsoil, beside paving

More Choices: pages 33, 37, 40, 41, 171, and 173

Options: *D. cooperi*—magenta flowers, *D. velutinum*—white flowers

Outstanding Features:
- ✳ Numerous daisylike flowers cover plants
- 🍃 Small, succulent leaves add texture
- ✔ Plants are heat and drought tolerant

This ground-hugging creeper needs very little water to survive and prefers poor, dry soil. Plant it to cover bare spots and enjoy orange-red flowers in summer.

Dianthus gratianopolitanus 'Bath's Pink'

Bath's Pink

Zones: 4-9

Light Needs: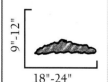

Mature Size:

9"–12"

18"-24"

Growth Rate:
medium to rapid

perennial

Needs: Plant in well-drained soil; plants won't thrive in soggy soil. Grow in full sun or partial shade. Too much shade discourages flowering. Pluck or shear wilted blooms to extend flowering and tidy up plants.

Good for: hillsides, growing over retaining walls, raised beds, berms, rock gardens, bordering planting beds, patios, walkways, courtyards, Xeriscaping

More Choices: pages 33, 35, 37, 39, 40, 41, 171, 172, and 173

Outstanding Features:
- 🍃 Fine-textured leaves are blue-green
- ✳ Pink, fringed flowers cover foliage in spring
- ✔ Tolerates heat, humidity, and drought

Plant this fragrant groundcover in sloping soil where water can drain quickly away. Pink flowers adorn blue-green mats of foliage each spring. If deadheaded, flowering will continue for more than six weeks. Bath's Pink is almost indestructible.

Erica carnea

Spring Heath

Zones: 4-8

Light Needs: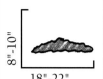

Mature Size:

8"-10" / 18"-22"

Growth Rate: medium

evergreen shrub

Needs: Plant in full sun and well-drained, fertile soil. Acidic preferred. Will tolerate alkaline soil, partial shade. In sparse snow cover, protect plants with evergreen branches. After flowering, prune branches to within an inch of previous season's growth.

Good for: entries, parking areas, walkways, positioning in front of larger shrubs

More Choices: pages 33, 39, 170, 171, 172, and 173

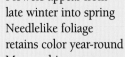

Outstanding Features:
- Flowers appear from late winter into spring
- Needlelike foliage retains color year-round
- Many cultivars are available

This groundcover puts on its flower show when winter is winding down, but plants are attractive all year long. Flower colors range from white to shades of pink and purple. Foliage is available in various hues as well.

Erigeron hybrid

Fleabane

Zones: 2-10

Light Needs:

Mature Size:

9"-30" / 24"

Growth Rate: rapid

perennial

Needs: Plant in full sun in well-drained, fertile soil. Soil should not dry out between waterings. Put plants in midday shade in warmer climates. Remove spent blooms to increase flowering. Shape plants by cutting stems back to just above a leaf.

Good for: entries, beside patios, along walkways, in front of taller shrubs, in mixed flower beds

More Choices: pages 33, 35, 41, 171, 172, and 173

E. speciósus

Outstanding Features:
- Daisylike flowers with bright yellow centers
- Grows in neat clumps of mounded foliage
- Suitable for moist growing areas

Summer flowers cover neat clumps of foliage. Locate Fleabane where you'll be able to water regularly. Plants are not drought tolerant. Group together in odd numbers of at least three plants for the best effect. Flowers are good for cutting.

Euonymus fortunei 'Coloratus'

Purple-Leaf Wintercreeper

Zones: 4-8

Light Needs:

Mature Size:

6"-24" / indefinite

Growth Rate: rapid

evergreen

Needs: Plant in full sun in any soil that is well-drained. It is tolerant of high and low soil pH. Trim midspring to keep it in bounds and to remove dead or damaged stems. Underplant with spring bulbs. Mulch for winter in colder growing zones.

Good for: filling in bare spots beneath trees, on hills, in dry areas surrounded with paving

More Choices: pages 33, 39, 40, 41, and 170

Outstanding Features:
- Leaves turn purplish red in fall and winter
- Foliage is dark green during warm months
- Tough, durable, and fast-spreading

This sprawling groundcover isn't picky about soil. Plant it in full sun so green foliage will turn wine red in fall and winter. Control scale with an insecticide spray labeled for Euonymus. This plant spreads fast, so be sure you want it.

Euphorbia cyparissias

Cypress Spurge

Zones: 4-8

Light Needs:

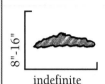

Mature Size:

8"-16"

indefinite

Growth Rate:
rapid

perennial

Needs: Plant in full sun or partial shade in well-drained soil. Tolerates dry, infertile growing conditions.

Good for: hillsides, dry areas, raised planters, banks, large planting beds

More Choices: pages 33, 35, 40, 171, and 173

Options: 'Orange Man'—flowers and fall leaves both tinted orange

Outstanding Features:

- Neat mounds of sea green foliage
- Yellow spring flowers blanket plants
- Adapts well to poor growing conditions

Here's a groundcover that won't stop for anything but dense shade and wet, boggy soil. Sprucelike needles fill in gaps in the landscape quickly. Avoid planting Cypress Spurge near flower beds. Underground roots enable this plant to spread.

Festuca glauca

Dwarf Blue Fescue

Zones: 4-9

Light Needs:

Mature Size:

6"-10"

6"-10"

Growth Rate:
medium to rapid

perennial

Needs: Plant in full sun in well-drained soil. Dig and divide plants every two or three years. Trim plants to the ground in early spring to allow emergence of new growth and clean up plants.

Good for: rock gardens, parking areas, entries, edging walkways, perennial beds, planting in front of shrubs

More Choices: pages 33, 37, 171, 172, and 173

Options: 'Elijah Blue'—6" to 10" high and wide, powdery blue foliage

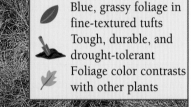

Outstanding Features:

- Blue, grassy foliage in fine-textured tufts
- Tough, durable, and drought-tolerant
- Foliage color contrasts with other plants

Add a little blue to your yard with Dwarf Blue Fescue. This ornamental grass is drought-tolerant and easy to grow. It forms tufts of fine-textured bluish leaves. Position plants close together to form a dense groundcover.

Fragaria 'Pink Panda'

Pink Panda Strawberry

Zones: 3-9

Light Needs:

Mature Size:

6"-8"

8"-10"

Growth Rate:
rapid

perennial

Needs: Plant in full sun or partial shade in fertile, well-drained soil. Divide by digging up tiny-rooted plants and clipping connecting stems. In spring, remove any dead or winter-damaged leaves before new growth emerges. Mulch plants in cold winters to help keep them evergreen.

Good for: entries, beside patios, along walkways, in containers

More Choices: pages 33, 35, 171, 172, and 173

Outstanding Features:

- Pink flowers through warm months
- Small, edible berries are sweet and tasty
- Glossy green foliage spreads quickly

If you have fertile, well-drained soil in partial shade, consider Pink Panda Strawberry. Enjoy pink flowers, miniature berries, and spreading foliage. Runners root wherever they touch soil. These plants need room.

Gaillardia x grandiflora

Blanket Flower

Zones: 2-9

Light Needs:

Mature Size:

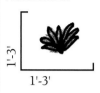

1'-3'
1'-3'

Growth Rate: rapid

perennial

Needs: Plant in well-drained soil. Poor, dry, and sandy soil is fine. Grow in full sun. This plant tolerates heat and drought. It is salt-tolerant. Divide every few years in the spring.

Good for: seaside gardens, hillsides, ditches, raised beds, berms, parking areas, seasonal accent, along sunny walkways or patios, containers, covering bare, dry hot spots

More Choices: pages 33, 37, 40, 41, 171, 172, and 173

Outstanding Features:
- Bright yellow, maroon, and reddish flowers
- Blooms nonstop throughout hot weather
- Thrives in hot, dry areas; tolerates cold

You can grow this bright bloomer anywhere soil stays dry. Hot, warm, or cold climates, it doesn't matter. Fiery flowers appear summer through frost. Flowers well even without regular deadheading.

Gaultheria procumbens

Wintergreen

Zones: 3-8

Light Needs:

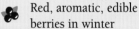

Mature Size:

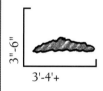

3"-6"
3'-4'+

Growth Rate: slow to medium

perennial

Needs: Plant in fertile, well-drained soil that's moist and acidic. Increase acidity by adding peat moss or composted oak leaves at planting time. Wintergreen grows best in partial shade; plants in full sun need extra water.

Good for: woodland areas, planting beneath acid-loving shrubs and trees, wintergreen fragrance, locating between stepping stones

More Choices: pages 35, 39, 171, and 173

Outstanding Features:
- White or pale pink flowers in summer
- Red, aromatic, edible berries in winter
- Wintergreen fragrance from leaves and fruit

Though it's a little picky about where it grows, Wintergreen requires very little maintenance if the situation is right. This groundcover is famous for fragrance, delicate flowers, and red winter berries.

Geranium sanguineum

Bloody Cranesbill

Zones: 3-8

Light Needs:

Mature Size:

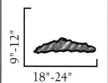

9"-12"
18"-24"

Growth Rate: medium

perennial

Needs: Plant in any soil that's well-drained; fertile soil is best. Grow in full sun or partial shade. Protect from afternoon sun in hotter climates. Trim plants after first bloom to extend flowering. This plant is pest- and disease-resistant.

Good for: planting beds, growing beneath shrubs or roses, beside patios, along walkways, in small spaces, formal or informal gardens, seasonal accents

More Choices: pages 33, 35, 41, 171, 172, and 173

Outstanding Features:
- Summer flowers in shades of pink
- Blooms abundantly in partial shade or sun
- Tolerates heat, drought, and harsh winters

This long-lived perennial—available in magenta, pink, and lavender—is perfect for small gardens or for covering ground beneath shrubs. Foliage grown in full sun turns red in autumn. Moist soil aids plants in spreading.

groundcovers 6

Geum reptans

Geum

Zones: 4-7

Light Needs:

Mature Size:

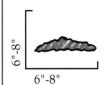

6"-8"

6"-8"

Growth Rate:
slow

evergreen perennial

Needs: Plant in fertile soils with excellent drainage. They prefer alkaline soil pH. Choose a spot in full sun unless your summers are hot—in those areas, midday shade is best. Dig established runners in spring or fall to expand the size of your plantings.

Good for: edging herb gardens, gravelly soils, walkways, patios, rock gardens, mass plantings

More Choices: pages 33, 170, 171, 172, and 173

Outstanding Features:

Foliage stays green year-round

Buttery yellow flowers in early summer

Fills areas quickly by spreading stolons

Low, tidy plants are decorated with cup-shaped blooms in early summer. Well-drained soil is a must, especially during the winter months.

Hedera helix

English Ivy

Zones: 5-9

Light Needs:

Mature Size:

4"-6"

indefinite

Growth Rate:
slow to rapid

evergreen

Needs: Grow in any soil that's moist or damp. Plant in full sun or partial shade where summers are cool; plant in partial or dense shade where summers are hot (protect from afternoon sun). Vines will adapt to poor, dry soil in shade.

Good for: hillsides, shady areas, planting beds, natural areas, formal gardens, aging new structures, clinging to and covering solid walls

More Choices: pages 33, 35, 40, 170, 171, and 173

Outstanding Features:

Coarse-textured, dark green glossy foliage

Provides thick coverage that smothers weeds

Controls erosion in shaded areas

Grow English Ivy to blanket shady beds or slopes with layers of dark, glossy foliage. Frame a lawn with an ivy-filled bed for a classic look. In areas with high rainfall, English Ivy is a nuisance plant that may climb and choke trees.

Helianthemum nummularium

Rock Rose

Zones: 5-8

Light Needs:

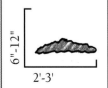

Mature Size:

6"-12"

2'-3'

Growth Rate:
medium

evergreen shrub

Needs: Plant in full sun in well-drained, alkaline to neutral soil. Work lime into soil to increase alkalinity. Shear plants after the flowers fade to keep plants neat and promote new growth.

Good for: rock gardens, raised beds, planters, hillsides, rock walls, and the front layer of shrub beds

More Choices: pages 33, 37, 39, 40, 41, 170, 171, and 173

Options: 'Buttercup'—golden yellow flowers

H. grandiflorum

Outstanding Features:
Blossoms in spring and early summer

Gray-green leaves last year-round

Adaptability to alkaline soils

Rock Rose is a heavy bloomer needing full sun and well-drained soil. Plants perform best in poor soils. Little care is required if good drainage is present. Water around roots can freeze, killing Rock Rose in colder climates.

Helleborus orientalis

Lenten Rose

Zones: 4-8

Light Needs:

Mature Size:

12"-18"

12"-18"

Growth Rate:
medium

evergreen perennial

Needs: Plant in moist soil and grow in partial shade. Protect from afternoon sun in hotter climates. Plants will fail in extreme heat or drought. Water regularly when conditions are dry. Mulch each spring to help conserve moisture.

Good for: winter interest, pathways, shady patios, natural areas, beneath trees, in raised beds or woodsy slopes

More Choices: pages 35, 41, 170, 171, 172, and 173

Tuck Lenten Rose in the shade for clusters of coarse-textured leaves to contrast with other plants. You'll enjoy delicate pink to cream-colored blossoms from January to March. Tolerates cold temperatures as well as warm.

Heuchera sanguinea

Coral Bells

Zones: 3-8

Light Needs:

Mature Size:

12"-18"

12"-18"

Growth Rate:
medium to rapid

evergreen perennial

Needs: Plant in well-drained, fertile soil. Coral Bells will not thrive in acidic soil; add lime to raise soil pH. In hotter climates, give plants partial shade. Grow in full sun elsewhere, but keep plants moist.

Good for: perennial beds, edging planting beds and walks, filling in narrow areas, combining with spring-blooming bulbs, foliage effect

More Choices: pages 33, 35, 39, 41, 170, 171, 172, and 173

Forming tidy mounds of heart-shaped leaves, this is grown more for the foliage than the flowers. Numerous cultivars are available with variations of foliage color. Delicate blooms in red, pink, or white open on stalks in spring or summer.

Hosta species

Hosta

Zones: 3-8

Light Needs:

Mature Size:

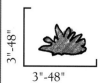

3"-48"

3"-48"

Growth Rate:
rapid

perennial

Needs: Plant in rich, moist soil. Mix compost at planting and mulch with humus each spring. Grow in partial or dense shade. Sun tolerance varies with the cultivar grown. Supply extra water during dry periods.

Good for: shade gardens, front layer of beds, natural areas, massing, specimen plants, coarse-textured accent, shady courtyards, entries, or patio areas

More Choices: pages 35, 41, 171, 172, and 173

If you find composing with textures to be an elusive concept, plant beds filled with Hostas. These large-leaved plants add coarse texture, a variety of hues, and erect stems of often fragrant flowers. Use care to avoid clashing foliage colors.

groundcovers 6

Houttuynia cordata 'Chameleon'

Houttuynia

Zones: 5-9

Light Needs:

Mature Size:

6"–18"

indefinite

Growth Rate:
rapid

perennial

Needs: Plant in well-drained soil that's rich in humus. Add peat moss or composted leaves at planting time and mulch beds heavily each spring. Keep moist at all times. Plants will tolerate partial shade, but full sun produces the most colorful leaves. In colder climates, apply a winter mulch when the ground freezes.

Good for: filling in bare, moist areas, planting near downspouts, growing in or along ponds, portable water gardens

More Choices: pages 33, 35, and 171

Options: 'Flore-Pleno'—leaves tinged purple, double white flowers

Outstanding Features:

- Colorfully variegated heart-shaped leaves
- Thrives in sunny areas with abundant water
- Spreads rapidly to cover large areas

For a moist, sunny spot, plant Houttuynia, and you can call that part of your yard complete. You'll enjoy care-free, colorful leaves throughout warm summer months. Houttuynia quickly spreads by underground roots and can be difficult to remove from areas where it isn't wanted. This plant is a vigorous grower.

Hypericum calycinum

Aaron's Beard

Zones: 5-9

Light Needs:

Mature Size:

12"–18"

indefinite

Growth Rate:
rapid

shrub

Needs: Plant in partial to dense shade in well-drained, fertile soil. In small gardens, divide plants every two to three years to keep in bounds. For best flowering, cut plants to the ground early each spring. Plants are quite drought-tolerant.

Good for: filling in bare shady areas, growing beneath trees, as a low layer in front of shrubs

More Choices: pages 35, 170, and 173

Outstanding Features:

- Bright yellow flowers in summer
- Dark green leaves—evergreen/deciduous
- Covers the ground in dry shady areas

Don't give up on flowers in the shade. Aaron's Beard produces bright yellow puffs of bloom with little sunlight, filling in bare spaces with layers of leaves. Plants spread quickly through stolons and can take over a planting bed.

Evergreen Candytuft

Zones: 4-8

Light Needs:

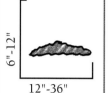

Mature Size:

6"-12"

12"-36"

Growth Rate:
slow to medium

evergreen perennial

Needs: Plant in any well-drained soil; fertile is best. Grow in full sun or partial shade. Every few years, prune heavily after blooming to encourage vigorous new growth.

Good for: rock gardens, edging walkways, patios, courtyards, narrow confined spaces, raised planters, retaining walls, slopes, perennial beds, stone pathways, entries, moonlight gardens

More Choices: pages 33, 35, 40, 41, 170, 171, 172, and 173

Outstanding Features:
- White flowers cover plants in early spring
- Fine-textured foliage stays green year-round
- Forms low, spreading mats

White is valuable for adding sparkle to landscapes; plant Candytuft to brighten areas or line walkways with snowy blooms in early spring. Plants will not thrive in soggy soil.

Japanese Blood Grass

Zones: 5-9

Light Needs:

Mature Size:

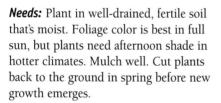

18"-24"

18"-24"

Growth Rate:
medium

perennial

Needs: Plant in well-drained, fertile soil that's moist. Foliage color is best in full sun, but plants need afternoon shade in hotter climates. Mulch well. Cut plants back to the ground in spring before new growth emerges.

Good for: accents and planting beds in front of walls, fences, and evergreen shrubs, massed plantings

More Choices: pages 33, 35, 41, and 171

Outstanding Features:
- Leaves are green at the bottom and red above
- Texture contrasts with other plants
- Very attractive massed planting

Though it dislikes hot, dry areas, Japanese Blood Grass will quickly fill an area with bright red foliage if conditions are right. It is most effective when planted in groups. Avoid poorly drained sites with this plant.

groundcovers 6

Juniperus conferta 'Blue Pacific'

Blue Pacific Shore Juniper

Zones: 5-9

Light Needs:

Mature Size:

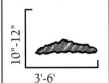

10"-12"

3'-6'

Growth Rate:
slow to medium

evergreen shrub

Needs: Plant in full sun and any well-drained soil, from acidic to alkaline. Little pruning required—remove dead or damaged branches as needed.

Good for: parking areas, entries, planting beds, hillsides, planter boxes, as a low layer in front of taller shrubs

More Choices: pages 33, 37, 39, 40, 41, and 170

Options: 'Emerald Sea'—emerald green leaves
'Silver Mist'—silvery foliage

Outstanding Features:
- Blue-green foliage lasts year-round
- Spreads to form very low, neat mats
- Tolerates salt and drought

Keep extra watering to a minimum, and this sun-loving groundcover will thrive. Blue-green foliage stays fresh looking year-round and provides great contrast with other foliage and flowers.

Juniperus horizontalis 'Bar Harbor'

Bar Harbor Juniper

Zones: 3-9

Light Needs:

Mature Size:

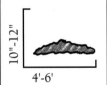

10"-12"

4'-6'

Growth Rate:
slow

evergreen shrub

Needs: Plant in full sun in well-drained soil. Slightly alkaline soil is preferred. Little pruning required—remove dead or damaged branches as needed. Supplemental water is not needed.

Good for: parking areas, coastal gardens, raised planters, hillsides, beside patios, filling in hot, dry beds, bare spots, and foundations

More Choices: pages 33, 39, 40, 41, 170, 171, and 172

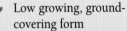

Outstanding Features:
- Foliage turns silvery plum in winter
- Tolerant of salt-spray and rocky locations
- Low growing, ground-covering form

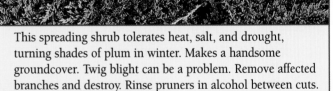

This spreading shrub tolerates heat, salt, and drought, turning shades of plum in winter. Makes a handsome groundcover. Twig blight can be a problem. Remove affected branches and destroy. Rinse pruners in alcohol between cuts.

Juniperus horizontalis 'Blue Chip'

Blue Chip Juniper

Zones: 3-9

Light Needs:

Mature Size:

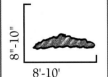

8"-10"

8'-10'

Growth Rate:
slow

evergreen shrub

Needs: Plant in full sun in any well-drained soil, including alkaline. Little pruning required. Extra water usually isn't needed.

Good for: parking areas, coastal gardens, raised planters, hillsides, beside patios, filling in hot, dry beds, bare spots, and foundations

More Choices: pages 33, 37, 39, 40, 41, 170, 171, and 172

Options: 'Prince of Wales'—bright green leaves turn purplish in winter

Outstanding Features:
- Blue summer foliage, ornamental in winter
- Plants stay low and grow wide
- Tolerant of drought and salt

Grow Blue Chip Juniper for its blue needlelike summer foliage that becomes tipped with purple during winter months. This plant loves sunny, dry locations and doesn't mind salt.

Juniperus horizontalis 'Plumosa Compacta'

Andorra Compact Juniper

Zones: 3-9

Light Needs:

Mature Size:

12"-18"

6'-10'

Growth Rate:
slow

evergreen shrub

Needs: Plant in full sun in any well-drained soil, including alkaline. Little pruning required—remove dead or damaged branches as needed. Extra water isn't usually needed.

Good for: parking areas, coastal gardens, raised planters, hillsides, beside patios, filling in hot, dry beds and bare spots, foundations

More Choices: pages 33, 39, 40, 41, 170, 171, and 172

Outstanding Features:

- Low plumes of foliage are blue- to gray-green
- Forms a dense mat of evergreen foliage
- Drought and salt tolerant

If you're looking for a groundcover for a bed surrounded by paving, look no further. This juniper won't mind the reflected heat as long as the soil drains well. Plants stay full in the center. It is susceptible to Kabatina twig blight.

Juniperus horizontalis 'Wiltonii'

Blue Rug Juniper

Zones: 3-9

Light Needs:

Mature Size:

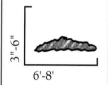

3"-6"

6'-8'

Growth Rate:
slow

evergreen shrub

Needs: Plant in full sun in any well-drained soil, including alkaline. Little pruning required—remove dead or damaged branches as needed. Extra water usually isn't needed.

Good for: parking areas, coastal gardens, dry planting beds, beside walkways and patios, behind retaining walls

More Choices: pages 33, 39, 40, 41, 170, 171, and 172

Outstanding Features:

- Flat, spreading growth creeps along ground
- Blue foliage turns purplish in winter
- Drought and salt tolerant

Here's a plant that's aptly named. Its intense blue foliage is flat just like a rug. Grow this juniper in hot, dry soil to carpet difficult spots or drape over retaining walls. This plant is susceptible to Kabatina twig blight.

Juniperus procumbens 'Nana'

Dwarf Japanese Garden Juniper

Zones: 4-9

Light Needs:

Mature Size:

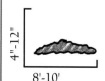

4"-12"

8'-10'

Growth Rate:
slow to medium

evergreen shrub

Needs: Plant in full sun in any well-drained soil, including acidic or alkaline. Little pruning required—remove dead or damaged branches as needed. Extra water is usually required.

Good for: parking areas, planting beds, growing beside walkways and patios

More Choices: pages 33, 39, 41, 170, 171, and 172

Options: 'Nana Greenmound'—resembles bright green cushions, 4" to 6" tall, 6' to 8' wide

Outstanding Features:

- Fine-textured bluish green foliage
- Tolerates heat and car exhaust
- Stays low with dense growth

This ground-hugging juniper has branches that are densely packed with blue-green foliage. Plants thrive in heat and dry soil; they'll even tolerate pollution. The brighter the sunlight, the better for this sun-loving plant.

groundcovers **6**

Lamiastrum galeobdolon 'Variegatum'

Yellow Archangel

Zones: 3-9

Light Needs:

Mature Size:

12"-18"

indefinite

Growth Rate:
rapid

perennial

Needs: Plant in moist, well-drained soil in dense or partial shade. Plants adapt to dry shade as well. Cut plants back after summer flowers fade to promote thick foliage growth.

Good for: planting beneath trees, covering bare, shady slopes; banks, containers

More Choices: pages 35, 171, and 173

Options: 'Herman's Pride'—green foliage with silver mottling, less invasive

Deep shade doesn't have to mean bare ground. Yellow Archangel will cover shady locations quickly. Hooded, yellow flowers appear in late spring and early summer. Avoid planting in flower beds; this plant can be quite invasive.

Outstanding Features:

 Silver and green leaves grow in dense shade
Trailing stems cover bare ground quickly
Adapts well to dry shade beneath trees

Lamium maculatum

Spotted Dead Nettle

Zones: 3-9

Light Needs:

Mature Size:

8"-12"

12"-24"

Growth Rate:
rapid

perennial

Needs: Plant in deep or partial shade in any soil that's well-drained. Plants will grow in full sun in colder climates if soil stays consistently moist.

Good for: planting beneath trees and covering bare, shady spots—even places with dry soil

More Choices: pages 35, 37, 41, 171, and 173

Options: 'White Nancy'—white flowers
'Beacon Silver'—pale pink blooms
'Pink Pewter'—pink flowers

Even shady spots kept dry by thirsty tree roots are no problem for this plant. Choose Spotted Dead Nettle for its silvery leaves and durability. Plants can be very vigorous and may outgrow some garden situations.

Outstanding Features:

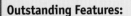 Leaves have white or silvery centers
Pink or purple blooms in spring to summer
Trailing stems cover shady ground quickly

Lonicera pileata

Royal Carpet Honeysuckle

Zones: 5-9

Light Needs:

Mature Size:

12"-24"

3'-8'

Growth Rate:
rapid

evergreen to semievergreen shrub

Needs: Plant in well-drained, fertile soil in full sun or partial shade. Prune after flowering to shape the plant. Tame wayward stems and control size anytime.

Good for: planting beds, foundation planting, attracting birds, covering banks and slopes

More Choices: pages 33, 35, 170, and 173

This groundcovering shrub is easy to grow. You'll enjoy creamy spring blossoms, purple berries in summer, and shiny green leaves year-round. Royal Carpet Honeysuckle isn't an invasive plant.

Outstanding Features:

Creamy yellow spring blooming flowers
Shiny, dark green leaves last year-round
Translucent purple berries in summer

Lysimachia nummularia

Moneywort

Zones: 3-8

Light Needs:

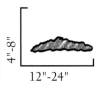

Mature Size:

4"-8"

12"-24"

Growth Rate: rapid

perennial

Needs: Plant in well-drained, fertile, moist soil. Choose a spot in dense or partial shade. Cut plants back after flowering to promote compact growth. For low maintenance, let plants grow.

Good for: shady, damp areas where grass won't grow, beside ponds and water features, near downspouts

More Choices: pages 35, 171, and 173

Options: 'Aurea'—lime-green to yellow leaves

Moneywort thrives in wet shade. Plants spread quickly and can take over small areas in no time. Plants are adaptable to sun or shade as long as moisture is available. It is also known as Creeping Jennie.

Mentha corsica

Corsican Mint

Zones: 6-9

Light Needs:

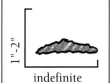

Mature Size:

1"-2"

indefinite

Growth Rate: medium

perennial

Needs: Plant in moist, fertile soil; like most mint, this too will adapt to any soil that isn't soggy or bone-dry. Grow in partial shade to shade. Water regularly in sunny locations.

Good for: growing between stepping stones, covering soil beneath roses and leggy perennials, planting beds, growing under benches

More Choices: pages 33, 41, 171, 172, and 173

Plant this mosslike mint where you'll be sure to see and smell it up close. Bright green leaves grow together to form low, creeping, fuzzy mats. Foliage is peppermint-scented. It may be sold as *M. requienii*.

Myosotis scorpioides

Forget-Me-Not

Zones: 3-8

Light Needs:

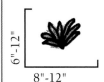

Mature Size:

6"-12"

8"-12"

Growth Rate: rapid

perennial

Needs: Plant in fertile, moist soil. Partial shade is best, but full sun in cooler areas where moisture is consistent. Cutting back after flowering promotes compact growth.

Good for: moist areas, planting beside water features, edges of woodlands, near downspouts, banks of streams

More Choices: pages 33, 35, 37, 171, and 173

Options: *M. sylvatica*—bedding plant, short-lived but reseeds, Zones 5-9

Damp, shady spots are ideal for Forget-Me-Not. They require abundant moisture to perform their best; the perfect location for these is near water or naturalized in moist woodlands. Prostrate plants will spread by stolons.

Nepeta x faassenii

Catmint

Zones: 4-8

Light Needs:

Mature Size:

12"-18"

18"-24"

Growth Rate:
rapid

perennial

Needs: Plant in well-drained, sandy soil in full sun or partial shade. Cut plants back after bloom to encourage a second flowering later. Dig and divide plants in early spring to make new plants.

Good for: Xeriscaping, rock gardens, filling in hot spots, edging planting beds, walkways, entries, or patios

More Choices: pages 33, 35, 37, 41, 171, 172, and 173

Options: 'Six Hills Giant'—violet blue blooms; 24" to 36" tall, 24" wide

Outstanding Features:

Grows in hot sun and dry, sandy soil
Great in combination with yellow and pink
Cascading, gray-green foliage is aromatic

Plant Catmint where you need a low-growing bloomer to tumble over the edges of patios, walkways, and rock walls. Purple-blue flowers bloom steadily in summer sun, forming a ribbon of blue where they are used.

Oenothera missouriensis

Sundrop Primrose

Zones: 4-8

Light Needs:

Mature Size:

6"-12"

8"-12"

Growth Rate:
rapid

perennial

Needs: Plant in well-drained soil or poor, rocky sites. Full sun for flowering. Mulch in late fall in areas with cold winters. Remove faded flowers for additional blooms. Dig and divide in spring or fall.

Good for: entry areas, parking areas, edging planting beds, walkways, rock walls, patios

More Choices: pages 33, 37, 171, 172, and 173

Outstanding Features:

Large, bright yellow flowers in summer
Tolerates heat, sun, and poor soil
Spreads quickly to cover large areas

Big, bright yellow flowers earn this plant its name. How appropriate to have drops of sunshine covering red-tinted foliage. It grows in hot, dry spots and comes back year after year. It is sometimes listed as *O. macrocarpa*.

Omphalodes verna

Blue-Eyed Mary

Zones: 5-9

Light Needs:

Mature Size:

2"-8"

8"- 12"

Growth Rate:
rapid

semievergreen perennial

Needs: Grow in partial shade. Plant in moist, fertile soil that's well-drained and somewhat acidic. Plants will tolerate poor soil or dry shady spots but won't spread as quickly. Dig and divide plants in fall or spring.

Good for: planting beneath trees and shrubs, pairing with spring flowering bulbs, woodland gardens

More Choices: pages 35, 39, 171, and 173

Options: 'Alba'—white flowers

Outstanding Features:

Bright blue flowers with white eyes
Spreads quickly to fill in bare, shady spots
Heart-shaped leaves are semievergreen

Try this groundcover for blue blossoms in shady places. Plants quickly fill bare areas and return each year without fail. Dig and divide stems to increase plantings or to control spread. Apply slug repellant in early spring.

Pachysandra terminalis

Pachysandra

Zones: 4-9

Light Needs:

Mature Size: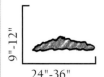
9"-12" | 24"-36"

Growth Rate: rapid

perennial

Needs: Plant in dense to partial shade—protect from afternoon sun in hotter climates. Moist, fertile soil is essential. Mix in peat moss or composted leaves at planting and tuck around plants each spring. Mulch new plantings for their first and second winters in colder areas.

Good for: filling in shady spots where grass won't grow, planting beneath trees, raised beds, growing in shade gardens

More Choices: pages 35, 171, and 173

Outstanding Features:
- ✔ Covers shady, bare areas
- 🍃 Rich green leaves stay low and neat
- ✿ Small white flowers in late spring

This groundcover fills in bare shady spots where grass won't grow—but only if the soil is moist. It makes a good companion to Hostas. Both are coarse-textured, grow in shade, and like the same type of soil.

Pennisetum alopecuroides

Fountain Grass

Zones: 5-9

Light Needs:

Mature Size:
18"-48" | 24"-36"

Growth Rate: rapid

perennial

Needs: Plant in average soil (dry is better than wet) and full sun. Allow leaves and seedheads to remain on plants through the winter. Cut them off in spring just as new growth is emerging.

Good for: growing in masses to fill bare sunny spots, adding winter color to landscapes, growing as accent plants, edging patios, containers

More Choices: pages 33, 37, 39, 41, 171, and 172

P. rubrum

Outstanding Features:
- ✔ Form spills up and over like a fountain
- 🍃 Fine-textured leaves turn red in fall
- ⚫ Maroon seedheads are showy through winter

Fountain Grass adds movement to the landscape with arching foliage that sways in the slightest breeze. Decorative seedheads are attractive, too. This plant is easy to grow in sunny spots. Also try *P. rubrum*—reddish purple foliage.

Phlox stolonifera

Creeping Phlox or Woodland Phlox

Zones: 2-8

Light Needs:

Mature Size: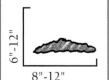
6"-12" | 8"-12"

Growth Rate: rapid

evergreen perennial

Needs: Plant in fertile, moist soil in partial to deep shade. Plants in cooler climates can tolerate more sun.

Good for: combining with spring flowering bulbs, shady areas, woodland plantings, growing at the base of shrubs and trees, moist locations

More Choices: pages 35, 39, 170, 171, 172, and 173

Options: 'Blue Ridge'—sky blue flowers; 12" tall stems

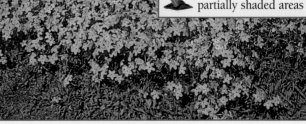

Outstanding Features:
- ✿ Becomes a carpet of flowers in spring
- 🍃 Foliage forms a dense, matted groundcover
- 🌱 Grows in deep to partially shaded areas

Creeping Phlox is the most shade tolerant of all phlox—either partial or deep shade. It thrives with abundant moisture, forming a dense groundcover that combines beautifully with bulbs and shrubs. Plants will not thrive in dry shade.

groundcovers 6

Phlox subulata

Moss Phlox

Zones: 2-9

Light Needs:

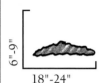

Mature Size:

6"-9"

18"-24"

Growth Rate:
rapid

evergreen perennial

Needs: Plant in full sun in average or poor, rocky soil that's dry. Alkaline soil is preferred. Dig and divide plants in fall or let them spread naturally. Shear plants after bloom to encourage dense growth and later rebloom.

Good for: Xeriscaping, slopes, ditches, erosion control, beside steps, edging planting beds, rock gardens, entries, creeping over walls

More Choices: pages 33, 37, 40, 41, 170, 171, 172, and 173

Outstanding Features:
- Becomes a carpet of flowers in spring
- Evergreen foliage forms a dense mat
- Grows in sunny, dry places

This matlike groundcover is the answer to dry hillsides and ditches. Plants are carpeted with white, pink, or lavender blooms in spring. Lush green foliage is present the remainder of the year.

Potentilla tabernaemontani

Spring Cinquefoil

Zones: 4-8

Light Needs:

Mature Size:

2"-4"

8"-12"

Growth Rate:
medium to rapid

perennial

Needs: Spring Cinquefoil will grow in soil that's rich or poor, even rocky, as long as it's dry. Full sun yields best flowering. Prune after blooms fade to reduce invasive tendencies. Divide in spring or fall.

Good for: Xeriscaping, rock gardens, slopes, edging planting beds, dry banks, rock walls

More Choices: pages 33, 37, 40, 171, 172, and 173

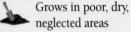
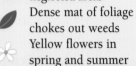

Outstanding Features:
- Grows in poor, dry, neglected areas
- Dense mat of foliage chokes out weeds
- Yellow flowers in spring and summer

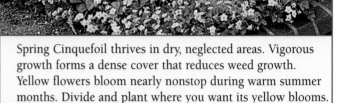

Spring Cinquefoil thrives in dry, neglected areas. Vigorous growth forms a dense cover that reduces weed growth. Yellow flowers bloom nearly nonstop during warm summer months. Divide and plant where you want its yellow blooms.

Primula japonica

Japanese Primrose

Zones: 5-8

Light Needs:

Mature Size:

12"-24"

12"-24"

Growth Rate:
medium

perennial

Needs: Plant in fertile soil that doesn't dry out. Soil should be acidic to neutral. Mix in composted oak leaves or peat moss at planting and add a 3-inch layer of mulch around plants each spring to keep soil rich in humus. Grow in a shady spot. Provide plants with extra water during dry periods.

Good for: wet, boggy areas, beside water features, adding color to shaded spots

More Choices: pages 35, 37, 171, and 173

Outstanding Features:
- Grows in wet, soggy soil near water
- Flowers from spring through midsummer
- Tiers of blooms in various shades

Soggy, shaded spots aren't problem areas if you plant Japanese Primrose in them. Colorful flowers in shades of pink, crimson, and white won't grow anywhere else.

Rosa Alba Meidiland

Alba Meidiland Rose

Zones: 4-8

Light Needs:

Mature Size:

1'-2'
3'-5'

Growth Rate:
medium

deciduous shrub

Needs: Plant in moist, fertile, well-drained soil and in sun or partial shade. Add super phosphate or bonemeal to planting hole to promote root growth. Reapply every fall. No pruning needed, but plants will need plenty of room.

Good for: slopes, planting behind retaining walls, along walkways, patios, the front layer of foundation planting, around low decks, in raised planters

More Choices: pages 33, 35, 40, 172, and 173

Outstanding Features:
- Clusters of cream-colored double blooms
- ✔ Blooms in sun or partial shade
- Mounded form spreads quickly

This sounds too good to be true—a rose that cascades thickly to cover the ground with fragrant flowers and shiny green foliage. Flowers appear from summer through fall.

Rosa wichuraiana

Memorial Rose

Zones: 4-9

Light Needs:

Mature Size:

10"-12"
18'-20'

Growth Rate:
medium

deciduous shrub

Needs: Plant in fertile, well-drained soil in full sun. Feed with rose food or bonemeal at planting and when blooms begin. Minimal care is needed. Remove any dead branches in spring after buds swell. Remove faded flowers to encourage fresh blooms.

Good for: front layers of planting beds, edging walkways and patios, combining with evergreens to show off rose hips for winter interest

More Choices: pages 33, 172, and 173

Outstanding Features:
- Single white flowers with yellow centers
- Shiny green leaves are disease-resistant
- Scarlet hips are showy in fall and winter

This old-fashioned rose is easy to grow. Simple, single flowers cover the long spreading canes in early summer. Scarlet hips last from fall through winter. Plants can be grown upright when provided support.

Rosa 'Flower Carpet'

Flower Carpet Rose

Zones: 4-10

Light Needs:

Mature Size:

24"-30"
30"-60"

Growth Rate:
medium

deciduous shrub

Needs: Plant in full sun in fertile, well-drained soil. No spraying required. Let plants grow together to form a mass. Remove branches that grow straight up.

Good for: filling in bare sunny beds, growing as the front layer of planting areas, growing on berms

More Choices: pages 33, 41, and 173

Options: 'Flower Carpet Pink' 'Flower Carpet White' 'Flower Carpet Appleblossom'

Outstanding Features:
- Available in a wide range of flower colors
- Disease-resistant, shiny green leaves
- Easy to grow; ideal for the novice rose grower

You don't need to know a lot about roses to succeed with these. Spreading plants need sun and soil that drains. They are often sold in pink plastic pots. Plants are thorny. Use two or three plants per square yard for groundcover.

groundcovers 6

Sedum acre

Goldmoss

Zones: 4-9

Light Needs:

Mature Size:

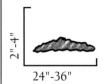
2"-4"
24"-36"

Growth Rate:
rapid

evergreen perennial

Needs: Grow in full sun in soil that's well-drained; slightly alkaline soil is best. Adapts to poor, dry locations. Tolerates drought and reflected heat.

Good for: slopes, ditches, rock gardens, tucking into crevices in paving or walls, parking areas, growing beside steps, cascading over retaining walls, filling in hot, dry areas; confined spaces, perennial gardens, containers

More Choices: pages 33, 37, 39, 40, 41, 170, 171, and 173

Here's a fast-growing groundcover that grows well in hot, dry pockets or barren slopes. Creeping plants produce gold flowers all summer. It may be sold as Stonecrop Sedum.

Sedum spectabile

Stonecrop

Zones: 3-10

Light Needs:

Mature Size:

12"-18"
18"-24"

Growth Rate:
medium to rapid

perennial

Needs: Plant in poor, dry soils that drain well; plants won't tolerate damp conditions. Grow in full sun. Divide plants in fall when clumps grow from outer edges instead of the center. Cut plants back in June for smaller plants with additional bloom and stems that don't flop over.

Good for: rock gardens, arid landscapes, Xeriscaping, slopes, entries, adding to the front layer of planting beds

More Choices: pages 33, 37, 40, 41, 171, and 173

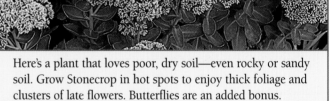

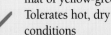
Here's a plant that loves poor, dry soil—even rocky or sandy soil. Grow Stonecrop in hot spots to enjoy thick foliage and clusters of late flowers. Butterflies are an added bonus. Support elongated stems of plants growing in partial shade.

Sedum spurium 'Dragon's Blood'

Dragon's Blood Sedum

Zones: 3-8

Light Needs:

Mature Size:

2"-6"
12"-18"

Growth Rate:
rapid

perennial

Needs: Plant in poor, dry soils that drain well—plants won't tolerate damp conditions. Grow in full sun. Plants are drought-tolerant and pest-free.

Good for: filling in hot, dry spots where nothing else will grow, rock gardens, arid landscapes, sunny slopes, Xeriscaping, edging beds, patios, or walkways, growing in containers, stone walls and crevices

More Choices: pages 33, 37, 40, 171, 172, and 173

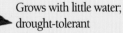
Red blooms appear in the heat of summer on this sedum. Grow it in poor, dry soil and in blazing sun. Spreads well, especially in northern gardens. It can be invasive in formal plantings. Divide plants any time during the growing season.

Stachys byzantina

Lamb's Ear

Zones: 4-8

Light Needs:

Mature Size:

12"-15"
12"-18"

Growth Rate:
medium to rapid

perennial

Needs: Plant in fertile soil that's moist but well-drained. Grow in full sun (with afternoon shade in hotter climates). Trim heat-damaged plants to encourage growth in fall. Dig and divide plants every three to four years.

Good for: entries, children's gardens, moonlight gardens, edging planting beds, patios, and walkways

More Choices: pages 33, 41, 171, 172, and 173

Outstanding Features:
- Velvety leaves are silvery and touchable
- Pink, white, or purplish flowers on stalks
- Dependable; plants return year after year

Lamb's Ears are as soft and fuzzy as their name suggests. Grow these in patches to fill in flower beds or to edge planting areas. Water plants early in the day so leaves will dry before nightfall.

Symphoricarpos x chenaultii 'Hancock'

Prostrate Chenault Coralberry

Zones: 4-7

Light Needs:

Mature Size:

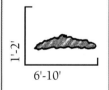
1'-2'
6'-10'

Growth Rate:
rapid

deciduous shrub

Needs: Plant in soil that's moist or dry, fertile or poor. Tolerates alkaline soil pH and will thrive in sun or shade. Prune in early spring to stimulate abundant bloom.

Good for: slopes, erosion control, woodland gardens, planting beds, bird habitats

More Choices: pages 33, 35, 37, 40, 41, and 173

Outstanding Features:

- Tolerates a wide range of soil conditions
- Multitudes of blooms in summer
- Pink and white berries attract birds

Grow this plant to cover ground that's moist or dry, in full sun or shade. Its self-layering habit forms a broad mound of foliage. White or pink flowers and berries add seasonal appeal. This plant tolerates air pollution.

Teucrium prostratum or chamaedrys

Germander

Zones: 4-9

Light Needs:

Mature Size:

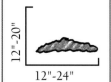
12"-20"
12"-24"

Growth Rate:
medium to rapid

evergreen shrub

Needs: Grow in full sun. Plant in well-drained, alkaline to neutral soil. Work lime into soil to increase alkalinity. For formal hedges, cut plants in early spring to within a few inches of the ground.

Good for: formal knot gardens, edging rose, herb, or flower beds, rock gardens, entries, edging patios or walkways

More Choices: pages 33, 39, 41, 170, 171, 172, and 173

T. chamaedrys

Outstanding Features:
- Tolerates pruning to form a low hedge
- Grows well in alkaline soil conditions
- Carmine rose blooms in mid- to late-summer

Grow Germander where you want a little row of green. Plants adapt to both a formal or informal way of life. Trim into desired forms or allow them to remain in their natural mounded form.

Thymus leucotrichus

Creeping Thyme

Zones: 5-9

Light Needs:

Mature Size:

6"-8"

8"-12"

Growth Rate:
medium to rapid

evergreen herb

Needs: Plant in full sun in alkaline to neutral soil. Work lime into soil to increase alkalinity. Plants won't thrive in damp soil; select a location that's well-drained.

Good for: tucking between stepping stones, beneath benches, edging planting beds or walkways, entries, filling in between roses, growing over tops of retaining walls, tucking into rock walls

More Choices: pages 33, 37, 39, 41, 170, 171, 172, and 173

Choose Creeping Thyme when you need a low-growing plant to tuck into hot, dry crevices or between stepping stones. Aromatic leaves stay gray-green year round and can tolerate light foot traffic. Pink flowers appear in spring.

Tiarella cordifolia

Allegheny Foam Flower

Zones: 4-9

Light Needs:

Mature Size:

6"-12"

12"-24"

Growth Rate:
rapid

evergreen perennial

Needs: Grow in deep or partial shade. Plant in well-drained, moist, fertile soil that's slightly acidic. To add organic matter, mix in peat moss or composted leaves at planting and apply a 3-inch-thick layer to the soil surface each spring. Avoid sunny, dry, alkaline conditions. Plants prefer cool locations.

Good for: moist shaded areas, planting beneath acid-loving shrubs and trees, woodland gardens, rock gardens, perennial flower borders

More Choices: pages 35, 39, 170, 171, and 173

Outstanding Features:

White plumes of foamy flowers in spring

Light-green leaves in spring, bronzy-red in fall

Thrives in acidic, damp, shady areas

Brighten those damp, shady spots with Allegheny Foam Flower. Feathery white flowers appear in spring above light green foliage. When grown with the proper conditions, plants spread quickly to make large, lush patches. Plants spread by underground stems and can quickly take over in moist, shady areas.

Littleleaf Periwinkle

Zones: 4-8

Light Needs:

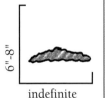

Mature Size:

6"-8"

indefinite

Growth Rate:
rapid

evergreen

Needs: Grow in sun or partial shade north of Zone 7; southward, grow in full or partial shade. Plant in well-drained, moist, fertile soil high in organic matter. Mix in peat moss or composted leaves at planting time.

Good for: bare shady spots, hillsides, erosion control, beneath trees, woodland gardens, underplanting with spring bulbs

More Choices: pages 33, 35, 40, 41, 170, 171, and 173

Options: 'Alba'—white flowers 'Aureola'—leaves veined with creamy yellow, lavender blossoms

Outstanding Features:

- Trailing stems form mats of glossy foliage
- Periwinkle blue flowers open in spring
- Little maintenance once established

Fill in bare shady areas with a dense blanket of glossy green leaves. Lavender blue flowers appear each spring. This plant grows slowly in poor soil and is not for coastal areas. It may be sold as Creeping Myrtle.

Dividing Groundcover Clumps

Dividing clump-forming groundcovers keeps plants vigorous and increases the quantity of plants you have to cover the ground. If your beds are already filled, share with a neighbor.

STUFF YOU'LL NEED

- ✔ Sharp shovel
- ✔ Utility knife (optional)
- ✔ Work boots
- ✔ Garden hose with sprayer attachment

What to Expect

You won't need to divide every year. Plants that decline, fail to bloom, or appear crowded should be divided. Every three years is usually enough.

1 **In late spring or early summer, dig up overgrown clumps of groundcover from crowded beds.** Dig and divide one clump at a time to keep roots from drying out. Spray roots with a stiff stream of water to wash soil away from roots. This makes it easier to see what you're doing.

2 **Lay the plant on its side.** Position the sharp shovel blade against the clump of roots and press down to cut it in half. (Large clumps can be divided several times.) You may need to use a utility knife if roots are tangled.

3 **Gently pull the severed root mass apart with your hands to form two plants.** Each plant should have its own roots and leaves. Replant and water right away to keep plants from drying out.

groundcovers

6

Add leafy layers of texture to your landscape by planting vines. Plant them to cover overhead arbors for added shade or position vines to dress up the vertical faces of walls, fences, and posts.

Vines

Add charming finishing touches to your landscape with the addition of vines. Observe landscapes in books and magazines, as well as eye-catching yards in your neighborhood. They usually have vines, sprawling up a post or over a wall, polishing off the composition with the lush look that makes you think an experienced gardener must live there.

Give your landscape that green-thumb look by learning about vines. Some climb by adhesive disks that will damage wood or stucco. Others climb by tendrils or twining stems, making them better choices for such supports.

The selection guides make it easy to pick the right vine for your yard. See pages 36-39 for vines for various soil types, page 33 for vines to grow in sun, page 35 for vines to grow in shade, and pages 28-29 for vines for privacy.

Dropmore Scarlet Honeysuckle
(Lonicera x brownii 'Dropmore Scarlet')
Page 210

Evergreen vines

Common Name	Zones	Page
Chocolate Vine	5-9	206
Akebia quinata		
Cross-Vine	6-9	207
Bignonia capreolata		
Dropmore Scarlet Honeysuckle	3-7	210
Lonicera x brownii 'Dropmore Scarlet'		

Deciduous vines

Common Name	Zones	Page
American Bittersweet	3-8	208
Celastrus scandens		
Blaze Climbing Rose	5-10	212
Rosa 'Blaze'		
Boston Ivy	4-8	211
Parthenocissus tricuspidata		
Chinese Wisteria	5-9	215
Wisteria sinensis		
Climbing Cecil Brunner Rose	6-10	213
Rosa 'Climbing Cecil Brunner'		
Climbing Hydrangea	4-7	209
Hydrangea petiolaris		
Climbing Iceberg Rose	4-10	213
Rosa 'Climbing Iceberg'		
Climbing Peace Rose	5-9	214
Rosa 'Climbing Peace'		
Hardy Kiwi	4-8	206
Actinidia arguta		
Hybrid Clematis	3-9	209
Clematis hybrid		
Joseph's Coat Climbing Rose	4-10	214
Rosa 'Joseph's Coat'		
Porcelain Vine	4-8	207
Ampelopsis brevipedunculata		
Silver Lace Vine	4-9	212
Polygonum aubertii		
Trumpet Honeysuckle	4-9	210
Lonicera sempervirens		
Trumpet Vine	4-9	208
Campis radicans		
Virginia Creeper	4-9	211
Parthenocissus quinquefolia		

Vines for wooden structures

Common Name	Zones	Page	Type
American Bittersweet *Celastrus scandens*	3-8	208	
Blaze Climbing Rose *Rosa 'Blaze'*	5-10	212	
Chocolate Vine *Akebia quinata*	5-9	206	
Climbing Cecil Brunner Rose *Rosa 'Climbing Cecil Brunner'*	6-10	213	
Climbing Iceberg Rose *Rosa 'Climbing Iceberg'*	4-10	213	
Climbing Peace Rose *Rosa 'Climbing Peace'*	5-9	214	
Cross-Vine *Bignonia capreolata*	6-9	207	
Dropmore Scarlet Honeysuckle *Lonicera x brownii 'Dropmore Scarlet'*	3-7	210	
Hardy Kiwi *Actinidia arguta*	4-8	206	
Hybrid Clematis *Clematis hybrid*	3-9	209	
Joseph's Coat Climbing Rose *Rosa 'Joseph's Coat'*	4-10	214	
Porcelain Vine *Ampelopsis brevipedunculata*	4-8	207	
Silver Lace Vine *Polygonum aubertii*	4-9	212	
Trumpet Honeysuckle *Lonicera sempervirens*	4-9	210	

Vines to avoid on wooden structures

Common Name	Zones	Page	Type
Boston Ivy *Parthenocissus tricuspidata*	4-8	211	stickers
Chinese Wisteria *Wisteria sinensis*	5-9	215	twiners
Climbing Hydrangea *Hydrangea petiolaris*	4-7	209	stickers
Trumpet Vine *Campsis radicans*	4-9	208	twiners
Virginia Creeper *Parthenocissus quinquefolia*	4-9	211	stickers

Availability varies by area and conditions (see page 21). Check with your garden center.

American Bittersweet
(Celastrus scandens)
Page 208

Putting an arbor in your yard gives vines a place to climb and frames the view looking from one garden area to another.

Twiners vs. Stickers

Twining vines grab onto whatever is handy to pull themselves up.
Some twining vines have stems that wrap themselves around supports. Other vines have straight stems but grow coiling tendrils that reach out to anchor the vine as it grows. Most twining vines won't hurt wooden structures, but beware of any vine that's described as rapid-growing and vigorous. Such a vine may develop strong, heavy stems that can eventually crush wooden structures. Twining vines don't grow well on flat walls because there's nothing for them to coil around. They do better on arbors, posts, and trellises. If you want to grow a twining vine on a flat, vertical surface, such as the back of your garage, attach a lattice panel to the wall. Insert 1-inch-thick blocks of wood, called spacers, between the lattice and the wall so that there is airspace between them. This provides a route for vines to follow as they weave their way through the lattice.

Sticking vines grow their own adhesive. Some grow aerial rootlets that plaster the vine against hard surfaces while others grow suction discs on the ends of special stems. Both methods allow vines to grow up flat supports, such as walls made of masonry or stone. However, you should think twice before planting sticking vines to grow up walls made of masonry, stucco, or stone because this kind of vine can damage hard surfaces. If you're willing to go to the trouble of repointing mortar after a number of years, then sticking vines are worth the beauty they add to flat walls. If you've already got a sticking vine growing on a flat wall, don't pull it off; you may do more damage during removal than the vine itself is causing. You'll also find it difficult to remove completely stubborn rootlets or discs that are left behind.

Boston Ivy
(Parthenocissus tricuspidata)
Page 211

Vines give garden spots a sheltered feeling,
adding leafy privacy and filtering sunlight.

Trumpet Honeysuckle
(Lonicera sempervirens)
Page 210

Choosing Vines for Seasonal Interest

Planting vines and climbers adds color and texture to your
landscape season after season. The selection guides that follow will
help you choose vines for their flowers, colorful foliage, fragrance,
and showy fruit in spring, summer, and fall.

Climbing Hydrangea
(Hydrangea petiolaris)
Page 209

Rapid-growing vines

Common Name	Zones	Page
American Bittersweet	3-8	208
Celastrus scandens		
Boston Ivy	4-8	211
Parthenocissus tricuspidata		
Chinese Wisteria	5-9	215
Wisteria sinensis		
Climbing Cecil Brunner Rose	6-10	213
Rosa 'Climbing Cecil Brunner'		
Cross-Vine	6-9	207
Bignonia capreolata		
Hardy Kiwi	4-8	206
Actinidia arguta		
Porcelain Vine	4-8	207
Ampelopsis brevipedunculata		
Silver Lace Vine	4-9	212
Polygonum aubertii		
Trumpet Honeysuckle	4-9	210
Lonicera sempervirens		
Trumpet Vine	4-9	208
Campsis radicans		
Virginia Creeper	4-9	211
Parthenocissus quinquefolia		

Fragrant vines

Common Name	Zones	Page
Blaze Climbing Rose	5-10	212
Rosa 'Blaze'		
Chinese Wisteria	5-9	215
Wisteria sinensis		
Chocolate Vine	5-9	206
Akebia quinata		
Climbing Cecil Brunner Rose	6-10	213
Rosa 'Climbing Cecil Brunner'		
Climbing Peace Rose	5-9	214
Rosa 'Climbing Peace'		
Cross-Vine	6-9	207
Bignonia capreolata		
Joseph's Coat Climbing Rose	4-10	214
Rosa 'Joseph's Coat'		

*Availability varies by area and
conditions (see page 21). Check
with your garden center.*

Spring-flowering vines

Common Name	Zones	Page
Chinese Wisteria	5-9	215
Wisteria sinensis		
Chocolate Vine	5-9	206
Akebia quinata		
Climbing Iceberg Rose	4-10	213
Rosa 'Climbing Iceberg'		
Cross-Vine	6-9	207
Bignonia capreolata		
Dropmore Scarlet Honeysuckle	3-7	210
Lonicera x brownii 'Dropmore Scarlet'		
Hybrid Clematis	3-9	209
Clematis hybrid		
Joseph's Coat Climbing Rose	4-10	214
Rosa 'Joseph's Coat'		
Trumpet Vine	4-9	208
Campsis radicans		

Summer-flowering vines

Common Name	Zones	Page
Blaze Climbing Rose	5-10	212
Rosa 'Blaze'		
Climbing Cecil Brunner Rose	6-10	213
Rosa 'Climbing Cecil Brunner'		
Climbing Hydrangea	4-7	209
Hydrangea petiolaris		
Climbing Iceberg Rose	4-10	213
Rosa 'Climbing Iceberg'		
Climbing Peace Rose	5-9	214
Rosa 'Climbing Peace'		
Dropmore Scarlet Honeysuckle	3-7	210
Lonicera x brownii 'Dropmore Scarlet'		
Hardy Kiwi	4-8	206
Actinidia arguta		
Silver Lace Vine	4-9	212
Polygonum aubertii		
Trumpet Honeysuckle	4-9	210
Lonicera sempervirens		

Vines for autumn interest

Common Name	Zones	Page	Type
American Bittersweet	3-8	208	B
Celastrus scandens			
Boston Ivy	4-8	211	FO
Parthenocissus tricuspidata			
Chocolate Vine	5-9	206	B
Akebia quinata			
Climbing Cecil Brunner Rose	6-10	213	FL
Rosa 'Climbing Cecil Brunner'			
Dropmore Scarlet Honeysuckle	3-7	210	FL/B
Lonicera x brownii 'Dropmore Scarlet'			
Hybrid Clematis	3-9	209	S
Clematis hybrid			
Porcelain Vine	4-8	207	B
Ampelopsis brevipedunculata			
Virginia Creeper	4-9	211	FO
Parthenocissus quinquefolia			

B: Berries FL: Flowers FO: Foliage S:Seeds

Pruning Vines

The first time you'll need to prune a vine is immediately after planting it. Though you might feel as though you're reducing your investment, you'll spur the vine onto new and faster growth if you cut it back to about half the size it was when you bought it. Most vines won't need much pruning for a season or two after that as they grow into their new homes. But if stems appear leggy with few leaves or flowers, trim them back to encourage new growth to develop more branches. However, most vines will eventually require trimming to shape them and keep their size under control. Here's how to prune some popular vines that thrive in Zones 5 and 6.

• American Bittersweet (*Celastrus scandens*)
Late winter or early spring is the time to cut back this vine to keep it in bounds, but trimming in fall produces pretty cuttings for arrangements. Trim stems as needed to keep vines the size and shape you desire. Overgrown vines require yearly pruning to keep them under control.

• Climbing Hydrangea (*Hydrangea petiolaris*)
Trim these vines only as needed to keep them growing in the area you want and to keep their aerial rootlets off wooden structures. Make cuts after flowering.

• Hardy Kiwi (*Actinidia arguta*)
No regular pruning is required except to maintain size. Trim stems back immediately after flowering to avoid cutting off next year's blossoms.

• Trumpet Honeysuckle (*Lonicera sempervirens*) and
• Dropmore Scarlet Honeysuckle (*Lonicera x brownii* 'Dropmore Scarlet')
Prune these vines only if they've outgrown their allotted space. You can cut them any time except just before a freeze, but the best time to prune honeysuckle is right after flowering finishes.

• Trumpet Vine (*Campsis radicans*)
Prune as needed in late winter or early spring to control this vigorous vine's size and reduce its weight. Cut back side shoots to develop a strong main framework of woody stems. Leave stubs with three or four buds when cutting off shoots.

• Virginia Creeper (*Parthenocissus quinquefolia*) and
• Boston Ivy (*Parthenocissus tricuspidata*)
Let these vines grow, but cut them back as needed to keep them off wooden structures. If you must control their size, cut the growing ends of stems back in early winter. Repeat if necessary at the beginning of summer. Never cut these vines at the base; if you do, you'll end up with the hard-to-remove dead stems clinging to the wall.

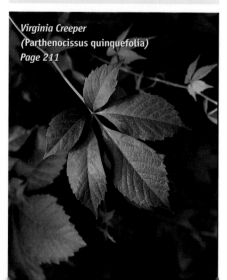

*Virginia Creeper
(Parthenocissus quinquefolia)
Page 211*

*Climbing Hydrangea
(Hydrangea petiolaris)
Page 209*

Actinidia arguta

Hardy Kiwi

Zones: 4-8

Light Needs:

Mature Size:

25'-30'

indefinite

Growth Rate:
rapid

deciduous vine

Needs: Plant in full sun or partial shade in any kind of soil. Growth rate is fastest in rich soil. To slow it down, plant in a poor location. Prune any time during the growing season to keep it in bounds.

Good for: screening, privacy, covering a fence, trellis, or arbor

More Choices: pages 29, 33, 35, 202, 203, 204, and 205

Options: 'Issai'— bears purple seed pods *A. chinensis* (also sold as *A. deliciosa*; Chinese Gooseberry or Kiwi Fruit)—bears edible fruit. Grow both male and female plants for fruit production.

Outstanding Features:

- Fast-growing screen for unsightly views
- Thick, beautiful, disease-free foliage
- Won't harm wood or supporting structures

For quick cover-ups, Hardy Kiwi is made to order. This deciduous, twining vine is not picky about its growing conditions. Poor or fertile soil, wet or dry, this vine will take off wherever it is planted. Attractive foliage adds coarse, textural background in the landscape. White flowers open in early summer. They are fragrant but not showy. Small fruit ripens from September to October. For added protection in colder climates, plant on southern walls only. Also try *A. kolomikta* (Variegated Kiwi Vine)—green leaves with pink and white blotches, grows to 15' high, Zones 5-8.

Akebia quinata

Chocolate Vine

Zones: 5-9

Light Needs:

Mature Size:

20'-40'

indefinite

Growth Rate:
medium to rapid

semievergreen flowering vine

Needs: Plant in full sun or partial shade in fertile soil that's moist but well-drained. Prune Chocolate Vine after flowering to control growth. Plant two vines to produce long, purple pods.

Good for: screening for privacy or blocking poor views, covering fences, trellises, or arbors, twining up posts and rails

More Choices: pages 28, 33, 35, 202, 203, 204, and 205

Options: 'Variegata'—leaves display patches of cream

Outstanding Features:

- Dark brown, purplish flowers in late spring
- Won't damage wooden structures
- Long, purple seed pods in fall

This vine earns its name with purplish brown blooms in spring that smell hauntingly of chocolate. Delicious and calorie-free. Delicate leaves make a fine-textured screen. Also sold as Fiveleaf Akebia.

Ampelopsis brevipedunculata

Porcelain Vine

Zones: 4-8

Light Needs:

Mature Size:

10'-25'

indefinite

Growth Rate:
rapid

deciduous vine

Needs: Vines will adapt to just about any soil except soggy. They grow best in full sun. Plant where root growth is restricted and climbing support is provided. Prune in winter to shape plants and encourage vigorous growth.

Good for: trellises, lattice, fences, arbors, entries, near patios, covering eyesores such as stumps or rock piles

More Choices: pages 33, 37, 39, 202, 203, 204, and 205

More Choices: pages 33, 37, 39, 202, 203, 204, and 205

Outstanding Features:
- Colorful fruit appearing in fall
- Fast-growing cover for all types of structures
- Adapts to a wide range of soils

The flowers on this vine aren't noticeable; but the fruit certainly is, forming in shades of yellow, lavender, and bright blue, all on the same vine. Round, colored fruit is showiest when vines are spread out, as on a trellis.

Bignonia capreolata

Cross-Vine

Zones: 6-9

Light Needs:

Mature Size:

30'-50'

indefinite

Growth Rate:
rapid

**semievergreen flowering vine
(evergreen in hotter climates)**

Needs: Plant in acidic soil that's moist but well-drained. This vine can tolerate standing water for short periods of time. Prune in winter. Grow in sun for best flowering.

Good for: screening, trellises, arbors, fences, walls, posts, rails, natural areas, seasonal accents, walls, erosion control on slopes, covering chain-link fences

More Choices: pages 28, 33, 35, 39, 202, 203, 204, and 205

More Choices: pages 28, 33, 35, 39, 202, 203, 204, and 205

Outstanding Features:
- Orange-red, funnel-shaped flowers in May
- Thick, glossy foliage provides dense coverage
- Fast growth covers structures quickly

This fast-growing vine features bright orange-red blooms in mid- to late-spring. Thick foliage hides whatever the plant grows over. Climbing by tendrils, plants will not damage wood. Flowers have a fragrance similar to mocha.

vines

6

Campsis radicans

Trumpet Vine

Zones: 4-9

Light Needs:

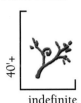

Mature Size:

40'+

indefinite

Growth Rate:
rapid

deciduous flowering vine

Needs: Plant in any conditions; Trumpet Vine grows in sun, shade, rich soil or poor. It will even thrive in sidewalk cracks. Prune as needed to control. Mow over stems in lawn.

Good for: camouflaging eyesores, attracting hummingbirds, growing on tall, blank masonry walls

More Choices: pages 29, 33, 35, 37, 202, 203, 204, and 205

Options: 'Flava'—yellow flowers 'Praecox'—red flowers

Outstanding Features:
- Grow in any soil type and lighting condition
- Blossoms attract hummingbirds
- Fast-growing for covering blank walls

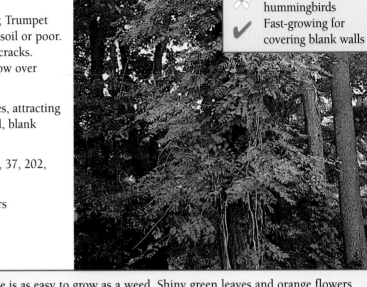

This blooming beauty of a vine is as easy to grow as a weed. Shiny green leaves and orange flowers are attractive from spring until frost. Rampant growth can destroy arbors and fences or choke trees. Keep this vine away from rooftops.

Celastrus scandens

American Bittersweet

Zones: 3-8

Light Needs:

Mature Size:

20'-60'

indefinite

Growth Rate:
rapid

deciduous vine

Needs: Plant in any kind of soil, damp or dry. This vine grows in sun or shade, but full sun yields the most fruit. Sturdy support is needed. Prune to control size and shape. Plant both males and females for fruit production.

Good for: autumn accent, growing on fences, trellises, or arbors, natural areas, hiding scars in the landscape

More Choices: pages 29, 33, 35, 37, 202, 203, 204, and 205

Outstanding Features:
- Ornamental red-and-yellow fruit in fall
- Vines cover arbors and fences quickly
- Good for cutting and use in arrangements

Maturing in autumn, bright red berries are nestled inside yellow capsules. The fruit is widely used in dried arrangements in fall and winter. Plants are easy to grow and very vigorous. Vines can girdle the trunks of young trees, killing them.

Hybrid Clematis

Zones: 3-9

Light Needs:

Mature Size:

10'-20'

indefinite

Growth Rate:
slow

deciduous flowering vine

Needs: Plant in fertile, well-drained soil that's rich in organic matter (add compost or composted manure). Set new plants about 2 inches deeper in the soil than they were in nursery pots. Keep roots cool and shaded but position vines to spread into sunny areas. After planting, cut back all stems to just above a pair of strong, healthy buds about a foot higher than soil level. Tie young plants to supports.

Good for: colorful accent, coarse texture, entries, growing up arbors, trellises, fences, posts, and poles

More Choices: pages 33, 35, 41, 202, 203, and 205

Outstanding Features:
- Large flowers available in many colors
- Fuzzy fall seedheads add seasonal interest
- Twining stems won't damage wood

When you think of flowering vines, Hybrid Clematis is probably the plant that comes to mind. Large, showy blossoms appear each spring. Numerous hybrids and a variety of colors are available. *Clematis armandii*, an evergreen vine, will grow in areas where coastal influences raise minimum temperature higher than typical conditions.

Climbing Hydrangea

Zones: 4-7

Light Needs:

Mature Size:

indefinite

indefinite

Growth Rate:
slow to medium

deciduous flowering vine

Needs: Plant in fertile, well-drained, moist soil in either full sun or shade. Prune as needed in late winter or early spring to control growth. This vine tolerates alkaline soil.

Good for: adding texture to brick or stone walls, chimneys, courtyard walls, and tree trunks, seasonal accent, provides a coarse-textured background

More Choices: pages 33, 35, 41, 202, 203, and 205

Outstanding Features:
- Lacy caps of white flowers in summer
- Coarse leaves, unusual growth habit
- Grows on hard surfaces without support

This hydrangea is an easy-growing and beautiful vine. It will cover buildings or tree trunks with yards of foliage and flowers. Older stems develop exfoliating bark. The combination of flowers, foliage, and bark makes this plant ideal for all seasons.

Vines

6

Lonicera sempervirens

Trumpet Honeysuckle

Zones: 4-9

Light Needs:

Mature Size:

10'-20'

indefinite

Growth Rate:
rapid

**deciduous flowering vine
(evergreen in frost-free zones)**

Needs: Plant in well-drained, moist soil that's rich in organic matter. Water regularly, especially during dry spells. Grow in full sun. Prune in late winter or early spring to control growth as needed.

Good for: entries, courtyards, sitting areas, covering fences, trellises, arbors, rails, and posts, attracting hummingbirds to the garden

More Choices: pages 29, 33, 202, 203, 204, and 205

Grow this gently twisting climber to cover fences, posts, arbors, or rails with blue-green foliage and scarlet summer flowers. It is easy to grow and nondamaging to garden structures.

Lonicera x brownii 'Dropmore Scarlet'

Dropmore Scarlet Honeysuckle

Zones: 3-7

Light Needs:

Mature Size:

7'-10'

indefinite

Growth Rate:
medium

semievergreen flowering vine

Needs: Plant in any type of soil that's well-drained. Grow in full sun. Water during dry periods. Fertilize using a balanced liquid fertilizer at half-strength every two months. New plants may require strings to help them start scaling posts.

Good for: climbing chain-link fences, trellises, scaling picket or privacy fences, arbors, posts, seasonal accents

More Choices: pages 28, 33, 202, 203, and 205

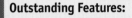

Enjoy the trumpet-shaped flowers as well as the hummingbirds they attract from June through September. Twining stems climb and clamber on vertical structures. This vine won't damage wood. Control major aphid infestations, if they occur, with insecticide or insecticidal soap. This vine may also be sold as Scarlet Trumpet Honeysuckle.

Parthenocissus quinquefolia

Virginia Creeper

Zones: 4-9

Light Needs:

Mature Size:

20'+

indefinite

Growth Rate:
rapid

deciduous vine

Needs: Grow in any soil, from alkaline to acidic, dry to moist. Rocky soil is fine. Plant in full sun or partial shade. More sun yields brighter fall color. Tolerates heat, drought, and salt spray.

Good for: natural areas, seaside gardens, masonry or stone walls, fences, or buildings, hiding blank walls, adding coarse texture, backgrounds, seasonal accents, groundcover for erosion control

More Choices: pages 29, 33, 35, 37, 39, 40, 202, 203, 204, and 205

This five-leaved native vine is easy to grow. Plant where it can climb on solid surfaces. This plant is often mistaken for poison ivy. The old saying—leaves of three let it be, leaves of five let it thrive—applies to this handsome plant. Also try *Parthenocissus* var. Englemannii; it boasts burgundy fall color and is hardy to Zone 3.

Parthenocissus tricuspidata

Boston Ivy

Zones: 4-8

Light Needs:

Mature Size:

20'+

indefinite

Growth Rate:
rapid

deciduous vine

Needs: Grow in any soil, from alkaline to acidic, dry to moist. Plant in full sun or partial shade. Full sun brings out intense fall color. Plants may require more water in hotter climates.

Good for: growing on masonry walls, fences, or buildings, hiding blank walls, adding coarse texture, backgrounds, seasonal accents, giving new homes an aged look

More Choices: pages 29, 33, 35, 37, 39, 202, 203, 204, and 205

Grow this vine to enjoy foliage that changes with the seasons. Large leaves are green in summer, turning rich red in fall. Bare winter stems lend pattern to hard surfaces for vertical interest. Adhesive disks can damage wood.

Vines 6

vines

6

Polygonum aubertii

Silver Lace Vine

Zones: 4-9

Light Needs:

Mature Size:

25-35'

indefinite

Growth Rate:
rapid

deciduous flowering vine

Needs: Plant in any kind of soil, including poor and dry. Grow in sun or shade. Plant vines near well-anchored supports. Prune in late winter or early spring to control growth.

Good for: coastal areas, Xeriscaping, dry shade, screening, privacy, growing on fences or arbors

More Choices: pages 29, 33, 35, 37, 40, 202, 203, 204, and 205

Outstanding Features:

- Foamy white flowers in midsummer
- Dense foliage for quick screening
- Grows in sun or shade, in any soil

Grow this quick climber in any kind of soil to cover just about anything. Blankets of white blooms appear mid- to late-summer. This vine can be hard to remove—be sure to plant it where you want it to be.

Rosa 'Blaze'

Blaze Climbing Rose

Zones: 5-10

Light Needs:

Mature Size:

12'-14'

12'-15'

Growth Rate:
rapid

deciduous flowering climber

Needs: Plant in well-drained, slightly acidic soil. Grow in full sun. Water roots generously during the growing season. Avoid wetting the foliage. Fertilize with rose food when blooming starts. Tie new canes to strong supports. Plants are disease-resistant and carefree.

Good for: fences, trellises, arbors, walls, pillars, specimen plants, seasonal accents, entries, beside patios

More Choices: pages 33, 39, 202, 203, 204, and 205

Outstanding Features:

- Large clusters of scarlet blooms in summer
- Tolerates the extremes of heat and cold
- Long, pliable canes are easily trained

Grow this rose for its abundant red blooms and tough disposition. Blaze Climbing Rose grows vigorously in cold, warm, or hot climates. It is the climbing hybrid of Memorial Rose. Flowers repeat throughout the hot months and have a light fragrance.

Climbing Cecil Brunner Rose

Zones: 6-10

Light Needs:

Mature Size:

20'-30'

12'-15'

Growth Rate:
rapid

deciduous flowering climber

Needs: Plant in well-drained, slightly acidic soil. Grow in full sun. Water generously during the growing season. Avoid wetting the foliage. Fertilize when blooming first starts. Tie new canes to supports. Provide winter protection in colder climates.

Good for: screening, camouflaging eyesores, growing on fences, arbors, pillars, or trees, specimen plants

More Choices: pages 29, 33, 39, 202, 203, 204, and 205

Outstanding Features:
- Large sprays of small, blush pink blooms
- Vigorous climber covers a lot of ground
- Small, pointed, dark green foliage

Grow this vigorous rose where you've got room to let it climb. Big sprays of small sweetheart pink roses cover stems in hot weather. Provide with a sturdy support and let it go.

Climbing Iceberg Rose

Zones: 4-10

Light Needs:

Mature Size:

14'-16'

12'-15'

Growth Rate:
rapid

deciduous flowering climber

Needs: Plant in well-drained, slightly acidic soil. Grow in full sun. Water generously during the growing season. Avoid wetting the foliage. Fertilize with rose food when blooming starts. Tie new canes to supports. Provide winter protection in colder climates.

Good for: arbors, fences, posts, railings, porches, entries, courtyards, growing beside patios or decks, specimen plants

More Choices: pages 33, 39, 202, 203, and 205

Outstanding Features:
- Clusters of pure white flowers
- Nearly continuous blooms in summer
- Vigorous canes with very few thorns

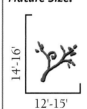

Described as one of the best climbers, this white flowering rose tolerates heat or cold. Climbing forms sometimes revert to the shrub form. If this happens, replant elsewhere and try again with another Climbing Iceberg Rose.

vines

6

Joseph's Coat Climbing Rose

Zones: 4-10

Light Needs:

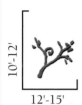

Mature Size:

10'-12'

12'-15'

Growth Rate:
rapid

deciduous flowering climber

Needs: Plant in well-drained, slightly acidic soil. Grow in full sun. Water generously during the growing season. Avoid wetting the foliage. Fertilize when blooming starts. Tie new canes to sturdy supports. Provide winter protection in colder climates.

Good for: fences, walls, arbors, entries, specimen plants, seasonal accents, as a climber or a sprawling shrub

More Choices: pages 33, 39, 202, 203, 204, and 205

Outstanding Features:

* Multicolored effect of clusters of blooms
✔ Blooms well through-out the growing season
* Upright form makes canes easy to train

You'll enjoy the multicolored effect of this appropriately named climbing rose. Clusters of blooms change from yellow to orange-gold to red. It is a colorful rose garden on just one plant.

Climbing Peace Rose

Zones: 5-9

Light Needs:

Mature Size:

14'-16'

12'-15'

Growth Rate:
rapid

deciduous flowering climber

Needs: Plant in well-drained, slightly acidic soil. Grow in full sun. Water generously during the growing season. Avoid wetting the foliage. Fertilize with rose food when blooming starts. Tie new canes to strong supports.

Good for: arbors, fences, entries, porches, pillars, seasonal accents, specimen plants, growing near patios, decks

More Choices: pages 33, 39, 202, 203, 204, and 205

Outstanding Features:

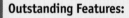

* Soft yellow blossoms edged with pink
✔ Fragrant flowers are long blooming
 Tolerates both hot and cold temperatures

Famous for its large flowers, soft coloring, and end of WWII legacy, Climbing Peace Rose is a rose worth growing. For maximum flower production, train plants around supports by bending long canes into horizontal positions.

Wisteria sinensis (W. chinensis)

Chinese Wisteria

Zones: 5-9	**deciduous flowering vine**
Light Needs:	**Needs:** Plant in fertile, moist, well-drained soil. Grow in full sun or partial shade. Plant near well-anchored, sturdy supports. Use a bloom-booster fertilizer for abundant blooms. Prune after flowering to control size or mow over vines spreading on the ground.

Mature Size:

30'+
12'-15'

Good for: growing on walls, sturdy fences, or arbors, shading sitting areas, adding texture to plain backgrounds

More Choices: pages 29, 33, 35, 202, 203, 204, and 205

Growth Rate: rapid

More Choices: pages 29, 33, 35, 202, 203, 204, and 205

Outstanding Features:

- Purple flowers dangle like grapes in spring
- Leaves cast cooling shade in summer
- Aged stems appear muscular and strong

If you're committed to keeping this strong vine within its bounds, you'll enjoy years of drooping spring flowers, summer shade, and sculptural stems. Keep Chinese Wisteria out of trees, away from eaves, and off delicate arbors.

Pruning Chinese Wisteria

Prune your Chinese Wisteria after it has grown as big as you want it to be.

After it has reached its desired size, promote flowering by thinning vines at least three times a year. If you only prune once a year, the vine will grow excessively thick foliage but yield few flowers.

Start by cutting new growth when Chinese Wisteria is dormant. You'll be able to identify new growth, even in winter, because the shoots at the end of vine tips are thinner than older branches. Locate the second bud on new growth; trim about half the shoots back to this point. In spring, remove all young branches that are leafless. Cut all side branches, leaving two or three buds and allowing all nubby spurs to remain; these are what the grapelike flowers will dangle from. Follow up with summer pruning to reduce the size of branches growing to the sides by one-half.

Good idea! If your vine isn't flowering, it just needs a little tough love. Use a shovel to sever roots about 18 inches around the base to a depth of 8 to10 inches. Severing the roots will stimulate root growth and shock the plant into a flowering cycle.

vines 6

General Index

Ⓐ

Acc/ent plants, 13, *13*
Acidic soil
  balancing, 49
  plants for, 38–39
Alkaline soil
  balancing, 49
  plants for, 39
Architect, landscape, 7
Austin, David, 156
Autumn interest
  Shrubs with, 125
  trees with, 67
  vines for, 205

Ⓑ

Base map, 16, *16*
Beds
  around trees, 65
  construction, 46–47
  designs, 44–45
  drainage, 51
  edging, 47, *47*, 49, *49*, 172
  preparation, 48–49
  raised, 49, *49*
  for shrubs, 110–113
  weed prevention, 46, 49
Buck, Griffith, 155
Budget, 17

Ⓒ

Cameras, 16
Catch basins, 51
Clay soil
  amending, 49
  plants for, 37
Climate Zones, 5
Color
  as accent, 13
  as design element, 10, *10*, 11, 12
  house color, choosing plants for, 11
  repetition of, 12
Composting, 69
Contrast as a design element, 13, *13*
Courtyards, shrubs for, 123

Ⓓ

Deciduous plants for screening, 27, 29
Design
  accents, 13, *13*
  beds, 44–45
  color, 10, *10*, 11, 12
  form, *10*, 11, 12, *12*
  line, 11
  planning, 6–7
  prioritizing plans, 18–19
  professional help, 7
  site assessment, 16–17
  style, 14–15
  symmetry, 14
  texture, 10–11, *11*, 12, *12*
  unity, *12*, 12–13
Digging bar, 64
Dividing groundcover clumps, 201
Downspouts, 51
Drainage, 51
Dry soil, plants for, 36–37

Ⓔ

Edging, 47, *47*, 172
  groundcover for, 172
Entries
  groundcover for, 172
  shrubs for, 123
Evergreens. *See also specific plants*
  groundcover, 170
  pruning, 116–117
  for screening, 26, *26*, 28, 29

shrubs, 28, 116–117
trees, 28
vines, 28, 202
Exposure, 17

Ⓕ

Fertilizing, 52–53
  with natural fertilizers, 53
  with synthetic fertilizers, 52–53
  troubleshooting, 53
Flowering plants
  groundcover, 173
  shrubs, fragrant, 120
  shrubs, pruning, 118–119
  shrubs, spring-flowering, 124
  shrubs, summer-flowering, 125
  trees, spring-flowering, 67
  trees, summer-flowering, 67
  vines, spring-flowering, 205
  vines, summer-flowering, 205
Form as a design element, *10*, 11, *12*, 12
Formal gardens
  shrubs for, 123
  style, 14, *14*, 15, *15*
Foundation plantings, 112–113
Fragrant plants
  shrubs, flowering, 120
  vines, 204
French drains, 51

Ⓖ

Grass removal from beds, 46–47
Groundcovers, 168–201
  for acidic soil, 39
  for alkaline soil, 39
  for clay soil, 37
  coarse-textured, 171
  design use of, 7
  dividing, 201
  for dry soil, 37
  for edging, 172
  encyclopedia of choices, 174–201
  evergreen, 170
  fine-textured, 171
  for full sun, 33
  perennial, 171
  planting, 169
  for rock gardens, 173
  salt-tolerant, 40
  for shade, 35
  for slopes, 40, 169
  for small spaces, 41
  for urban areas, 41
  for wet soil, 37
  for woodlands, 173
  for Zone 5, 23
  for Zone 6, 25
Gypsum, 49

Ⓗ

Hedges
  pruning, 117
  selection guide, 111
Herbicide, 46, 47, 49
Hoes, 48

Ⓘ

Informal style, 15, *15*, 42–43
Irrigation, 50

Ⓛ

Landscape architect, 7
Landscape assessment quiz, 17
Leaves, composting, 69
Limestone, 49
Line as a design element, 11

Ⓜ

Map, base, 16, *16*
Mass plantings, shrubs for, 122
Mulch, 49, 55, 63, 65, 115

Ⓝ

Nitrogen, 52, 53

Ⓟ

Patios
  groundcovers for, 172
  shrubs for, 123
  trees for, 68
Peat moss, 49
Percolation test, 36
PH, soil, 38–39
Phosphorus, 52, 53
Pinching, 116
Planning, 6–7. *See also* Design
  budget, 17
  needs inventory, 17
  prioritizing, 18–19
  site analysis, 16–17
Planting
  bed construction, 46–47
  bed design, 44–45
  bed preparation, 48–49
  fall, 61
  groundcovers, 169
  roses, bare-root, 54
  roses, climbing, 55
  roses, containerized, 55
  shrubs, 111–115
  trees, 61–65
Potassium, 52, 53
Privacy. See also Screening
  filtering views, 26–27
  needs, determining, 26
  plant selection guides for, 28–29
Private spaces, landscaping, *18*, 18–19, *19*
Pruning, 56–57
  azaleas, 117
  Bradford pear, 100
  Chinese wisteria, 215
  evergreen shrubs, 116–117
  flowering shrubs, 118–119
  hard, 119
  hedges, 117
  hydrangeas, 118
  pinching, 116
  roses, 56-57
  selective, 116
  shearing, 116
  tool sterilization, 56
  tools, 119
  trees, 64
  vines, 205, 215
Public spaces, landscaping, 18, *18*, 19, *19*

Ⓡ

Raised beds, 49, *49*
Repetition, value of, 12–13
Rock gardens, groundcover for, 173
Root stimulator, 52

Ⓢ

Salt-tolerant plants, 40
Screening, 26–29
  deciduous shrubs for, 29
  deciduous trees for, 29
  deciduous vines for, 29
  evergreen shrubs for, 28
  evergreen trees for, 28
  evergreen vines for, 28
  filtering view, 26–27, 29, *29*
  needs, determining, 26
  plant selection guides, 28–29
Selection guides-groundcovers
  for acidic soil, 39
  for alkaline soil, 39
  for clay soil, 37
  coarse-textured, 171
  for dry soil, 37
  for edging, 172

evergreen, 170
fine-textured, 171
flowering, 173
for full sun, 33
perennial, 171
for rock gardens, 173
salt-tolerant, 40
for shade, 35
for slopes, 40
for small spaces, 41
for urban areas, 41
for wet soil, 37
for woodlands, 173
for Zone 5, 23
for Zone 6, 25
Selection guides-shrubs
  for acidic soil, 38–39
  for alkaline soil, 39
  with autumn color, 125
  for clay soil, 37
  coarse-textured, 121
  for dry soil, 37
  for entries, courtyards, and patios, 12
  fine-textured, 121
  for formal gardens, 123
  foundation plantings, 112–113
  fragrant flowering, 120
  for full sun, 32–33
  hedges, 111
  for mass planting, 122
  rapid-growing, 121
  salt-tolerant, 40
  for screening, deciduous, 29
  for screening, evergreen, 28
  for shade, 34
  for slopes, 40
  slow-growing, 121
  for small spaces, 41
  spring-flowering, 124
  summer-flowering, 125
  for urban areas, 41
  for wet soil, 37
  for windbreaks, 43
  with winter fruit, 125
  for woodland gardens, 123
  for Zone 5, 22–23
  for Zone 6, 24–25
Selection guides-trees
  accent, 69
  for acidic soil, 38
  for alkaline soil, 39
  with autumn interest, 67
  for clay soil, 37
  for dry soil, 36–37
  for filtering views, 29
  for full sun, 32
  for open areas, 69
  patio, 68
  rapid-growing, 59
  salt-tolerant, 40
  for screening, evergreen, 28
  shade, 69
  for shade, 34
  for slopes, 40
  for small spaces, 41
  spring-flowering, 67
  streetside, 69
  summer-flowering, 67
  for urban areas, 41
  for wet soil, 37
  for windbreaks, 43
  with winter interest, 67
  for Zone 5, 22
  for Zone 6, 24
Selection guides-vines
  for acidic soil, 39
  for alkaline soil, 39

for autumn interest, 205
deciduous, 202
for dry soil, 37
evergreen, 202
fragrant, 204
for full sun, 33
rapid-growing, 204
salt-tolerant, 40
for screening, deciduous, 29
for screening, evergreen, 28
for shade, 35
for small spaces, 41
spring-flowering, 205
summer-flowering, 205
for wooden structures, 203
for Zone 5, 23
for Zone 6, 25
Selection of plants, 20–43
    climate factors, 21
    maintenance requirements and, 21
    needs, determining, 20
    salt-tolerant, 40
    screening and privacy, 26–29
    slopes and, 40
    for small spaces, 41
    soil conditions and, 36–39
    sunlight conditions and, 30–35
    for urban areas, 41
    for windbreaks, 42–43
    for Zone 5, 22–23
    for Zone 6, 24–25
Shade
    groundcovers, 35
    requirements, 30–31
    shrubs, 34
    trees, 34, 69
    vines, 35
Shearing, 116
Shovels, 47, 63
Shrubs, 110–167
    for acidic soil, 38–39
    for alkaline soil, 39
    with autumn color, 125
    beds, planning, 110–111
    for clay soil, 37
    coarse-textured, 121
    design use of, 6
    for dry soil, 37
    encyclopedia of choices, 126–167
    for entries, courtyards, and patios, 123
    fine-textured, 121
    for formal gardens, 123
    foundation plantings, 112–113
    fragrant flowering, 120
    for full sun, 32–33
    hedges, 111
    for mass planting, 122
    planting, 114-115

pruning, 116–117
rapid-growing, 121
salt-tolerant, 40
for screening, deciduous, 29
for screening, evergreen, 28
for shade, 34
slopes and, 40, 115
slow-growing, 121
for small spaces, 41
spacing, 110–111
spring-flowering, 124
summer-flowering, 125
for urban areas, 41
for wet soil, 37
for windbreaks, 43
with winter fruit, 125
for woodland gardens, 123
for Zone 5, 22–23
for Zone 6, 24–25
Site analysis, 16–17
Slopes
    plant selection for, 40
    planting groundcovers on, 169
    planting shrubs on, 115
    planting trees on, 63
Small spaces, plants for, 41
Sod cutter, 47
Soil
    acidic soil, plants for, 38–39
    alkaline soil, plants for, 39
    amending, 48–49, 62, *62*, 64, *64*
    assessment, 17
    bed preparation, 48–49
    clay soil, plants for, 37
    dry soil, plants for, 36–37
    percolation test, 36
    pH, 38–39
    types, 36
    wet soil, plants for, 37
Spraying herbicides, 46, 49
Spring-flowering shrubs, 118, 124
Spring-flowering trees, 67
Spring-flowering vines, 205
Staking trees, 63
Streetside trees, 69
Style
    combined, 15
    formal, 14, *14*, 15, *15*
    informal, 15, *15*, 42–43
    regional, 14
Summer-flowering shrubs, 125
Summer-flowering trees, 67
Summer-flowering vines, 205
Sunlight requirements, 30–35. *See also* Shade
    groundcover for full sun, 33
    shrubs for full sun, 32–33
    trees for full sun, 32
    vines for full sun, 33

Symmetry, 14, *14*
T
Terminology, 4
Texture
    as design element, 10–11, *11*, 12, *12*
    groundcovers, 171
    repetition of, 12
    shrubs, 121
Tilling, 46, *46*, 48, *48*
Tools
    camera, 16
    digging bar, 64
    hoes, 48
    pruning, 119
    shovels, 47, 63
    sod cutter, 47
    sprayer, 46
    sterilizing with alcohol, 56, 119
    tillers, 46, *48*
Topping trees, 64
Transplant shock, 64
Trees, 58–109
    accent, 69
    for acidic soil, 38
    for alkaline soil, 39
    with autumn interest, 67
    buying, 60–61
    for clay soil, 37
    climate effect from, 59
    composting leaves, 69
    design use of, 6
    for dry soil, 36–37
    encyclopedia of choices, 70–109
    for filtering views, 29
    for full sun, 32
    legacy, 59
    mortality, 61
    for open areas, 69
    patio, 68
    planting, season for, 61
    planting balled-and-burlapped, 64–65
    planting container grown, 62–63
    planting on a slope, 63
    rapid growers, 59
    salt-tolerant, 40
    for screening, evergreen, 28
    for seasonality, 66–67
    shade, 34, 69
    for slopes, 40
    for small spaces, 41
    spring-flowering, 67
    staking, 63
    streetside, 69
    summer-flowering, 67
    topping, 64
    transplant shock, 64
    for urban areas, 41
    for wet soil, 37

for windbreaks, 43
with winter interest, 67
for Zone 5, 22
for Zone 6, 24
U
Unity, design, *12*, 12–13
Urban areas, plants for, 41
V
Vines, 202–215
    for acidic soil, 39
    for alkaline soil, 39
    for autumn interest, 205
    deciduous, 202
    design use of, 7
    for dry soil, 37
    encyclopedia of choices, 206–215
    evergreen, 202
    fragrant, 204
    for full sun, 33
    pruning, 205
    rapid-growing, 204
    salt-tolerant, 40
    for screening, deciduous, 29
    for screening, evergreen, 28
    for shade, 35
    for small spaces, 41
    spring-flowering, 205
    summer-flowering, 205
    twiners versus stickers, 203
    for wooden structures, 203
    for Zone 5, 23
    for Zone 6, 25
W
Watering
    deep, 50
    drainage, 51
    irrigation, 50
    shrubs, 114, 115
    timing, 50
    trees, 61, 65
    troubleshooting, 50
    winter, 50
Weed prevention, 46, 49
Wet soil, plants for, 37
Windbreaks, 42–43
    positioning, 42
    shrubs for, 43
    snow accumulation and, 43
    trees for, 43
Winter fruit, shrubs with, 125
Winter interest, trees with, 67
Winter watering, 50
Wooden structures, vines for, 203
Woodlands
    groundcovers for, 173
    shrubs for, 123

Plants by Common and Botanical Names

Numbers in **boldface** indicate Plant Encyclopedia entries. Numbers in *italics* indicate photographs.

A
Aaron's Beard (*Hypericum calycinum*), 35, 170, *170*, 173, *188*, **188**
Abelia x grandiflora (Glossy Abelia), 28, 33, 34, 39, 41, 111, 113, 121, 122, 125, 126, **126**
Abies concolor (White fir), *20*, 28, 32, 37, 43, *70*, **70**
Abies fraseri (Frasier fir), 28, 32, 34, *70*, **70**
Acer buergerianum (Trident maple), 32, 38, 67, 68, 69, *71*, **71**

Acer griseum (Paperbark maple), 32, 37, 41, 67, 68, 72, *72*
Acer palmatum (Japanese maple), 34, 41, 67, 68, 69, *73*, **73**
Acer platanoides (Norway maple), 32, 34, 36, 37, 39, 41, 43, 67, 69, 72, *72*
Acer rubrum (Red maple), 29, 34, 36, 38, 41, 59, 67, 68, 69, *74*, **74**
Acer saccharinum (Silver maple), 29, 32, 34, 36, 37, 38, 39, 59, 67, 69, *75*, **75**
Acer saccharum (Sugar maple), 32, 34, 38, 67, 69, *75*, **75**
Acer tataricum ginnala (Amur maple), 32, 34, 67, 68, *71*, **71**
Actinidia arguta (Hardy kiwi), 29, 33, 35, 202, 203, 204, 205, *206*, **206**

Actinidia chinensis (Chinese gooseberry), 206
Actinidia kolomikta (Variegated kiwi vine), 206
Adiantum pedatum (Maidenhair fern), 35, 39, 41, 171, 173, *174*, **174**
Aegopodium podagraria 'Variegatum' (Snow-on-the-mountain), 35, 37, 39, 40, 171, 173, *174*, **174**
Aethionema 'Warley Rose' (Warley Rose), 33, 39, 170, 171, 172, 173, *174*, **174**
Ajuga (*Ajuga reptans*), 33, 35, *169*, 170, 171, 173, *175*, **175**
    'Alba,' 175
    'Atropurpurea,' 175
    'Burgundy Lace,' 175
    'Tricolor,' 175
Akebia quinata (Chocolate vine), 28, 33, 35, 104, 202, 203, 205, *206*, **206**

Alba Meidiland rose (*Rosa* Alba Meidiland), 33, 35, 40, 172, 173, *197*, **197**
Alchemilla mollis (Lady's mantle), 35, 171, 172, *172*, 173, *175*, **175**
Allegheny foam flower (*Tiarella cordifolia*), 35, 39, 170, 171, 173, *200*, **200**
Almond. *See* Dwarf flowering almond (*Prunus glandulosa* 'Rosea')
Amelanchier alnifolia (Serviceberry), 29, 33, 34, 39, 111, 123, 124, 125, *126*, **126**
Amelanchier arborea (Downy Serviceberry), 32, 34, 38, 67, 69, *76*, **76**
American arborvitae (*Thuja occidentalis*), 30, 34, 39, 41, 45, *107*, *122*, **107**
   'Emerald,' *107*, 166
   'Globosa,' 166
   'Golden Globe,' 166
   'Little Giant,' 28, 33, 37, 39, 43, 113, 121, 123, 125, *166*, **166**
   'Pyramidalis,' *107*
   'Techny,' 107
American beech (*Fagus grandifolia*), 32, 34, 38, 67, *85*, **85**
American bittersweet (*Celastrus scandens*), 29, 33, 35, 37, 202, 203, *203*, 204, 205, *208*, **208**
   pruning, 205
American hornbeam (*Carpinus caroliniana*), 78
American sweetgum. *See* Fruitless American sweetgum (*Liquidambar styraciflua* 'Rotundiloba')
Ampelopsis brevipedunculata (Porcelain vine), 33, 37, 39, 202, 203, 204, 205, 207, **207**
Amsonia tabernaemontana (Blue star), 35, 171, 173, *175*, **175**
Amur chokecherry (*Prunus mackii*), 32, 34, 59, 67, 69, *97*, **97**
Amur maple (*Acer tataricum ginnala*), 32, 34, 67, 68, *71*, **71**
   'Flame,' 71
   'Red Fruit,' 71
Anchusa myosotidiflora (Siberian forget-me-not), 35, 171, 173, *176*, **176**
Andorra compact juniper (*Juniperus horizontalis* 'Plumosa Compacta'), 33, 39, 40, 41, 170, *170*, 171, 172, *191*, **191**
Andromeda (*Pieris japonica*), 32, 34, 38, 111, 123, 124, *151*, **151**
   'Purity,' 151
   'Valley Rose,' 151
   'Valley Valentine,' 151
Andromeda polifolia (Bog Rosemary), 35, 39, 170, 173, *176*, **176**
Andromeda rosmarinifolia. *See* Bog Rosemary
Androsace lanuginosa (Rock jasmine), 35, 37, 170, 171, 172, 173, *176*, **176**
Annabelle hydrangea (*Hydrangea arborescens* 'Annabelle'), 32, 34, 37, 38, 40, 41, *118*, 121, *121*, 122, 123, 124, 125, *139*, **139**
Anthony Waterer spirea (*Spiraea japonica* 'Anthony Waterer'), *12*, 32, 34, 37, 41, 122, 123, 124, 125, *161*, **161**
   'Alpina,' 161
   'Little Princess,' 161
Arabis caucasica (Rockcress), 33, 35, 170, 171, 172, 173, *177*, **177**
Arborvitae. *See* American arborvitae (*Thuja occidentalis*)
Arctostaphylos uva-ursi (Kinnikinick), 33, 35, 37, 40, 170, 171, 173, *177*, **177**
Arenaria montana (Mountain sandwort), 33, 37, 170, 171, 173, *177*, **177**
Arenaria purpurascens (Pink sandwort), 177
Armeria maritima (Sea thrift), 35, 37, 40, 170, 171, 172, 173, *178*, **178**
Arnold's Red tatarian honeysuckle (*Lonicera tatarica* 'Arnold's Red'), 29, 32, 111, 120, 121, 122, 123, 124, 125, *148*, **148**
   'Alba,' 148
   'Hack's Red,' 148
   'Parvifolia,' 148
   'Virginalis,' 148

Artemisia ludoviciana, 178
Artemisia schmidtiana 'Silver Mound,' 178
Artemisia stelleriana (Silver brocade artemisia), 33, 37, 40, 41, 170, 171, 172, 173, *178*, **178**
Arum (*Arum italicum*), 33, 35, 41, 171, 172, 173, *178*, **178**
   'Marmoratum,' 178
   'Pictum,' 178
Ash. *See* Green ash (*Fraxinus pennsylvanica*)
Aspen. *See* Quaking aspen (*Populus tremuloides*)
Asperula odorata (Sweet Woodruff), 33, 35, *35*, 39, *170*, 171, 173, *179*, **179**
Athyrium nipponicum 'Pictum' (Japanese painted fern), 35, 41, 171, 173, *179*, **179**
Azaleas
   Azalea carolinianum (Carolina azalea), 32, 38, 113, 122, 123, 124, 125, *127*, **127**
   Azalea 'Exbury Hybrids' (Exbury azalea), 32, *38*, 39, 111, 113, 121, 122, 124, 125, *127*, **127**
   Azalea kurume, 127
      'Hino Crimson,' 127
   Azalea mucronulatum 'Cornell Pink' (Cornell Pink Azalea), 29, 32, 39, 113, 121, 122, 123, 124, 125, *128*, **128**
   Azalea 'Northern Lights' (Northern Lights azalea), 33, 39, 111, 113, 120, *120*, 121, 122, 123, 124, 125, *128*, **128**
   pruning, 117

B

Baby's Breath spirea (*Spiraea thunbergii*), 29, 32, 34, 111, 121, 122, 123, 124, 125, *162*, **162**
   'Compacta,' 162
Bald Cypress (*Taxodium distichum*), 29, 32, 36, 37, 69, *106*, **106**
Bar harbor juniper (*Juniperus horizontalis* 'Bar Harbor'), 33, 39, 40, 41, 170, 171, 172, *190*, **190**
Barberry. *See* Japanese barberry (*Berberis thunbergii*)
Bath's pink (*Dianthus gratianopolitanus* 'Bath's Pink), 33, 35, *35*, 37, 39, 40, 41, 171, 172, 173, *182*, **182**
Bayberry, northern (*Myrica pensylvanica*), 28, 29, 33, 34, 37, 40, 43, 111, 113, 121, 122, 123, 125, *149*, **149**
Bearberry. *See* Kinnikinick (*Arctostaphylos uva-ursi*)
Bearberry cotoneaster (*Cotoneaster dammeri*), 33, 35, 37, 39, 40, 41, 170, 171, 173, *182*, **182**
   'Coral Beauty,' 135
Beautyberry. *See* Chinese beautyberry (*Callicarpa dichotoma*)
Beech. *See* American beech (*Fagus grandifolia*)
Berberis thunbergii (Japanese barberry), 33, 34, 37, 111, 113, 121, 122, 125, 129, **129**
Bergenia cordifolia (Saxifrage), *20*, 33, 35, 171, 173, *179*, **179**
Betty Proir rose (*Rosa* 'Betty Prioir'), 32, 111, 120, 122, 125, *155*, **155**
Betula mandschurica japonica 'Whitespire' (Whitespire birch), 32, 37, 38, 59, 67, 68, *77*, **77**
Betula nigra (River birch), 29, 32, 34, 36, *36*, 37, 38, 59, 67, *67*, 68, 69, *76*, **76**
Betula papyrifera (Canoe birch), 32, 38, 59, 67, 77, **77**
Bignonia capreolata (Cross-vine), 28, 33, 35, 39, 202, 203, 204, 205, 207, **207**
Birch
   Canoe birch (*Betula papyrifera*), 32, 38, 59, 67, *77*, **77**,
   River birch (*Betula nigra*), 29, 32, 34, 36, *36*, 37, 38, 59, 67, 68, 69, *76*, **76**
   Whitespire birch (*Betula mandschurica japonica* 'Whitespire'), 32, 37, 38, 59, 67, 68, *77*, **77**
Bird's nest spruce (*Picea abies* 'Nidiformis'), 32, 37, 121, *150*, **150**
Blanket flower (*Gaillardia x grandiflora*), 33, 37, 40, 41, 171, 172, 173, *185*, **185**
Blaze climbing rose (*Rosa* 'Blaze'), 33, 39, 202, 203, 204, 205, *212*, **212**

Bloody cranesbill (*Geranium sanguineum*), 33, 35, 41, 171, 172, 173, *185*, **185**
Blue atlas cedar (*Cedrus libani* 'Glauca'), 28, 32, 36, 37, *79*, **79**
   'Pendula,' 79
Blue Chip juniper (*Juniperus horizontalis* 'Blue Chip'), 33, 39, 40, 41, 170, 171, 172, *190*, **190**
   'Prince of Wales,' 190
Blue-eyed Mary (*Omphalodes verna*), 35, 39, 171, 173, *194*, **194**
   'Alba,' 194
Blue holly (*Ilex x meserveae*), 28, 32, 34, 38, 67, *88*, **88**
   'Blue Boy,' 88
   'Blue Girl,' 88
Blue Pacific Shore juniper (*Juniperus conferta* 'Blue Pacific'), 33, 37, 39, 40, 41, 170, *190*, **190**
   'Emerald Sea,' 190
   'Silver Mist,' 190
Blue Rug juniper (*Juniperus horizontalis* 'Wiltonii'), 33, 39, 40, 41, 170, 171, 172, *191*, **191**
Blue spruce. *See* Colorado blue spruce (*Picea pungens glauca*)
Blue star (*Amsonia tabernaemontana*), 35, 171, 173, *175*, **175**
Blue Star juniper (*Juniperus squamata* 'Blue Star'), 32, 37, 121, 122, *146*, **146**
Bog Rosemary (*Andromeda polifolia*), 35, 39, 170, 173, *176*, **176**
   'Alba,' 176
Border forsythia (*Forsythia x intermedia*), 29, 32, 37, 38, 39, 40, 41, 111, 121, 122, 123, 124, *137*, **137**
Boston ivy (*Parthenocissus tricuspidata*), 29, 33, 35, 37, 39, 202, 203, 204, *204*, 205, *211*, **211**
   pruning, 205
Boxwood, *120*
   Edging boxwood (*Buxus sempervirens* 'Suffruticosa'), 32, 34, 111, 121, 123, *131*, **131**
   Green Beauty boxwood (*Buxus microphylla* 'Green Beauty'), 33, 34, 111, 121, 123, *130*, **130**
   Japanese boxwood (*Buxus microphylla japonica*), 33, 34, 111, 121, 123, *130*, **130**
   Korean boxwood (*Buxus microphylla koreana*), 39, 41, 111, 113, 121, 122, 123, *131*, **131**
Bradford pear (*Pyrus calleryana* 'Bradford'), 29, 32, 41, 59, 67, 68, 69, *100*, **100**
   'Aristocrat,' 100
   'Autumn Blaze,' 100
   'Capital,' 100
   'Chanticleer,' 100
   'Cleveland Select,' 100
   pruning, 100
Bridalwreath spirea (*Spiraea prunifolia*), 29, 32, 34, 111, 121, 122, 123, 124, 125, *162*, **162**
Brunnera macrophylla. *See* Siberian forget-me-not (*Anchusa myosotidiflora*)
Buddleia davidii (Butterfly bush), 32, 41, 124, 125, *129*, **129**
Bunchberry (*Cornus canadensis*), 35, 39, 171, 173, *181*, **181**
Burning bush (*Euonymus alatus*), *110*, 136
Butterfly bush (*Buddleia davidii*), 32, 41, 124, 125, *129*, **129**
   'Black Knight,' 129
   'Empire Blue,' 129
   'Fascination,' 129
   'Harlequin,' 129
   'Royal Red,' 129
   'White Bouquet,' 129
   'Wilsonii,' 129
Buxus microphylla 'Green Beauty' (Green Beauty boxwood), 33, 34, 111, 121, 123, *130*, **130**
Buxus microphylla japonica (Japanese boxwood), 33, 34, 111, 121, 123, *130*, **130**
Buxus microphylla koreana (Korean boxwood), 39, 41, 111, 113, 121, 122, 123, *131*, **131**

Buxus sempervirens 'Suffruticosa' (Edging boxwood), 32, 34, 111, 121, 123, *131*, **131**

C

California Incense cedar (*Calocedrus decurrens*), 28, 32, 34, 43, *78*, **78**

Callicarpa dichotoma (Chinese beautyberry), 32, 34, 121, 123, 125, *132*, **132**

Callicarpa japonica (Japanese beautyberry), 132

Calluna vulgaris (Scotch heather), 33, 39, 170, 171, 172, 173, *180*, **180**

Calocedrus decurrens (California Incense cedar), 28, 32, 34, 43, *78*, **78**

Campsis radicans (Trumpet vine), 29, 33, 35, 37, 202, 203, 204, 205, *208*, **208**

Canadian hemlock (*Tsuga canadensis*), 28, 32, 34, 38, 43, 67, *108*, **108**
  'Pendula,' 108

Canoe birch (*Betula papyrifera*), 32, 38, 59, 67, 77, **77**

Carefree Beauty rose (*Rosa* 'Carefree Beauty'), 32, 111, 113, 120, 122, 125, *155*, **155**

Carex morrowii 'Variegata' (Variegated Japanese sedge), 33, 35, 40, 41, 170, 171, 172, 173, *180*, **180**

Carol Mackie daphne (*Daphne x burkwoodii* 'Carol Mackie'), 32, 34, 37, *37*, 39, 120, 121, 123, 124, *136*, **136**

Carolina azalea (*Azalea carolinianum*), 32, 38, 113, 122, 123, 124, 125, *127*, **127**
  var. *album*, 127
  var. *luteum*, 127

Carpinus betulus (European hornbeam), 32, 34, 37, 38, 39, 41, 67, 68, 69, *78*, **78**

Carpinus caroliniana (American hornbeam), 78

Catawba rhododendron (*Rhododendron catawbiense*), 28, 32, 34, 38, *38*, 113, 121, 122, 123, 124, *154*, **154**
  'Mollis' hybrids, 154
  'P.J.M.,' 154
  'P.J.M. White,' 154

Catmint (*Nepeta x faassenii*), 33, 35, 37, 41, 171, 172, 173, *194*, **194**
  'Six Hills Giant, 194

Cedrus deodara (Deodar cedar), 28, 32, 36, 38, 39, 69, *79*, **79**

Cedrus libani 'Glauca' (Blue atlas cedar), 28, 32, 36, 37, *79*, **79**

Celastrus scandens (American bittersweet), 29, 33, 35, 37, 202, 203, *203*, 204, 205, *208*, **208**

Celtis laevigata (Sugarberry), 32, 34, 36, 37, 39, 41, 67, 69, *80*, **80**

Celtis occidentalis, 80

Ceratostigma plumbaginoides (Plumbago), 33, 170, 171, 173, *180*, **180**

Cercidiphyllum japonicum (Katsura tree), 32, 38, 39, 59, 67, 69, *80*, **80**

Cercis canadensis (Redbud), 29, 32, 34, 36, 37, 38, 39, 41, 59, 67, 68, 69, *81*, **81**
  'Alba' (White flowering redbud), *13*

Chamaecyparis obtusa 'Nana Gracilis' (Dwarf Hinoki false cypress), 32, 37, 39, *120*, 121, 123, *132*, **132**

Cherry
  Cornealian cherry (*Cornus mas*), 29, 32, 111, 113, 121, 123, 124, *134*, **134**
  Kwanzan cherry (*Prunus serrulata* 'Kwanzan'), 32, 67, 68, 69, *98*, **98**
  Sargent cherry (*Prunus sargentii*), 32, 34, 67, 69, *98*, **98**
  Weeping cherry (*Prunus subhirtella* 'Pendula'), 32, 34, 67, 68, 69, *99*, **99**

Chinese beautyberry (*Callicarpa dichotoma*), 32, 34, 121, 123, 125, *132*, **132**
  var. *albifructus*, 132

Chinese elm (*Ulmus parvifolia*), 29, 32, 36, 39, 41, 59, 67, 68, 69, *109*, **109**
  'Drake,' 109
  'Sempervirens,' 109

Chinese fringe tree (*Chionanthus retusus*), 32, 34, 38, 67, 69, *81*, **81**

Chinese gooseberry (*Actinidia chinensis*), 206

Chinese wisteria (*Wisteria sinensis*), 29, 33, 35, 202, 203, 204, 205, *215*, **215**
  pruning, 215

Chionanthus retusus (Chinese fringe tree), 32, 34, 38, 67, 69, *81*, **81**

Chocolate vine (*Akebia quinata*), 28, 33, 35, 104, 202, 203, 205, *206*, **206**
  'Variegata,' 206

Chokecherry. *See* Amur chokecherry (*Prunus macckii*)

Chrysogonum virginianum (Green and gold), 35, 39, 170, 171, 173, *181*, **181**

Cinquefoil. *See* Shrubby cinquefoil (*Potentilla fruiticosa*); Spring cinquefoil (*Potentilla tabernaemontani*)

Cladastris lutea (Yellowwood), 32, 34, 37, 67, 68, 69, *82*, **82**

Clematis (*Clematis* hybrid), 33, 35, 41, 202, 203, 205, *209*, **209**

Clethra alnifolia (Summersweet), 29, 34, 37, 39, 40, 120, 121, 122, 123, *124*, 125, *133*, **133**

Climbing Cecil Brunner rose (*Rosa* 'Climbing Cecil Brunner'), 33, 39, 202, 203, 204, 205, *213*, **213**

Climbing hydrangea (*Hydrangea petiolaris*), 27, 33, 35, 41, 202, 203, *204*, 205, *205*, *209*, **209**
  pruning, 205

Climbing Iceberg rose (*Rosa* 'Climbing Iceberg'), 33, 39, 202, 203, 205, *213*, **213**

Climbing Peace rose (*Rosa* 'Climbing Peace'), 33,39, 202, 203, 204, 205, *214*, **214**

Colorado blue spruce (*Picea pungens glauca*), 28, 32, 43, *95*, **95**
  'Hoopsii,' 95
  'Koster,' 95

Common lilac (*Syringa vulgaris*), 29, 32, 34, 37, 111, 120, 121, 123, 124, 125, *165*, **165**

Common Witch Hazel (*Hamamelis virginiana*), 32, 34, 113, 123, 125, *138*, **138**

Compact Japanese holly (*Ilex crenata* 'Compacta'), 32, 34, 41, 113, 121, 123, *143*, **143**

Concolor fir. *See* White fir (*Abies concolor*)

Convallaria majalis (Lily-of-the-valley), 35, 37, 171, 172, 173, *181*, **181**

Coral bells (*Heuchera sanguinea*), 33, 35, 39, 41, 170, 171, 172, 173, *187*, **187**

Coral Embers willow (*Salix alba* 'Britzensis'), 29, 32, 37, 40, 121, *160*, **160**

Coralberry, prostrate Chenault (*Symphoricarpos x chenaultii* 'Hancock'), 33, 35, 37, 40, 41, 173, *199*, **199**

Coralberry (*Symphoricarpos orbiculatus*), 29, 32, 34, 37, 40, 111, 121, 122, 123, 125, *163*, **163**

Cornealian cherry (*Cornus mas*), 29, 32, 111, 113, 121, 123, 124, *134*, **134**

Cornell Pink Azalea (*Azalea mucronulatum* 'Cornell Pink'), 29, 32, 39, 113, 121, 122, 123, 124, 125, *128*, **128**

Cornus alba (Redtwig dogwood), 29, 33, 37, 121, *133*, **133**

Cornus alternifolia, 83

Cornus canadensis (Bunchberry), 35, 39, 171, 173, *181*, **181**

Cornus florida (Flowering dogwood), 34, 38, 39, 40, 41, 67, 68, 69, *82*, **82**

Cornus kousa (Kousa dogwood), *21*, 32, 34, 38, 67, 68, 69, *83*, **83**

Cornus mas (Cornealian cherry), 29, 32, 111, 113, 121, 123, 124, *134*, **134**
  'Aureo-elegantissima,' 134
  'Variegata,' 134

Cornus racemosa (Gray dogwood), 29, 33, 111, 113, 121, 124, 125, *134*, **134**

Cornus stolonifera 'Cardinal,' 133

Cornus stolonifera 'Flaviramea' (Yellow-twig dogwood), 29, 33, 34, 37, 121, 123, 125, *135*, **135**

Corsican mint (*Mentha corsica*), 33, 41, 171, 172, 173, *193*, **193**

Cotoneaster dammeri (Bearberry cotoneaster), 33, 35, 37, 39, 40, 41, 170, 171, 173, *182*, **182**
  'Coral Beauty,' 135

Cotoneaster horizontalis (Rockspray cotoneaster), 33, 40, 41, 121, 122, 124, 125, *135*, **135**

Crabapple
  Japanese flowering crabapple (*Malus floribunda*), 32, 39, 41, 67, 68, 69, *92*, **92**
  Plumleaf crabapple (*Malus prunifolia*), 32, 38, 41, 67, 69, *92*, **92**

Crataegus phaenopyrum (Washington hawthorn), 32, 34, 36, 38, 39, 41, 67, 68, 69, *83*, **83**

Creeping Jenny. *See* Moneywort (*Lysimachia nummularia*)

Creeping phlox (*Phlox stolonifera*), 35, 39, 170, 171, 172, 173, *195*, **195**
  'Blue Ridge,' 195

Creeping thyme (*Thymus leucotrichus*), 33, 37, 39, 41, 170, 171, 172, 173, *200*, **200**

Cross-vine (*Bignonia capreolata*), 28, 33, 35, 39, 202, 203, 204, 205, *207*, **207**

X *Cupressocyparis leylandii* (Leyland cypress), 28, 32, 43, *84*, **84**

Cutleaf lilac (*Syringa x laciniata*), 29, 32, 34, 111, 120, 121, 123, 124, *164*, **164**

Cypress. *See* Bald Cypress (*Taxodium distichum*); Leyland cypress (X *Cupressocyparis leylandii*)

Cypress spurge (*Euphorbia cyparissias*), 33, 35, 40, 171, 173, *184*, **184**
  'Orange Man,' 184

D

Daphne x burkwoodii 'Carol Mackie' (Carol Mackie daphne), 32, 34, 37, *37*, 39, 120, 121, 123, 124, *136*, **136**

David viburnum (*Viburnum davidii*), 167

Dawn redwood (*Metasequoia glyptostroboides*), 32, 37, 59, 69, *93*, **93**

Dead nettle. *See* Spotted dead nettle (*Lamium maculatum*)

Delosperma cooperi, 182

Delosperma nubigenum (Hardy ice plant), 33, 37, 40, 41, 171, 173, *182*, **182**

Delosperma velutinum, 182

Deodar cedar (*Cedrus deodara*), 28, 32, 36, 38, 39, 69, *79*, **79**
  'Aurea,' 79

Dianthus gratianopolitanus 'Bath's Pink (Bath's pink), 33, 35, 37, 39, 40, 171, 172, 173, *182*, **182**

Dogwood
  Flowering dogwood (*Cornus florida*), 34, 38, 39, 40, 41, 67, 68, 69, *82*, **82**
  Gray dogwood (*Cornus racemosa*), 29, 33, 111, 113, 121, 124, 125, *134*, **134**
  Kousa dogwood (*Cornus kousa*), *21*, 32, 34, 38, 67, 68, 69, *83*, **83**
  Redtwig dogwood (*Cornus alba*), 29, 33, 37, 121, *133*, **133**
  Yellow-twig dogwood (*Cornus stolonifera* 'Flaviramea'), 29, 33, 34, 37, 121, 123, 125, *135*, **135**

Doublefile viburnum (*Viburnum plicatum tomentosum*), 29, 32, 37, 121, 123, 124, 125, *167*, **167**

Douglas fir (*Pseudotsuga menziesii*), 28, 32, 38, *99*, **99**
  'Fastigiata,' 99
  'Oudemansii,' 99
  var. *glauca*, 99

Downy Serviceberry (*Amelanchier arborea*), 32, 34, 38, 67, 69, *76*, **76**

Dragon's Blood sedum (*Sedum spurium* 'Dragon's Blood'), 33, 37, 40, 171, 172, 173, *198*, **198**

Drooping leucothoe (*Leucothoe fontanesiana*), 34, 39, 120, 122, 123, 124, *147*, **147**
  'Rainbow,' 147

Dropmore Scarlet honeysuckle (*Lonicera x brownii* 'Dropmore Scarlet'), 28, 33, 202, *202*, 203, 205, *210*, **210**
  pruning, 205

Dwarf Alberta spruce (*Picea glauca* 'Conica'), 32, 34, 37, 39, 41, 121, 123, *150*, **150**

plant names

Dwarf blue fescue (*Festuca glauca*), 33, 37, 171, 172, 173, *184*, **184**
　'Elijah Blue,' 184
Dwarf Burford holly (*Ilex cornuta* 'Burfordii Nana'), 28, 32, 34, 37, 39, 41, 111, 113, 123, 125, *141*, **141**
Dwarf burning bush (*Euonymus alatus* 'Compacta'), 29, 32, 34, 39, 41, *120*, 121, *121*, 122, 123, 125, *136*, **136**
Dwarf flowering almond (*Prunus glandulosa* 'Rosea'), 32, 34, 124, *153*, **153**
Dwarf fothergilla (*Fothergilla gardenii*), 138
Dwarf Hinoki false cypress (*Chamaecyparis obtusa* 'Nana Gracilis'), 32, 37, 39, *120*, 121, 123, *132*, **132**
　'Nana Lutea,' 132
Dwarf Japanese garden juniper (*Juniperus procumbens* 'Nana'), 33, 39, *40*, 41, 170, 171, 172, *191*, **191**
　'Nana Greenmound,' 191
Dwarf winged euonymus. *See* Dwarf burning bush (*Euonymus alata* 'Compacta')

E

Eastern red cedar (*Juniperus virginiana*), 28, 32, 36, 37, 38, 39, 40, 43, 67, 69, 84, *89*, **89**
Edging boxwood (*Buxus sempervirens* 'Suffruticosa'), 32, 34, 111, 121, 123, *131*, **131**
Elaeagnus angustifolia (Russian Olive), 32, 38, 40, 59, 67, 68, 69, 84, **84**
Elm. *See* Chinese elm (*Ulmus parvifolia*)
English ivy (*Hedera helix*), 33, 35, 40, 170, 171, 173, *186*, **186**
Erica carnea (Spring heath), 33, 39, 170, 171, 172, 173, *183*, **183**
Erigeron hybrid (Fleabane), 33, 35, 41, 171, 172, 173, *183*, **183**
Euonymus alatus 'Compacta' (Dwarf burning bush), 29, 32, 34, 39, 41, *120*, 121, *121*, 122, 123, 125, *136*, **136**
Euonymus alatus (Burning bush), *110*, 136
Euonymus fortunei 'Coloratus' (Purple-leaf winter-creeper), 33, 39, 40, 41, 170, *183*, **183**
Euonymus kiautschovicus 'Manhattan' (Manhattan spreading euonymus), 28, 33, 34, 37, 111, 125, *137*, **137**
Euphorbia cyparissias (Cypress spurge), 33, 35, 40, 171, 173, *184*, **184**
European cranberrybush (*Viburnum opulus* 'Roseum'), 29, 32, 37, 121, 123, 124, 125, *167*, **167**
European hornbeam (*Carpinus betulus*), 32, 34, 37, 38, 39, 41, 67, 68, 69, *78*, **78**
　'Asplenifolia,' 78
　'Columnaris,' 78
　'Fastigata,' 78
　'Pyramidalis,' 78
European mountain ash (*Sorbus aucuparia*), 32, 34, *34*, 37, 38, 40, 67, 68, 69, *104*, **104**
Evening primrose (*Oenothera speciosa*), 194
Evergreen candytuft (*Iberis sempervirens*), 33, 35, 40, 41, 170, 171, 172, 173, *189*, **189**
Exbury azalea (*Azalea* 'Exbury Hybrids'), 32, *38*, 39, 111, 113, 121, 122, 124, 125, *127*, **127**
　'Berry Rose,' 127
　'Firefly,' 127
　'Gibraltar,' 127
　'White Swan,' 127

F

Fagus grandifolia (American beech), 32, 34, 38, 67, *85*, **85**
Fagus sylvatica pendula (Weeping beech), 85
Fagus sylvatica 'Purpurea Pendula,' 85
Fagus sylvatica 'Purpurea Tricolor,' 85
Fagus sylvatica 'Roseomarginata,' 85
Fagus sylvatica 'Tricolor' (Tricolor beech), 85
Fairy rose (*Rosa* 'The Fairy'), 33, 34, 41, 121, 123, 125, *159*, **159**

Fern
　Japanese painted fern (*Athyrium nipponicum* 'Pictum'), 35, 41, 171, 173, *179*, **179**
　Maidenhair fern (*Adiantum pedatum*), 35, 39, 41, 171, 173, *174*, **174**
Festuca glauca (Dwarf blue fescue), 33, 37, 171, 172, 173, *184*, **184**
Firethorn. *See* Yukon Belle firethorn (*Pyracantha angustifolia* Yukon Belle)
Firs
　Douglas fir (*Pseudotsuga menziesii*), 28, 32, 38, *99*, **99**
　Frasier fir (*Abies fraseri*), 20, 28, 32, 34, *70*, **70**
　White fir (*Abies concolor*), 28, 32, 37, 43, *70*, **70**
Fiveleaf Akebia. *See* Chocolate vine (*Akebia quinata*)
Fleabane (*Erigeron* hybrid), 33, 35, 41, 171, 172, 173, *183*, **183**
Flower Carpet rose (*Rosa* 'Flower Carpet'), 33, 41, *41*, 173, *197*, **197**
Flowering dogwood (*Cornus florida*), 34, 38, 39, 40, 41, 67, 68, 69, *82*, **82**
　'Cherokee Chief,' 82
　'Plena,' 82
Foam flower. *See* Allegheny foam flower (*Tiarella cordifolia*)
Forget-me-not (*Myosotis scorpioides*), 33, 35, 37, 171, 173, *193*, **193**
Forsythia x intermedia (Border forsythia), 29, 32, 37, 38, 39, 40, 41, 111, 121, 122, 123, 124, *137*, **137**
Fothergilla gardenii (Dwarf fothergilla), 138
Fothergilla major (Large fothergilla), 29, 33, 39, 113, 120, 122, 124, 125, *138*, **138**
Fountain grass (*Pennisetum alopecuroides*), 33, 37, 39, 41, 171, 172, *195*, **195**
Fragaria 'Pink Panda' (Pink Panda strawberry), 33, 35, 171, 172, 173, *184*, **184**
Frasier fir (*Abies fraseri*), 28, 32, 34, *70*, **70**
Fraxinus americana Autumn Purple, 86
Fraxinus pennsylvanica (Green ash), 29, 32, 36, 37, 38, 39, 41, 59, 67, 69, *86*, **86**
Fru Dagmar Hastrup rose (*Rosa* 'Fru Dagmar Hastrup'), 32, 37, 40, 111, 120, 122, 125, *156*, **156**
Fruitless American sweetgum (*Liquidambar styraciflua* 'Rotundiloba'), 32, 38, 67, 68, 69, *90*, **90**

G

Gaillardia x grandiflora (Blanket flower), 33, 37, 40, 41, 171, 172, 173, *185*, **185**
Gallium. *See* Sweet Woodruff (*Asperula odorata*)
Gallberry. *See* Inkberry (*Ilex glabra* 'Compacta')
Gaultheria procumbens (Wintergreen), 35, 39, 171, 173, *185*, **185**
Geranium sanguineum (Bloody cranesbill), 33, 35, 41, 171, 172, 173, *185*, **185**
Germander (*Teucrium prostratum*), 33, 39, 41, 170, 171, 172, 173, *199*, **199**
Geum (*Geum reptans*), 33, 170, 171, 172, 173, *186*, **186**
Ginkgo (*Ginkgo biloba*), 32, 36, 37, 38, 39, 41, 66, 67, 68, 69, *86*, **86**
　'Autumn Gold,' 86
　'Fastigiata,' 86
Gleditsia triacanthos inermis (Honeylocust), 32, 39, 40, 41, 59, 67, *68*, 69, *87*, **87**
Glossy Abelia (*Abelia x grandiflora*), 28, 33, 34, 39, 41, 111, 113, 121, 122, 125, *126*, **126**
　'Edward Goucher,' 126
　'Francis Mason,' 126
　'Prostrata,' 126
　'Sherwood,' 126
Golden vicary privet (*Ligustrum x vicaryi*), 28, 33, 111, 113, 125, *148*, **148**
Goldenstar. *See* Green and gold (*Chrysogonum virginianum*)
Goldmoss (*Sedum acre*), 33, 37, 39, 40, 41, 170, 171, 173, *198*, **198**
Goutweed. *See* Snow-on-the-mountain (*Aegopodium podagraria* 'Variegatum')

Graham Thomas rose (*Rosa* 'Graham Thomas'), 33, *110*, 111, 120, 122, 123, 125, *156*, **156**
Grancy Graybeard. *See* Chinese fringe tree (*Chionanthus retusus*)
Gray dogwood (*Cornus racemosa*), 29, 33, 111, 113, 121, 124, 125, *134*, **134**
　'Slavinii,' 134
Green and gold (*Chrysogonum virginianum*), 35, 39, 170, 171, 173, *181*, **181**
Green ash (*Fraxinus pennsylvanica*), 29, 32, 36, 37, 38, 39, 41, 59, 67, 69, *86*, **86**
　'Marshall's Seedless,' 86
　'Summit,' 86
Green Beauty boxwood (*Buxus microphylla* 'Green Beauty'), 33, 34, 111, 121, 123, *130*, **130**
　'Compacta,' 130
　'Green Pillow,' 130
　'Winter Gem,' 130
Green Lustre Japanese holly (*Ilex crenata* 'Green Lustre'), 28, 33, 34, 41, 43, *43*, 111, 121, 123, *142*, **142**

H

Hackberry. *See* Sugarberry (*Celtis laevigata*)
Hamamelis virginiana (Witch Hazel), 32, 34, 113, 123, 125, *138*, **138**
Hardy ice plant (*Delosperma nubigenum*), 33, 37, 40, 41, 171, 173, *182*, **182**
Hardy kiwi (*Actinidia arguta*), 29, 33, 35, 202, 203, 204, 205, *206*, **206**
　'Issai,' 206
　pruning, 205
Hedera helix (English ivy), 33, 35, 40, 170, 171, 173, *186*, **186**
Helianthemum nummularium (Rock rose), 33, 37, 39, 40, 41, 170, 171, 173, *186*, **186**
Helleborus orientalis (Lenten rose), 35, 41, 170, 171, 172, 173, *187*, **187**
Heller Japanese holly (*Ilex crenata* 'Helleri'), 33, 34, 41, 121, 123, *142*, **142**
Hemlock. *See* Canadian hemlock (*Tsuga canadensis*)
Heuchera sanguinea (Coral bells), 33, 35, 39, 41, 170, 171, 172, 173, *187*, **187**
Hibiscus syriacus (Rose of Sharon), 29, 33, 34, 37, 39, 41, 121, 125, *139*, **139**
Hick's upright yew (*Taxus x media* 'Hicksii'), 28, 33, 34, 37, 39, 43, 111, 121, 123, *166*, **166**
Holly
　Blue holly (*Ilex x meserveae*), 28, 32, 34, 38, 67, *88*, **88**
　Compact Japanese holly (*Ilex crenata* 'Compacta'), 32, 34, 41, 113, 121, 123, *143*, **143**
　Dwarf Burford holly (*Ilex cornuta* 'Burfodii Nana'), 28, 32, 34, 37, 39, 41, 111, 113, 123, 125, *141*, **141**
　Green Lustre Japanese holly (*Ilex crenata* 'Green Lustre'), 28, 33, 34, 41, 43, *43*, 111, 121, 123, *142*, **142**
　Heller Japanese holly (*Ilex crenata* 'Helleri'), 33, 34, 41, 121, 123, *142*, **142**
　Nellie R. Stevens holly (*Ilex x* 'Nellie R. Stevens'), 28, 33, 34, 37, 39, 41, 43, 123, *144*, **144**
　Savannah holly (*Ilex opaca* 'Savannah'), 28, 32, 34, 37, 38, 41, 67, 68, 69, *88*, **88**
Honeylocust (*Gleditsia triacanthos inermis*), 32, 39, 40, 41, 59, 67, *68*, 69, *87*, **87**
　'Shademaster,' 87
　'Skyline,' 87
　'Sunburst,' 87
Honeysuckle
　Arnold's Red tatarian honeysuckle (*Lonicera tatarica* 'Arnold's Red'), 29, 32, 111, 120, 121, 122, 123, 124, *148*, **148**
　Dropmore Scarlet honeysuckle (*Lonicera x brownii* 'Dropmore Scarlet'), 28, 33, 202, 203, 205, *210*, **210**
　Royal Carpet honeysuckle (*Lonicera pileata*), 33, 35, 170, 173, *192*, **192**
　Trumpet honeysuckle (*Lonicera sempervirens*), 29, 33, 202, 203, 204, 205, *210*, **210**

Hornbeam. *See* American hornbeam (*Carpinus caroliniana*); European hornbeam (*Carpinus betulus*)

Hosta (*Hosta*), 13, 35, 41, *170*, 171, 172, 173, *187*, **187**

Houttuynia (*Houttunynia cordata* 'Chameleon'), 33, 35, 171, *188*, **188**
    'Flore-Pleno,' 188

Hybrid clematis. *See* Clematis hybrid

Hydrangea arborescens 'Annabelle' (Annabelle hydrangea), 32, 34, 37, 38, 40, 41, *118*, 121, *121*, 122, 123, 124, 125, *139*, **139**

Hydrangea macrophylla 'Nikko Blue' (Nikko Blue hydrangea), 33, 34, 40, 121, 122, 123, *123*, 125, *140*, **140**

Hydrangea paniculata 'Grandiflora' (PeeGee hydrangea), 29, 33, 34, 39, 121, 122, 123, 125, *140*, **140**

Hydrangea petiolaris (Climbing hydrangea), *27*, 33, 35, 41, 202, 203, *204*, 205, *205*, *209*, **209**

Hydrangea quercifolia (Oakleaf hydrangea), 34, 39, 121, 122, 123, 125, *141*, **141**

Hydrangeas, pruning, 118

Hypericum calycinum (Aaron's Beard), 35, 170, *170*, 173, *188*, **188**

I

Iberis sempervirens (Evergreen candytuft), 33, 35, 40, 41, 170, 171, 172, 173, *189*, **189**

Iceberg rose (*Rosa* 'Iceberg'), 33, 111, 120, 122, 124, 125, *157*, **157**

Ilex cornuta 'Burfordii Nana' (Dwarf Burford holly), 28, 32, 34, 37, 39, 41, 111, 113, 123, 125, *141*, **141**

Ilex crenata 'Compacta' (Compact Japanese holly), 32, 34, 41, 113, 121, 123, *143*, **143**

Ilex crenata 'Green Lustre' (Green Lustre Japanese holly), 28, 33, 34, 41, 43, *43*, 111, 121, 123, *142*, **142**

Ilex crenata 'Helleri' (Heller Japanese holly), 33, 34, 41, 121, 123, *142*, **142**

Ilex decidua (Possum Haw), 32, 34, 37, 38, 39, 41, 59, 67, 68, *87*, **87**

Ilex glabra 'Compacta' (Inkberry), 28, 33, 34, 37, 39, 40, 41, 43, 113, 122, 123, *143*, **143**

Ilex x meserveae (Blue holly), 28, 32, 34, 38, 67, *88*, **88**

Ilex x 'Nellie R. Stevens' (Nellie R. Stevens holly), 28, 33, 34, 37, 39, 41, 43, 123, *144*, **144**

Ilex opaca 'Savannah' (Savannah holly), 28, 32, 34, 37, 38, 41, 67, 68, 69, *88*, **88**

Ilex verticillata (Winterberry), 29, 33, 34, 37, 39, 111, 121, 122, 123, 125, *125*, *144*, **144**

Imperata cylindrica 'Red Baron' (Japanese blood grass), 33, 35, 41, 171, *189*, **189**

Inkberry (*Ilex glabra* 'Compacta'), 28, 33, 34, 37, 39, 40, 41, 43, 113, 122, 123, *143*, **143**
    'Nigra,' 143
    'Shamrock,' 143

Ivy
    Boston ivy (*Parthenocissus tricuspidata*), 29, 33, 35, 37, 39, 202, 203, *204*, 205, *211*, **211**
    English ivy (*Hedera helix*), 33, 35, 40, 170, 171, 173, *186*, **186**

J

Japanese barberry (*Berberis thunbergii*), 33, 34, 37, 111, 113, 121, 122, 125, *129*, **129**
    'Crimson Pygmy,' 129
    'Rose Glow,' 129
    var. *atropurpurea*, 129

Japanese beautyberry (*Callicarpa japonica*), 132

Japanese black pine (*Pinus thunbergii*), 28, 32, 36, 37, 40, 43, 67, *96*, **96**
    'Oculus-draconis,' 96

Japanese blood grass (*Imperata cylindrica* 'Red Baron'), 33, 35, 41, 171, *189*, **189**

Japanese boxwood (*Buxus microphylla japonica*), 33, 34, 111, 121, 123, *130*, **130**

Japanese flowering crabapple (*Malus floribunda*), 32, 39, 41, *66*, 67, 68, 69, *92*, **92**
    'Pink Spires,' 92
    'Prairie Fire,' 92
    'Profusion,' 92
    'Red Splendor,' 92
    'Royalty,' 92
    'Spring Snow,' 92

Japanese maple (*Acer palmatum*), 34, 41, 67, 68, 69, *73*, **73**
    'Atropurpurea, ' 73
    'Bloodgood,' 73, *73*
    'Burgundy Lace,' 73
    'Crimson Queen,' 73
    'Dissectum' (threadleaf), 73
    'Ever Red,' 73
    'Inaba Shidare,' 73
    'Linearilobum,' 73
    'Oshio Beni,' 73
    'Sango Kaku,' 73
    'Shishio,' 73
    var. heptalobum, 73
    'Viridis,' 73

Japanese painted fern (*Athyrium nipponicum* 'Pictum'), 35, 41, 171, 173, *179*, **179**

Japanese pieris. *See* Andromeda (*Pieris japonica*)

Japanese primrose (*Primula japonica*), 35, 37, 171, 173, *196*, **196**

Japanese skimmia (*Skimmia japonica*), 34, 37, 39, 122, 124, 125, *160*, **160**
    'Bronze Knight,' 160
    'Fructo Albo,' 160
    'Rubella,' 160

Japanese snowbell (*Styrax japonicum*), 32, 34, 38, 40, 67, 68, 69, *105*, **105**

Japanese snowdrop tree. *See* Japanese snowbell (*Styrax japonicum*)

Japanese stewartia (*Stewartia pseudocamellia*), 32, 34, 38, 67, 68, 69, *105*, **105**

Japanese tree lilac (*Syringa reticulata*), 32, 38, 67, *67*, 68, 69, *106*, **106**
    'Ivory Silk,' 106
    'Regent,' 106
    'Summer Snow,' 106

Japanese zelkova (*Zelkova serrata*), 29, 38, 39, 41, 59, 67, 68, 69, *109*, **109**

Joseph's Coat climbing rose (*Rosa* 'Joseph's Coat'), 33, 39, *39*, 202, 203, *204*, 205, *214*, **214**

Juniperus chinensis 'Parsonii' (Parson's juniper), 33, 37, 41, 111, 121, 122, 123, *145*, **145**

Juniperus chinensis 'Sea Green' (Sea Green juniper), 33, 37, 40, 43, 113, 121, 122, 123, *145*, **145**

Juniperus conferta 'Blue Pacific' (Blue Pacific Shore juniper), 33, 37, 39, 40, 41, 170, *190*, **190**

Juniperus horizontalis 'Bar Harbor' (Bar harbor juniper), 33, 39, 40, 41, 170, 171, 172, *190*, **190**

Juniperus horizontalis 'Blue Chip' (Blue Chip juniper), 33, 39, 40, 41, 170, 171, 172, *190*, **190**

Juniperus horizontalis 'Plumosa Compacta' (Andorra compact juniper), 33, 39, 40, 41, 170, *170*, 171, 172, *191*, **191**

Juniperus horizontalis 'Wiltonii' (Blue Rug juniper), 33, 39, 40, 41, 170, 171, 172, *191*, **191**

Juniperus procumbens 'Nana' (Dwarf Japanese garden juniper), 33, 39, *40*, 41, 170, 171, 172, *191*, **191**

Juniperus sabina 'Tamariscifolia' (Tam juniper), 33, 37, 43, 111, 121, 123, *146*, **146**

Juniperus scopulorum 'Skyrocket' (Skyrocket juniper), 28, 32, 36, 41, 43, 69, *89*, **89**

Juniperus squamata 'Blue Star' (Blue Star juniper), 32, 37, 121, 122, *146*, **146**

Juniperus virginiana (Eastern red cedar), 28, 32, 36, 37, 38, 39, 40, 43, 67, 69, 84, *89*, **89**

K

Kalmia latifolia (Mountain laurel), 28, 33, 34, 39, 113, 121, 122, 123, 124, *147*, **147**

Katsura tree (*Cercidiphyllum japonicum*), 32, 38, 39, 59, 67, 69, *80*, **80**

Kinnikinick (*Arctostaphylos uva-ursi*), 33, 35, 37, 40, 170, 171, 173, *177*, **177**
    'Massachusetts,' 177

Kiwi. *See* Hardy kiwi (*Actinidia arguta*)

Knap Hill hybrid azalea. *See* Exbury azalea (*Azalea* 'Exbury hybrids')

Korean boxwood (*Buxus microphylla koreana*), 39, 41, 111, 113, 121, 122, 123, *131*, **131**
    'Suffructicosa,' 131
    'Tide Hill,' 131
    'Wintergreen,' 131

Korean spice viburnum (*Viburnum carlesii*), 33, 34, 39, 113, 120, 121, 123, 124, *167*, **167**

Kousa dogwood (*Cornus kousa*), *21*, 32, 34, 38, 67, 68, 69, *83*, **83**

Kwanzan cherry (*Prunus serrulata* 'Kwanzan'), 32, 67, 68, 69, *98*, **98**
    'Mt. Fuji,' 98
    'Shirofugen,' 98

L

Lady's mantle (*Alchemilla mollis*), 35, 171, 172, *172*, 173, *175*, **175**

Lamb's ear (*Stachys byzantina*), 33, 41, 171, 172, *172*, 173, *199*, **199**

Lamiastrum galeobdolon 'Variegatum' (Yellow archangel), 35, 171, 173, *192*, **192**

Lamium maculatum (Spotted dead nettle), 35, 37, 41, 171, 173, *192*, **192**

Large fothergilla (*Fothergilla major*), 29, 33, 39, 113, 120, 122, 124, 125, *138*, **138**
    'Mt. Airy,' 138

Lenten rose (*Helleborus orientalis*), 35, 41, 170, 171, 172, 173, *187*, **187**

Leucothoe fontanesiana (Drooping leucothoe), 34, 39, 120, 122, 123, 124, *147*, **147**

Leyland cypress (X *Cupressocyparis leylandii*), 28, 32, 43, *84*, **84**

Ligustrum sinense 'Variegatum' (Variegated Chinese privet), 148

Ligustrum x vicaryi (Golden vicary privet), 28, 33, 111, 113, 125, *148*, **148**

Lilac
    Common lilac (*Syringa vulgaris*), 29, 32, 34, 37, 111, 120, 121, 123, 124, *165*, **165**
    Cutleaf lilac (*Syringa x laciniata*), 29, 32, 34, 111, 120, 121, 123, 124, *164*, **164**
    Japanese tree lilac (*Syringa reticulata*), 32, 38, 67, 68, 69, *106*, **106**
    Miss Kim lilac (*Syringa patula* 'Miss Kim'), 29, 33, 34, 111, 120, 121, 123, 124, 125, *164*, **164**
    Persian lilac (*Syringa x persica*), 29, 33, 34, 39, 111, 121, 124, *164*, **164**
    rejuvenating overgrown, 165

Lily-of-the-valley bush. *See* Andromeda (*Pieris japonica*)

Lily-of-the-valley (*Convallaria majalis*), 35, 37, 171, 172, 173, *181*, **181**

Linden. *See* Littleleaf linden (*Tilia cordata*)

Liquidambar formosana, 90

Liquidambar styraciflua, 90

Liquidambar styraciflua 'Rotundiloba' (Fruitless American sweetgum), 32, 38, 67, 68, 69, *90*, **90**

Little Giant arborvitae (*Thuja occidentalis* 'Little Giant'), 28, 33, 37, 39, 43, 113, 121, 123, 125, *166*, **166**

Littleleaf linden (*Tilia cordata*), 32, 37, 38, 39, 40, 41, 67, 68, 69, *108*, **108**

Littleleaf periwinkle (*Vinca minor*), 33, 35, 40, 41, 170, 171, *172*, 173, *201*, **201**
    'Alba,' 201
    'Aureola,' 201

Lonicera pileata (Royal Carpet honeysuckle), 33, 35, 170, 173, *192*, **192**

Lonicera sempervirens (Trumpet honeysuckle), 29, 33, 202, 203, 204, *204*, 205, *210*, **210**

Lonicera tatarica 'Arnold's Red' (Arnold's Red tatarian honeysuckle), 29, 32, 111, 120, 121, 122, 123, 124, *148*, **148**

Lonicera x brownii 'Dropmore Scarlet' (Dropmore Scarlet honeysuckle), 28, 33, 202, *202*, 203, 205, *210*, **210**

Lysimachia nummularia (Moneywort), 35, 171, 173, *193*, **193**

Ⓜ

Magnolia grandiflora (Southern magnolia), 28, 32, 34, 36, 37, 40, 67, 69, *90*, **90**

Magnolia kobus (Northern Japanese magnolia), 91

Magnolia stellata (Star magnolia), 34, 38, 41, 67, 68, 69, *91*, **91**

Magnolia x soulangiana (Saucer magnolia), 29, *29*, 32, 34, 37, 38, 41, 59, 67, 69, *91*, **91**

Maidenhair fern (*Adiantum pedatum*), 35, 39, 41, 171, 173, *174*, **174**

Malus floribunda (Japanese flowering crabapple), 32, 39, 41, *66*, 67, 68, 69, *92*, **92**

Malus prunifolia (Plumleaf crabapple), 32, 38, 41, 67, 69, *92*, **92**

Malus x robusta 'Red Siberian,' 92

Manhattan spreading euonymus (*Euonymus kiautschovicus* 'Manhattan'), 28, 33, 34, 37, 111, 125, *137*, **137**

Maples
 Amur maple (*Acer tataricum ginnala*), 32, 34, 67, 68, *71*, **71**
 Japanese maple (*Acer palmatum*), 34, 41, 67, 68, 69, *73*, **73**
 Norway maple (*Acer platanoides*), 32, 34, 36, 37, 39, 41, 43, 67, 69, *72*, **72**
 Paperbark maple (*Acer griseum*), 32, 37, 41, 67, 68, *72*, **72**
 Red maple (*Acer rubrum*), 29, 34, 36, 38, 41, 59, 67, 68, 69, *74*, **74**
 Silver maple (*Acer saccharinum*), 29, 32, 34, 36, 37, 38, 39, 59, 67, 69, *75*, **75**
 Sugar maple (*Acer saccharum*), 32, 34, 38, 67, 69, *75*, **75**
 Trident maple (*Acer buergerianum*), 32, 38, 67, 68, 69, *71*, **71**

Margo Koster rose (*Rosa* 'Margo Koster'), 33, 111, 120, 122, 125, *157*, **157**
 'Nearly Wild,' 157

Memorial rose (*Rosa wichuraiana*), 33, 172, 173, *197*, **197**

Mentha corsica (Corsican mint), 33, 41, 171, 172, 173, *193*, **193**

Mentha requienii, 193

Metasequoia glyptostroboides (Dawn redwood), 32, 37, 59, 69, 93, **93**

Miss Kim lilac (*Syringa patula* 'Miss Kim'), 29, 33, 34, 111, 120, 121, 123, 124, 125, *164*, **164**

Moneywort (*Lysimachia nummularia*), 35, 171, 173, *193*, **193**
 'Aurea,' 193

Moss phlox (*Phlox subulata*), 33, 37, 40, 41, 170, 171, 172, 173, *196*, **196**

Mountain ash. *See* European mountain ash (*Sorbus aucuparia*)

Mountain laurel (*Kalmia latifolia*), 28, 33, 34, 39, 113, 121, 122, 123, 124, *147*, **147**
 'Alba,' 147
 'Myrtifolia,' 147
 'Ostbo red,' 147
 'Pink Charm,' 147
 'Polypetala,' 147
 'Sharon Rose,' 147

Mountain pieris (*Pieris floribunda*), 33, 34, 39, 111, 120, 122, 123, *123*, 124, *151*, **151**

Mountain sandwort (*Arenaria montana*), 33, 37, 170, 171, 173, *177*, **177**

Mugo pine (*Pinus mugo*), 33, 34, 37, 43, 121, 123, *152*, **152**
 'Compacta,' 152
 'Gnome,' 152
 'Mops,' 152

Myosotis scorpioides (Forget-me-not), 33, 35, 37, 171, 173, *193*, **193**

Myosotis sylvatica, 193

Myrica pensylvanica (Northern bayberry), 28, 29, 33, 34, 37, 40, 43, 111, 113, 121, 122, 123, *124*, 125, *149*, **149**

Ⓝ

Nellie R. Stevens holly (*Ilex x* 'Nellie R. Stevens'), 28, 33, 34, 37, 39, 41, 43, 123, *144*, **144**

Nepeta x faassenii (Catmint), 33, 35, 37, 41, 171, 172, 173, *194*, **194**

Nikko Blue hydrangea (*Hydrangea macrophylla* 'Nikko Blue'), 33, 34, 40, 121, 122, 123, *123*, 125, *140*, **140**
 'Pia,' 140

Northern bayberry (*Myrica pensylvanica*), 28, 29, 33, 34, 37, 40, 43, 111, 113, 121, 122, 123, *124*, 125, *149*, **149**

Northern Japanese magnolia (*Magnolia kobus*), 91

Northern Lights azalea (*Azalea* 'Northern Lights'), 33, 39, 111, 113, 120, *120*, 121, 122, 123, 124, 125, *128*, **128**
 'Golden Lights,' 128
 'Northern Hi-Lights,' 128
 'Orchid Lights,' 128
 'Rosy Lights,' 128
 'White Lights,' 128

Northern maidenhair fern. *See* Maidenhair fern (*Adiantum pedatum*)

Northern red oak (*Quercus rubra*), 32, 38, 41, 59, 67, 69, *103*, **103**

Norway maple (*Acer platanoides*), 32, 34, 36, 37, 39, 41, 43, 67, 69, *72*, **72**
 'Crimson King,' 72, *72*
 'Deborah,' 72
 'Royal Red,' 72
 'Schwedleri,' 72

Norway spruce (*Picea abies*), 28, 32, 37, 38, 43, *93*, **93**
 'Aurea,' 93
 'Pendula,' 93

Ⓞ

Oak
 Northern red oak (*Quercus rubra*), 32, 38, 41, 59, 67, 69, *103*, **103**
 Pin oak (*Quercus palustris*), 29, 32, 34, 36, 37, 38, 41, 59, 67, 69, *102*, **102**
 Scarlet oak (*Quercus coccinea*), 29, 32, 59, 67, 69, *101*, **101**
 Shumard oak (*Quercus shumardii*), 29, 32, 38, 39, 41, 59, 67, 68, 69, *103*, **103**
 White oak (*Quercus alba*), 32, 37, 38, *59*, 67, 69, *101*, **101**
 Willow oak (*Quercus phellos*), 29, 32, 37, 38, 39, 41, 43, 59, 68, 69, *102*, **102**

Oakleaf hydrangea (*Hydrangea quercifolia*), 34, 39, 121, 122, 123, 125, *141*, **141**

Oenothera macrocarpa. *See Oenothera missouriensis* (Sundrop primrose)

Oenothera missouriensis (Sundrop primrose), 33, 37, 171, 172, 173, *194*, **194**

Oenothera speciosa (Evening primrose), 194

Omphalodes verna (Blue-eyed Mary), 35, 39, 171, 173, *194*, **194**

Otto Luyken laurel (*Prunus laurocerasus* "Otto Luyken"), 34, 41, 113, 122, 123, 124, *153*, **153**

Ⓟ

Pachysandra (*Pachysandra terminalis*), 35, 171, 173, *195*, **195**

Paperbark maple (*Acer griseum*), 32, 37, 41, 67, 68, *72*, **72**

Parson's juniper (*Juniperus chinensis* 'Parsonii'), 33, 37, 41, 111, 121, 122, 123, *145*, **145**

Parthenocissus quinquefolia (Virginia creeper), 29, 33, 35, 37, 39, 40, 202, 203, 204, 205, *205*, *211*, **211**

Parthenocissus tricuspidata (Boston ivy), 29, 33, 35, 37, 39, 202, 203, 204, *204*, 205, *211*, **211**

Parthenocissus var. Englemannii, 211

Peace rose (*Rosa* 'Peace'), 33, 111, 120, 122, 123, 125, *158*, **158**

Pear. *See* Bradford pear (*Pyrus calleryana* 'Bradford')

PeeGee hydrangea (*Hydrangea paniculata* 'Grandiflora'), 29, 33, 34, 39, 121, 122, 123, 125, *140*, **140**
 'Tardiva,' 140, *140*

Pennisetum alopecuroides (Fountain grass), 33, 37, 39, 41, 171, 172, *195*, **195**

Pennisetum rubrum, 195

Periwinkle, littleleaf (*Vinca minor*), 33, 35, 40, 41, 170, 171, 173, *201*, **201**

Persian candytuft. *See* Warley Rose (*Aethionema* 'Warley Rose')

Persian lilac (*Syringa x persica*), 29, 33, 34, 39, 111, 121, 124, *165*, **165**

Phlox stolonifera (Creeping phlox), 35, 39, 170, 171, 172, 173, *195*, **195**

Phlox subulata (Moss phlox), 33, 37, 40, 41, 170, 171, 172, 173, *196*, **196**

Photinia x fraseri (Redtip photinia), 28, 33, 34, 111, 121, 124, *149*, **149**

Picea abies 'Nidiformis' (Bird's nest spruce), 32, 37, 121, 150, **150**

Picea abies (Norway spruce), 28, 32, 37, 38, 43, *93*, **93**

Picea glauca 'Conica' (Dwarf Alberta spruce), 32, 34, 37, 39, 41, 121, 123, *150*, **150**

Picea glauca (White spruce), 28, 32, 34, 37, 38, 43, *94*, **94**

Picea omorika (Serbian spruce), 28, 32, 34, 38, 39, 41, 69, *94*, **94**

Picea pungens glauca (Colorado blue spruce), 28, 32, 43, *95*, **95**

Pieris floribunda (Mountain pieris), 33, 34, 39, 111, 120, 122, 123, *123*, 124, *151*, **151**

Pieris japonica (Andromeda), 32, 34, 38, 111, 123, 124, *151*, **151**

Pin oak (*Quercus palustris*), 29, 32, 34, 36, 37, 38, 41, 59, 67, 69, *102*, **102**

Pine
 Japanese black pine (*Pinus thunbergii*), 28, 32, 36, 37, 40, 43, 67, *96*, **96**
 Mugo pine (*Pinus mugo*), 33, 34, 37, 43, 121, 123, *152*, **152**
 White pine (*Pinus strobus*), 28, 32, 37, 43, *43*, *95*, **95**

Pink Meidiland rose (*Rosa* 'Pink Meidiland'), 33, *57*, 111, 122, 125, *158*, **158**

Pink Panda strawberry (*Fragaria* 'Pink Panda'), 33, 35, 171, 172, 173, *184*, **184**

Pink sandwort (*Arenaria purpurascens*), 177

Pinus mugo (Mugo pine), 33, 34, 37, 43, 121, 123, *152*, **152**

Pinus strobus (White pine), 28, 32, 37, 43, *43*, *95*, **95**

Pinus thunbergii (Japanese black pine), 28, 32, 36, 37, 40, 43, 67, *96*, **96**

Plum. *See* Purple-leaf plum (*Prunus cerasifera* 'Atropurpurea')

Plumbago (*Ceratostigma plumbaginoides*), 33, 170, 171, 173, *180*, **180**

Polygonum aubertii (Silver lace vine), 29, 33, 35, 37, 40, *40*, 202, 203, 204, 205, *212*, **212**

Populus tremuloides (Quaking aspen), 32, 40, 59, 67, 69, *96*, **96**

Porcelain vine (*Ampelopsis brevipedunculata*), 33, 37, 39, 202, 203, 204, 205, *207*, **207**

Possum Haw (*Ilex decidua*), 32, 34, 37, 38, 39, 41, 59, 67, 68, *87*, **87**
 'Warren's Red,' 87

Potentilla fruiticosa (Shrubby cinquefoil), 33, 34, 111, 113, 121, 122, 125, *125*, *152*, **152**

Potentilla tabernaemontani (Spring cinquefoil), 33, 37, 40, 171, 172, 173, *196*, **196**

Primula japonica (Japanese primrose), 35, 37, 171, 173, *196*, **196**
Privet
    Golden vicary privet (*Ligustrum x vicaryi*), 28, 33, 111, 113, 125, *148*, **148**
    Variegated Chinese privet (*Ligustrum sinense* 'Variegatum'), 148
Prostrate Chenault coralberry (*Symphoricarpos x chenaultii* 'Hancock'), 33, 35, 37, 40, 41, 173, *199*, **199**
Prunus avium, 98, 99
Prunus bireiana, 97
Prunus cerasifera 'Atropurpurea' (Purple-leaf plum), 29, 32, 38, 39, 41, 59, 68, 69, *97*, **97**
Prunus glandulosa 'Rosea' (Dwarf flowering almond), 32, 34, 124, *153*, **153**
Prunus laurocerasus "Otto Luyken" (Otto Luyken laurel), 34, 41, 113, 122, 123, 124, *153*, **153**
Prunus mackii (Amur chokecherry), 32, 34, 59, 67, 69, *97*, **97**
Prunus sargentii (Sargent cherry), 32, 34, 67, 69, *98*, **98**
Prunus serrulata 'Kwanzan' (Kwanzan cherry), 32, 67, 68, 69, *98*, **98**
Prunus subhirtella 'Pendula' (Weeping cherry), 32, 34, 67, 68, 69, *99*, **99**
Prunus x yedoensis (Yoshino cherry), 98
Pseudotsuga douglasi. See Douglas fir (*Pseudotsuga menziesii*)
Pseudotsuga menziesii (Douglas fir), 28, 32, 38, *99*, **99**
Purple-leaf plum (*Prunus cerasifera* 'Atropurpurea'), 29, 32, 38, 39, 41, 59, 68, 69, *97*, **97**
    'Thundercloud,' 97
    'Versuvias,' 97
Purple-leaf wintercreeper (*Euonymus fortunei* 'Coloratus'), 33, 39, 40, 41, 170, *183*, **183**
Pyracantha angustifolia Yukon Belle (Yukon Belle Firethorn), 33, 34, 111, 121, 122, 125, *154*, **154**
Pyramidal Japanese yew (*Taxus cuspidata* 'Capitata'), 28, 32, 34, 36, 40, 41, 69, *107*, **107**
Pyrus calleryana 'Bradford' (Bradford pear), 29, 32, 41, 59, 67, 68, 69, *100*, **100**

Q

Quaking aspen (*Populus tremuloides*), 32, 40, 59, 67, 69, *96*, **96**
Quercus alba (White oak), 32, 37, 38, *59*, 67, 69, *101*, **101**
Quercus coccinea (Scarlet oak), 29, 32, 59, 67, 69, *101*, **101**
Quercus palustris (Pin oak), 29, 32, 34, 36, 37, 38, 41, 59, 67, 69, *102*, **102**
Quercus phellos (Willow oak), 29, 32, 37, 38, 39, 41, 43, 59, 68, 69, *102*, **102**
Quercus rubra (Northern red oak), 32, 38, 41, 59, 67, 69, *103*, **103**
Quercus shumardii (Shumard oak), 29, 32, 38, 39, 41, 59, 67, 68, 69, *103*, **103**

R

Red maple (*Acer rubrum*), 29, 34, 36, 38, 41, 59, 67, 68, 69, *74*, **74**
    'Autumn Flame,' 74
    'Bowhall,' 74
    'Columnare,' 74
    'Indian Summer,' 74
    'October Glory,' 74
    'Red Sunset,' 74
Red oak, northern (*Quercus rubra*), 32, 38, 41, 59, 67, 69, *103*, **103**
Redbud (*Cercis canadensis*), 29, 32, 34, 36, 37, 38, 39, 41, 59, 67, 68, 69, *81*, **81**
    'Alba,' *13*, 81
    'Forest Pansy,' 81
Redtip photinia (*Photinia x fraseri*), 28, 33, 34, 111, 121, 124, *149*, **149**
Redtwig dogwood (*Cornus alba*), 29, 33, 37, 121, *133*, **133**

    'Aurea,' 133
    'Elegantissima,' 133
Redwood. *See* Dawn redwood (*Metasequoia glyptostroboides*)
Rhododendron catawbiense (Catawba rhododendron), 28, 32, 34, 38, *38*, 113, 121, 122, 123, 124, *154*, **154**
River birch (*Betula nigra*), 29, 32, 34, 36, *36*, 37, 38, 59, 67, *67*, 68, 69, *76*, **76**
    'Heritage,' 76
Rock jasmine (*Androsace lanuginosa*), 35, 37, 170, 171, 172, 173, *176*, **176**
Rock rose (*Helianthemum nummularium*), 33, 37, 39, 40, 41, 170, 171, 173, *186*, **186**
    'Buttercup,' 186
Rockcress (*Arabis caucasica*), 33, 35, 170, 171, 172, 173, *177*, **177**
    'Variegata,' 177
Rockspray cotoneaster (*Cotoneaster horizontalis*), 33, 40, 41, 121, 122, 124, 125, *135*, **135**
    'Little Gem,' 135
    'Robusta,' 135
    'Saxatilis,' 135
    'Tom Thumb,' 135
Rocky Mountain juniper. *See* Skyrocket juniper (*Juniperus scopulorum* 'Skyrocket')
Rosa Alba Meidiland (Alba Meidiland rose), 33, 35, 40, 172, 173, *197*, **197**
Rosa 'Betty Prioir' (Betty Proir rose), 32, 111, 120, 122, 125, *155*, **155**
Rosa 'Blaze' (Blaze climbing rose), 33, 39, 202, 203, 204, 205, *212*, **212**
Rosa 'Carefree Beauty' (Carefree Beauty rose), 32, 111, 113, 120, 122, 125, *155*, **155**
Rosa 'Climbing Cecil Brunner' (Climbing Cecil Brunner rose), 33, 39, 202, 203, 204, 205, *213*, **213**
Rosa 'Climbing Iceberg' (Climbing Iceberg rose), 33, 39, 202, 203, 205, *213*, **213**
Rosa 'Climbing Peace' (Climbing Peace rose), 33, 39, 202, 203, 204, 205, *214*, **214**
Rosa 'Flower Carpet' (Flower Carpet rose), 33, 41, *41*, 173, *197*, **197**
Rosa 'Fru Dagmar Hastrup' (Fru Dagmar Hastrup rose), 32, 37, 40, 111, 120, 122, 125, *156*, **156**
Rosa glauca. See Rosa rubrifolia
Rosa 'Graham Thomas' (Graham Thomas rose), 33, *110*, 111, 120, 122, 123, 125, *156*, **156**
Rosa 'Iceberg' (Iceberg rose), 33, 111, 120, 122, 124, 125, *157*, **157**
Rosa 'Joseph's Coat' (Joseph's Coat climbing rose), 33, 39, *39*, 202, 203, 204, 205, *214*, **214**
Rosa 'Margo Koster' (Margo Koster rose), 33, 111, 120, 122, 125, *157*, **157**
Rosa 'Peace' (Peace rose), 33, 111, 120, 122, 123, 125, *158*, **158**
Rosa 'Pink Meidiland' (Pink Meidiland rose), 33, 57, 111, 122, 125, *158*, **158**
Rosa rubrifolia, 33, 111, 120, 122, 125, *159*, **159**
Rosa 'The Fairy' (The Fairy rose), 33, 34, 41, 121, 123, 125, *159*, **159**
Rosa wichuraiana (Memorial rose), 33, 172, 173, *197*, **197**
Rose of Sharon (*Hibiscus syriacus*), 29, 33, 34, 37, 39, 41, 121, 125, *139*, **139**
    'Aphrodite,' 139
    'Blue Bird,' 139
    'Diana,' 139
    'Oiseau Bleu,' 139
    'Paeoniflora,' 139
Roses (*Rosa*)
    Alba Meidiland, 33, 35, 40, 172, 173, *197*, **197**
    Betty Proir, 32, 111, 120, 122, 125, *155*, **155**
    Blaze climbing, 33, 39, 202, 203, 204, 205, *212*, **212**
    Carefree Beauty, 32, 111, 113, 120, 122, 125, *155*, **155**
    climbing, care of, 55
    Climbing Cecil Brunner, 33, 39, 202, 203, 204, 205, *213*, **213**

    Climbing Iceberg, 33, 39, 202, 203, 205, *213*, **213**
    Climbing Peace, 33, 39, 202, 203, 204, 205, *214*, **214**
    Fairy, The, 33, 34, 41, 121, 123, 125, *159*, **159**
    feeding, 57
    Flower Carpet, 33, 41, *41*, 173, *197*, **197**
    Fru Dagmar Hastrup, 32, 37, 40, 111, 120, 122, 125, *156*, **156**
    Graham Thomas, 33, *110*, 111, 120, 122, 123, 125, *156*, **156**
    Iceberg, 33, 111, 120, 122, 124, 125, *157*, **157**
    Joseph's Coat, 33, 39, *39*, 202, 203, 204, 205, *214*, **214**
    light requirement, 31
    Margo Koster, 33, 111, 120, 122, 125, *157*, **157**
    Memorial, 33, 172, 173, *197*, **197**
    Nearly Wild, 158
    Peace, 33, 111, 120, 122, 123, 125, *158*, **158**
    Pink Meidiland, 33, 57, 111, 122, 125, *158*, **158**
    planting bare-root, 54
    planting containerized, 55
    problem solving, 57
    pruning, 56–57
    rubrifolia, 159
Rothschild Hybrid Azalea. *See* Exbury Azalea (*Azalea* 'Exbury Hybrids')
Royal Carpet honeysuckle (*Lonicera pileata*), 33, 35, 170, 173, *192*, **192**
Russian Olive (*Elaeagnus angustifolia*), 32, 38, 40, 59, 67, 68, 69, *84*, **84**

S

Salix alba 'Britzensis' (Coral Embers willow), 29, 32, 37, 40, 121, *160*, **160**
Salix babylonica (Weeping willow), 32, 37, 40, 59, 68, 69, *104*, **104**
Sandwort. *See* Mountain sandwort (*Arenaria montana*)
Sargent cherry (*Prunus sargentii*), 32, 34, 67, 69, *98*, **98**
    'Columnaris,' 98
Saucer magnolia (*Magnolia x soulangiana*), 29, *29*, 32, 34, 37, 38, 41, 59, 67, 69, *91*, **91**
Savannah holly (*Ilex opaca* 'Savannah'), 28, 32, 34, 37, 38, 41, 67, 68, 69, *88*, **88**
Saxifrage (*Bergenia cordifolia*), 20, 33, 35, 171, 173, *179*, **179**
    'Bressingham Ruby,' 179
Scarlet oak (*Quercus coccinea*), 29, 32, 59, 67, 69, *101*, **101**
Scarlet trumpet honeysuckle. *See* Dropmore Scarlet honeysuckle (*Lonicera x brownii* 'Dropmore Scarlet')
Schip laurel 'Schipkaensis,' 153
Scotch heather (*Calluna vulgaris*), 33, 39, 170, 171, 172, 173, *180*, **180**
    'Allegro,' 180
    'Beoley Gold,' 180
    'Country Wicklow,' 180
Sea Green juniper (*Juniperus chinensis* 'Sea Green'), 33, 37, 40, 43, 113, 121, 122, 123, 145, *145*
Sea thrift (*Armeria maritima*), 35, 37, 40, 170, 171, 172, 173, *178*, **178**
    'Alba,' 178
    'Dusseldorf Pride,' 178
    'Laucheana,' 178
Sedge. *See* Variegated Japanese sedge (*Carex morrowii* 'Variegata')
Sedum acre (Goldmoss), 33, 37, 39, 40, 41, 170, 171, 173, *198*, **198**
Sedum spectabile (Stonecrop), 33, 37, 40, 41, 171, 173, *198*, **198**
Sedum spurium 'Dragon's Blood' (Dragon's Blood sedum), 33, 37, 40, 171, 172, 173, *198*, **198**
Serbian spruce (*Picea omorika*), 28, 32, 34, 38, 39, 41, 69, *94*, **94**
    'Nana,' 94

Serviceberry, downy (*Amelanchier arborea*), 32, 34, 38, 67, 69, *76*, **76**

Serviceberry (*Amelanchier alnifolia*), 29, 33, 34, 39, 111, 123, 124, 125, *126*, **126**

'Regent,' 126

Shibori spirea (*Spiraea japonica* 'Shibori'), 33, 34, 122, 123, *161*, **161**

Showy mountain ash (*Sorbus decora*), 104

Shrubby cinquefoil (*Potentilla fruiticosa*), 33, 34, 111, 113, 121, 122, 125, *125*, *152*, **152**

'Abbottswood,' 152

'Goldfinger,' 152

'Jackman's Variety,' 152

'Primrose Beauty,' 152

'Tangerine,' 152

Shumard oak (*Quercus shumardii*), 29, 32, 38, 39, 41, 59, 67, 68, 69, *103*, **103**

Siberian forget-me-not (*Anchusa myosotidiflora*), 35, 171, 173, *176*, **176**

Silver brocade artemisia (*Artemisia stelleriana*), 33, 37, 40, 41, 170, 171, 172, 173, *178*, **178**

'Powis Castle,' 178

Silver lace vine (*Polygonum aubertii*), 29, 33, 35, 37, 40, *40*, 202, 203, 204, 205, *212*, **212**

Silver maple (*Acer saccharinum*), 29, 32, 34, 36, 37, 38, 39, 59, 67, 69, *75*, **75**

'Silver Queen,' 75

'Skinneri,' 75

Skimmia japonica (Japanese skimmia), 34, 37, 39, 122, 124, 125, *160*, **160**

Skyrocket juniper (*Juniperus scopulorum* 'Skyrocket'), 28, 32, 36, 41, 43, 69, *89*, **89**

Snow-on-the-mountain (*Aegopodium podagraria* 'Variegatum'), 35, 37, 39, 40, 171, 173, *174*, **174**

Snowberry (*Symphoricarpos albus*), 33, 34, 40, 41, 121, 122, 123, 125, *163*, **163**

Sorbus aucuparia (European mountain ash), 32, 34, *34*, 37, 38, 40, 67, 68, 69, *104*, **104**

Sorbus decora (Showy mountain ash), 104

Southern balsam fir. *See* Frasier fir (*Abies fraseri*)

Southern magnolia (*Magnolia grandiflora*), 28, 32, 34, 36, 37, 40, 67, 69, *90*, **90**

'Bracken's Brown Beauty,' 90

'D.D. Blancher,' 90

'Little Gem,' 90

Spiraea japonica 'Anthony Waterer' (Anthony Waterer spirea), *12*, 32, 34, 37, 41, 122, 123, 124, 125, *161*, **161**

Spiraea japonica 'Shibori' (Shibori spirea), 33, 34, 122, 123, *161*, **161**

Spiraea prunifolia (Bridalwreath spirea), 29, 32, 34, 111, 121, 122, 123, 124, 125, *162*, **162**

Spiraea thunbergii (Baby's Breath spirea), 29, 32, 34, 111, 121, 122, 123, 124, 125, *162*, **162**

Spiraea x vanhouttei (Vanhoutte spirea), 29, 33, 34, 37, 111, 121, 122, 123, 124, 125, *162*, **162**

Spotted dead nettle (*Lamium maculatum*), 35, 37, 41, 171, 173, *192*, **192**

'Beacon Silver,' 192

'Pink Pewter,' 192

'White Nancy,' 192

Spring cinquefoil (*Potentilla tabernaemontani*), 33, 37, 40, 171, 172, 173, *196*, **196**

Spring heath (*Erica carnea*), 33, 39, 170, 171, 172, 173, *183*, **183**

Spruce

Bird's nest spruce (*Picea abies* 'Nidiformis'), 32, 37, 121, *150*, **150**

Colorado blue spruce (*Picea pungens glauca*), 28, 32, 43, *95*, **95**

Dwarf Alberta spruce (*Picea glauca* 'Conica'), 32, 34, 37, 39, 41, 121, 123, *150*, **150**

Norway spruce (*Picea abies*), 28, 32, 37, 38, 43, *93*, **93**

Serbian spruce (*Picea omorika*), 28, 32, 34, 38, 39, 41, 69, *94*, **94**

White spruce (*Picea glauca*), 28, 32, 34, 37, 38, 43, *94*, **94**

Spurge. *See* Cypress spurge (*Euphorbia cyparissias*)

Stachys byzantina (Lamb's ear), 33, 41, 171, 172, *172*, 173, *199*, **199**

Star magnolia (*Magnolia stellata*), 34, 38, 41, 67, 68, 69, *91*, **91**

Stewartia pseudocamellia (Japanese stewartia), 32, 34, 38, 67, 68, 69, *105*, **105**

Stonecrop (*Sedum spectabile*), 33, 37, 40, 41, 171, 173, *198*, **198**

Strawberry. *See* Pink Panda strawberry (*Fragaria* 'Pink Panda')

Styrax japonica (Japanese snowbell), 32, 34, 38, 40, 67, 68, 69, *105*, **105**

Sugar hackberry. *See* Sugarberry (*Celtis laevigata*)

Sugar maple (*Acer saccharum*), 32, 34, 38, 67, 69, *75*, **75**

'Bonfire,' 75

'Flax Mill Majesty,' 75

'Green Column,' 75

'Green Mountain,' 75

'Legacy,' 75

Sugarberry (*Celtis laevigata*), 32, 34, 36, 37, 39, 41, 67, 69, *80*, **80**

Summersweet (*Clethra alnifolia*), 29, 34, 37, 39, 40, 120, 121, 122, 123, *124*, 125, *133*, **133**

'Ruby spice,' 133

Sundrop primrose (*Oenothera missouriensis*), 33, 37, 171, 172, 173, *194*, **194**

Sweet pepperbush. *See* Summersweet (*Clethra alnifolia*)

Sweet Woodruff (*Asperula odorata*), 33, 35, *35*, 39, 170, 171, 173, *179*, **179**

Sweetgum. *See* Fruitless American sweetgum (*Liquidambar styraciflua* 'Rotundiloba')

Symphoricarpos albus (Snowberry), 33, 34, 40, 41, 121, 122, 123, 125, *163*, **163**

Symphoricarpos orbiculatus (Coralberry), 29, 32, 34, 37, 40, 111, 121, 122, 123, 125, *163*, **163**

Symphoricarpos x chenaultii 'Hancock' (Prostrate Chenault coralberry), 33, 35, 37, 40, 41, 173, *199*, **199**

Syringa x laciniata (Cutleaf lilac), 29, 32, 34, 111, 120, 121, 123, 124, *164*, **164**

Syringa patula 'Miss Kim' (Miss Kim lilac), 29, 33, 34, 111, 120, 121, 123, 124, 125, *164*, **164**

Syringa x persica (Persian lilac), 29, 33, 34, 39, 111, 121, 124, *164*, **164**

Syringa reticulata (Japanese tree lilac), 32, 38, 67, *67*, 68, 69, *106*, **106**

Syringa vulgaris (Common lilac), 29, 32, 34, 37, 111, 120, 121, 123, 124, *165*, **165**

T

Tam juniper (*Juniperus sabina* 'Tamariscifolia'), 33, 37, 43, 111, 121, 123, *146*, **146**

'Arcadia,' 146

Taxodium distichum (Bald Cypress), 29, 32, 36, 37, 69, *106*, **106**

Taxus cuspidata 'Capitata' (Pyramidal Japanese yew), 28, 32, 34, 36, 40, 41, 69, *107*, **107**

Taxus x media 'Densiformis,' 166

Taxus x media 'Hicksii' (Hick's upright yew), 28, 33, 34, 37, 39, 43, 111, 121, 123, *166*, **166**

Teucrium chamaedrys. *See Teucrium prostratum* (Germander)

Teucrium prostratum (Germander), 33, 39, 41, 170, 171, 172, 173, *199*, **199**

Thuja occidentalis (American arborvitae), 30, 34, 39, 41, 45, *107*, **122**, 107

Thymus leucotrichus (Creeping thyme), 33, 37, 39, 41, 170, 171, 172, 173, *200*, **200**

Tiarella cordifolia (Allegheny foam flower), 35, 39, 170, 171, 173, *200*, **200**

Tilia cordata (Littleleaf linden), 32, 37, 38, 39, 40, 41, 67, 68, 69, *108*, **108**

Tricolor beech (*Fagus sylvatica* 'Tricolor'), 85

Trident maple (*Acer buergerianum*), 32, 38, 67, 68, 69, *71*, **71**

Trumpet honeysuckle (*Lonicera sempervirens*), 29, 33, 202, 203, 204, *204*, 205, *210*, **210**

pruning, 205

Trumpet vine (*Campsis radicans*), 29, 33, 35, 37, 202, 203, 204, 205, *208*, **208**

'Flava,' 208

'Praecox,' 208

pruning, 205

Tsuga canadensis (Canadian hemlock), 28, 32, 34, 38, 43, 67, *108*, **108**

U

Ulmus parvifolia (Chinese elm), 29, 32, 36, 39, 41, 59, 67, 68, 69, *109*, **109**

V

Vanhoutte spirea (*Spiraea x vanhouttei*), 29, 33, 34, 37, 111, 121, 122, 123, 124, 125, *162*, **162**

Variegated bishop's weed. *See* Snow-on-the-mountain (*Aegopodium podagraria* 'Variegatum')

Variegated Chinese privet (*Ligustrum sinense* 'Variegatum'), 148

Variegated Japanese sedge (*Carex morrowii* 'Variegata'), 33, 35, 40, 41, 170, 171, 172, 173, *180*, **180**

'Fisher,' 180

Variegated kiwi vine (*Actinidia kolomikta*), 206

Viburnum carlesii (Korean spice viburnum), 33, 34, 39, 113, 120, 121, 123, 124, *167*, **167**

Viburnum davidii (David viburnum), 167

Viburnum opulus 'Roseum' (European cranberry-bush), 29, 32, 37, 121, 123, 124, 125, *167*, **167**

Viburnum plicatum tomentosum (Doublefile viburnum), 29, 32, 37, 121, 123, 124, 125, *167*, **167**

Vinca minor (Littleleaf periwinkle), 33, 35, 40, 41, 170, 171, *172*, 173, *201*, **201**

Virginia creeper (*Parthenocissus quinquefolia*), 29, 33, 35, 37, 39, 40, 202, 203, 204, 205, 205, *211*, **211**

pruning, 205

W

Warley Rose (*Aethionema* 'Warley Rose'), 33, 39, 170, 171, 172, 173, *174*, **174**

Washington hawthorn (*Crataegus phaenopyrum*), 32, 34, 36, 38, 39, 41, 67, 68, 69, *83*, **83**

Weeping beech (*Fagus sylvatica pendula*), 85

Weeping cherry (*Prunus subhirtella* 'Pendula'), 32, 34, 67, 68, 69, *99*, **99**

'Autumnalis,' 99

'Yae-shidare-higan,' 99

Weeping willow (*Salix babylonica*), 32, 37, 40, 59, 68, 69, *104*, **104**

'Niobe,' 104

White fir (*Abies concolor*), 20, 28, 32, 37, 43, *70*, **70**

White flowering redbud (*Cercis canadensis* 'Alba'), 13

White oak (*Quercus alba*), 32, 37, 38, 59, 67, 69, *101*, **101**

White pine (*Pinus strobus*), 28, 32, 37, 43, *43*, *95*, **95**

'Nana,' 95

White spruce (*Picea glauca*), 28, 32, 34, 37, 38, 43, *94*, **94**

Whitespire birch (*Betula mandschurica japonica* 'Whitespire'), 32, 37, 38, 59, 67, 68, *77*, **77**

Willow

Coral Embers willow (*Salix alba* 'Britzensis'), 29, 32, 37, 40, 121, *160*, **160**

Weeping willow (*Salix babylonica*), 32, 37, 40, 59, 69, *104*, **104**

Willow oak (*Quercus phellos*), 29, 32, 37, 38, 39, 41, 43, 59, 68, 69, *102*, **102**

Winterberry (*Ilex verticillata*), 29, 33, 34, 37, 39, 111, 121, 122, 123, 125, *125*, *144*, **144**

'Sparkleberry,' 144

'Winter Red,' 144

Wintercreeper. See Purple-leaf wintercreeper (*Euonymus fortunei* 'Coloratus')

Wintergreen (*Gaultheria procumbens*), 35, 39, 171, 173, *185*, **185**

Wisteria chinensis. See Chinese Wisteria (*Wisteria sinensis*)

Wisteria sinensis (Chinese wisteria), 29, 33, 35, 202, 203, 204, 205, *215*, **215**

Witch Hazel. See Common Witch Hazel (*Hamamelis virginiana*)

Woodland phlox (*Phlox stolonifera*), 35, 39, 170, 171, 172, 173, *195*, **195**

Y

Yellow archangel (*Lamiastrum galeobdolon* 'Variegatum'), 35, 171, 173, *192*, **192**

Herman's Pride', 192

Yellow-twig dogwood (*Cornus stolonifera* 'Flaviramea'), 29, 33, 34, 37, 121, 123, 125, *135*, **135**

'Isanti,' 135

Yellowwood (*Cladastris lutea*), 32, 34, 37, 67, 68, 69, *82*, **82**

'Rosea,' 82

Yew. *See* Hick's upright yew (*Taxus x media* 'Hicksii'); Pyramidal Japanese yew (*Taxus cuspidata* 'Capitata')

Yoshino cherry (*Prunus x yedoensis*), 98

Yukon Belle firethorn (*Pyracantha angustifolia* Yukon Belle), 33, 34, 111, 121, 122, 125, *154*, **154**

'Gnome,' 154

Z

Zelkova serrata (Japanese zelkova), 29, 38, 39, 41, 59, 67, 68, 69, *109*, **109**

Acknowledgements

Hetherington Studios
3520 S.W. 9th
Des Moines, Iowa 50315
515-243-6329
dhetherington@earthlink.net

Doug Hetherington
Mara Hetherington
Sophia Hetherington
Johanna Hetherington
Steve Hetherington
John Hetherington
Matt Johnson
Matt Miller
Ella Hall
Amy Hawes

Thank you
Mary Howell Williams
Kenna Neighbors

Jackson & Perkins Wholesale, Inc.
P.O. Box 9100
2518 South Pacific Highway
Medford, OR 97501
800-854-1766
www.jproses.com
www.surfinia.com
www.jacksonandperkins.com

City of Carlsbad
1200 Carlsbad Village Drive
Carlsbad, CA 92008-1989
760-720-9461
www.ci.carlsbad.ca.us

Missouri Botanical Garden
4344 Shaw Blvd.
P.O. Box 299
St. Louis, MO 63166-0299
314-577-5100
www.mobot.org

Minnesota Landscape Arboretum
Andersen Horticultural Library
3675 Arboretum Drive
P.O. Box 39
Chanhassen, MN 55317-0039
952-443-1400
www.arboretum.umn.edu

The Morton Arboretum
4100 Illinois Route 53
Lisle, IL 60532-1293
630-719-2400
www.mortonarb.org

Heard Gardens Ltd.
8000 Raccoon River Drive
West Des Moines, IA 50266
515-987-0800
www.heardgardens.com

The Dawes Arboretum
7770 Jacksontown Road S.E.
Newark, OH 43056-9380
800-443-2937
www.dawesarb.org

The Holden Arboretum
9500 Sperry Road
Kirtland, OH 44094-5172
216-256-1110
www.holdenarb.org

Iowa Arboretum, Inc.
1875 Peach Avenue
Madrid, IA 50516
515-795-3216
www.iowaarboretum.com

Bellevue Botanical Garden
P.O. Box 40536
Bellevue, WA 98015-4536
206-454-7603
www.bellevuebotanical.org

The Butchart Gardens
Box 4010
Victoria, BC V8X3X4
Canada
250-652-4422
www.butchartgardens.com

Reiman Gardens
1407 Elwood Drive
Ames, IA 50011
515-294-0028
www.ag.iastate.edu/departments/hort/rgardens/rgframe.html

The State Botanical Garden of Georgia
2450 S. Milledge Avenue
Athens, GA 30605
706-542-1244
www.uga.edu/~botgarden

Powell Gardens
1609 NW. U.S. Highway 50
Kingsville, MO 64061
816-697-2600
www.powellgardens.org

Fullerton Arboretum
P.O. Box 6850
Fullerton, CA 92834-6850
714-278-3579
www.arboretum.fullerton.edu

Des Moines Botanical Center
909 East River Drive
Des Moines, IA 50316
515-323-8900

Des Moines Waterworks
2201 Valley Drive
Des Moines, IA 50325
515-283-8755

Photo Credits

T=Top C=Center B=Bottom L=Left R=Right

Front Cover
Karlis Grants
CoverL
Doug Hetherington
Cover Background, CoverR
Rick Taylor
CoverC

Back Cover
Doug Hetherington
Cover Background

Craig Allen: 207B
Cathy Wilkinson Barash: 197T
Ernest Braun: 17CR, 27TR, 49TR, 53BR
Dave Cavagnaro: 80T, 197C, 198T
Chuck Crandall: 19BR
Crandall & Crandall: 58TR, 130T, 154T, 213B
Stephen Cridland: 19TR, 168BL, 173TR
Michael Dirr: 176T, 177B, 178B, 127T, 78T, 182C, 185C, 86B, 142B, 143T, 87B, 88T, 145T, 193B, 195B, 196B, 151T, 153B, 98T, 98B, 101B, 198B, 199C, 161B, 164B, 165T, 122TL
Harrison L. Flint: 89B, 123CL, 176M
Randolph Foulds: 12TL, 20TL, 52TL, 53CL, 170TL
Galen Gates: 176B, 166B
Susan Gilmore: 13BC, 111TR, 112T
Jay Graham: 204TL
Karlis Grants: 110TL, 203TR
Caroll Highsmith: 44TR
Barbara Hogenson Agency: 28T
Roy Inman: 120TR
J&P™ roses presented by Jackson & Perkins Wholesale, Inc.: 39TR, 214T, 157B
Jon Jensen: 10TR
Mike Jensen: 18T, 52BL
Stark Jett: 169BR, 7BL
Peter Krumhardt: 42T
Barbara Martin: 26TR
Jennie Massey McIlwain: 193C
Tim Murphy: 202T
Jerry Pavia: 174B, 194B, 214B, 159B, 160T, 156T
Mary Carolyn Pindar: 124TL
Julie Maris Semel: 4BC, 11TR, 11BL, 66BR, 110CR, 113TR, 170BL
Bill Stites: 15TR, 27CL, 31TR, 59TC, 61TR, 119TL
Rick Taylor: 10CR, 14TR, 14BR, 44TL, 58TL, 111CR
Al Teufen: 18CR
Zane Williams: 12BR

Nathan D. Ehrlich
Atlanta, GA

Troy Jackson
Olathe, KS

Lorn Patterson
San Marcos, CA

Timothy J. Cappuccio
Independence, MO

Bradley Phillips
Bloomington, MN

Steven J. Esguerra
San Diego, CA

Carolyn Evans
Escondido, CA

Many thanks to
the employees
of The Home Depot.
whose "wisdom of the
aisles" has made
Landscaping 1-2-3™
the most useful
book of its kind.

Sherry Gugerty
Downers Grove, IL

Chris Hopkins
Orange, CA

Lissett Urso
Arlington Heights, IL

Rebecca M. Tainter
Atlanta, GA

Cindy Broaddus
Gladstone, MO

Matt Anthony
Atlanta, GA

Neil Hayes
Kansas City, MO

James M. Ary
Duluth, GA

Shari K. Willman
Atlanta, GA

Mike Mitchell
Bothell, WA

Plant Shapes—Quick Reference Guide

Entries for plants in this book use the icons below to indicate the shape of the mature plant.

Trees

Bradford Pear	Columnar Standard	Columnar	Pyramidal	Pyramidal Standard

Rounded	Spreading	Upright Multi-Trunk	Upright Single-Trunk	Weeping